A CULTURAL HISTORY OF THE SOUL

A CULTURAL HISTORY *of the Soul*

EUROPE AND NORTH AMERICA FROM 1870 TO THE PRESENT

KOCKU VON STUCKRAD

Columbia University Press *New York*

Columbia University Press
Publishers Since 1893
New York Chichester, West Sussex
cup.columbia.edu

Library of Congress Cataloging-in-Publication Data
Names: Stuckrad, Kocku von, 1966– author.
Title: A cultural history of the soul: Europe and
North America from 1870 to the Present / Kocku von Stuckrad.
Description: New York : Columbia University Press, 2021. | Includes
bibliographical references and index.
Identifiers: LCCN 2021014475 (print) | LCCN 2021014476 (ebook) |
ISBN 9780231200363 (hardback) | ISBN 9780231200370 (trade paperback) |
ISBN 9780231553575 (ebook)
Subjects: LCSH: Soul—History. | Europe—Civilization—History. |
North America—Civilization—History.
Classification: LCC BD421 .S85 2021 (print) | LCC BD421 (ebook) |
DDC 128/.1—dc23
LC record available at https://lccn.loc.gov/2021014475
LC ebook record available at https://lccn.loc.gov/2021014476

Columbia University Press books are printed on permanent
and durable acid-free paper.
Printed in the United States of America

Cover image: *Blue Fox*, 1911 (oil on canvas), by Franz Marc (1880–1916).
Courtesy Von der Heydt Museum, Wuppertal, Germany / Bridgeman Images.
Cover design: Lisa Hamm

For Hans G. Kippenberg on the occasion

of his eightieth birthday

CONTENTS

PART II: FROM EUROPE TO AMERICA AND BACK: THE SOUL GOES MAINSTREAM

ACKNOWLEDGMENTS

A Cultural History of the Soul is the English version of a text that came out in 2019 under the German title *Die Seele im 20. Jahrhundert: Eine Kulturgeschichte* (Wilhelm Fink Press). For the English edition, I went through the text thoroughly once more and revised it in a number of ways, both in response to feedback from readers (including the peer reviews for Columbia University Press) and in order to strengthen and clarify my argument. I also adjusted some of the content for an English-speaking readership. I want to thank Wendy Lochner from Columbia University Press for her interest in this work and for her continued support and encouragement.

Most of the research for this book was carried out during a sabbatical I spent in Berlin, a city I also call my home. Berlin is a place where history is omnipresent, where light and shadow exist—and are allowed to exist—side by side, as in hardly any other city. It is a city that reinvents itself again and again with an incredible vitality, without ever being pretentious; a city where failure and renewal have become a way of life that frees creativity and provides air to breathe. Berlin has a presence that unfolds in encounters between places and people. The first part of this book is full of people who have shaped Berlin and with whom the city has made history.

Many of the people who have helped to write this book do not belong to the human species. The birds, foxes, squirrels, mice, dogs, trees, and plants of Wilmersdorf are my constant companions. To them I address my gratitude. I would especially like to thank our Yorkie Genki, whom we had to let go in 2017, and little Oskar, who has found a firm place in our midst; both were and are a constant source of wisdom, joy, and life energy.

Other places besides Berlin have contributed to this book. In recent years I have visited many places where the boundaries between the levels of reality are permeable. Among these "thin places" are the west coast of the United States, especially the Redwood Forests, but also Scotland and northern Scandinavia. I would especially like to thank Mount Gisuris, who today, together with Mount Akka and Mount Nijak, protects the entrance to Sarek National Park, and who has been one of Lapland's inhalation and exhalation points for sixty-five million years.

In this book I continue research that has kept me busy for the last twenty years. Many conversations with colleagues and students have helped me to formulate and improve my arguments. Special thanks go to Whitney A. Bauman, a good friend and colleague with whom I cofounded the research hub Counterpoint: Navigating Knowledge in 2018. I have also received valuable suggestions for this book from Jay Johnston, Bron Taylor, Jens Schlieter, Claudia Bruns, and the members of a research group on new animism, above all Sarah Pike, Graham Harvey, and David Haberman. With deep appreciation I remember the many conversations with my friend and colleague Dylan Burns, either during our lunch breaks in the cafeteria at the Freie Universität Berlin or over drinks and dinner.

Anne Koch, Helmut Zander, Andreas Sommer, and Stefan Mekiffer read the whole manuscript—or parts of it—and provided me with important feedback, which I tried to implement as well as I could. I am very grateful for this exchange of ideas.

Special thanks go to Hans G. Kippenberg. I will never forget how I visited him in his office at the University of Bremen in 1995 to propose a dissertation project on ancient astrology. He was immediately interested, although he did not know me at all. His enthusiasm for cultural studies research, even and especially when it goes against the grain of traditional wisdom, has motivated and inspired me ever since. It was also Hans G. Kippenberg who put me on the track of discursive studies of religion, and most of what I have learned since my time as a doctoral student can be traced back to him, either directly or indirectly. Over the years, we have developed a friendship that fills me with gratitude. On the occasion of his eightieth birthday, I dedicate this book to him.

I owe heartfelt thanks to Alissa Jones Nelson. She was not only a patient listener every time I bothered her with questions about the history of the soul, but she has also introduced me to authors, topics, and questions that have become part of this book in many ways. For the English version of the book, she offered invaluable help in preparing an accessible, readable manuscript. Most importantly, however, she shares the adventure of life with me. Love is touching souls.

PROLOGUE

The Crisis of the Soul in the Twentieth Century

This book began with an observation: if you want to know what psychology today has to say about the "soul," you will soon be disappointed. Many psychological dictionaries do not even include an entry on the soul. This is true of the well-regarded *Oxford Dictionary of Psychology*, for instance. The American Psychological Association's online resources also seem to make do without a concept of the soul.[1] One hundred years ago, things were very different. The soul was a key term in learned debates across disciplines in Europe, from psychology and philosophy to the natural sciences, medicine, art and literature, and even politics.

Over against this "forgotten soul" in psychology, a second observation is also striking: in contemporary European and North American culture—and elsewhere too, as a result of global entanglements—the soul is enjoying a considerable boom. How can we explain this discrepancy? What happened to the soul in the twentieth century? When did psychology lose its soul, as it were? And why is there such a great interest in the soul outside the universities? This leads to another important question: Can a historical analysis of these processes help us to better understand the intersections of science, philosophy, spirituality, art, and politics today? I think so, and this book is an exploration of the dynamics underlying this question.

In order to see the relevance of these developments, we need to have a closer look at the role that the concept of the soul has played in cultural debates since the nineteenth century, and how this arrangement has changed over the course of time. Where do we see continuities and discontinuities? What did the concept of the soul have to offer twentieth-century societies in their changing dispositions? What other concepts was it linked to, which gave new meanings to the soul or preserved old meanings in new vessels? In *A Cultural History of the Soul*, I attempt to provide answers to these questions. What I am doing here is not a history of psychology. There are plenty such histories, many of them excellent. My book is a cultural history, which means I am locating and analyzing the soul in very different places—from literature and poetry to the sciences and the humanities, from spiritual practices to political documents. It is exactly this confluence of cultural locations, the mutual dependency of these systems, that creates meaning for large sections of many societies today. Put differently, it is in processes of societal negotiation that cultural knowledge about the soul is organized and established. The results of such processes are orders of knowledge that provide many people with direction, and often even with blueprints for action. These orders are always in flux, but they also reveal a certain persistence that historical analysis can identify.

Talking of orders of knowledge does not mean that we have to decide which claims about the soul are "true" or how we should properly define the soul. I use "orders of knowledge" in the way the term has been established in cultural studies and the sociology of knowledge, namely, as a description and a reconstruction of that which groups and societies in a given context conceive of and accept as knowledge. The term has an important function in discourse research as well, and reference is often made to Michel Foucault, who was interested in the "genealogy" of our stores of knowledge and who provided important contributions to their cultural "archaeology." By looking at very diverse—yet influential—historical contributions to societal discussions, I reconstruct the genealogies of today's orders of knowledge about the soul. I describe how changing historical contexts have given meaning to the concept of the soul. In other words, what is at stake here are the ways in which shared knowledge about the soul was legitimized or delegitimized, stabilized or modified, and how it was entangled with other stores of knowledge.

Hence this book is not only a cultural history; it is also a discursive history of the soul. Since the use of the term *discourse* has become so common as to lose some of its meaning, let me briefly explain how I use the term in this book.[2] For me, an "open" definition of discourse is very helpful, for instance, in the way Franz X. Eder has suggested: discourses are practices "that systematically organize and regulate statements about a certain theme; by doing so, discourses determine the conditions of possibility of what (in a social group at a certain period of time) can be thought and said."[3] Consequently, discourse analysis looks not only at the textual and linguistic dimensions of a topic, but also at the practices that support or change orders of knowledge. This includes institutions. For instance, if a new discipline called "psychology" is established at universities, this represents a societal manifestation (or "reification," from the Latin for "becoming a thing") of a certain order of knowledge; conversely, the existence of such a subject of study legitimizes and further stabilizes this very order of knowledge. The same is true for the creation of associations and organizations, for the publication of popular books and journals, and for juridical and political decisions.

Discourse researchers sometimes call these institutional vehicles of discourse "dispositives." Dispositives constitute the "infrastructure" that carries a discourse and helps to spread it. Dispositives can change discourses simply by existing—examples would include the United Nations as a new global organization, the Internet as a new technology, or even algorithms, which currently constitute a dispositive with a lot of power over "the conditions of possibility of what (in a social group at a certain period of time) can be thought and said," as Eder's definition of discourse has it.

Thus meanings of and knowledge about the soul emerge from highly diverse sources and contributions to societal discussions. In these conversations, the term *soul* never arrives on its own. The simple term *soul* has no meaning in and of itself. As is the case with all discourses, the concept of the soul gains its specific meaning only in combination with other terms. For instance, if *soul* is combined with *cosmos* and conceptualized as the *world soul*, or if it is linked to concepts such as *life*, *breath*, or *mind*, such an arrangement changes the order of knowledge that gives meaning to the concept of the soul. Discourse researchers call this a "discursive knot": discursive knots combine or entangle several discourse strands (i.e., individual concepts such as *soul* or *life*), resulting in a discursive arrangement that generates meaning only through the entanglement of its individual strands.

What I am doing in this book is actually quite simple: I look at a large number of historical sources and analyze the respective discursive knots that generate meaning around the concept of the soul. I have not limited my selection of sources to specific genres; rather, everything that has the potential to influence shared social opinions is a candidate for discourse analysis. This procedure of putting relevant data together is what Michel Foucault calls "grouping." In *The Archaeology of Knowledge*, he notes that this analytical method frees us from associations and connotations that are often taken for granted, subsequently enabling us "to describe other unities, but this time by means of a group of controlled decisions. Providing one defines the conditions clearly, it might be legitimate to constitute, on the basis of correctly described relations, discursive groups that are not arbitrary, and yet remain invisible."[4]

In combination with textual or other historical documents, I also look at the respective dispositives that support and spread the ideas under consideration. The popular work of a Nobel laureate in physics or a best-selling novel have more discursive impact (and hence "power") than some other sources; the establishment of a university discipline, as well as of associations and academies, is an institutionalization of stores of knowledge that in turn influence discourses.

Reiner Keller, a sociologist of knowledge, once said in a discussion that discourse analysis is manual labor. This is certainly true. The amount of material one could use to reconstruct a discourse is huge, and the decisions about which discursive formations one wants to study in depth (Foucault's "controlled decisions") are very much dependent on the concrete needs of the respective study as well as on scholarly preferences. Hence, there can be no such thing as *the* discursive history of the soul (or of any other term). The present book is just one of many possible cultural histories of the soul in the twentieth century. I do not claim that my analysis is comprehensive—not least because this study does not cover all possible aspects of the theme. As the modern concept of the soul originates from Euro-American histories, I address contributions (often with very different terms and meanings) from outside this cultural location only if they are directly entangled with Euro-American discourses on the soul, mainly through processes of colonialism and globalization.[5]

The first part of *A Cultural History of the Soul* focuses mainly on Europe, where major developments took place between the rise of Romanticism and the end of World War II, creating a discursive arrangement that is still operative today, despite a number of changes, which I address in my analysis. Within Europe, much of my data comes from German-speaking countries and from the United Kingdom; discourse communities in Austria, Switzerland, Germany, and the United Kingdom have been crucial in the formation of the orders of knowledge this book engages. While I also include some material from France, southern Europe, and the Netherlands, the intellectual contexts of these countries are not the main focus of my study; the same is true for Scandinavia and central and eastern Europe. I invite colleagues with the respective expertise to compare my account with data from those areas and thus to paint a more nuanced historical picture. In the second part of the book, the focus shifts to the United States of America, because it was in this context that discourses on the soul experienced their most important adaptations and transformations after World War II. I should also say that, for pragmatic reasons, I have excluded the whole field of music, as the discursive history of "soul" in music would require a book of its own (not to mention expertise I do not have); and finally, while I include quite a bit of literature and poetry in my analysis, I touch upon the arts only when there is a direct link to my line of argument.

Hence it should be clear that although I cover a broad range of data and topics, my analysis is still limited in scope. Nevertheless, despite these caveats about the nature of my approach, I am convinced that the knowledge arrangements I have reconstructed here—the groupings and new unities—are representative of influential cultural developments in Europe and North America. They demonstrate how the concept of the soul was instrumental in the negotiation of key ideas about the human position in the world, about the link between material and spiritual dimensions of reality, and about the evolution of human and planetary life. They also show that scientific and nonscientific ideas and practices have strongly influenced and enriched each other. What we see at work here is a discourse community that has created meanings around the term *soul* through the interplay of various cultural productions. In *A Cultural History of the Soul*, I reconstruct some of the main lines of this discursive formation.

To reveal the various discourse strands in the sources I introduce, I sometimes have to include longer quotations. I do not want to assert a certain discursive arrangement without sufficient evidence, but rather to reconstruct it from the sources. Readers can then make up their own minds about the continuities and discontinuities in the cultural and discursive history of the soul in the twentieth century. In the first chapter, I introduce the basic components of what would become the strands constituting the discourse on the soul in the twentieth century. For instance, in order to understand the close link between the two discourse strands of "soul" and "animism" in my analysis, it is important to know that the soul had animistic connotations in ancient Greek philosophy, and that these connotations have influenced our understanding of the soul up to the present day. Readers who are already familiar with—or simply less interested in—this historical context may wish to begin with the second chapter.

The patterns this reconstruction and regrouping help to uncover are even more significant for contemporary culture than I had expected at the beginning of my research. At first glance, it is perhaps not self-evident why we should be interested in a history of the term *soul*. But once we see how intricately ideas of the soul are woven together with concepts such as consciousness, evolution, nature, matter, energy, art, and cognition, things start to look quite different. This reconstruction becomes even more interesting when we extend our analysis to allegedly "secular" contexts—to areas that have done away with old-fashioned "religion" but are still interested in metaphysical and ethical questions that integrate the human being into larger frameworks, even cosmic ones.[6] This is why I am particularly interested in those discourses that emerge from entanglements of "secular-scientific" and "spiritual-metaphysical" contributions, rather than in discourses on the soul that have formed in more traditionally "religious" locations—mainly in Christian theology.[7] Indeed, it is precisely the ability of discourses on the soul to playfully bridge "religious" and "secular" points of view that makes the cultural and discursive history of the soul from the Romantic period until today so fascinating.[8]

My main argument is that analyzing the soul in its discursive arrangement with other concepts enhances our understanding of the place and the function of the metaphysical in human thought and action in the twentieth and twenty-first centuries. One implication of such an approach is that this book is not only about the soul; it is also a contribution to the discursive history of nature, science, consciousness, politics, spirituality, ecology, religion, and philosophy. Put differently, this book is about discursive arrangements that transmit knowledge about the soul; my grouping of discourse strands into historical arrangements of knowledge allows me to reconstruct the data in a way that showcases the enormous influence of these ideas and cultural practices. Sometimes I give names to (specific forms of) these arrangements, such as the "Orphic web" I use as a blueprint to analyze continuities and changes. Moreover, grouping discourse strands allows me to identify a "discourse on the soul" even where the term *soul* has been replaced by related terms, such as *consciousness*, *psyche*, or *life force*. The orders of knowledge are still intact, even if the terms in the arrangements change.

Therefore, readers who are specifically interested in my take on what the soul "really" is, or how we should conceptualize it, may be disappointed. But readers who are interested in how our understanding of the soul has been shaped by philosophy, science, the arts, politics, spirituality, and religion between 1870 and today will, I hope, find some inspiration in the following chapters.

The soul continues to be part of a complex arrangement of knowledge. In the end, maybe it is not the soul that is in crisis. Maybe our academic and cultural perception simply needs to catch up.

A CULTURAL HISTORY OF THE SOUL

PART I

THE SOUL IN ITS CULTURAL SETTING BETWEEN 1870 AND 1930

1

NATURE RESEARCH, PSYCHOLOGY, AND OCCULTISM IN THE NINETEENTH CENTURY

The Soul in European Cultural History

The history of the soul reaches far back into antiquity, and it has seen many different phases on its way to the present day. Babylonian, Egyptian, and Greek philosophies and religions formed a broad basis on which ideas about the soul were developed in late antiquity and have affected European culture—and subsequently other regions—ever since. What we today call the soul had various names back then: the Greek *pneuma* referred to "air," "breeze," or "breath." The old Greek noun *psychē* and the corresponding verb *psychein* (to breathe) carry the same connotation, but they can also mean "life" itself. We see similar links in Latin, in which *anima* (breath) was the word for "soul" (see also the Hindu *atman* or the Germanic *Atem*).[1] The intrinsic connection between the soul and ideas about life and animation has retained its importance up to the present day. In my analysis, I treat this connection as respective discourse strands that together establish the discursive meaning of "soul."

Underlying these terms are fundamental questions that have been raised over and over again. Are humans more than their bodies? Is there a separate authority within the human body that controls thinking and sensing? And if so, where is it located? Is there anything that endures after a person's death? And if what endures is the soul, then what happens to it?

Questions such as these resonated in ancient mythology, religion, and philosophy, but also in everyday life. Burkhard Gladigow describes the crucial importance of these discussions as follows: "The concept of the soul is probably one of the most universal and influential concepts in Europe. The basic patterns, the set pieces of the discourse, so to speak, were practically already formed in antiquity: standardization and internal differentiation (the soul is 'one,' but has 'parts'), the soul as a knowledge-accumulating self that 'lasts' and that has its own history of encumbrance and ascent."[2]

The decisive turn that Gladigow refers to was initiated by Greek philosophers in response to the Pre-Socratics: whereas earlier thinking had assumed the existence of a variety of souls, for these Greeks the *one* soul enabled human cognition of the world. As a second important turn, Greek thinking developed the idea that the soul could exist independently of the body. This idea, first attributed to Socrates, had a huge impact on subsequent cultural history; it enabled the "invention of the inner person" and the distinction between the "mere" bodily person and the soul as the "real" core of the human being.[3]

In the aftermath of this turn, we can distinguish two main trajectories in European ideas about the soul. The first goes back to Plato (428/427 BCE–348/347 BCE) and is interested in the unity between macrocosm and microcosm, and hence also in the human soul as a representation of the cosmic soul. This idea, formulated by Plato and subsequently developed by Plotinus (204–70), reappears in holistic concepts of the "world soul" and in mystical visions of the cosmos (which I will address in subsequent chapters).[4] Plotinus was intrigued by the question of how the individual soul relates to the absolute, or to the world soul. He explained this relation by arguing that the soul had separated from the purely spiritual—intelligible—world by directing its productive power to something that is distinct from the absolute, but it nevertheless remains tied to the spiritual world because, as a partial soul, it still represents the whole. Originating from the *nous* ("mind," "intellect," "reason"), the soul is therefore positioned between the spiritual and the material worlds. As Clemens Zintzen explains: "We can understand it as a hinge between two worlds, as it were; its essence is characterized by *energeia*, asserting its power at the juncture between *nous* and matter. That is why Plotinus attributed both divisibility and indivisibility to the soul: if the soul turns to the material world, it becomes divisible; if it turns to the *nous*, it remains indivisible."[5] Indeed, the influence of this line of argument on European cultural history can hardly be overestimated. It introduced not only the separation of body and soul, but also the idea that the soul can be divided. Without the latter, a theory of multiple personalities would be unthinkable.[6]

Building on Plato's conviction that the soul was, as it were, exiled in the body, or that the body even was "the soul's grave,"[7] Plotinus and other Neoplatonists also introduced the motif of redemption. In its Christian iteration, this meant the soul's turn toward God, which was also a journey back to the home of light, its place of origin.[8] For the more "official" Christian theology and philosophy, however, a second trajectory of interpretation became important. This trajectory starts with Aristotle and propagates a dualism between body and soul. Christian philosophy in the Middle Ages—known as scholasticism—reinforced this dualism, which continues to be an important aspect of (mainly Catholic) theology.[9] Thomas Aquinas (1225–1274) plays a crucial role in this development.[10] His teaching, which the Catholic Church still recognizes as its official psychology, assumes two souls within the human being. With birth comes the *anima vegetativa*, a soul that animals and even plants also have. Only with baptism, however, in a sort of divine act of creation, does the human being receive the *anima rationalis* or *anima intellectiva*, a rational soul unique to humans. Linked to this distinction, the triplicity of memory, thinking, and volition represents the Christian trinity.

With these theological approaches, the Catholic Church made important contributions to the emergence of psychology, as distinct from Islamic approaches, in which this specific European discourse on the soul is much less prominent. This strong tie with Christian theology is also the reason why concepts of the soul have enjoyed a high degree of continuity in official Catholic thought.[11] During the last quarter of the twentieth century, a theological debate about eschatology took place, in which Cardinal Joseph Ratzinger, who later became Pope Benedict XVI, vigorously pleaded for retaining the concept of the soul, even though that concept may have gone out of fashion outside Catholicism. As a result of this discussion, ideas about the soul and redemption are still firmly rooted in many Christian cultures, particularly outside Europe and North America.

A problem emerged from this historical constellation—one similar to what I have described elsewhere as the "tragedy of nominalism."[12] On the one hand, Thomas Aquinas's scholastic philosophy offered the possibility of a philosophically and empirically grounded psychology, as far as the physical, vegetative human systems are concerned. On the other hand, it restricted any higher knowledge of the soul, which can only be achieved as theological knowledge of God. The *anima rationalis* as the "true" soul must be perfect because it is divine; any illness or deformation of the soul can therefore only be caused by physical nature and external factors—or, theologically speaking, by the workings of evil. The idea that the mentally ill dwell in an utterly soulless body and therefore cannot be treated as full-fledged human beings—and even the idea that their souls can only be "saved" by burning their bodies at the stake—still formed the guiding principle in assessing psychological deviation in the nineteenth century. With a nod to Michel Foucault, we can call this a discourse by which institutions such as hospitals and the Church legitimize hegemonic control over human beings; in turn, this discursive practice perpetuates the underlying construction of the soul.

The basic lines of this discourse on the soul run through the philosophical and religious debates of the early modern period. They were also addressed during the European Enlightenment, forming important aspects of a history of the soul, which historical psychology can reconstruct.[13] René Descartes (1596–1650) provided a crucial building block for modern ideas about the soul, nature, and matter when he introduced the dichotomy between *res cogitans* (Latin for "the thinking thing") and *res extensa* (Latin for "the extended thing"): extended material things cannot think, and the thinking self—the soul—cannot have a material extension. I will come back to this influential dichotomy, which animist discourses on nature have critiqued in the twentieth century. But in early modern and Enlightenment Europe, scholars had already developed alternatives to this model. We may think of Gottfried Wilhelm Leibniz (1646–1716), whose "monadology" conceived of the monad as a point without material extension that nevertheless had agency. This doctrine also influenced the young Immanuel Kant

(1724–1804) before he subscribed to a strict separation between thinking and the body.

The details of this prehistory of modern discourses on the soul fall outside the scope of this book. Suffice it to say that at the turn of the nineteenth century, various alternatives were discussed. The dominant position of Enlightenment philosophies—particularly German idealism, which identified the human mind as the sole authority in understanding and acting—was met with increasing suspicion. What became Romantic thought was more influenced by scholars such as Friedrich Wilhelm Joseph Schelling (1775–1854) and Johann Wolfgang von Goethe (1749–1832), while it wrestled with Descartes and Kant. This led to a discursive arrangement that perpetuated the soul's association with life, livelihood, animation, immateriality, and the cosmos—known from Mediterranean and European cultural history—on the one hand, and on the other tied the soul even more tightly to questions of natural philosophy.

The Soul and Nature in Romantic Philosophy

Both Schelling and Goethe are good points of departure if we want to gauge the Romantic discourse on the soul and on nature. Around 1800, the University of Jena was a center of German *Naturphilosophie*, or "natural philosophy." Many students who later became prominent Romantic thinkers flocked to Jena to witness the heated debates between Schelling, Johann Gottlieb Fichte (1762–1814), and Georg Wilhelm Friedrich Hegel (1770–1831). Among the natural philosophers who attended Schelling's lectures in Jena and later integrated his views into their own work were Lorenz Oken (1779–1851), Friedrich Hufeland (1774–1839), Dietrich Georg von Kiefer (1779–1862), Gotthilf Heinrich von Schubert (1780–1860), and Ignatius Paul Vital Troxler (1780–1866). They were all fascinated by Schelling's model of nature as an organism, and they built on the idea of a living, animated cosmos.

Lorenz Oken is a good example. In his *Lehrbuch der Naturphilosophie* (Textbook of Natural Philosophy), published in 1809, he presents natural philosophy as a necessary condition of philosophy of mind

(*Geistesphilosophie*).[14] The eternal and the absolute form a unity with the real and the material because the material (or organic) real emerges from the eternal–absolute.[15] But the emergence of the organic–real follows the basic principle of all being, which is polarity—a creative dynamic that exists from the beginning, "an idea, a moving thought of God, the very primordial act with all its implications," as he says in section 88. Since nothing exists without this dynamic and this movement, Oken agrees with Schelling and notes: "There is nothing in the world that is actually dead; dead is only what does not exist, only nothingness."[16]

Hence matter is also alive, as far as it exists at all. And it can only exist "through continuous emerging, through life. There is no dead matter; matter is alive through its being, through the eternal within it." And in a pantheistic manner he specifies: "Matter as such has no existence; only the eternal within it exists. All of this is God, and outside God there is absolutely nothing."[17] Oken calls the matter that fills the entire universe "*primordial matter*, world matter, cosmic matter, *ether*."[18]

If all being emerges from the rhythmic dynamic of becoming, the only difference between the organic and the inorganic is the fact that the inorganic lacks movement; it is only mass. For Oken, the organic is alive and animated: "The movement is . . . the soul, and through the soul the organic rises above the inorganic."[19] At this point, we clearly see how the discourse strands of soul and nature are tied to those of the organic and the inorganic, but also to scientific concepts such as "ether." At all its levels of evolution, the organic world mirrors nature in its totality. Nevertheless, Oken conceives of the human being as the highest level, the one that unites all the other levels—including the realms of animals and plants. "The higher organism is a small universe; in the deepest, truest sense a *small world*, a *microcosm*."[20]

While Schelling was still concerned with an analytical approach to nature, which aimed to include the *concept* of nature in an overall philosophical framework, Oken's understanding of nature comes across as more aesthetic and emotional.[21] Odo Marquard refers to this as the "Romantic nature" overcoming the "control nature." Control nature, as "the nature of rational laws and rules" based on "the laws of nature,"[22] is evident in Descartes's claim that "we are becoming the masters and owners of nature,"[23] as well as in Kant's influential definition of nature as "the being of things, as far as it is determined by general laws"—hence a nature subjected to human control.[24] Marquard juxtaposes this controlling approach to nature with the "Romantic nature," which he defines as nature "seen mainly as an organism, as sublime or beautiful, and certainly as a liveliness that is holistic and beyond historical change." This nature can be accessed through art and emotion.[25]

An example of this trend is Gotthilf Heinrich von Schubert and his *Symbolik des Traumes* (Symbolism of Dreams, published in 1814), as well as his *Geschichte der Seele* (History of the Soul, published in 1830). Similarly to Goethe's *Werther*, in these books, the human feeling and experiencing of nature become the basic authority for any knowledge about nature. Schubert presents the symbolic language of dreams, also accessible in ancient mythology, as a means by which to decode the language of nature. "With this relationship it may also be possible to regain the lost key to that part of the sign language of nature that has not been unraveled yet, and that would mean much more for us than a simple extension of our archaeological and mythological knowledge—we would gain an understanding of the nature around us that our average nature studies would never have dreamed of."[26]

At first glance, such an understanding of nature appears subjective and random. But we can also interpret it as a kind of research that does not subject nature as an object to the human gaze; rather, it is open to being challenged, changed, and inspired by natural "objects." Amanda Jo Goldstein calls this approach "sweet science," using William Blake's expression. She demonstrates how this nondomesticating approach to nature found particularly strong expression in Johann Wolfgang von Goethe and Percy Bysshe Shelley (1792–1822). To be sure, such natural research opposed the "control nature" in Marquard's sense, but the alternative was not simple empathy and an aestheticization of nature, as Marquard assumed. The alternative is more complex, and also subversive:

> Romantic, revisionary poetic sciences . . . challenged emergent life-scientific and aesthetic protocols to understand "raw" sensation itself as susceptible and generative of social and rhetorical transformation; to countenance the mutual, material influence between the subjects and

> objects of experiment; and to position vulnerability—to impression, influence, and decay—as central, not inimical, to biological life. Against the vitalist ideal of self-generating "organic form" with which Romantic biology is frequently identified, sweet sciences conceive of animation as a relational effect of contact and context; against the twinned, post-Kantian scientific and aesthetic ideals of impartial observation, they pose an ethos of ineluctable participation in that which is felt or known.[27]

Goethe depicts this approach to nature as *zarte Empirie*, or "tender empiricism." Here is his definition from *Wilhelm Meisters Wanderjahre*: "There is a tender empiricism that intimately merges with its object and through this very identification becomes proper theory. This growth of mental abilities, however, belongs to a highly educated era."[28] In his book *Natur und Gott* (Nature and God), published in 1931, Arthur Titius noted that for Goethe, knowledge of nature and intuition belonged together. "By applying Spinoza's 'intuitive perception,' Goethe thought he had direct access to the understanding of things, so that he could find the divine in plants and stones."[29]

Goethe's approach is reminiscent of Novalis's Romantic understanding of science, too. In *Die Lehrlinge zu Saïs*, Novalis speaks of the visionary perception (*Beschauung*) of the eternal ebb and flow of nature that creates in the observer "a new revelation of love's genius, a new band of the You and the Me. The careful description of this inner world history is the true *theory* of nature. Through the internal association of the world of thoughts and its harmony with the universe, a *thought system* that exactly mirrors and formulates the universe is automatically created."[30] Therefore, Goldstein makes a valid point when she asserts that this is a critical response to the objectifying approaches that Kant in particular had propagated:

> The "tenderness" in Goethe's "tender empiricism" is a double-sided virtue that will recall the sweet science of Blake's Antamon: a mode of "beholding" an object in "beautiful flexible hands" that averts the violence of experimentalist practice not only by handling objects gently but also by acknowledging the experimenter's own tractable softness and vulnerability to their touch. Indeed, . . . Goethe's "objectively active" poetic science slyly exposes the Kantian ethics of distanced "impartiality"

> in aesthetic and scientific observation as built to guard against tenderness in the second sense.[31]

Goldstein is one of many voices in a recent reevaluation of Romanticism that tries to free this period from the stereotypes so often linked with it. As Kate Rigby, another scholar in this field, aptly notes: "Romanticism, understood as a defined 'movement,' does not exist outside of the pages of literary historiography."[32] Moreover, we should not forget that our understanding of objectivity as a method "independent of the observer" was only developed recently. As Lorraine Daston and Peter Galison point out:

> It first emerged in the mid-nineteenth century and in a matter of decades became established not only as a scientific norm but also as a set of practices, including the making of images for scientific atlases. However dominant objectivity may have become in the sciences since *circa* 1860, it never had, and still does not have, the epistemological field to itself. Before objectivity, there was truth-to-nature; after the advent of objectivity came trained judgment.[33]

Natural philosophy as "tender empiricism" and "truth-to-nature" leads Gotthilf Heinrich von Schubert to interesting considerations in his *Geschichte der Seele.* Schubert refutes Descartes's and Kant's opinion that animals are inanimate "machines." Instead, he notes that "the organic whole of the animal body also has a start and end point with regard to the intentional movements and the emotions; an organ that, more than any other part of the body, can be called a soul organ. Neither crystals nor plants have such a defining center of physical becoming."[34] The souls of animals, equipped with agency, push for the understanding they presume in the human being. "The look, even of the dying animal, tells its 'rational' caretaker or killer that it may not understand the spooky depth of the human being, but that it can sense it."[35] Animals have an "independent mental capacity of memory," and they can, "in the singing nightingale, in the darkest night, sense the longing of the beings who listen."[36] The world of animals and plants is tied to the world of humans in that "the animal kingdom, in all its searching and moving, is an external reflection of the activity of the human mind, while the dealings of the soul are mirrored in the lives of plants."[37]

For Schubert, the organic whole is at stake here. "The entire history of the emergence, growth, and work of organic beings is a continuous repetition of the creation of the visible and sensually perceivable from the invisible and supernatural."[38] Schubert thus bridges the gap between the empirical and the quantifiable on the one hand, and the transcendental on the other. Do these two domains actually influence each other? Do they constitute two dimensions of one *singular* reality that could be incorporated into a universal scientific understanding? Questions such as these gained increasing significance in the second half of the nineteenth century. Debates soon crystallized around the concept of "occultism," a discourse that would become highly important for the history of the soul in the twentieth century. Recent studies have convincingly demonstrated that occultism played a decisive role not only in the emergence of academic psychology, but also in the development of the natural sciences, art, and politics.[39] As I will explain in more detail in subsequent chapters, historical discourse analysis confirms these observations. Therefore it should suffice at this point to briefly address the prehistory of these philosophical and scientific debates.

The Pivotal Place of Occultism

If we want to understand the late-nineteenth-century fascination with the link between the metaphysical and the material, between the supernatural and the empirically measurable, we have to keep in mind that during this period, a number of discoveries and inventions dominated the public discussions that illustrated exactly this relationship. Ulrich Linse asserts that the discovery of electromagnetic waves, X-rays, and radioactivity presented a particular challenge to philosophical and scientific approaches to invisible and mental phenomena.

> On the one hand, materialism led to a reductionist categorization of psychological and mental processes as "power and matter" (*Kraft und*

> *Stoff*, Ludwig Büchner, 1855); on the other hand, the traditional Christian worldview disconnected the material-natural domain from the mental-spiritual. Spiritualism, however, connected the physical and the supernatural worlds and denied a deep gap between them; indeed, it even postulated their mutual intersection. The spirits could "materialize," and with the new image of death the difference between this world and the hereafter—both, according to Carl du Prel, "only subjectively divided worlds"—became highly fluid.[40]

Linse rightly mentions Carl du Prel (1839–1899), whose works were situated at the interface between cultural history, natural science, mysticism, and occultism.[41] His best-known book, *Philosophie der Mystik* (1885), was translated into English as *The Philosophy of Mysticism* and earned its author international recognition. The book became a source of inspiration for Sigmund Freud (1856–1939) and other scholars. But du Prel also wrote more popular works on "Socrates's Demon" or "Modern Temple Sleep," which helped establish these discourses in the context of a wider academic and public debate.[42]

When it comes to the introduction of the term *occultism* itself, we have to mention Karl Kiesewetter (1854–1895), particularly with regard to the learned discussion in Germany. His works—both his nine-hundred-page book *Der Occultismus des Altertums* (Ancient Occultism) and his equally thick work *Geschichte des neueren Occultismus* (Recent History of Occultism)—had a significant impact. In the latter book, Kiesewetter presents a comprehensive story of occultism between 1500 and 1900, thus enabling critical research on such phenomena. For Kiesewetter, occultism is the field of "the occult phenomena of the inner life [*Seelenleben*]," which have often led to attempts "to construct a supernatural worldview."[43]

In many ways, Kiesewetter's reconstruction of occult traditions resembles more recent attempts to file these phenomena under the rubric of esotericism. Kiesewetter himself uses this term as a sort of "secret science" (*Geheimwissenschaft*): occultism, in its "essence," has been the same for thousands of years, but "of course its *forms* have changed under the influence of different state religions, and therefore we need to demonstrate the same *esoteric center* under the changing garb of *dogmas*, as well as its progressive development and maturation."[44] Hence Antoine Faivre's differentiation between occultism and esotericism does not seem to align with this example: "The term *occultism* is properly used to refer to a large number of practices, ranging from astrology and alchemy to occult medicine and magic, that are based in one way or another on the homo-analogical principle, or doctrine of correspondences. . . . Occultism, as a group of practices, is to be distinguished from esotericism, which is, roughly speaking, the theory that makes these practices possible."[45] Karl Hoheisel's remarks on the subject seem more appropriate; he argued that, since Kiesewetter, occultism has functioned as a collective term to describe "all kinds of doctrines and practices that address 'metaphysical' or 'supernatural' powers"; thus it overlapped with "esotericism" to a significant degree and was often practically identical to "parapsychology."[46] However, it is important to emphasize that this observation mainly holds true for the German use of the term.

After a brief description of medieval and early modern sources—from Roger Bacon to Albertus Magnus, from Marsilio Ficino to Giovanni Pico della Mirandola, Johannes Reuchlin, and Johannes Trithemius—Kiesewetter aptly begins his detailed report on "recent occultism" with Heinrich Cornelius Agrippa von Nettesheim (1486–1535). This is because, as Kiesewetter tells us, "in his *Occulta Philosophia* Agrippa summarized everything that the old philosophers, mystics, church fathers, scholastics, and natural philosophers had written and taught about the doctrines of transcendental phenomena, and he integrated this into a system by presuming—as quoted in the inscription to this present book—that the spirit that lives within us causes magic and miracles."[47]

Kiesewetter's approach widens the understanding of occultism and weaves a discursive knot consisting of occultism, soul, transcendence, phenomenology, spirit, magic, miracle, and wonder; but this knot also includes philosophy, mysticism, supernatural worldviews, and secret sciences.[48] This represents a trend that had captured the attention of large segments of European and also North American societies by the end of the nineteenth century.[49] Alex Owen also stresses the extent to which occultism was tied to a new concept of subjectivity, "that innovative sense of self that so often characterized those self-identified 'we moderns' of the fin de siècle." Occultism, according to Owen, was "integral to much that was most self-consciously new at the turn of the century."[50] As she concludes:

> By the 1890s the terms *mysticism* and *mystical revival* were in general use to refer to one of the most remarked trends of the decade: the widespread emergence of a new esoteric spirituality and a proliferation of spiritual groups and identities that together constituted what contemporaries called the new "spiritual movement of the age." Characteristic of this "spiritual movement" was an upsurge of interest in medieval and Renaissance Christian mysticism, heterodox inspirational neo-Christianity, and, most notably, a nondenominational—sometimes non-Christian—interest in "esoteric philosophy," or occultism.[51]

This blending of the discourse strand of "spirituality" with the discourse strand of "mysticism" is a prelude to what would occur on a broader scale later in the twentieth century (which I will discuss in part 2). These new discursive formations were also instrumental in the establishment of academic psychology. Many areas of societal debate at the time were highly interested in the soul. Certain questions were subjects of heated debate: What are the features of a "science of the soul"? Should the professional study of psychology be integrated in faculties of science, philosophy, or medicine? What methods are appropriate for such an academic discipline?

The Scientification of the Soul and the Institutionalization of Academic Psychology

The scientification and institutionalization of socially accepted knowledge are two dimensions of discourse history that intersect in many ways. Steven Shapin points out that the mechanisms of attributing "truth" and validity to certain shared communal opinions have changed significantly since the seventeenth century. Whereas personal relationships and social values used to drive the acceptance of truth, since the nineteenth century societies have trusted institutions most—the same phenomenon Niklas Luhmann calls "systemic trust." Today, even specialized knowledge is usually deemed trustworthy only when experts communicate it to the public with the support of trusted institutions.[52]

Therefore the institutional stabilization of societal discourse on the soul is indicative of processes of legitimizing and delegitimizing stores of knowledge. Kurt Danziger also stresses the social and organizational dimensions of knowledge about the soul.

> There is an intimate relationship between the general forms of presuppositions, knowledge goals, and investigative practices and their specific embodiment. As the community of knowledge producers grows it develops internal norms and values that reflect its external alliances. Its professional project is directed at carving out and filling a particular set of niches in the professional ecosystem of its society, and its internal norms reflect the conditions for the success of this project. These norms tend to govern both the production of knowledge and the production of the producers of knowledge through appropriate training programs.[53]

Most histories of psychology start with the establishment of the discipline at European universities around 1900.[54] However, the scientification and professionalization of psychological research had already begun at the beginning of the nineteenth century.[55] Indeed, the institutionalization of psychological knowledge in new centers and programs of study should be seen as a materialization and a stabilization of discourses that gained importance during the second half of the nineteenth century. And the development of the underlying processes was by no means linear. There were bitter quarrels about the features and methodological characteristics of psychology, which led to the emergence of various "schools" that continued to regulate the discipline in the twentieth century.

The concept of the soul clearly played a role in these arguments. Helmut Zander makes a very similar point when he titles the relevant section of his historical account of European ideas of reincarnation "Fin de Siècle: The Great Laboratory of the Transmigration of Souls."[56] With reference to Bruno Latour, one could also say that in order to understand these processes, we need a "symmetrical anthropology"[57] that refrains from presenting this process as the "evolution" of psychology toward a normative discipline that would subsequently define what counts as "soul" or "psyche." Rather, this interpretation emphasizes the concurrent existence of diverse approaches at the turn of the twentieth century, each developing in its own way.

Around 1850, psychology was already quite established in its theories and methods, and the concept of the soul was increasingly tied to ideas of consciousness and to empirical methods. But scholars were still speculating about the soul's material presence, as we see in Joseph Beck's *Grundriß der Empirischen Psychologie und Logik* (Outline of Empirical Psychology and Logic), published in 1846:

> The medium by which the soul, as an *internally existing entity, only visible in its temporal activity, i.e., as a mental power*, connects to the *external material world* is actually the whole body; through the body and its organs, the soul receives impressions from outside and generates movement toward the outside world. But from physiology and experience, we know that the soul engages in mutual exchange with many parts of the body, be it in *mediated* or *immediate* ways, and that especially the *nervous system* communicates this exchange in the healthy body; that is why it is preferably called the *soul organ*.[58]

Johann Friedrich Herbart (1776–1841), who succeeded Immanuel Kant as professor of philosophy in Königsberg in 1809, was very influential during this period. In his *Lehrbuch der Psychologie* (Textbook of Psychology), published in 1834, Herbart differentiated between psychology as a discipline of "inner experience" and natural philosophy as a discipline of "outer experience." He notes: "As both domains of experience are distinct and related at the same time, so are these two sciences. In their main concepts, both depend on general metaphysics; but psychology relates to metaphysics in the odd way that it answers some of the questions metaphysics raises and claims as its own. Therefore we prefer to hear the psychological lecture before the metaphysical one—trying to eschew the metaphysical concept of *soul* (the substance of the mind) as long as possible."[59]

Herbart argues that we cannot localize the soul in spatial terms or define it in terms of time.[60] Even the "simple *What* of the soul will forever remain completely unknown; as an object, it is relevant neither for speculative nor for empirical psychology."[61] For him, empirically based research into inner experience is only possible by means of conceptual clarity. "If the concepts we use to describe *what happens within us* have emerged in an unscientific way, and if we add to these *our skills and potentials*, psychology will be turned into a *mythology*; while nobody would want to confess that they seriously believe in it, still the most important research depends on it in such a way that all clarity would be lost if we were to remove that basis."[62]

We see a similar line of argument in Friedrich Eduard Beneke (1798–1854), who defined psychology as "the natural science of the human soul"[63] and thus organized his textbook around the soul as its conceptual center. Neither was the concept of the soul critically juxtaposed with the idea of natural science or empiricism in his *Lehrbuch der Psychologie als Naturwissenschaft* (Textbook of Psychology as a Natural Science), published in 1833. Beneke could still define the soul "as a quite immaterial being," "consisting of certain basic systems that are consistent in themselves and also completely united with one another, or in fact they form this One Being." This being is "a sensory being, i.e., the soul's primordial powers are able to receive certain stimulations from outside, which these powers then incorporate and retain."[64] Nevertheless, one can also characterize Beneke as a forerunner of empirically based psychology—it was he who introduced the term *new psychology*. What Friedrich Herbart, Friedrich Eduard Beneke, and Jakob Friedrich Fries (1773–1843, not discussed here) have in common is their attempt "to disprove Kant's critique of the possibility of a 'scientific psychology' by reinterpreting this very critique as a manual for developing a scientific psychology."[65]

In the course of the emergence of scientific psychology, the concept of the soul increasingly came under pressure. Wilhelm Wundt (1832–1920), who accepted Beneke's notion of "new psychology," was especially important in this development. Many historians describe the foundation of Wundt's Institute for Experimental Psychology at the University of Leipzig in 1879 as the birth of modern psychology, even though earlier programs had laid the foundations for this step.[66] In Wundt's "Lectures on the Souls of Humans and Animals"—which he characterized as a "juvenal sin" in the preface to the second edition, correcting the most obvious mistakes in the light of his more recent research into experimental psychology—the term *soul* does only occur in the title and nowhere else in the book. Leaving that term behind, the author explains human emotions and sensual impressions as physiological processes. In the lecture 22, Wundt addresses the trickier phenomena of dreams, somnambulism, hypnosis, and suggestion. He claims their significance is highly overrated:

> From all life situations, we know that humans tend to perceive the exceptional as more miraculous than the familiar and the regular. What is exceptional has the glamor of a riddle simply because it is rare, while the familiar phenomena that often contain the more difficult problems are taken for granted. This is why in earlier periods, depending on the context, the mentally ill were perceived as blessed by the gods and equipped with higher knowledge, or as possessed by demons; even today, some of these opinions, originating from various forms of mental illness, influence the subjective ideas of the mad patients themselves.[67]

In this context, Wundt leaves no doubt as to what he thinks of occult theories:

> This leads to even more leeway for fantastic hypotheses, triggered by the surprising features that some irregular phenomena exhibit for the layperson. And among these psychological laypersons, unfortunately, there are also those who devote their time to the observation of hypnosis. Most hypnosis researchers are either medical doctors who use hypnosis for curative means or philosophers who like to see hypnotism as a source of new worldviews, and instead of investigating these phenomena in the light of clearly defined psychological laws, they want to base their entire psychology on hypnotism. Thus it is not surprising that much of the modern psychology of hypnotism has become a branch of spiritualism. Clairvoyance and long-distance magical influence from soul to soul have played a worrying role in this psychology, and even if more sober observers do not participate in all of these confusions, the disturbing influence of this business is revealed in the fact that some of them present such superstitious phenomena as "open questions," worthy and in need of further investigation, at the very least. Just as scientific superstitions have

> done in all eras, this one also likes to dress itself up in garments borrowed from real science.[68]

This position echoes Wundt's pamphlet against spiritualism, written almost twenty years earlier.[69]

At the end of the nineteenth century, the newly established field of empirical-scientific psychology was already able to assume a position from which to judge medical and philosophical approaches to explaining the soul. The discursive processes of including and excluding knowledge are clearly visible when Wundt criticizes attempts to call the field of hypnotic mysticism "experimental psychology" or to found "societies for psychological research" that amounted to nothing more than a legitimation of hypnotic experiments carried out by laypersons. "We can only hope that such abuses and confusions will gradually disappear, as this field is taken out of the hands of dilettante laypersons and physicians, and transferred to the experts called to investigate it—in this case, the psychologically and scientifically trained representatives of medicine."[70]

We see a similar process in Wilhelm Jerusalem's (1854–1923) work.[71] In his *Lehrbuch der Psychologie* (Textbook of Psychology; third edition 1902), the central vehicles of meaning are the discourse strands of consciousness, the nervous system, sensation, perception, imagination, thinking, language, emotion, and volition. It is only in the appendix that he engages with "Psychological Interruptions and Distortions." Here he addresses sleep, dreams, hypnosis, hallucinations, illusions, distortions of speech, and mental illnesses.[72] He uses the term *soul* only in passing, and only for one reason:

> Belief in a soul as a being detached from the body, which leaves the body after death and continues an independent existence, is deeply anchored in human nature, and in fact finds expression in the most primitive peoples who have remained on the lowest cultural level. Almost every religious system around the world has turned this belief into a dogma, and it has also been incorporated into many philosophical systems as a self-evident presupposition. Hence scientific psychology is confronted with the *concept of the soul* and has to comment on it.[73]

But according to Jerusalem, psychology could never grant scientific status to the soul.

> Just as mechanics can say nothing about the essence of matter, as it only investigates the laws of balance and movement, so psychology has to refrain from any claims about the essence of the soul. For the psychologist, the soul is nothing more than the referential arrangement of inner life [*Seelenleben*]. Questions about the soul's essence and origin, or its fate after death, exceed the boundaries of experience. These are questions for *metaphysics*, whose job it is to tie the facts of experience to a coherent system. Psychology limits itself to the investigation of psychological laws.[74]

Here we witness the discursive differentiation between psychology and metaphysics. This is especially noteworthy when the authors are themselves philosophers. Indeed, "the intrusion of physiology into the domain of philosophy . . . was embraced by philosophy itself."[75] A telling example is Friedrich Jodl (1849–1914), a professor of philosophy at the University of Vienna. In his *Lehrbuch der Psychologie* (Textbook of Psychology), first published in 1896, he argues:

> Usually we condense the sum of the phenomena of consciousness achieved by internal perception into the substantive "soul," and we regard the soul as the substantial carrier of conscious processes. This is unproblematic, as long as the symbolic character of this expression is strictly warranted, and as long as we always keep in mind that it is nothing more than a linguistic abbreviation of the totality of what is given in the phenomena of consciousness itself, and what presents itself . . . as the experience, state, or activity of an ego or a person. Whether or not the attempt to turn the term's logical-grammatical validity into an ontological one is justified, hence to construct the soul as a real subject that steers the totality of consciousness and to juxtapose it with the physical organism as an independent substance distinct and separated from it, can only be decided upon further discussion.[76]

The soul as the "linguistic abbreviation of the totality of consciousness," the "ego," or the "person": the new discursive arrangement is unmistakable. Here "consciousness" itself, along with "sensation," presented as the new core concept of psychology, is also defined physiologically (which marks a difference from understandings of the soul as consciousness in the second half of the twentieth century, as discussed in part 2). Jodl sees consciousness as "a connection of singular stimulations, a summation of impressions, ideas, and directed movements through ideas," which is why the claim that animals may also have consciousness must be "repudiated in the most resolute way."[77]

Otto Klemm (1884–1939), a lecturer in philosophy at the University of Leipzig, also regarded consciousness as psychology's central category and object.[78] We can see discourses on the soul and discourses on physiological explanations of consciousness drifting apart in Klemm's *Geschichte der Psychologie* (History of Psychology), in two trajectories that he differentiates historically—"metaphysical psychology" over against "empirical psychology." Klemm argues that the antagonism of these two trajectories has been historically relevant, but has found its end in the emergence of "scientific" psychology.

> To be sure, psychology as the science of the soul entered the hierarchy of the sciences surprisingly early, but for centuries its doctrines have reflected only the presuppositions and conclusions of philosophical systems. When considerations of a metaphysical worldview were applied to the field of the contents of consciousness, these contents were proof of the phenomena and activities of a soul that was usually conceived of as substantial. From the conceptual essence of the soul, expressed in this definition, one deduced the various phenomena. As an alternative to this *metaphysical* psychology, *empirical* psychology keeps the psychological phenomena as contents of self-observation in place and tries to find a scientific frame for them. The metaphysical and empirical directions of psychology by no means exclude one another.[79]

With such an approach, Klemm and his colleagues found themselves in an ambiguous position at the turn of the century: on the one hand, the term *soul*—thanks to its widespread, general use—seemed to be indispensable; on the other hand, the term did not qualify as a scientific concept to be used in empirical psychology. One response to this dilemma is to replace the concept of the soul with the term *consciousness*—an influential combination of psychology and discourses on the soul in the twentieth century, as I will explain in chapter 6.[80] But for Wundt, Jerusalem, Klemm, and others, the scientification of the soul goes hand in hand with its elimination. Put differently, discourses on the soul and discourses on psychology slowly drifted apart, resulting in the concept of the soul—if used at all—becoming an empty word, void of meaning and with no ontological point of reference.

People noted this development immediately. In a textbook published in 1900, K. O. Beetz spoke of the "transition to a 'psychology without soul'": "The persistent attempt to free itself from the chains of metaphysics therefore pushes psychology ever more decidedly onto the general warpath of experience. . . . From this side, new terms are developed and new laws become the foundation of all research. Soon psychology could no longer evade this influence, and so it happened that the movement (introduced by Herbart) that denied the soul any potentials and powers consequently ended in the abandonment of the soul itself."[81]

Another critic was Wilhelm Dilthey (1833–1911). As early as 1894, he condemned the new experimental psychology—of which "Herbart is a splendid example"[82]—for its "soullessness." A truly scientific psychology, Dilthey argued, could never be built on experimentation and claims to "explain"; rather, it would always have to be oriented toward "understanding," which implied a descriptive-hermeneutic approach. "The methods of explanatory psychology derive from an unjustified expansion of scientific concepts to the field of the inner life [*Seelenleben*] and to history. Knowledge of nature became a science when it started to construct equations between cause and effect in the area of movement." This was "forced upon our living thinking."[83] Dilthey's critique is directed against Herbart, but also—and particularly—against Wilhelm Wundt, whose psychology basically does away with the concept of the soul, as we have seen.

Although space does not permit me to do more than give brief hints at a complex discussion, it is clear that at the end of the nineteenth century, questions regarding the direction academic psychology should take and where it should be embedded institutionally and methodologically were still undecided. Even within the field of psychology itself, there were so many different positions that William James (1842–1910) lamented in a letter to his friend and colleague Théodore Flournoy (1854–1920) in 1893: "Everyone seems to be publishing a Psychology in these days."[84] Sonu Shamdasani summarizes the situation as follows:

> At the end of the nineteenth century, many figures in the West sought to establish a scientific psychology that would be independent of philosophy, theology, biology, anthropology, literature, medicine, and neurology, whilst taking over their traditional subject matters. The very possibility of psychology rested upon the successful negotiation of these disciplinary crossings. . . . Through becoming a science, it was hoped that psychology would be able to solve questions that had vexed thinkers for centuries, and to replace superstition, folk wisdom, and metaphysical speculation with the rule of universal law.[85]

These struggles over psychology's scientific status were vehement in part because more was at stake. At the turn of the century, the possibilities presented by the scientific method and an explanation of nature itself hinged on these very debates about psychology, as Lorraine Daston points out.[86]

The broad spectrum of possible iterations of psychology allowed for more extreme and more moderate positions. At one end of this spectrum stood Romantic psychology, with its metaphysical orientation (which was interested in the "dark side of the soul"); at the other pole stood Wilhelm Wundt's version of experimental psychology (interestingly, Wundt later turned to mysticism himself).[87] But there were also more modest positions that claimed scientific status for psychology while also questioning its feasibility. A good example of this is Théodore Flournoy, who took up the chair of psychology at the University of Geneva (the very first chair of psychology to be located in a faculty of sciences) in 1892. As was the case for his friend William James—who had published his influential two-volume work *The Principles of Psychology* in 1890—it was evident to Flournoy that psychology deserved scientific status and had implemented experimental testing, but he was not at all sure psychology could ever meet these expectations.[88]

For his part, James fully subscribed to an experimental, "scientific" approach to the soul and to psychology, which also informed his pragmatist philosophy (on the basis of which he became highly influential in the United States). At the same time, he acknowledged the limits of empirical science. "Round about the accredited and orderly facts of every science," he wrote in 1890, "there ever floats a sort of dust-cloud of exceptional observations, of occurrences minute and regular, and seldom met with, which it always proves less easy to attend to than to ignore."[89] As Andreas Sommer comments: "In fact, while it would be safe to state that James's psychical research was to a considerable extent motivated by broadly religious considerations and concerns, like his colleagues in England, France and Germany he insisted on the legitimacy of psychical research in terms of the scientific duty to attend to anomalies, or the 'Unclassified Residuum' of science."[90] In a new study of James's interest in "psychical" research, Krister Dylan Knapp confirms this impression.[91] James was instrumental in the formation of critical research on psychic phenomena—which he studied for almost thirty years—and helped to build up a philosophically informed academic psychology in the United States.[92] His balanced position between the radical poles of the debate (particularly in Germany) led him to the opinion that occult phenomena should be taken seriously, but that the soul itself would escape empirical research. He identified the soul of traditional metaphysics as the "pure ego," the individual "I." While the human self is part of a continuous stream of consciousness that constitutes a person, the pure ego cannot be an object of science, and furthermore should not be regarded as a substance.[93]

From the perspective of a cultural and discursive history of the soul—which has different aims and interests than an institutional history of psychology—it is striking that the entanglement of psychological and occult discourses ignited and sustained a fascination with the soul, both within and beyond academic milieus. Thus ever-more-professional empirical psychology and philosophical-mystical-occult psychology, with its wide societal impact, influenced each other in many ways. Andreas Sommer pertinently summarizes this situation: in the last two decades of the nineteenth century, we see competing strands of psychological experimentation that also reveal

> a considerable permeability of boundaries between psychical research and what has come to be known as "scientific" experimental psychology. "Fathers" of scientific psychology such as James and Théodore Flournoy sought to expand the new discipline to integrate psychical research, psychological societies in France and Germany conducted investigations of telepathy and related areas, and psychical research associations made significant empirical and methodological contributions to contemporary psychological knowledge.[94]

Moreover, fascinating new technologies and scientific theories seemed to offer undreamt-of opportunities. All of this led to a situation in which occultism and the psychological and philosophical positions attached to it became a mass movement—especially in Germany, as Corinna Treitel has consistently shown.[95] The soul became the center of a particular fascination in religion, art, philosophy, and science.

This first chapter has been a veritable tour de force. Many details of the long genealogy of ideas about the soul in European cultural history had to be left out for the sake of the chapter's main purpose: to introduce the basic components of the discursive arrangement that crystallized around the "soul" at the end of the nineteenth century, as well as the institutional settings of this discourse. The ideas about the soul—and the discursive knots formed around them—that had been built up over more than two thousand years of cultural history provide a pool of associations and possible arrangements that could easily be "reactivated" in the twentieth century. Linking "soul" to discourse strands of life–nature–knowledge–cosmos had been common for many centuries; intellectual debate in the nineteenth century rearranged these discourse strands and tied concepts of science–psychology–occultism (and a few others) into the new arrangement.

Equipped with these tools of analysis, we can now begin our discursive journey through the twentieth century.

2

FASCINATION WITH THE SOUL IN RELIGION, ART, PHILOSOPHY, AND SCIENCE

The soul was an object of intense discussion around 1900, not only in the newly established field of psychology, but also in other societal locations. From the perspectives of cultural and discursive history, the soul cannot be limited to psychology and philosophy in any case; the respective discourses also clearly materialize in religion, art, and literature. These cross-references, which perpetuated Romantic thinking and brought it into conversation with new developments in the sciences and the arts, are the topic of this chapter.

The discursive arrangements I have addressed so far had an impact on historical imagination, particularly with reference to the preparatory stages of "modern" culture in antiquity or in the phases of so-called prehistory. Historiography is, and has always been, work on the present. Ancient mythology turned out to be a treasure trove for cultural theories and psychological patterns of interpretation. We can almost speak of a mythologization of the soul at the turn of the century, which also affected philosophy and science. An influential example of this phenomenon is the mythical figure of Orpheus: In the nineteenth century, this hero who specialized in communication with animals and with nature became a counterfigure to the Enlightenment—Orpheus the artist, who through his art gains access to hidden dimensions of reality; a traveler in time and space, conceived as an antidote to the Enlightenment's "purely rational human." Indeed, the discourse strands that form what I call an "Orphic web" have been so important for the cultural history of the soul that I will address them repeatedly. One such example is the shamanic movement in North America and Europe (see chapter 8), in the context of which Michael Harner stresses that "the Greek Orpheus myth is a version of the same myth found in a variety of shamanic cultures all over the world."[1] Piers Vitebsky also notes that "this essentially shamanic theme can be found in painters from Titian to Picasso, and in the work of writers and poets from Ezra Pound to Edgar Allen Poe."[2]

But how did this discursive knot emerge in the first place?

Orpheus and Dionysus as Cultural Heroes

Orpheus fascinated nineteenth-century audiences in several ways. The Romantics made him the emblem of heroic love. He used his animated lyre playing to calm wild animals and the gods of the underworld in order to free his beloved Eurydice from the land of the dead. But he had given himself over to love so completely that he failed tragically—he could not keep his promise not to turn around and look at Eurydice, and so he lost his lover again. In addition to these aspects of the Orpheus myth, modern interpreters were particularly fascinated by Orpheus as a seer and a traveler who opened up unknown and invisible worlds with his music. This idea inspired many French Romantics, from Victor Hugo to Honoré de Balzac to Alphonse de Lamartine.[3] A similar movement emerged in Germany as in France, a movement that experienced "modernity" as a cultural crisis and propagated a return to ancient mythology. These European movements formed the cradle of academic disciplines such as sociology and the study of religion.[4]

We can study the influence of this discourse in the work of Friedrich Nietzsche (1844–1900).[5] Nietzsche picked up a theme that had already been under discussion for some time, one that combined the figure of Orpheus with those of Apollo and Dionysus.[6] Nietzsche's thinking made Orpheus the principle of "the Dionysian," thus rendering the Greek god the opposite pole to what Nietzsche called "the Apollonian." This polarity became one of his most important tools for interpreting ancient culture—and in fact all culture. He laid the basis for this cultural theory in *The Birth of Tragedy from the Spirit of Music* (German edition 1872). Two years earlier, in his treatise *The Dionysian Worldview*, he had introduced the opposition between the "Apollonian" and the "Dionysian" as a means to interpret Greek tragedy. For Nietzsche, Dionysus embodies unconquered nature, framed as a wild, ecstatic cult that had come from Asia to Greece. He describes this cult as follows:

> Dionysian art . . . is based on the play with intoxication/ecstasy [*Rausch*], with rapture [*Verzückung*]. There are two powers in particular that trigger the oblivious ecstasy [*Rausch*] of the naïve natural person—the drive of spring and the narcotic drink. Their impacts are symbolized by the figure of Dionysus. In both states, the *principium individuationis* is broken; the subjective disappears entirely under the force of the general-human, indeed the general-natural that breaks forth. The festivals of Dionysus not only create a bond between humans, they also reconcile the human with nature.[7]

The conscious transgression of boundaries is a central characteristic of Dionysian experience of the world. By giving up their individuality, the participants become part of the community; at the same time, they experience the mystical power of nature. The close links between Dionysus and the themes of mystical community and nature become explicit when Nietzsche writes: "In ever larger droves, the gospel of 'world harmony' is rolling from place to place: singing and dancing, the human being expresses himself as a member of a higher, ideal community: he has forgotten how to walk and to speak. Moreover, he feels enchanted, and indeed he has become something else. Just as the animals talk and the earth gives milk and honey, something supernatural sounds from him. He feels like a god; what used to live only in his imagination, he now feels in himself."[8]

In the next chapter I will demonstrate how, based on this theme, the "national soul" was loaded with mythical meaning; the discursive entanglements we see here reveal the inner links between *völkisch* religion around 1900 and the veneration of nature that had always been part of this movement. Nietzsche, however, stressed that the Dionysian needed the Apollonian, which he identified as the sublimation and "taming" of the wild Dionysian. Dionysus became the Dionysian, and Apollo became the Apollonian. "In the summer of 1870, with the transformation of the stylistic characteristics of art—the Apollonian and the Dionysian—into metaphysical powers of life, Friedrich Nietzsche made the decisive step in his intellectual biography. From then on, he held in his hand the key he thought he could use to understand the trade secrets of all cultures, their history, and their future."[9]

Like Arthur Schopenhauer (1788–1860) and other Romantics, Nietzsche found the essence of the world in music. Music was the link to the ultimate primordial reality, which he tried to conceptualize as the Dionysian. While in antiquity the Apollonian refinement of the wild rage and sublimation of the animal drive in the human being was the task of the tragedy, in his own epoch Nietzsche found a similar task realized in the musical dramas of Richard Wagner (1813–1883). Wagner's projects offered a true experience of art and an antidote to the increasing intellectualism and commercialization of music in the nineteenth century. For Nietzsche, of course, this experience of music must not be mixed up with the simple pleasure of listening; it means listening to the "ventricle of the World's Will."[10] Such music does not aim at superficial beauty, but at making contact with the "horrible" (*Ungeheure*) and the "deep." He wrote to his close friend Erwin Rohde on October 27, 1868, after having listened to the overture to Wagner's *Meistersinger*: "Every fiber, every nerve twitched; I haven't had such a long-lasting feeling of rapture [*Entrücktheit*] for a long time."[11] *Entrückung, Ekstase, Rausch*: these are the three terms that—not only for Schopenhauer and Nietzsche, but subsequently also for Rohde and others—became the master keys for interpreting Greek "irrationalism."[12]

Shortly after his experience with the *Meistersinger*, Nietzsche got in touch with Wagner and began to present the latter's music—until the end of their friendship in 1878—as the quintessential example of the Dionysian-Apollonian initiation. In *The Birth of Tragedy* he writes: "The tragedy sucks the highest orgiastic feeling of music into itself."[13] In contrast to those who stick to the surface of music and stylize that experience as the "pleasure of art," Nietzsche addresses those who, like himself, have "music as their native language":

> To those real musicians I pose the question of whether they can imagine someone who would be able to perceive the third act of *Tristan and Isolde* without the aid of any text or image, simply as an incredible symphonic movement, and who would not breathe out their life in a compulsive spreading of all the wings of their soul? Someone who put their ear to the ventricle of the World's Will, who felt the raging desire for being as a roaring river or as a most sublime creek pouring into all the veins of the world—and who would not immediately break? Someone who could endure hearing, in the miserable glass shell of the human individual, the echo of countless cries of lust and pain from the "wide space of the world's night"—and who would not at such a shepherd's round dance of metaphysics flee inescapably to their original home?[14]

These sentences mark the red thread that links Romanticism to early-twentieth-century German literature, such as Thomas Mann's *Tod in Venedig* and Hermann Hesse's *Das Glasperlenspiel*.[15]

Nietzsche's discursive web of soul, music, transgression, ecstasy, and metaphysics also includes nature. As Jürgen Habermas points out: "Art opens the way to the Dionysian only at the price of ecstasy—at the price of painful dedifferentiation, of overcoming the individual's limits, of melting with an amorphous nature, both inside and outside."[16] It is therefore not accidental that Peter Sloterdijk and Thomas H. Macho included the passage "Before Sunrise" from Nietzsche's *Thus Spoke Zarathustra* in their collection *Weltrevolution der Seele* (World Revolution of the Soul) under the rubric "In the Eighth Heaven: Frequencies of Ecstasy."[17]

I also want to mention another piece of evidence here, namely, Nietzsche's comments on the music of the "German masters." In his forth Untimely Meditation, Nietzsche notes that this music "is a return to nature, and at the same time it is the purification and transformation of nature, because in the soul of the most loving human beings the necessity for such a return emerged, and *nature transformed into the sounds of love in their art*."[18] For

Nietzsche, nature comes to its teleological culmination in human consciousness, even if that consciousness remains broken due to the impossibility of its actually incorporating the horrible.

This conception had an enormous impact in the twentieth century. Even if it is a bit of an oversimplification, Safranski is right when he concludes: "Nietzsche's 'Dionysus,' Heidegger's 'Being,' and Adorno/Horkheimer's 'nature' are different names for the same thing—for the horrible [*das Ungeheure*]."[19] At the same time, the horrible had immense potential to gauge the absolute being and to contact the ultimate ground of reality—a potential that certainly maintained its fascinating appeal in the twentieth century. In a new study, Adam Lecznar describes this appeal in the works of intellectuals as diverse as Jane Ellen Harrison, D. H. Lawrence, Martin Heidegger, Richard Schechner, and Wole Soyinka. As Lecznar puts it: "In Nietzsche's beginning was his end, and in his end is our beginning: while Nietzsche danced for Dionysus in Turin, he initiated a series of associations, manipulations, reincarnations and receptions that would make the Greek god into a symbol of the vital modernity that forms the subject of this book."[20] Indeed, all of these intellectuals—and many more whom I address in my own analysis—contributed to the emergence of an order of knowledge with an impact that can still be seen today.

The Orphic Web in Rainer Maria Rilke

At the turn of the twentieth century, there is nowhere better to observe the fascination with this discursive arrangement than in the poetic work of Rainer Maria Rilke (1875–1926).[21] As Walter Strauss notes, "Rilke's work represents the confluence of the French and German Orphic currents; as Nerval was, in some respects, the logical successor to Novalis, so Rilke may be looked upon as the heir of Mallarmé."[22] To this list we can also add the Peruvian poet César Vallejo, who died in Paris in 1938.[23] Rilke's engagement with the ancient material was not only inspired by Romanticism; it also responded to discourses on modernity, which were typical of the fin-de-siècle, and then escalated existentially after the experience of World War I.

In his comparison of Rilke and D. H. Lawrence, Ian R. Leslie points out: "The *Sonnets to Orpheus* mention the gods as a fact, ousted by industrialization from human life."[24] In addition to the *Sonnets to Orpheus*, written in February 1922, the poem "Orpheus. Eurydice. Hermes" (1904) is particularly important for the theme of the soul.

Just as Virgil had done before him, Rilke also places Orpheus's tragic mistake of turning around to see his lover at the center of the story. However, in "Orpheus. Eurydice. Hermes," Eurydice rather than Orpheus is the main character, which leads to a conscious change in perspective.[25] Moreover, the external events transform into an internal process, which makes the soul the true theme of the poem. This is already clear in the first stanza:

> That was the deep uncanny mine of souls.
> Like veins of silver ore, they silently
> moved through its massive darkness. Blood welled up
> among the roots, on its way to the world of men,
> and in the dark it looked as hard as stone.
> Nothing else was red.[26]

This "mine of souls" is a world of its own—a world of the dead and of shadows, characterized by emptiness and mourning:

> There were cliffs there,
> and forests made of mist. There were bridges
> spanning the void, and that great gray blind lake
> which hung above its distant bottom
> like the sky on a rainy day above a landscape.
> And through the gentle, unresisting meadows
> one pale path unrolled like a strip of cotton.
>
> Down this path they were coming.[27]

Even before Orpheus makes his decisive mistake, Eurydice already belongs to this other world. She is so immersed in this parallel world that later she cannot even understand the implications of Orpheus's behavior. Rilke describes the lyre as the link to the world of the soul:

> A woman so loved that from one lyre there came
> more lament than from all lamenting women;
> that a whole world of lament arose, in which
> all nature reappeared: forest and valley,
> road and village, field and stream and animal;
> and that around this lament-world, even as
> around the other earth, a sun revolved
> and a silent star-filled heaven, a lament-
> heaven, with its own, disfigured stars—:
> So greatly was she loved.[28]

Rilke adapts the theme of transience, as known from older lyrical traditions, in the sense that Eurydice herself embodies the creation of life and the state of being bound to the Earth. Here death is no longer the end or the antithesis of life, but an integral part of it. This is an assessment of the soul's inner transformation, quite similar to the poem "The Man Watching" ("Der Schauende"), which states:

> Whoever was beaten by the Angel
> (who often simply declined the fight)
> went away proud and strengthened
> and great from that harsh hand,
> that kneaded him as if to change his shape.
> Winning does not tempt that man.
> This is how he grows: by being defeated, decisively,
> by constantly greater beings.[29]

Two elements are important for the discourse on the soul: on the one hand, the model of reality that conceives of an invisible, parallel world alongside the visible world, accessible through art and mysticism; on the other hand, the role of the Psychopompos as a virtuoso of living and dying.

How is this theme presented in the *Sonnets to Orpheus*? Rilke composed this cycle of fifty-five poems in less than three weeks. "The entire first part," Rilke writes to Xaver von Moos, "was written down in a single breathless submission between the second and the fifth of February 1922, without a single word being doubtful or in need of alternation."[30] The Eurydice of the Sonnets is Wera Knoop, a dancer who died at the age of nineteen. Rilke's dedication—"Written as a monument [*Grab-Mal*] to Wera Ouckama Knoop"—anticipates in a single line the thematic triad of love–art–death for which Orpheus has stood since ancient times.

For our purpose here, it must suffice to have a quick look at the motifs of nature and art, as these take up and amend discourses on the soul in specific ways. The first sonnet strikes a note that will sound through the entire cycle of poems:

> A tree ascended there. Oh pure transcendence!
> Oh Orpheus sings! Oh tall tree in the ear!
> And all things hushed. Yet even in that silence
> a new beginning, beckoning, change appeared.
>
> Creatures of stillness crowded from the bright
> unbound forest, out of their lairs and nests;
> and it was not from any dullness, not
> from fear, that they were so quiet in themselves,
>
> but from simply listening. Bellow, roar, shriek
> seemed small inside their hearts. And where there had been
> just a makeshift hut to receive the music,
>
> a shelter nailed up out of their darkest longing,
> with an entryway that shuddered in the wind—
> you built a temple deep inside their hearing.[31]

Rilke presents Orpheus's ability to calm wild animals not as a powerful demonstration of his superiority, but as the creation of concord, a harmony between entities that is born from love and poetry. And from "this single harmony of song and lyre," Eurydice appeared "and made herself a bed inside my ear / And slept in me. Her sleep was everything."[32] This again refers to the hidden reality that "Orpheus. Eurydice. Hermes" had already conceived, and that Eurydice embodies: "She slept the world." Renate Breuninger emphasizes the way in which Rilke's conception of reality was influenced by Nietzsche's critique of civilization, as well as his "diagnosis of a chasm between the inner and the outer. There is no longer an essence hidden in the physical, sensual world, which would abandon its enveloped or hidden status and become visible in the physical world. . . . The concept of 'reality' that underlies Rilke's ideas of 'reality' is clearly monistic"[33]—a reality, we may add, that is only accessible through art.

The animals in the poem further stress the mystical unity of the two worlds. Orpheus does not defeat them; rather, his death paradoxically leads them to life. Something similar occurs with the maenads: when the maenads in their rage rip him to pieces, he "wove their shrieking into wider harmonies, / and brought from that destruction a song to build with."[34] The poem continues:

> Hounded by hatred, you were torn to pieces
> while your music still rang amidst rocks and lions,
> trees and birds. There you are singing still.
> O dear lost god, you endless path!
> Only because you were broken and scattered
> have we become the ears of nature, and her voice.[35]

With these last verses of the first part of the *Sonnets*, Rilke emphasizes how important nature in general and animals in particular are to the Orphic mythology (it is by no means accidental that the first part of the sonnets begins with the "ascending tree" and ends with nature). Orpheus's lyre combines art, music, and poetry, and it enables humans to participate in a primordial unity as the "ears" and "voice" of nature. Superficially, it seems that this unity is destroyed; but when we look deeper, it becomes clear that it still sounds in every stone, tree, and bird. Hence Rilke is talking of nature itself, not just of the poet, when he writes: "It is Orpheus in the singing, once and for all time."[36]

The second part picks up this aspect again. It describes nature as entirely resonant with Orpheus's singing, a power that the animals and the elements carry within them. Sonnet 28 says that nature

> was stirred
> to total hearing just when Orpheus sang.
> You were still moved by those primeval words
> and a bit surprised if any tree took long
>
> to step with you into the listening ear.[37]

Sonnets 14, 20, and 21 again address the mystical union with ensouled animals and plants, and in Sonnet 17 the poet asks: "Are there then trees to which angels frequently go / And which slow occult gardeners so strangely rear, / That, without belonging to us, for us they bear?"[38] And from Sonnet 26 we can derive what is at stake here: a plurality of realities that flow together in dreamlike states. On the cry of birds, Rilke writes:

> How it can stir us—the cry of a bird . . .
> Any of creation's primal cries. . . .
>
> Cry of chance. Between the edges
> Of the world-space, (into which it seems
> Unbroken bird-cries pass, as people do in dreams—)
> They drive their wedges, their shrieking wedges.
>
> . . . Lead the crier,
> Singing god! That he wakes resounding,
> A current bearing the head and the lyre.[39]

Ultimately, the entire work ends with a connection to the elements:

> And if the earthly no longer knows your name,
> whisper to the silent earth: I'm flowing.
> To the flashing water say: I am.[40]

Rainer Maria Rilke's poetic work contributed to the solidification of a discursive arrangement that entangled the concept of the soul with motifs of animated nature, art, and a vision of absolute reality. Rilke was part of a broad intellectual movement at the beginning of the twentieth century. Motivated by a critique of civilization, this movement gave metaphysical meaning to the soul and regarded the soul as a vehicle by which to achieve knowledge of nature. Hermann Hesse (1877–1962) was part of this movement, too. As early as 1904 he wrote the poem "Sometimes," which we can read as yet another animistic testimony:

> Sometimes when a bird cries out,
> Or the wind sweeps through a tree,
> Or a dog howls in a far-off farm,
> I hold still and listen a long time.
>
> My soul turns and goes back to the place
> Where, a thousand forgotten years ago,
> The bird and the blowing wind
> Were like me, and were my brothers.
>
> My soul turns into a tree,
> And an animal, and a cloud bank.
> Then changed and odd it comes home
> And asks me questions. What should I reply?[41]

It says a lot about the consistency of this discourse that ninety years later, Hesse's poem (in English) was printed in the course brochure of the Scandinavian Center for Shamanic Studies in Copenhagen (Fall/Winter 1998/1999), and that Joan Halifax quotes it in her book *The Fruitful Darkness*.[42] The tone that Rilke, Hesse, and others had struck found its echo in shamanic and nature-based spiritualities throughout the twentieth century. As I will analyze in more detail in chapters 9 and 10, English-language authors in particular helped to consolidate this discourse.

But let me once more return to Rilke and his artistic network, which is one of the crystallization points of the discourse that interests us here.[43]

Rilke—who for some time had also been secretary to the Parisian sculptor Auguste Rodin—was part of the scene in bohemian Berlin, and had excellent contacts with artists and intellectuals, as well as with Princess Taxis, Edith Andreae (Walter Rathenau's sister), Anton and Katharina Kippenberg,[44] and others. At the end of World War I, he met the sculptor and artist Renée Sintenis in Berlin. Sintenis (1888–1965) was a rising star at the time, and Rilke was intrigued by the dynamic originality of her work. For many observers, Sintenis embodied the "new woman"—an androgynous, queer, self-confident, modern personality who playfully evaded prescribed gender roles.[45] She became "one of the women you had to know in Berlin, someone to talk about if you want to have a say."[46] Rilke's enthusiasm for her art helped her gain further success as an artist.

Among other things, Sintenis is known for the small animal sculptures she created from 1915 onward. The figure of a bear standing upright with front paws raised became the landmark of Berlin: large bronze sculptures of this bear were erected beside Berlin highways in 1957 and again in 1962. The sculpture is also the model for the Berlin International Film Festival's Golden Bear award to this day.

Sintenis enjoyed her greatest successes in the 1920s. Members of the Freie Secession, the most important artist association in Berlin—which included Max Beckmann, Max Liebermann, and Karl Schmidt-Rottluff—held her work in high esteem. When her gallery opened in Berlin in 1922, she became one of the most important people in the Flechtheimer Kunstkreis. She subsequently exhibited her work at the National Gallery in Berlin, in Paris, at the Tate Gallery in London, and at the Museum of Modern Art in New York, as well as in Glasgow and Rotterdam. In 1931 she was the first female sculptor—and only the second woman, after Käthe Kollwitz—to be accepted into the Berlin Academy of Arts.

Renée Sintenis was the most photographed woman of the Weimar Republic. Her art and lifestyle are an example of the Orphic combination of nature, art, death, and love. Quite like Rilke, Sintenis brought ancient mythology into conversation with modernity, for instance, in *Des Longus Hirtengeschichten von Daphnis und Chloë* (Longus's Shephard's Tales of Daphne and Cloë), published in 1939 with thirty-one woodcuts by Sintenis. In his acknowledgment of her work, the lyricist and essayist Paul Appel tied the theme of death—"unconsciously at first, then more and more consciously, death must have hovered around her"[47]—to the themes of nature, soul, mysticism, and religion. For him, Sintenis embodied "the modern soul [*modernes Seelentum*]."[48] Her "animals and humans are creatures, they are whole, they are given to themselves, and they suffice in themselves."[49] And he adds: "How deeply Renée Sintenis is characterized by a dense soulhood [*dichtes Seelentum*], which we can see in the fact that the animals she makes, while representing the species they belong to, are at the same time a far more general expression of all animal beings. I often see her animals as *one* single animal."[50] This was closely linked to the "mystical genius," which Sintenis uniquely embodied. Paul Appel's enthusiasm culminates in the statement:

> Can it then be surprising to say that Renée Sintenis's oeuvre appeals to me as something highly religious? I feel floods of piety. The dumbness, the taciturnity of the animal heads is piety. The trembling of the very young creatures is piety. Their grace, their soft, wild charm are piety. All those tresses of mane and tail, how pious they are! I will stop here; I will simply say: if Renée Sintenis were given a pedagogical mission on Earth, it would be to free the concept of the religious from its clumsy, miserable narrowness, so that it would become young, whole, unspoiled, and legible again.

Both Rilke's poetic work and Sintenis's sculptural and graphic work hit the nerve of their day. As artists, they contributed to an Orphic discourse that wove together the strands of art, nature, death, and soul. The intellectual fascination with such a discursive arrangement also captured scholars of religion, who reinforced these orders of knowledge in their own ways.

Frenzy, Ecstasy, and Dance in the Study of Religion

The fascination with frenzy and ecstasy, which had a strong proponent in Nietzsche's concept of the Dionysian at the end of the nineteenth century, also clearly influenced the study of culture and religion at the time.

Scholars of religion, in turn, invented the theories that lent scientific plausibility to the aesthetic, artistic, and political dedifferentiation of the soul and connected themes.[51] The discursive web that resulted from this combination can hardly be overestimated. It also had an impact on culture in the United States at the time, as Lytton Naegele McDonnell has recently demonstrated.[52]

In the field of classics and cultural studies, Nietzsche's considerations were propagated by Erwin Rohde (1845–1898) in particular. Rohde, who sometimes addressed Nietzsche as his "dear brother in Dionysus," contributed to the writing of Nietzsche's *Birth of the Tragedy*, and the two self-declared "brothers in arms," at war with the bourgeois establishment, subsequently continued their exchange of ideas.[53] In his influential two-volume study *Psyche: The Cult of Souls and Belief in Immortality Among the Greeks* (German edition 1894), Rohde puts Nietzsche's program into practice and applies it, with a few adjustments, to the interpretation of ancient Greek culture. Interestingly, Nietzsche's name is entirely absent from *Psyche*. Rohde refers to the original Greek meaning of *ecstasy* and calls it "a 'temporary madness,' while madness is a lasting ecstasy. But ecstasy, the temporary *alienatio mentis* of the Dionysian cult, is not regarded as a fluttering soul, wandering around in spaces of empty delusion, but as hieromania, a sacred madness."[54] The Dionysian cult held a particular attraction for women. Through the "liberation of the soul from the restrictive imprisonment of the body," Rohde explains, the female participants experience an enormous energy boost, which enables them to travel into spheres that are hidden from everyday perception. "Now [the soul] can socialize freely as a spirit among spirits, and with the liberation from temporality it is able to see what only the eyes of spirits can see, things that are temporally and spatially distant."[55]

Nietzsche's and Rohde's constructions of Dionysian dedifferentiation were enthusiastically received in the study of religion, a discipline that had just begun to establish itself at universities. Of particular interest for us is the use of these theories in the United Kingdom, especially in the work of the historian of antiquity Jane Ellen Harrison (1850–1928). Harrison was a top scholar in the history of religion at the time, applying culture-theoretical, anthropological, and philosophical questions to the interpretation of ancient culture. "By exploring the Nietzschean resonances in Harrison's writing and thought," Adam Lecznar points out, "it will be possible to glimpse a powerful route by which Nietzsche's Greeks came to underwrite modernist praxis."[56]

Harrison's fascination with the theme of Dionysian rage and with Orpheus's death at the hands of the maenads also originated from the gender relations of her time. For Camille Paglia, Harrison was the inventor of the "chthonian gods," as opposed to the Olympian gods—this differentiation offered a blueprint for interpreting the symbolic categories of male and female sexuality.[57] Ulrike Brunotte argues similarly and maintains that, for Harrison, the Dionysian antiquity was "a laboratory of female models of identity and community, located between or rather beyond matriarchy and patriarchy. . . . The utopia of such a network of women acquired concrete social evidence in the context of life in the women's colleges of Newnham and Girton, the newly founded women's clubs, and the female groups that were formed in artistic milieus and among the suffragettes."[58] The liberation of the soul from the "chains of the body" could almost be read as the epitome of the dedifferentiation of gender constructions and the formation of new forms of community. What the anthropologist Victor Turner would later call *communitas*, Harrison had already theoretically anticipated at the beginning of the twentieth century; particularly in dance, music, and ritual, Harrison found the decisive means for individual metamorphosis and the creation of new forms of community.[59]

One important influence on this thinking was Erwin Rohde, whose two volumes on the Greek concept of the soul Harrison reviewed for *Classical Review* in 1890 and 1894.[60] On the importance of this concept of ecstasy and dance for becoming one with the divine, Harrison's biographer remarks: "These ideas of Rohde became seminal for Harrison's *Themis*, published eighteen years later. The importance to her of Rohde, however, went beyond the intellectual stimulus. . . . Rohde's conception of spirituality became a model for her own, and parallel to her writing on the religion of the Greeks can be discerned the development of a personal spiritual quest, which for the rest of her life she sought to bring into line with the latest in sociological and psychological research."[61]

Theories about the dedifferentiation of the soul in ritual, dance, and music were cornerstones of historical and anthropological research into religion among the so-called Cambridge Ritualists, a group to which Harrison belonged. But these theories also made a significant contribution to the emergence of religious phenomenology. Mysticism—from the fascination with ancient mystery cults to the discovery of "Eastern" wisdom traditions—played an important role in this process. Mysticism became "the means of overthrowing the rule of reason over man and achieving a lifestyle without rationalist damage, by blending the essence of man with god."[62] Hans G. Kippenberg correctly refers to Martin Buber (1878–1965), who in his influential collection *Ekstatische Konfessionen* (Ecstatic Confessions, 1909) had provocatively noted that ecstasy was God's highest gift to humanity.[63] Buber was absolutely serious about this. He asked: "But is myth a phantasm? Isn't it a revelation of the final reality of being? The experience of the ecstatic, isn't it an emblem of the primordial experience of the world spirit? Aren't both an experience? We hearken unto ourselves—and we don't know which sea's surge we are hearing."[64] In the work of Buber and other Jewish intellectuals of his generation, we see Nietzsche's inspiration once again.[65]

What we can describe as a sort of internalization of the ecstatic in religious emotion also found expression in the work of Rudolf Otto (1869–1937). His book *Das Heilige: Über das Irrationale in der Idee des Göttlichen und sein Verhältnis zum Rationalen* (published in English in 1923 as *The Idea of the Holy*) came out in 1917, during World War I, and immediately commanded a large audience.[66] It was an attempt to rehabilitate religious experience over against the materialistic and rationalist tendencies of the time.

> The book's inconsistency of grasping something inexpressible in words identifies Rudolf Otto as a genuine representative of "German mysticism." Over a long time, a tradition had developed in Germany that God was revealed not only in the Holy Scriptures, but also in the world and in the soul of the individual. Despite its contrary claim of an inexpressible experience, this "German mysticism" was philosophical in argumentation and literary in presentation. *Pace* Schleiermacher, Otto adopted it into religious studies. As all known historical religions had risen out of the ground of a "pre-religion," so religion reemerged anew in every individual.[67]

Phenomenology of religion, which emerged from this tradition, sees the sacred as a reality, the impact of which becomes visible and accessible in the history of religion in general, and in the individual soul in particular. This approach closely tied the study of religion to psychology, which materialized in the United States in William James's work and in Europe in Carl Gustav Jung's. I will come back to this.

At this point, let me bring in the Dutch theologian and scholar of religion Gerardus van der Leeuw (1890–1950), as his studies reveal phenomenology of religion's contribution to the discourse on the soul.[68] Van der Leeuw was appointed chair of the history of religion and theology at the University of Groningen in 1918, which in 1945 was renamed the chair of phenomenology of religion. Van der Leeuw's influence was not limited to the study of religion, but included the political and cultural sectors as well. He served as minister of education, arts, and sciences in the first Dutch cabinet after World War II. He was instrumental in the foundation of the Dutch Association for the Study of Religion (in 1947, the first association of its kind worldwide) and the International Association for the History of Religion (1950). Moreover, he was the president of the Dutch Bach Association, the Groningen Orchestra Association, and other organizations as well. He played the organ and was an active singer. During his term as minister, he personally supported a number of Dutch artists. Overall, this makes for a significant discursive impact. Also interesting for us is the fact that van der Leeuw participated in the Eranos conferences in 1948, 1949, and 1950 in Ascona, Switzerland (on which see chapter 5).

Although the details differ, phenomenology of religion in the twentieth century has always argued against reductionist approaches in the empirical social sciences. Many phenomenologists regard religion as a category sui generis—as a unique and incomparable category. When it comes to the theoretical formulation of these views, van der Leeuw was much more nuanced than Rudolf Otto, for instance. Furthermore, he did not regard phenomenology of religion as an aspect of theology; rather, he insisted that science must study human action, and not the alleged power of the sacred itself.

For van der Leeuw, religion was entwined in cultural processes. He was particularly interested in religion as an aesthetically communicated phenomenon, which places him squarely in the midst of the discursive arrangement that had formed around art, mysticism, and ecstasy. In his book about mysticism (published in Dutch in 1924 as *Mystiek*), he referred back to Goethe as the pinnacle of the scientific understanding of religion and mysticism, the successor to Plato and Plotinus.[69] We find similar ideas in his book *Uren met Novalis* (Hours with Novalis, 1943). As a public intellectual, van der Leeuw often mixed genres in his publications. For him, it was evident that science had to find answers to the most urgent questions of the day. His fascination with dance, eroticism, and mysticism was clearly tied to a diagnosis of "modernity." In his book *Sacred and Profane Beauty: The Holy in Art* (1963, first published in Dutch as *Wegen en Grenzen: Een studie over de verhouding van religie en kunst*, 1932), he asserts that art and dance are the oldest forms of expression in human communication with the sacred. "For us, with the exception of our children, the dance is a problem. We still understand the effect, the magical power, of the dance best when we are dealing with the erotic dance."[70] Dance as a "natural" form of access to the sacred, which was a normal thing in "primitive" stages of human culture, is no longer a real possibility for modern people. A return to the "primitive" state is not an option, and yet: "At times the dance, as an independent art form, has been lost. But only at times, for it cannot die. The more one becomes conscious of the unity of body and soul, the more the dance will again achieve its rightful position as a function of life."[71] This also explains van der Leeuw's enthusiasm for the Californian dancer Isadora Duncan (1877–1927), who enjoyed a celebrated career in Europe, performing in Richard Wagner's *Tannhäuser* in Bayreuth as well as in other productions. Van der Leeuw writes about her:

> In this connection I shall again mention with honor the name of the person who for the first time revealed to us the majesty of the dance, and that is Isadora Duncan. She has already had many excellent successors, but she was the first. Only when the dance as an art has once again achieved respect, when the possibilities within it for universal expression have again been revealed by beautiful examples, only then will it all be able once more to become an expression of the holy. The metaphysics of music we can experience, those of the dance only, and not without effort,

> understand. But why should not mankind speak again in its most ancient language of the great mystery of movement and countermovement: the one movement which proceeds from this world to God, and the other movement which proceeds from God to this world?[72]

In his hermeneutic of religious dance, van der Leeuw entangles discourse strands on the soul with those of art, dance, religion, metaphysics, and the unity of body and soul. With direct reference to Nietzsche's considerations, he distinguishes between "Apollonian" and "Dionysian movement."[73] Dionysian-ecstatic movement can link the soul to the absolute and the divine. "For this reason," van der Leeuw maintains, "Plato describes the eternal ascent of the souls of gods and men to true being as a gigantic procession." And for the same reason, "we can understand the metaphysics of this dance when we listen to the highest forms of dance music. Beethoven's Seventh, justifiably called the apotheosis of the dance, is inspired with a truly Dionysiac passion which seems not to rest until the entire world dances with it."[74]

A bit unexpectedly, as the title sounds very theological, van der Leeuw gets even more explicit in his book *Sakramentales Denken: Erscheinungsformen und Wesen der außerchristlichen und christlichen Sakramente* (Sacramental Thinking: The Manifestations and Essence of Non-Christian and Christian Sacraments, published in German in 1959). Building on his earlier ideas about the current state of civilization, van der Leeuw here writes against what he sees as the prudish theology and cultural studies of his time. First, with reference to Rudolf Otto, he clarifies: "The sacramental is the counterpole of the technical."[75] Then he notes that the sexual act is the moment at which the human comes closest to the primordial act of creation. "Now, the danger of our time is that it becomes something trivial."[76] Ancient and "primitive" cultures, however, provided "the sexual moment" with a prominent place.

> People who are influenced on the one hand by the rise of modern technology, and on the other hand by the Platonic-Christian idea—now solidified as prudery—of the sexual act as *the* sin, are naively surprised about this prominent place. Fortunately, the modern world once again views the sexual with more equanimity, and this in particular nourishes the

> hope that our time will rediscover the sacramental in this context. It is easier for us than for people in the time of Queen Victoria, when, according to Punch, the question of whether women had legs was unresolved, and when the sexual was a matter about which one either remained silent or smirked.[77]

Hence, from the perspective of this professor's male gaze, the unification of body and soul with the sacred—which modern civilization is more in need of than any previous cultural era—had to come from the Dionysian-ecstatic restoration of sexuality, dance, and sacramental action.

The Soul and Nature in Neoromantic Philosophy

The new interest in mysticism, transcendence, and nature, which was so prominent at the beginning of the twentieth century, captured philosophy as well. Ideas originating from philosophy of life and Neoromantic philosophy were widely discussed. In Germany, Eugen Diederichs press played a significant role in this development, firmly establishing itself at the confluence of philosophy, religion, mysticism, and science.[78] These publications—and also those of other publishing houses, such as S. Fischer (founded in 1886) and Ernst Rowohlt (founded in 1908, renewed in 1919)—had significant discursive impact in part because Diederichs provided a platform for experts to reach a large audience.

When it comes to discourses on the soul, Karl Joël's (1864–1934) works provide a relevant example. Joël studied philosophy with Wilhelm Dilthey in Breslau, defended his doctoral dissertation in Leipzig in 1886, and earned his habilitation in 1893 in Basel, where he was also appointed professor of philosophy in 1897. In his writings, Joël gauged the implications of new scientific and technological developments for the very foundations of philosophy, attempting to apply them productively in the creation of an integrative philosophy. In physics, for instance, the discovery that colors and sounds are based on vibration led him to interpret the entire world as an interrelated, coherent organism. Taking up ideas from evolutionary theory and electrodynamics as well as psychology, he developed a dynamic worldview that combined the soul and the cosmos into one system. The title of his main work, *Seele und Welt: Versuch einer organischen Auffassung* (Soul and World: An Attempt at an Organic Understanding), published with Diederichs in 1912, aptly summarizes this project. But six years earlier, in his *Der Ursprung der Naturphilosophie aus dem Geiste der Mystik* (The Birth of Natural Philosophy from the Spirit of Mysticism), he had already signaled this specific discursive arrangement. In this book, also published with Diederichs, Joël puts forward the thesis that natural philosophy's three big epochs—which he identifies as the Pre-Socratics, the Renaissance, and Romanticism—formulate the essential unity of the divine, the soul, and nature in a way that modern humans, hampered by the influence of rationalism and technological developments, have to regain.[79] Referring to "our newest friends, the Romantics,"[80] Joël seeks to prove that holism, mysticism, and pantheism have been constant factors in European intellectual history.[81] He celebrates Sebastian Franck and Jacob Boehme because "deepest, most pious mysticism here urges a valuation of nature that even the materialist cannot surpass. They discovered nature by seeking God in it."[82] Consequently, for him the core of natural philosophy is mystical: "To feel something is nothing less than to grasp it in unity with oneself."[83]

In *Seele und Welt*, Joël expands on this idea and develops a large philosophical-cosmological program. In his first chapter, titled "The Soul as Modern Specter," he takes reductionist psychology to task:

> Under the green lampshade [a humorous reference to the desk lamps many scholars used at the time], the modern researcher assesses the belief in the soul in all times, peoples, and religions, including the breath-soul and the blood-soul of the native peoples, as well as the Old Egyptian conversation with the soul, written down thousands of years ago. He collects all the intimacy of mysticism, all the eschatological longing, the bliss of all heavens and the horror of all hells, puts it into neatly edited, well-annotated booklets—just as one collects and labels the remains of pile dwellings. From the high pulpit, one allows the "soul" to speak once more—but when the soul speaks, well, it is no longer the soul that is speaking; only the little old ladies in the Gothic twilight below nod to the old soul, nod till they doze off. But outside

> the streetcar drones: Do the moderns really have time for the words of past emotions? Who today would still believe in the soul? Every other period spoke of the soul, even sensed something high and secret, something of heaven and hell, trembling within it. Speaking of the soul today is almost as indecent as speaking of virtue; it sounds almost theological. But if they simply cannot avoid the topic, our medical doctors speak of the psyche at most. This is because the most devoted followers of humanistic education are the materialists—since the safest recipe for sanitizing old idealist terms is translating them into Greek.[84]

This is a miserable situation, and Joël has also identified the culprit: "But to finish the job of slaughtering the soul, a special science was invented and called psychology. And with experimental torture from the abysses of a hundred laboratories, it has been possible to exorcise the soul, and psychology has only become the most flourishing of all modern sciences since there has no longer been a soul."[85] With this assessment, he seems to be channeling his teacher Dilthey's critique of academic psychology (as mentioned in the previous chapter). Over against a psychology that has entirely distanced itself from any worldview or philosophy, Joël reminds his readers that concepts of the soul and its links to the world have always formed the core of philosophical thinking. "The way you see the soul is the way you see the world. The riddle of the world determines all other riddles. Only the moderns think they can be blind to the question of the soul, that it is enough to analyze the soul internally, with no synthesis with the outside world."[86]

What we see here is the entanglement of the discourse strands of soul, nature, world, philosophy, and mysticism, and the positioning of this arrangement over against a negative view of professional psychology and modern civilization. Thus Joël contributed to the formation of a discursive pattern that would prove highly influential in the second half of the twentieth century.

World War I further strengthened these positions. The traumatic experience of a brutal war of annihilation revealed modernity's ambiguity and enhanced the search for a holistic, metaphysical philosophy, a moral-spiritual haven of peace.[87] Once again it was Diederichs press that dominated the German discussion of this issue, this time with its series *Gott—Natur: Schriftenreihe zur Neubegründung der Naturphilosophie* (God—Nature: Book Series for the Renewal of Natural Philosophy). A new edition of Karl Joël's book of 1906 was printed in this series in 1926, and the same year saw the appearance of Christoph Bernoulli and Hans Kern's collection *Romantische Naturphilosophie* (Romantic Philosophy of Nature), which the editors dedicated to Ludwig Klages (1872–1956). This volume is remarkable insofar as it documents the rift within German philosophy at the time—the deep gaps that had opened between Neo-Kantians, Neo-Hegelians, and nature mystics harking back to Romanticism. For the latter, Goethe was the uncontested authority, and his light far outshone the endeavors of all other philosophers, poets, and scientists. Joël had already argued this, but Bernoulli and Kern added their voices to this eulogy for Goethe (at the same time enthroning Ludwig Klages as the new shining light). The reception of Goethe's work thus served as a bridge between natural philosophy and theosophical-mystical tendencies, which we can also see in Rudolf Steiner's Anthroposophy, in which a veritable Goethe cult developed.

Bernoulli and Kern set themselves apart not only from Kant—"as we think, on the whole, [he was] an almost disastrous influence on subsequent philosophy"[88]—but also from Schelling. They blame Schelling for following Kant and Fichte's "bloodless, arrogant ideology" too far and for elevating language over experience. But Romanticism had done away with this: "Enough! The later mutilations of Schelling's natural philosophy by its own originator demonstrate that he was indeed *logocentric* rather than *biocentric* (to use Ludwig Klages's beautiful word)."[89] The reference to Klages, as well as the editors' further explanations in their introduction, indicates that more is at stake here than was at stake in Romanticism or in turn-of-the-century American transcendentalism: not only a sensitive relationship to nature, from which a biocentric ethic can be derived, but also a metaphysical-existentialist understanding of nature as the location of absolute knowledge, which takes on gnostic overtones. In Germany, this line of thought extended from Friedrich Nietzsche to Ludwig Klages to Martin Heidegger. The "age of extremes" (as Hobsbawm puts it) had left its first traces.[90]

Klages's biocentric ethic emerged from a critique of civilization in which natural philosophy and mysticism played an important role. Klages's famous welcoming address to the Erster Freideutscher Jugendtag (First Free German Youth Day), given in 1913 on Hoher Meißner Mountain, was programmatic. Under the title "The Human Being and the Earth," the philosopher laments the extinction of species, both in Germany and across the planet, triggered by the modern "war of annihilation" waged by religion and "civilization." "Under the most feeble-minded of all pretexts, that innumerable animal species were 'harmful,' humans exterminated almost everything" that was not immediately useful in terms of hunting and eating.[91] Furthermore: "What the Germans call old-growth forest is actually reforested sticks. The real old-growth forest, however, which for us has become a pious fable, is approaching its end all around the globe."[92] "An unparalleled orgy of devastation has seized humankind, 'civilization' bears the traits of murder unleashed, and the abundance of the Earth withers from its poisonous breath. So this is what the fruits of 'progress' look like!"[93] The destructive rage of the human "civilization" does not exclude humans themselves. "No doubt, we have entered the age of the *demise of the soul.*"[94]

Klages identifies Christianity as the cause of this technical and "civilizing" alienation of humans from nature.

> If "progress," "civilization," and "capitalism" are just different aspects of one single direction of the will, we should remember that these aspects have been carried out exclusively by *peoples of Christendom*. It was only within that culture that invention was heaped upon invention, that "exact," that is to say, numerical, science flourished, and that the urge for expansion was ruthlessly stirred, an urge that seeks to subjugate the non-Christian races and economically exploit the whole of nature. . . . With its stress on human value and "humanity," Christianity covers up its real opinion: that all nonhuman life is worthless, unless it *serves* humankind! What is more, its "love" has never prevented Christianity from persecuting the pagan worship of nature with deadly hatred, and does not prevent it from dismissing the sacred customs of simple peoples today.[95]

The argument that Christianity has been the main cause of the contemporary ecological catastrophe is often connected with the American historian Lynn White. The "Lynn White thesis" was first presented in 1967, in

White's *Science* article "The Historical Roots of Our Ecologic Crisis," and has influenced the political, ecological, and philosophical discussion to this day.[96] But this should not obscure the fact that the thesis has a discursive prehistory, and that Ludwig Klages decisively contributed to this, even if that fact is often overlooked in the historiography of ecology and environmentalism.

We may note something else in this context. Via the "Munich Cosmic Circle," Ludwig Klages was in close contact with Rainer Maria Rilke, Stefan George, Karl Wolfskehl, Franziska Reventlow, and also Max Weber. From Weber he picked up the idea of the "disenchantment of the world" to explain the modern human being's distance from the "cosmogonic Eros."[97] In 1913 Weber spent his vacation at Monte Verità in Switzerland and visited the alternative pagan commune there. Weber even asked Klages to interpret his handwriting psychologically. This shows that Weber was anything but a representative of the "secularization thesis." For him, magic and enchantment had never really left the modern world; they had simply moved on to new "providers of meaning," mainly in science, art, and other societal domains.[98]

The multifaceted nature of the developments described in this chapter shows that we are indeed dealing with an influential discursive arrangement. During the first decades of the twentieth century, the strands of soul–ecstasy–art–music–nature–knowledge were tied together into a discursive knot that provided meaning for large segments of European societies. These orders of knowledge were developed and further stabilized in the domains and institutions of the study of religion, the sciences, and the arts. Discourse communities comprising philosophers, academics, and artists created arrangements such as the Orphic web. However, as I will explain in the following chapter, this discursive knot (with slight adjustments) also manifested in political and nationalist arrangements at the time.

3

THE MOBILIZATION OF THE SOUL IN POLITICAL AND NATIONALISTIC SETTINGS

In the course of the investigation so far, I have followed the basic lines of the discursive arrangements that had formed around the soul at the end of the nineteenth century. Concepts of the soul prove to be inscribed in scientific, philosophical, and literary-artistic debates. In this chapter, I will demonstrate how these debates also impacted political developments and influenced constructions of state and nation. The idea of the nation-state was linked with considerations of collective structures of the soul. But other social groups, such as the Jewish minority—construed as a "nation"—could also be identified with collective characteristics of the soul. In these processes, self-perception and outside perception often intersect and influence each other. The soul becomes a vehicle for what Benedict Anderson calls "imagined communities."

With his book *Imagined Communities: Reflections on the Origin and Spread of Nationalism*, published in 1983, Benedict Anderson initiated a radical change in nation and nationalism research. His ideas were not without precedent, but the thesis that communities were "imagined" had not yet been presented in this way. As an imagined community, a nation produces a feeling of togetherness, even if most of its members never really meet. The community, Anderson maintains, is determined by two ideas: on the one hand by its limitations, because there must always be people who do not belong to the community if it wants to become a visible entity (in contrast to religions, which often see the whole of humanity as potential members); and on the other hand by its sovereignty, by the need to regulate its own affairs. This is also the reason why nations develop the idea of a national state.

Anderson does not claim "that the appearance of nationalism towards the end of the eighteenth century was 'produced' by the erosion of religious certainties." He adds: "Nor am I suggesting that somehow nationalism historically 'supersedes' religion. What I am proposing is that nationalism has to be understood by aligning it, not with self-consciously held political ideologies, but with the large cultural systems that preceded it, out of which—as well as against which—it came into being."[1] Here the religious community and the dynastic empire have a special role to play. Inspired by his Marxist interpretation, it is clear to Anderson that nation and nationalism were not somehow "invented" by ideologues (a position that Ernest Gellner held), but that they were based on materialistic conditions—above all capitalism, language, infrastructure, and media—that create a coherent framework for communication and life. Furthermore, this dynamic is underpinned by a national history of origin that legitimizes the entire project. Anderson calls this the nation's "biography."

Even thirty-five years after the publication of *Imagined Communities*, Anderson's reflections on the emergence of communities as "nations" are still relevant. Today they are combined with postcolonial and cultural studies approaches.[2] Regarding the connection between soul and nation that interests us here, the processes of evoking a common prehistory (including the creation of moments of memory), which has produced an identity and a "soul" that is distinguishable from other peoples and nations, are of great importance. The same is true for the visualization of a common space of experience—for example, in constructions of nature (and national parks) or in the media of film and theater—and the material connectedness of a community through transport, infrastructure, language, and even war. In Europe, we encounter all of these factors in the period between the formation of nation-states (the German Empire was founded in 1871) and the rise of National Socialism and European fascism in the 1920s and 1930s.

Ernest Renan: The Nation as "Soul and Spiritual Principle"

European historiography has repeatedly addressed the "culture war" at the end of the nineteenth century, in which a sheer irreconcilable contrast is constructed between Germany and France in particular. The term also had a very tangible political function in Bismarck's war against Catholic politics. But the talk of "culture war," or *Kulturkampf*, sometimes overlooks the similarities in the formation of a general discourse across European countries. The phenomena of colonialism, nation-building, criticism of monarchies, and the struggle for democratic rights, coupled with industrialization, capitalism, and new scientific developments, were by no means confined to a few countries in Europe, but led to a pan-European process that also connected Europe to a global discursive space. In other words, even though the rhetorical connection between soul and nation was sharpened and used to mobilize diverse national identities and "struggles" in the nineteenth and early twentieth centuries, the processes that steered this mobilization across Europe were quite similar in nature.

We can see what this means concretely in the life and work of Ernest Renan (1823–1892), "a great teacher of humanity and a sage of the West," according to one of his biographers.[3] Renan first studied Catholic theology and was accepted into various seminaries. But he left the seminary in 1845 because he had rejected the interpretation of the Bible as historical truth and considered Catholic historiography wrong. He contrasted this conservative historiography with the positions of German idealism and the critical biblical exegesis that was forming at the time. Increasingly he began to address historical-linguistic questions. The connection between the history of language and the history of culture that fascinated many nineteenth-century authors is also evident in Renan's early work *L'Âme bretonne à travers la poésie des races celtiques* (The Breton Soul Through the Poetry of the Celtic Peoples, 1854). A year later, Renan published a systematic historical concordance of Semitic languages, which brought him international fame. He was admitted to the Prussian Academy of Sciences as a corresponding member in 1859, and in 1860 the Bavarian Academy of Sciences elected him a foreign member.

In 1863 the first volume of his eight-volume major work *Histoire des origines du Christianisme* (History of the Origins of Christianity) was published. Under the title *Vie de Jésus*, Renan took up perspectives from life of Jesus research and described in novelistic form the person and development of Jesus as a human being in the ancient context. Renan's thesis that Jesus' followers proclaimed him "God" only after his death made the book instantly famous, but it also got Renan into trouble, because the episcopate of the Catholic Church in France fought the historical-critical exploration of early Christianity. His appointment to a chair of Oriental languages at the Collège de France in 1862 was blocked, and Renan was only rehabilitated in 1870. In 1879 he became a member of the Académie Française, and from 1883 until his death he served as director of the Collège de France.

Ernest Renan became known not only as a scholar, but also as a politically active intellectual. He regularly took a stand on questions of nationality, the "spirit of a people," and race. At first he promoted the merging of the "Gallic" and the "Germanic" spirits, which he thought could serve as a role model for the wider world. His German biographer Eduard Platzhoff wrote in 1900 that the solution would come from the "lessons of history," which in all eras had "proved its worth as the salvation of France." What we see is

> the re-fertilization by the Germanic spirit, whose mingling with the Gallic spirit always became its blessing and often enough helped it to fully unfold its wealth. This time, however, it is not the Anglo-Saxon form of the Germanic spirit that can assume the mission, but the Teutonic form: the Germany of poets and thinkers, the home of poetry and idealism, the cradle of all serious diligence and all faithful work. If only France were far-sighted enough to recognize this greatness admiringly and to let it have a humbling effect on itself! But it only sees the naïve customs of its neighbors on the left [*sic*!] bank of the Rhine, their often tactless, clumsy nature, and their stiff, shortsighted ponderousness.[4]

This interpretation of Renan's views says a lot about German reception and the developing culture wars at the turn of the century (which also involved scientists such as Rudolf Virchow and Ernst Haeckel). In 1921, Walther

Küchler dedicated an entire chapter in his biography to the subject of "Renan between France and Germany." He maintained: "Renan was not brought up in love with the fatherland."[5] His values were different: "The fatherland vanishes from the Faustian-enamored young man to make way for the science devoted enthusiastically to the exploration of the eternal and the divine," and the fatherland and the individual faded "before the infinite collective being that is humankind."[6] Küchler laments that after 1870, Renan developed a much more critical opinion of Germany and came to regard France as the model for the world.

In fact, Renan's views on soul and nation were much more differentiated than Platzhoff, Küchler, and others presented them. On March 11, 1882, Renan gave a speech at the Sorbonne in Paris on the question "Qu'est-ce qu'une nation?" (What is a nation?), which, according to Raoul Girardet, became a "major text in the history of the national idea in France."[7] In this speech, Renan opposes the widespread equation of "race" with "nation" and points out that "fatherland" (*patrie*) was historically constituted by completely different criteria than what was to become the nation only in the nineteenth century. According to Renan, the modern nation is the result of a series of quite heterogeneous developments, among which the French Revolution was of critical importance.

> We should not be displeased if others imitate us in this. It was we who founded the principle of nationality. But what is a nation? Why is Holland a nation, when Hanover, or the Grand Duchy of Parma, are not? How is it that France continues to be a nation, when the principle which created it has disappeared? How is it that Switzerland, which has three languages, two religions, and three or four races, is a nation, when Tuscany, which is so homogeneous, is not one? Why is Austria a state and not a nation? In what ways does the principle of nationality differ from that of races?[8]

On the problem of "race," Renan notes:

> The truth is that there is no pure race and that to make politics depend upon ethnographic analysis is to surrender it to a chimera. The noblest countries, England, France, and Italy, are those where the blood is the

> most mixed. Is Germany an exception in this respect? Is it a purely Germanic country? This is a complete illusion. The whole of the south was once Gallic; the whole of the east, from the river Elbe on, is Slav. Even those parts which are claimed to be really pure, are they in fact so? We touch here on one of those problems in regard to which it is of the utmost importance that we equip ourselves with clear ideas and ward off misconceptions.[9]

He concludes: "Race, as we historians understand it, is therefore something which is made and unmade. The study of race is of crucial importance for the scholar concerned with the history of humanity. It has no applications, however, in politics."[10] This statement is almost visionary in view of later political developments in Europe. Having also outlined the impossibility of defining the nation through language, religion, communities of interest, geography, or military necessities, he formulates the answer to his initial question:

> A nation is a soul, a spiritual principle [*Une nation est une âme, un principe spirituel*]. Two things, which in truth are but one, constitute this soul or spiritual principle. One lies in the past, one in the present. One is the possession in common of a rich legacy of memories; the other is present-day consent, the desire to live together, the will to perpetuate the value of the heritage that one has received in an undivided form. Man, Gentlemen, does not improvise. The nation, like the individual, is the culmination of a long past of endeavours, sacrifice, and devotion.[11]

According to Renan, the nation is "a large-scale solidarity, constituted by the feeling of the sacrifices that one has made in the past and of those that one is prepared to make in the future."[12] The place of metaphysical and theological speculations, which had rightly been expelled from politics, is now occupied by humans and their desires and needs. Another visionary statement follows: "The nations are not something eternal. They had their beginnings and they will end. A European confederation will very probably replace them. But such is not the law of the century in which we are living."[13]

Renan's discursive contribution consists in linking the concept of the soul with the discourse strands of nation, community, people, race, politics, spirit, history, and sacrifice. His specific use of this discursive arrangement was a warning against nationalistic and racist employments of the concept of nation and an insistence on the time-bound and temporary nature of both "race" and "nation."

It is tempting to compare Renan's understanding with the work of his American contemporary W. E. B. Du Bois (1868–1963), a leading sociologist, civil rights activist, and Pan-Africanist. Particularly Du Bois's *The Souls of Black Folk*, a collection of fourteen essays that came out in 1903, represents a very similar engagement with the discourse strands of soul, nation, and race. As Brent Hayes Edwards notes in a new edition of this key publication in the struggle against racism and for civil rights in the United States: "The title of the book itself announces a departure from the rhetoric of race, derived from nineteenth-century social Darwinism, to the spiritual vocabulary of German Romanticism."[14] Edwards agrees with Du Bois's biographer David Levering Lewis, who states that "the German influences are unmistakable with their suggestion of materializing spirit and dialectical struggle, the whole surging process coming to concretion in *das Volk*—a mighty nation with a unique soul. It is as though the voices of Schopenhauer and Sojourner Truth were blended."[15]

Indeed, Du Bois repeatedly refers to European discourses on race, nation, and soul, applying them to the North American situation. "After the Egyptian and Indian, the Greek and Roman, the Teuton and Mongolian, the Negro is a sort of seventh son, born with a veil, and gifted with second-sight in this American world," he writes. And he adds: "It is a peculiar sensation, this double-consciousness, this sense of always looking at one's self through the eyes of others, of measuring one's soul by the tape of a world that looks on in amused contempt and pity. One ever feels his two-ness,—an American, a Negro; two souls, two thoughts, two unreconciled strivings; two warring ideals in one dark body, whose dogged strength alone keeps it from being torn asunder."[16] In the course of his argumentation, Du Bois is as critical as Renan (whom he does not mention in his book) about the common link between nation and race. While he acknowledges the existence and the influence of physical differences—which was the discourse of the day—like Renan he doubts the equation of race, soul, and nation. It is questionable what the "real" differences are between races, groups, and nations, when

> no mere physical distinctions would really define or explain the deeper differences—the cohesiveness and continuity of these groups. The deeper differences are spiritual, psychical, differences—undoubtedly based on the physical, but infinitely transcending them. The forces that bind together the Teuton nations are, then, first, their race identity and common blood; secondly, and more important, a common history, common laws and religion, similar habits of thought and a conscious striving together for certain ideals of life. The whole process which has brought about these race differentiations has been a growth, and the great characteristic of this growth has been the differentiation of spiritual and mental differences between great races of mankind and the integration of physical differences.[17]

Consequently, and reminiscent of Renan's visionary conclusion, Du Bois notes: "If we carefully consider what race prejudice really is, we find it, historically, to be nothing but the friction between different groups of people."[18] Race distinctions are no basis for politics and nation-building; different racial identities may exist together fruitfully in one nation, and African Americans should be cherished as "the first fruits of this new nation, the harbinger of that black to-morrow which is yet destined to soften the whiteness of the Teutonic to-day."[19] These complex approaches to racial identity, which is both fluid and socially visible, underpin Carol Wayne White's argument that W. E. B. Du Bois, along with Anna Julia Cooper and James Baldwin, can be seen as a pioneer of a potential African American Religious Naturalism that links "Black Lives and Sacred Humanity."[20]

The discursive arrangement that Renan and Du Bois engaged was a cornerstone of orders of knowledge about the soul, the nation, and the "people" around 1900. But many used the same discursive arrangement in a very different way—precisely in the sense of a mythical twist given to the discursive knot of people–nation–soul. Let us take a look at Germany, where the discourse emerged (and derailed) on the basis of what Du Bois called the "Teutonic."

The "German Soul" from Romanticism to National Socialism

The mythical amplification of the soul was particularly strong in Germany. One reason for this may be the fact that the adjective "German," applied to the marking of national peculiarities, referred only to the linguistic unity of a group and not—as with "English," "French," or "Italian"—to an ethnic category. Thus Dieter Borchmeyer states: "Hardly any other nation has asked itself the question of its own identity as often as the German one. The problem of 'what is German' was discussed in countless tracts in the nineteenth and twentieth centuries. No wonder, as probably no other European nation had become conscious and certain of itself so late. And as always, when one is not sure of one's cause, this uncertainty is often offset by exaggeration, by overemphasis on what one lacks right now."[21]

The evocation of a "German soul" is part of this identity work. Since the end of the eighteenth century, especially in Romantic thinking, an influential discourse had been connecting the soul with nature and nation. No wonder that Elias Canetti devotes a chapter of his work of 1960 *Masse und Macht* (published in English as *Crowds and Power*) to this very connection. The forest in particular was repeatedly invoked with regard to national identity, in an interplay of cultural theory, art, literature, philosophy, and politics.[22] As an example from early Romanticism, let me quote Johann Gottfried Herder's "Der Wanderer" (The Wanderer) as representative of many other instances:

> Do spirits roar in the air?
> Does the nymph speak to me in the spring?
> Or do gods descend?
> For my gaze becomes pure and bright.

With the spruce summit
My soul rises heavenward;
With the birch branches my heart
Gently bends down to rest.

And the green paper carpet
Cradles me on silken moss;
Beside this golden flower
I am blessed, and how greatly!

Hark! From that old oak tree
a bard's tone sounds,
And the spruce tops swish
Ethereally; the forest becomes a choir:

"We, the spirits of paradise,
Abiding here in peace,
Bless you. Merrily enjoy
Our holy, quiet forest!"[23]

Here the forest becomes a temple from which the soul rises up to heaven and in which the human heart connects with sublime nature. We can clearly see the effects of Herder, but also of Friedrich Gottlieb Klopstock and others, on the nineteenth-century emergence of a discourse that closely associates the German soul with the "German forest," and therein with the "German oak": "From the heroes of the Teutoburg Forest one takes the strength to rebel against cultural alienation, later also against Napoleonic foreign rule. Thus, at the beginning of an awakening German national consciousness, there is a recollection." But the visualization of a Germanic past based on forest romanticism presupposes "that the forest can be experienced as a place withdrawn from the immediate present."[24]

Initially, in the formative period after 1871, the renewal of the idea of the Reich and the longing for imperial power did not necessarily show a clear tendency to make the forest and nature the center of the construction of the "German soul." Other identification factors, such as the big city, were added as alternatives, and these shaped the culture of German Art Nouveau. Friedrich Rothe identifies the youth movements around 1900 as protest movements, which transformed the enthusiasm for nature into a national zeal for war in the run-up to World War I. "The love of nature was not pure at all, but merely a compensation for a desire for destruction that had to be suppressed. The countless enthusiastic war volunteers of 1914 were in this sense not deceived youths whose selfless idealism was exploited; rather, in the unbroken transition from peacetime to war, a willing move toward aggression, which had previously been fended off by a penchant for nature and a misled idealism, came into play."[25] The nationalistic turn of this enthusiasm for nature is even evident in the work of avant-garde artists, such as Franz Marc in his *Briefe aus dem Feld* (1920, published in English as *Letters from the War*). In Karl Kraus's *Die letzten Tage der Menschheit* (1919, published in English as *The Last Days of Mankind*), the "dead forest" embodies the accusation that the glory of the forest had also perished in the World War.[26]

The same discursive constellation also includes Ludwig Klages (already introduced in the previous chapter), whose book *Vom kosmogonischen Eros* (On the Cosmogonic Eros, written in the last year of World War I, published in 1921) describes his metaphysical and ecstatic experience of the forest as follows: "A hundred times I may have seen the forest in front of my window, without experiencing anything other than just the thing, the same thing that the botanist also refers to; but once, while it flames in the glow of the evening sun, the sight can snatch me from my ego; and there my soul suddenly sees what I have never seen before, perhaps only for a minute, yes, maybe only for seconds; but whether long or short, what I beheld then was the archetype of the forest, and *this* image never returns for me, or for anyone else."[27]

After Germany lost the war, an intensified politicization of the "German soul" took place, often with a close link to the ideas of nature and forest.[28] The National Socialist movement in particular, which was formed in the 1920s, took up the existing discourse strands and radicalized them in a way that prepared the ground for a *Führer* cult, anti-Semitism, and an enthusiasm for war. Countless examples of this new order of discourse could be mentioned here, but perhaps in no other place do we see the power of this rhetoric as clearly as in the writings of Alfred Rosenberg (1892–1946). In the period of the Weimar Republic, Rosenberg had already become known as an author of anti-Semitic and nationalist publications, and he played a central role in the history of the National Socialist German Workers' Party (NSDAP). It is for good reason that Ernst Piper describes Rosenberg in his biography as "Hitler's chief ideologist."[29]

In 1930, the same year in which Rosenberg was elected to the Reichstag as a member of the NSDAP, he published the book that would make him famous as the leading thinker (and demagogue) of National Socialism. The book also triggered criticism, of course—such as Kurt Hutten's defense in 1935 of Christianity in the "struggle for the German soul."[30] *Der Mythus des 20. Jahrhunderts*, subtitled *Eine Wertung der seelisch-geistigen Gestaltenkämpfe unserer Zeit* (translated into English as *The Myth of the Twentieth Century: An Evaluation of the Spiritual-Intellectual Confrontations of Our Age*) is a sweeping attempt at a political, philosophical, religious, and biological legitimization of the "German rebirth," which was supposed to find its perfect expression in the National Socialist program. At more than seven hundred pages, this volume—which Rosenberg conceived as a continuation of Houston Stewart Chamberlain's *The Foundations of the Nineteenth Century* (1899)—contains three "books" that sketch an image of the "German soul," with inextricable links to racial thinking and mystically connoted religion. The "Great War" of 1914 is described as the "beginning of a world revolution in all domains," but according to Rosenberg in his introduction to the first edition of 1930, the war "has revealed the tragic fact that millions have sacrificed their lives, but that this has benefited other forces than the armies were prepared to die for. The dead of war are the victims of the catastrophe of an epoch that has lost all of its values, but at the same time—and this is beginning to be understood in Germany, even if only by a few thus far—they are the martyrs of a new dawn, of a new faith."[31]

It is no coincidence that Rosenberg begins his "First Book: The Conflict of Values" with the chapter "Race and Racial Soul." Against Darwinism and positivism, Rosenberg conjures up a soul that dissolves individual structures and merges into the collective. "Humankind, the All-Church, and the autocratic ego detached from the bonds of blood are no longer absolute values for us. They are dubious, even moribund dogmas without any polarity, representing a rape of nature in favor of abstractions."[32] And he goes on:

> Race is the parable of a soul, the entire racial good an intrinsic value without reference to bloodless values that overlook the fullness of nature, or with reference to material worshipers who apprehend only discrete events in time and space, without experiencing these events as the greatest and most profound of all secrets.
>
> Therefore, racial history is natural history and soul mysticism at the same time; but the history of the religion of the blood, conversely, is the great narrative of the rise and fall of peoples, their heroes and thinkers, their inventors and artists.[33]

The discursive entanglement of soul, nature, mysticism, religion, and race is unlikely to appear as clearly in any other document of the time as in *The Myth of the Twentieth Century*. Rosenberg's book also provides a clear example of the role of national history or "biography" as Benedict Anderson observed it. In this narrative, the Great War of 1914 was merely the beginning of a movement that would ultimately bring about the revolutionary restoration of the original German soul. In an idiosyncratic rhetorical construction of history, Rosenberg goes back to the origins of human history and sketches a line of confrontation between different races and concepts of consciousness in which the Nordic-Aryan race would assert itself as a vital principle. Rosenberg proclaims that "the deepest law of every *genuine* culture" is that "*it is the shaping of the consciousness of the vegetal vitality of a race*."[34] That which is specifically "German"—and which he distinguishes above all from the "Semitic" and the "Jewish"—is expressed in all cultural, artistic, religious, and scientific aspects of life.

> Since Nordic man starts from precisely this nascent life, from the *day*, he is quite "naturally" a vitalist. The greatest achievement of his history, however, was the *Germanic* realization *that nature could not be mastered by magic* (as people in the Near East thought could be done), *or by mental schemes* (as the later Greeks thought), *but only by the most intimate observation of nature*. Here the pious Albrecht von Bollstedt (Albertus Magnus) comes close to Goethe; the enthusiast Francis of Assisi to the religious skeptic Leonardo. The Germanic Occident did not let itself be robbed of this vitalism even by the Roman Church, despite

> excommunication, poison, and the stake. And this mystical vitalism was at the same time cosmic; or conversely, *because* Germanic man felt cosmic-solar, therefore he also discovered laws in the eternal becoming on Earth.[35]

The National Socialist program served the purpose of "re-northing [*Wiedervernordung*] the German people."[36] This would be accomplished by means of a "sacrificial love," which aided "the *cultivating* nobility of the soul." Rosenberg uses the term *nobility of the soul* (*Seelenadel*) in his discussion of the teachings of Jesus of Nazareth in the period before, as he claims, "Jewish" influences destroyed Christianity.

> His greatest successor, Meister Eckhart, also proceeded from the "nobility of the soul," and his love in the service of this value was likewise a strong, conscious, quite unsentimental one. This love did not serve in "trembling fear," as Ignatius demanded; it did not serve a system of soul enslavement and racial annihilation. It served only honor-conscious freedom. And Martin Luther also knew only too well what he was saying when, shortly before his death, he wrote: "These three words—free, Christian, German—are nothing but vain poison, death, devil, and hell to the pope and the Roman court."[37]

Meister Eckhart, Luther, Herder, and Goethe—these are the national heroes who serve as models for the mystical "German soul." For the mastermind of the National Socialists, these heroes are also examples of the Germanic spirit, committed solely to freedom. There is no place for women here, for they are bound to nature and are merely passive preservers of the race. Rosenberg never tires of emphasizing this claim in long antifeminist chapters, and in doing so, he enhances the stereotype of the "German mother."

It is interesting to note that the term *Führer* (leader) is not used here; rather, it is loyalty to oneself that enables "an internal and external German rebirth to take place."[38] "Honor and freedom are ideas, loyalty an activity. Honor expresses itself in free loyalty to oneself."[39] We can implicitly conclude that Adolf Hitler, whose name is not mentioned in the book—although the publishing house advertises his *Mein Kampf* in the appendix as the "standard work of National Socialism"—is somehow part of the German soul itself. Therefore the German people can unconditionally surrender to this most highly visible part of its own soul.

After 1933, staging this bond of souls became an integral part of Nazi propaganda. This was evident in public rituals, but also in cinematic aestheticizations, such as Leni Riefenstahl's *Triumph des Willens* (*Triumph of the Will*, 1935). Such aestheticization was frequently combined with discourses on nature and the forest, for example, in the documentary film *Ewiger Wald* (Eternal Forest, directed by Hanns Springer and Rolf von Sonjevski-Jamrowski in 1936). When the camera pans up from young soldiers' legs to rows of trees, it communicates the spirit of the National Socialist "blood and soil" ideology: "Eternal forest, eternal people—the tree lives, like you and me; it strives for space, like you and me."[40] We may also recall the biologist and conservationist Walter Schoenichen, who propagated National Socialist ideology in the sense of "keeping nature pure." In 1934 he published *Urwaldwildnis in deutschen Landen: Bilder vom Kampf des deutschen Menschen mit der Urlandschaft* (Primeval Forest Wilderness in German Territories: Images of the German Struggle with the Primeval Landscape), a book with photographs of trees as symbols of the German soul.[41] National Socialist nature conservation laws were the strictest that modern states had developed at that time. In Benedict Anderson's sense, these political instruments demonstrate the means of generating an "imagined community." They are discursive actions that consolidate and legitimize the order of knowledge built around soul, nature, and people.

When it comes to the German soul, German Classicism and Romanticism are conjured up over and over again. One example of many is Günther Müller, who in 1939 noted in his *Geschichte der deutschen Seele: Vom Faustbuch zu Goethes Faust* (History of the German Soul: From the *Faust* Book to Goethe's *Faust*): "But what Klopstock and Lessing had experienced on their distinct paths, what Hamann and Herder proclaimed in their emotions, could not be eliminated from the consciousness of the people as a whole by this classical taming." Subsequently, it was the spirit of Goethe's age that provided the pinnacle of the realization of the German soul:

> Among the leading literary influencers . . . it is above all the experience of one's own inwardness, of the suprapersonal laws of life, that enforces new means of creativity. It is not only the duality of intellect and emotion that demands a new balance and union for deeper reasons. The emotional and cognitive forces of the soul also lead back to a common and unpredictable source, and united, they lift themselves up to a nonconceptual and nonemotional capability, which one can probably call a visionary spirit [*Schaugeist*].[42]

The National Socialist ideology constituted the climax of an invocation of the "German soul," but this invocation had a long prehistory. What is more, the discursive entanglement of soul and nation was by no means aimed at nation-states alone; it could also affect other groups. Imagined communities are not only national, but also social entities. In the next section, I explain this dynamic with reference to Jewish identity work at the beginning of the twentieth century.

The "Jewish Soul" and Jewish Intellectuals' Self-Orientalization

Processes of national mobilization of the soul also entail the creation of categories of alterity that legitimize the exclusion of groups that do not belong to the imagined community of the "people." In the National Socialist theme of the "revolutionary rebirth of the German people," race, sexual orientation, and religion served as central markers of alterity, and Jews in particular were excluded from the "German people" as pariahs and declared enemies. From cultural studies and postcolonial research we know that such processes are not a one-way street; rather, the groups excluded as underprivileged develop strategies to secure their identity. A "Third Space" (Homi Bhabha) emerges in which new identities and points of reference are negotiated. Again we may think of W. E. B. Du Bois, who described such a situation very clearly with regard to African American identity under conditions of segregation and racism:

> Here, then, is the dilemma, and it is a puzzling one, I admit. No Negro who has given earnest thought to the situation of his people in America has failed, at some time in life, to find himself at these cross-roads; has failed to ask himself at some time: What, after all, am I? Am I an American or am I a Negro? Can I be both? Or is it my duty to cease to be a Negro as soon as possible and be an American? If I strive as a Negro, am I not perpetuating the very cleft that threatens and separates Black and White America? Is not my only possible practical aim the subduction of all that is Negro in me to the American? Does my black blood place upon me any more obligation to assert my nationality than German, or Irish or Italian blood would?[43]

Questions of the assimilation or emancipation of underprivileged groups, which Du Bois implicitly discusses here, have been an important component of negotiations of Jewishness as well. In this context, discourses on the "Jewish soul," as differentiated from the "German soul" or the "European soul," had a clear impact on Jewish life and thought at the time, and Jews attempted to create a Third Space as a response to anti-Semitism.

In his study of Orientalism and Jewish-Hebrew imagination, Yaron Peleg states: "At a time when Europe was being divided along ethnic lines, rearranging itself evermore into political entities according to hitherto unacknowledged criteria such as history, language, culture, and ethnicity, the Orient or East became an important point of reference as an ultimate Elsewhere."[44] In this reordering of knowledge and politics at the end of the nineteenth century, categories of alterity and "figures of the Third" emerged. One of the most important categories in this regard, as Klaus Holz explains, was the "Jew" as the "Third of the Nations."[45] Views on what was considered Jewish can be found in complex discursive structures of gender, Orientalism, and the emergence of nation-states.[46]

In order to understand this dynamic, we have to go back to the early nineteenth century.[47] When Abraham Geiger, Immanuel Wolf, Leopold Zunz, and others presented the newly founded *Wissenschaft des Judentums* (Judaic Studies) as an instrument for the emancipation of German Jews, a discussion began among Jewish intellectuals, leading to heated debates that continued into the twentieth century. Discourses on nationalism,

"Germanness," gender, Orientalism, and also mysticism and "gnosis" came together in an attempt to clarify what Jewish identity was and the extent to which Judaism could be assimilated into European culture.

Jews were an important factor in German colonial fantasies. Jewish emancipation could assume the function of an "internal colonization."[48] Both Jewish historians and Christian theologians (mostly Protestants) took part in debates on this issue. Judaic studies in the nineteenth century was an attempt to create a subversive Third Space. In this emerging space, the debate about whether Jews should adhere to the rational Jewish Enlightenment (*Haskalah*) or whether mystical, ecstatic, and kabbalistic forms of Jewish tradition provided an alternative way of "being Jewish" became a central motif of identity work. As Michael Brenner notes: "Gnosticism, a seemingly remote and obscure religious phenomenon of late antiquity, became another disputed topic in Jewish scholarship where present interests and conceptions often overshadowed the research into the past."[49] While Heinrich Graetz was of the opinion that Gnosticism was a non-Jewish element and a danger to "real" Judaism, Moritz Friedländer stressed the Jewish origins of gnosis and Gnosticism.

Over the course of the nineteenth century, Jewish scholars became increasingly interested in Eastern European Jewish traditions, and quite a few of them considered *shtetl* Judaism to be a more authentic form of Jewish religion than what had developed in Western Europe. This Orientalist discourse was reflected in the works of many writers around 1900, among them Franz Kafka, Alfred Döblin, Joseph Roth, Lion Feuchtwanger, and Arnold Zweig.[50] Many of these writers were in correspondence with scholars who also constructed the "eastern Jew" as a counterconcept to the "bloodless rational" Judaism of Western Europe.

A case in point is the correspondence between Arnold Zweig (1887–1968) and Martin Buber. When Zweig was stationed at a German press department in Lithuania in 1918, he experienced Eastern European Jewish life for the first time. He wrote to Martin Buber that he would like to draft a report about his experiences, which two years later appeared under the title *Das ostjüdische Antlitz* (The Eastern Jewish Face), enriched with lithographs by Hermann Struck, who was stationed with Zweig in Lithuania. In their preface, Struck and Zweig made it clear that the book is to be regarded as a resistance to anti-Semitism and the ongoing anti-Jewish pogroms. In the book we find descriptions of "real" and "original" Judaism as Oriental-ecstatic, in contrast to modern European rational Judaism. The following passage stands for many others:

> The prayer robe, the Tallit, in the "liberal" West often only a flirtatious and superfluous ritual ornament, shamefacedly folded into a narrow stole and flashing with its gold or silver border—in the East it envelops the praying man, disintegrates the contour of his figure, separates him from the world, and, often pulled over his head, extinguishes the light of this world, so that the divine light may shine all the brighter for him. Yes, prayer is still loud in the east, at every hour of prayer the embers of the rush to the heights of the Lord ignite, and for superficial Western eyes and ears this is an embarrassing and distasteful impression, these ruthless voices, these shaking figures, these strangely articulated, howled, moaned strands of a melody, which roar together into a wild screaming chorus, and which even outside the walls of the house sound like the roar of distant surf, like the shouting of wild crowds. But anyone who has ever stayed in a mosque in the Islamic countries and was allowed to do so during prayer, recognizes in the Jew the Oriental. The rhythm that moves the bodies there is more spiritless, less personal, more regulated by the precept, has entered into the objective part of prayer; with the Jew it remained subjective, more formed by the impulse and breaking out of the individual soul of the praying man according to the power of the hour. But this is also found in the Orient, and in short, the praying eastern Jew in his extreme ecstasy is closer to the dervish than any modern Jew.[51]

In ecstasy the soul dissolves its boundaries and becomes one with the divine. It is clear to the "truly pious," says Zweig, "that the bridge to God is not grounded in any spatial category, but in the soul of the praying person."[52]

Martin Buber fully endorsed this interpretation. We have already seen in the previous chapter that Buber—in his reading of Friedrich Nietzsche—regarded ecstasy as a means of self-delimitation and a mystical vision of the world spirit. In a handwritten addition to his dissertation, he described Jacob Boehme's mysticism in Dionysian terms:

> For Boehme God and nature are one, much like soul and body, or better yet, as energy and organism are one. . . . What we call God is nothing less than the eternal energy of the natural powers, the eternal energy, the effective principle of [existence]. Because the unity of all the powers is revealed in nature, . . . the world is not being (*Sein*), but becoming (*Werden*). Hence, with each day reality is born de novo. And with every tomorrow reality presents itself once again to our formative hands. Thus we are not slaves, but the beloved of our world [*So sind wir nicht Sklaven, sondern die Geliebten unserer Welt*].[53]

In a way, Buber develops a pantheism that unites the individual soul with the world spirit and with nature. Paul R. Mendes-Flohr states: "Such a pantheistic twist to Nietzsche's thought was common among his disciples of the fin de siècle, we may mention Stefan George, Rainer Maria Rilke, Karl Wolfskehl, and Karl Joël—all in their own fashion pantheistic Nietzscheans."[54] Here Buber braids together the same discourse strands that we have already found in many other contexts, especially in connection with vitalism and science (more on that in chapter 5). But he gives these discourses his own twist by taking the view that the "essence" of Judaism embodies the full realization of that mystical potential in the human being. Similarly to the strategy Anderson sees at work in the imagination of community, Buber maintains in his *Reden über das Judentum* (Speeches on Judaism) that original Judaism was characterized by the ideas of "unity," "deed," and "future." This original Judaism was at the same time eastern Judaism. In the speech *Das Judentum und die Menschheit* (Judaism and Humanity), he points to Asia as the origin of this spirit:

> For this is the original process of the Jew, the original process that the great Jews, in whom the deepest Judaism came to life, brought to manifestation in their personal lives with all the force of Asian genius: the unification of the soul. The great Asia lived in them as an example for the Occident, the Asia of boundlessness and holy unity, the Asia of

> Laotse and Buddha, which is the Asia of Moses and the Isaiahs, of John, Jesus, and Paul. In the pursuit of unity, the creative powers are ignited in the Jew. His creative deed is rooted in the unification of the soul.[55]

This is why Buber regarded everything creative in Christianity as ultimately Jewish, and everything non-Jewish in Christianity as ultimately uncreative. A "dialogue" between Judaism and Christianity was therefore pointless.[56] Original Judaism, according to Buber, was "the apostle of the Orient for humankind," because the Jewish experience of inner division and redemption had given Judaism the strength and the passion to "teach the human world the one thing that is necessary."[57] In "The Renewal of Judaism" he writes: "This may absolutely be regarded as a fundamental difference between Orient and Occident: for the Oriental it is the deed, for the Occidental it is faith that serves as the decisive connection between the human being and God. This difference has become particularly pronounced with the Jew," namely, in the Jewish accentuation of the deed.[58]

With his depiction of eastern Judaism as the original teacher of humankind, Buber participates in an Orientalist discourse that is also visible in Helena P. Blavatsky and others. But in contrast to the often anti-Jewish positions of the Theosophical Society, Buber glorifies the eastern Jewish tradition. Even if he regarded Judaism as a "nation" in which "blood is to be addressed as the soul's deepest layer of power,"[59] he thought that eastern Judaism could serve as a model for all humankind. "Everyone who wins the unity of his soul contributes to the great process of Judaism,"[60] as do those who liberate the "original Jew" (*Urjude*) from the sphere of influence of the "Galut Jew" (*Galutjude*, from the Hebrew *galut* = exile). "But *Urjude* I call the one who becomes conscious in himself of the great powers of original Judaism and decides for them, for their activation, for their becoming effective [*Werkwerden*]."[61]

All three of the basic ideas of Judaism that Buber propagated are associated with a kind of rebirth of the Jewish soul: "The tendency of unity by forming our soul into a unity so that it will be able to conceive unity; the tendency of deed by filling our soul with unconditional will so that it will be able to prove the deed; the tendency of the future by untying our soul from the machinations of purpose and turning it toward the goal so that it will be able to serve the future."[62]

Similar to Arnold Zweig, Martin Buber had created a Third Space by defining the "Jewish essence" at a critical distance from the spirituality of Western Europe. Despite very different ideological objectives, Buber can therefore be compared with the historians of the *Wissenschaft des Judentums*.[63]

We see similar "boundary work" in Buber's younger contemporary Gershom Scholem (1897–1982). Scholem, however, propagated a spiritualized form of Zionism as the best response to the failure of Jewish emancipation and assimilation in Europe. Kabbalah, mysticism, and esotericism became the cornerstones of his "counter-history,"[64] which we can again regard as the establishment of a Third Space for European Jews, or an imagined community founded on a distinctive historical and cultural construction of the Jewish "soul." In his diary entry for January 4, 1916, Scholem writes: "If, in an Oriental spirit, we were to sacrifice science to serve the renewal of the Orient, I would have nothing against it."[65] Shortly thereafter he states: "It seems, by the way—does it only seem so, or *is* it really the case?—to be a paradox that I, who am absolutely and unremittingly an enemy of Europe and a follower of the new Orient, which on its strong wave will also carry the new Judah, must for the time being be content with the intention of going there as a teacher of this very European science."[66]

Against this background, Klaus Samuel Davidowicz speaks of Scholem's and Buber's "utopian retreat": "The utopian retreat into one's own history was called Zionism for Scholem. For Buber, however, Zionism meant looking into one's own person in order to unearth the 'other' tradition."[67] This can also be seen in the way Scholem regarded "forlornness" and "loneliness" almost as a human condition, from which the Jewish religion in general and the Zionist movement in particular offered a way out. On March 16, 1918, Scholem notes in his diary: "In the final analysis, all precious people are sunk in some inescapable abyss of misfortune, cut off from doctrine and tradition among humans. To change this would be the first and most essential of all the work that can be done on others. It is precisely in its deepest layer that Zionism is supposed to turn the misfortune of our existence into *tikkun*."[68]

Jewish self-Orientalization took place in direct reference to a more general movement that directed its gaze to the East in order to obtain spiritual inspiration and wisdom teachings that could be juxtaposed with rationalized European culture. It is no coincidence that Buber and Scholem later appeared at the Eranos conferences, which in turn emerged from what Thomas Hakl calls a "yearning for the East" in movements such as Monte Verità and Hermann Graf Keyserling's "School of Wisdom."[69]

In this chapter, I have traced attempts to define collective qualities of the soul. The discursive entanglements between constructions of the soul and the mobilization of these notions for nationalist and collective demarcation are an important feature of the period between 1880 and 1930. They also prepared the ground for what later became mass psychology and media theory.[70] This development is accompanied by academic research on the collective soul. The concept of *Völkerpsychologie* (folk psychology) had been discussed since the beginning of the nineteenth century, among others by Wilhelm von Humboldt, Herder, Hegel, and Herbart. But it was Wilhelm Wundt who, with an essay in German ("On the Aims and Ways of *Völkerpsychologie*," 1888), continued this research in the field of psychology. His ten-volume *Völkerpsychologie: Eine Untersuchung der Entwicklungsgesetze von Sprache, Mythus und Sitte* (Folk Psychology: An Investigation of the Laws of Development in Language, Myth, and Custom, 1900–1920) then takes a comprehensive look at the fields of art, society, law, culture, and history.[71] Although this work constituted a significant contribution to the discursive formation of national and collective psychologies, another thinker is even more important for the cultural and discursive history of the soul in the twentieth century: Carl Gustav Jung.

4

CARL GUSTAV JUNG

Psychology as a Comprehensive Empirical Science of the Soul

Carl Gustav Jung (1875–1961) deserves a prominent place in any discursive history of the soul in the twentieth century. His broad interest in psychology, philosophy, and the history of religion led him to engage extensively with the cultural and intellectual issues of the time. He took up discussions from other disciplines—from ethnology to quantum theory—and integrated them into a system in which psychology served as the scientific foundation. Jung repeatedly emphasized the links between psychology and other disciplines, above all philosophy and the study of religion.

> I have been told sometimes that interpretation at the subject level is a philosophical problem, and the implementation of this principle comes up against the barriers of worldview and therefore ceases to be science. It does not seem surprising to me that psychology touches upon philosophy, for the thinking that underlies philosophy is a psychic activity, which as such is the subject of psychology. When I think of psychology, I always think of the whole extent of the soul, and that involves philosophy, and theology, and so many other things. For over against all philosophies and all religions, there are the facts of the human soul, which perhaps have the final word on truth and error.[1]

When it comes to Jung's work, one encounters a whole arsenal of different evaluations and assessments, which often differ considerably not only from one another, but also from what Jung actually wrote in his enormous oeuvre. One sees this dynamic at work even in the name of the "school" Jung is said to have founded. While he initially used the term *analytical psychology* for his endeavor, from 1930 onward he spoke of *complex psychology*, which he used to refer to a psychological interpretation that empirically explores the workings of the unconscious in many cultural contexts. Jung never intended to found a "school," and the fact that today one still speaks of "analytical psychology" in the singular is, as Sonu Shamdasani reminds us, a highly misleading anachronism.[2]

Only in recent years has there been a fundamental reorientation in historical research on Jung.[3] This also has to do with the fact that previously inaccessible original texts written by Jung are now available to researchers and have been published—particularly the legendary *Red Book* (*Liber Novus*), which thoroughly enriches our understanding of Jung's spiritual and mystical interests.[4] *The Red Book* was edited by Sonu Shamdasani, and Shamdasani is also a leading voice in new research on Jung's work. For a discursive history of the soul, a certain tension arises from this data situation, because on the one hand historical contexts and new sources need to be studied carefully, and on the other hand—and sometimes above all—"creative misunderstandings" also influence subsequent generations and contribute to the establishment of orders of knowledge, which may differ significantly from their historical origins. The latter is certainly the case with Carl Gustav Jung. *The Red Book*, for example, allows us to draw important conclusions about the actual extent of Jung's interest in alchemy, mysticism, iconography, and comparative religion, but we can prove the book's discursive influence only indirectly—namely, through Jung's activities and the work he actually published.

Whatever his true opinions may have been, it is clear that a simplified, even simplistic interpretation of Jung's positions has generated clichés that left deep grooves in the second half of the twentieth century. "The Figure of 'Jung' stands at the interfaces of academic psychology, psychiatry, psychotherapy, popular psychology, and New Age psychologies. The rise of these disciplines and movements is one of the decisive developments in twentieth-century Western society. It may well be its most curious legacy."[5] While Jung's theories fell into oblivion in academic psychology and psychiatry (especially in Europe) after his death, outside mainstream academic research the name Carl Gustav Jung stands for a nonreductionist psychology—a holistic psychology that integrates the human soul into suprapersonal, even cosmic dimensions and takes spiritual experiences seriously rather than pathologizing them.

For this reason, in terms of discourse theory it makes sense to locate Jung's work within his lifetime and to study the interrelationships between broader intellectual debate and his views on the soul, psychology, and science. Jung is no exception to the discourse of his time, and he himself never claimed to have presented original theories. Rather, his positions were developed as part of an international network of scholars with a clear reference to nineteenth-century theoretical precedent.[6] What is more, Jung spent an important part of his career outside academic institutions. Between 1914 (when he gave up both his lectureship at the University of Zurich and the chair of the International Psychoanalytical Association) and 1933 (when he was appointed professor at ETH Zurich), Jung conducted research independently of the psychiatric hospital on the one hand and the university on the other—institutions that later became leading vehicles for the development of psychiatry (the hospital) and psychology (the university).[7] During this time Jung formulated his most important psychological theories. The fact that he also undertook extensive travels—to visit the Pueblo peoples in North America in 1924–1925, to North and East Africa to study the ethnic groups at Mount Elgon in 1925–1926, and then to India in 1937—significantly contributed to the formation of his theories.

There are two subject areas in particular in which Jung has decisively influenced discourse on the soul in the twentieth century. One has to do with the psychology opening up to collective and suprapersonal factors, the other with the idea that the soul displays regularities and patterns that can be found in all cultures and at all times. Both topics are connected with the question of the extent to which psychology can be a science.

From Biography to the Collective

Jung's work can only be meaningfully interpreted in the context of the discussions of his time. Like almost no one else, Jung took up psychological, historical, religious, and scientific research and tried to incorporate all of this into an integrative science. His library in Küsnacht, Switzerland—which still exists today—is a testimony to his broad interests. During his early medical studies in Basel (from 1895), he dealt with the phenomena of occultism and spiritualism. He took part in his cousin Hélène ("Helly") Preiswerk's séances, and for two years he attended the weekly séances of a "glass- and table-turning circle" formed around a fifteen-year-old psychic. Further so-called poltergeist phenomena, which he experienced, led him to study such phenomena intensively.[8] After his state examination, Jung worked as an assistant to Eugen Bleuler in the *Irrenheilanstalt* (mental hospital) Burghölzli in Zurich. He used his experiences in the occult and spiritualist fields in his studies on multiple personality disorder, and in 1902 he submitted his dissertation, *Zur Psychologie und Pathologie sogenannter occulter Phänomene* (On the Psychology and Pathology of So-Called Occult Phenomena).

In his further research, initially as a continuation of Wilhelm Wundt's study of association theory, Jung worked closely with Franz Beda Riklin in Zurich, Pierre Janet in Paris, and Théodore Flournoy in Geneva.[9] This is important because Jung's work is often interpreted through the lens of his collaboration and involvement with Sigmund Freud. However, Jung himself emphasized that it was mainly Bleuler, Janet, and Flournoy who helped him formulate and significantly influenced his theories.[10] Among the range of scientists who provided important inspiration for Jung's ideas was also William James. In his essay "Über den Archetypus mit besonderer Berücksichtigung des Animabegriffs" (On the Archetype, with Special Consideration of the Concept of Anima, 1936), Jung wrote:

> It was mainly thanks to these two researchers [Flournoy and James] that I learned to understand the nature of mental disorder within the

> framework of the whole human soul. I myself performed experimental work for several years, but through my intensive occupation with neuroses and psychoses I had to admit—as desirable as quantitative determination is—it is not possible without the qualitative descriptive method. . . . The soul does not come to an end where the range of a physiological or other precondition ends, i.e., in each individual case that we study scientifically, we have to consider the full manifestation of the soul.[11]

Although Jung worked closely with Freud between 1906 and 1912, the theoretical differences that ultimately led to the break between them were evident from the beginning. Jung could not understand Freud's fixation on sexual theory and his principle rejection of any metaphysical phenomena—positions Jung later attributed to Freud's neurotic personality structure.[12] What was at stake for Jung was, as we have already seen, "the whole of the human soul," and therefore psychological dynamics could not be reduced to the sex drive or to purely biographical experiences (despite the importance Jung also attributed to the sex drive). If one reduces the human soul to the individual biography and individual manifestations, Jung concluded, it will be difficult to establish psychology as a scientific discipline, since one is dealing with a mere stringing together of subjective experiences. Therefore Jung further developed the idea of the unconscious and added a collective dimension to this concept. Initially in a lecture for the International Psychoanalytical Association in 1916, and later in various other contexts, he worked on a concept of the "collective unconscious," which holds suprapersonal experiences and collective memories that can be recalled in dreams and other individual situations.

But Jung did not come up with the concept of the unconscious all on his own. As we have already seen in many sources, considerations of the connection between the individual soul and collective and cosmic structures were already firmly established in the second half of the nineteenth century. Jung himself repeatedly emphasized that his ideas on the collective unconscious are part of a long line of thought stretching from Carl Gustav Carus to Eduard von Hartmann, Arthur Schopenhauer, and Friedrich Nietzsche, while it had little connection to Freud. In a foreword to Olga von Koenig-Fachsenfeld's book *Wandlungen des Traumproblems von der*

Romantik bis zur Gegenwart (Transformations in the Problem of Dreams from Romanticism to the Present, 1935), which he recommends as a very good contribution to the "problematic of modern complex psychology," Jung describes his psychology as Romantic and alchemical, but at the same time scientific:

> It is the great merit of the present work to have opened up the treasure trove of contemplative, Romantic poetry for modern psychology. The parallelism with my psychological views justifies calling my ideas "Romantic." A corresponding investigation from a philosophical point of view would also justify this designation, because every psychology that understands the soul as an experience is "Romantic" and "alchemical" in a historical sense. Below the level of experience, however, my psychology is also scientific-rationalistic, which I would ask the willing reader not to overlook.[13]

In his treatise "Über die Archetypen des kollektiven Unbewussten" (On the Archetypes of the Collective Unconscious), first published in the *Eranos-Jahrbuch* in 1934, we also find a very clear expression of the discursive knot that is relevant for us here. Jung begins his reflections as follows:

> The hypothesis of a collective unconscious is one of those concepts that first bewilder the audience, but then soon become common notions in their vocabulary and use, as has happened with the concept of the unconscious in general. After the philosophical idea of the unconscious, as it is mainly found in C. G. Carus and E. v. Hartmann, had disappeared under the dominant wave of materialism and empiricism without leaving any significant traces, it gradually reappeared in scientifically oriented, medical psychology.
>
> Initially, the concept of the unconscious was limited to denoting the state of repressed or forgotten content. In Freud's work, the unconscious, although it already appears—at least metaphorically—as an acting subject, is essentially nothing but the place where these same forgotten and repressed contents are collected, which is the only reason for the practical significance of the unconscious. Consequently, according to this view,

> it is exclusively personal in nature, although on the other hand Freud had already seen the unconscious' archaic-mythological way of thinking.
>
> A somewhat superficial layer of the unconscious is undoubtedly personal. We call it the *personal unconscious*. But this rests on a deeper layer, which no longer comes from personal experience and acquisition, but is innate. This deeper layer is the so-called collective unconscious. I have chosen the term *collective* because this unconscious is not individual but general, i.e., in contrast to the personal psyche, it evinces contents and behaviors that are more or less the same everywhere and in all individuals. It is, in other words, identical in all human beings and thus forms a general spiritual basis of a suprapersonal nature that is present in everyone.[14]

These quotations make it clear that, following Romantic discourses on the soul and in contrast to materialist and empirical-reductionist approaches, Jung wanted to establish psychology as a *science* that, interestingly enough, pays special attention to natural-scientific approaches. This understanding, however, recognizes the suprapersonal (as manifested in the soul) as well as psychology's metaphysical references. As for the history of philosophy, we can note with Marilyn Nagy: "It may fairly be said that the direct line of descent to Jung's own theory begins early in the eighteenth century with Berkeley and with Leibniz, passing then through Kant to Schopenhauer and von Hartmann and to turn-of-the-century academic quarrels about whether Kant had intended to affirm or deny the reliability of our knowledge of phenomena."[15]

Another aspect is noteworthy here: since the collectively unconscious contents of the human soul are hereditary and thus based on evolution, there is no fundamental difference between the human soul and the animal soul. In his treatise "Über das Unbewußte" (On the Unconscious), for example, first published in 1918 and written with a strong reference to World War I, Jung speaks about "the animal within us" and the human alienation from the animal soul, which Christianity in particular had precipitated in European culture. Christianity had suppressed pre-Christian, "pagan" symbols, "but as soon as the validity of the Christian faith appears to be shaken, that element takes center stage again."[16] Whenever the animalistic is suppressed, as happened in Europe, its primeval power breaks out in an uncontrollable way, as the World War had shown. "Our worldview has proved to be too narrow to grasp these powers in a cultural form."[17]

Thus it was no coincidence that Christianity "has no relationship to animals,"[18] in stark contrast to Buddhism.

> Through repression into the unconscious, into the sources from which it flowed, the animal becomes even more animalistic, which is probably why no other religion is so besmirched with innocent, cruelly spilt blood as is the Christian church, and the world has never seen a bloodier war than the war of the Christian nations. That is why the repressed animal appears in dangerous forms when it comes to the surface on its own, and when it breaks through, it leads to self-destruction, to the suicide of nations. But if every individual had a better relationship with their "animal," they would have a different appreciation of life. Then "life" would be an unconditional, moral principle for them, and they would instinctively resist any institution or organization that has the power to destroy life on a large scale.[19]

In "Über die Psychologie des Unbewussten" (On the Psychology of the Unconscious), first published in 1917 as *Die Psychologie der unbewußten Prozesse* (The Psychology of Unconscious Processes), Jung connects these considerations with the terms *instinct* and *drive*, particularly as Nietzsche and Freud had coined them. The Dionysian and the ecstatic, he argues, are not really helpful here because they cannot integrate the animal soul. An "ecstatic animal is an absurd thing. An animal fulfills its law of life, no more and no less. You can call it obedient and pious. The ecstatic person, however, transgresses the law of life and behaves, according to nature, in a disorderly fashion."[20]

With these remarks Jung continues the Orphic-Dionysian discourse I discussed earlier, but he gives it his own twist. For him, the "inner animal" stands for human drives and instincts, while ecstasy is a transgression of the animal soul and not—as in Nietzsche, Rilke, and others—the realization of the Dionysian power in the human being. Despite these differences, Jung strengthens the connection between animal soul, evolution, and cultural hermeneutics in a way that plunges him straight into the discursive stream of his day. In addition, his numerous interpretations of animals in dreams enabled his emphasis on the "inner animal," which would later become visible once again in many forms of shamanic and nature-based spiritualities.

If the human soul has suprapersonal components, it must also have tangible structures and recurring patterns, which complex psychology explores in an interdisciplinary way. This is the second subject area for which Jung's thinking was of great importance.

Alchemy and the Basic Patterns of the Soul

Jung regarded the collective unconscious as a culturally bound inner event, the dynamics of which are related to inherited structures. What is inherited here, however, are not the concrete images and representations of collective structures, but "*inherited instinctive drives and forms*, as can be observed in all living beings."[21] From his broad interest in comparative research on myth and religion, Jung came to the conviction "that certain ideas occur almost everywhere and at all times, and can even form spontaneously by themselves, completely independent of migration and tradition. They are not made by the individual, but they happen to them, indeed they virtually impose themselves on the individual consciousness. This is not Platonic philosophy, but empirical psychology."[22]

In order to represent the dynamics behind collective structures, Jung developed the concept of the *Archetypus* or "archetype," which was probably the best-known feature of Jung's psychology in the second half of the twentieth century. The archetype, as Jung says in a text that first appeared in the *Eranos-Jahrbuch* in 1946, is a numinous factor underlying the psychological structure, a factor that "determines the nature and sequence of the formation [of unconscious processes], with an apparent preknowledge or *in the a priori possession of the goal*."[23] He adds: "The archetype is pure, unadulterated nature, and it is nature that causes the human being to speak words and to perform actions whose meanings are unconscious to them, so unconscious that they do not even think about them."[24] In *Die Wandlung der Libido* (The Transformation of the Libido, first published in 1912), Jung states: "Of course, it is not a matter of inherited ideas, but of an innate disposition toward parallel formations of imagination, or rather universal, identical structures of the psyche, which I later called the collective unconscious. These structures I called archetypes. They correspond to the biological concept of the 'pattern of behavior.'"[25] The collective unconscious as "the enormous mental heritage of human development, reborn in every individual brain structure," contains the archetypes as "the source of the driving mental forces and the forms or categories regulating them." According to Jung, the archetypes are responsible for all of "humankind's strongest ideas and concepts." He claims that "even the scientific, philosophical, and moral key concepts are no exception to this. In their present form, they are variants of the original ideas that have arisen through conscious application and adaptation, for it is the function of consciousness not only to take up and recognize the outer world through the gates of the senses, but also to creatively translate the inner to the outer world."[26]

In European cultural history, alchemy provided Jung with proof of the existence of archetypes; in cultures outside Europe, he found similar confirmation in shamanism and Indigenous religious systems, and particularly in Buddhism. Thanks to the publication of *The Red Book*, we know that Jung conducted his alchemical research on a very personal level. *The Red Book*, which Jung called *Liber Novus* (Latin for "the new book"), was written between 1914 and 1930. After his break with Sigmund Freud, Jung began an experiment he called "confrontation with the unconscious," in which he recorded his fantasies or "active imaginations" as notes and sketches in notebooks he called "black books." He later revised these notes and supplemented them with further thoughts, and then transferred them in calligraphic medieval script into a book bound in red leather, with elaborate illustrations. Hence the name "Red Book." In 2009 *Liber Novus* was presented to the public for the first time at the Rubin Museum of Art in New York, followed by an exhibition at the Rietberg Museum in Zurich in 2010–2011.[27]

Liber Novus is an impressive document that demonstrates the seriousness with which Jung sought to fathom the deep layers of his unconscious and to build a bridge to art on the one hand, and to the history of alchemy, mysticism, and natural philosophy on the other.[28] But on the whole, Jung's project was not a private matter: "The making of *Liber Novus* was by no means a peculiar and idiosyncratic activity, nor the product of a psychosis. Rather, it indicates the close intersections between psychological and artistic experimentation with which many individuals were engaged at this time."[29] In his "experiment," Jung found a spiritual teacher in the figure of Philemon, as reported in his memoirs, which were recorded by Aniela Jaffé: "Soon after this fantasy, another figure emerged from the unconscious. It had developed from the figure of Elijah. I called it Philemon. Philemon was a pagan and brought up an Egyptian-Hellenistic mood with a Gnostic tinge. His figure first appeared to me in a dream. . . . Philemon and other fantasy figures brought me the decisive insight that there are things in the soul that I do not create, but that create themselves and have their own lives. Philemon represented a force that was not me."[30]

In November 1914 Jung also reread Nietzsche's *Thus Spoke Zarathustra*, which he knew from his youth. This reading exerted a strong influence on the structure of *Liber Novus*. "Like Nietzsche in *Zarathustra*, Jung divided the material into a series of books comprised of short chapters. But where Zarathustra proclaimed the death of God, *Liber Novus* depicts the rebirth of God in the soul. . . . The role of Philemon in Jung's work has analogies to that of Zarathustra in Nietzsche's work and Virgil in Dante's."[31] Yet another psychological connection to Nietzsche should be mentioned here: at the same time Jung was working on Nietzsche, Ludwig Klages described Nietzsche's philosophy as actual psychology—namely, as a universal scientific approach, in Jung's sense. Klages quotes Nietzsche's demand in *Beyond Good and Evil* "that psychology be recognized again as the mistress of the sciences, for whose service and foundation the other sciences exist."[32] For Klages, it is a fact "that only with Nietzsche had soul research (= psychology) in its own right actually begun."[33]

In his published work, Jung picked up the experiences and thoughts in *Liber Novus* in many ways, but they always remained implicit. For example, in 1954 Jung wrote in the preface to one of his most influential works on alchemy, *Mysterium Coniunctionis*, that it took more than ten years for "everything that belongs to this central problem to be collected and shaped to some extent."[34] After reading the essay by Karl Kerényi "Aegean Festival in Goethe's *Faust*" and Goethe's recourse in this scene to Christian Rosenkreutz's "chymical wedding," Jung subsequently devoted extensive study to the connections between alchemy and the interpretation of dreams, between Hermeticism and psychology.

> On this occasion, I have hinted at the wealth of ideas and symbols hidden in the neglected tracts of this often misunderstood "art" more than I have presented it in detail, as it would have deserved; after all, it was a more urgent concern to first prove that the alchemical world of symbols by no means or exclusively belongs to the rubble heaps of the past, but rather has an extremely vivid relation to the latest experiences and insights of the psychology of the unconscious. As it turns out, it is not only that this modern psychological discipline provides the key to the mystery of alchemy, but also that the latter provides the former with a meaningful historical basis.[35]

This insight is urgently needed, for "not only was alchemy as a natural philosophy and as a religious movement almost completely unknown, but the modern discovery of the archetypes was also hidden, or at least misunderstood by most."[36] The discourse on alchemy at the beginning of the twentieth century combined natural science, philosophy, and spirituality.[37] Therefore Wouter J. Hanegraaff's assertion that "academic study of the 'occult sciences' had seemed all but dead by the end of the nineteenth century, but Jung's psychology seemed capable of making the Waste Land revive" seems a bit exaggerated.[38] In contrast, with Mark S. Morrisson, we could point to the remarkable overlap in the scientific and alchemical interests of the time: "Indeed, to understand how the science of radioactivity came to be so tied to alchemical tropes and images, we must turn to an apparently unscientific phenomenon: the major fin-de-siècle revival of interest in alchemy and esoteric religion. Stunning landmarks of atomic science occurred alongside an efflorescence of occultism that ascribed deep significance to questions about the nature of matter and energy."[39] Jung was part of this broader movement, combining the existing discourse strands of alchemy, natural philosophy, religion, and vitalism with his concepts of dreams, the unconscious, and archetypes.

The interpretation of symbols resulting from this approach has significantly contributed to the popularity of Jung's psychology. An example of this is the tree symbol. Jung dedicated an entire treatise to the "philosophical tree" and used a quote from Goethe's *Faust* as an epigraph: "All theory, dear friend, is grey, but the golden tree of actual life springs ever green." In a detailed collage of pictures drawn by his patients, enriched with examples from cultural history and especially from alchemy, Jung seeks to prove the existence of collective structures because, "the diversity of the symbol notwithstanding, characteristic features emerge."[40] It is interesting how Jung weaves together discourse strands with reference to basic patterns of the soul (archetypes)–consciousness–alchemy–shamanism: "My casuistic material is unprejudiced because in no single case was there any knowledge of alchemy or shamanism. The pictures are spontaneous products of free-floating imagination, and their only conscious motive is the intention to express that experience, which arises when unconscious contents are taken up in the consciousness in such a way that these [contents] are not uprooted from it and the unconscious is not mutilated."[41]

Jung takes up the criticism of contemporary uprooting of the unconscious, which is implied here, later in his study. He states that both the historical alchemist and the modern metaphysician need psychology as a unifying, explanatory science. The authors of the alchemical texts "obviously recognized a parallelism between the alchemical process and religious ideas, a relationship that, however, is not easy for us to understand." It is the "psychological" that, as *tertium comparationis*, is capable of building a bridge between these different fields.

> The alchemist, of course, would have been just as indignant at the implication that his ideas about chemical matter were fantasies, as the metaphysician of today, who also believes that his statements are more than anthropomorphisms. Just as the alchemist could not distinguish between things in and of themselves and the ideas he had about them, so the metaphysician of today still believes that his views validly express their metaphysical object. Apparently, neither of them has ever noticed that their

> objects have always been the subject of the most diverse views. If nothing else helped, people were content with stating that the other was, of course, wrong. In contrast to the metaphysicians and especially the theologians, the alchemists do not express any polemical tendencies, but at most complain about the opacity of an author they do not understand.
>
> It is obvious to any reasonable person that in both cases we are dealing primarily with fantasies, which does not mean that their unidentified object does not exist. No matter what the fantasies refer to, they are always governed by the same mental laws, namely, by the *archetypes*. This is what the alchemists have noticed in their way of insisting on the parallelism between their own and religious beliefs.[42]

A discourse analysis is not much interested in assessing the historical validity of this representation of alchemy.[43] Rather, what is at stake for us is the question of how social knowledge about alchemy is being reorganized here. In this respect, Jung's understanding of alchemy as a system that enables individual cognition with the help of archetypes of the soul must be regarded as highly significant in its impact on Euro-American cultural history in the twentieth century.

Psychology and Natural Science: The World Soul, Quantum Mechanics, and Hermeticism

In his efforts to develop psychology as a fundamental discipline for both the humanities and the natural sciences, Carl Gustav Jung took a keen interest in new developments in the physics, chemistry, and biology of his time. With the advent of the theory of relativity and quantum mechanics, Newtonian mechanics—which was characterized by its basic assumption that natural processes were deterministic—was presented with a radical alternative. The implications of the paradigm shifts that accompanied this turn, as Thomas Arzt wrote at the end of the twentieth century, "have hardly become part of a collective consciousness thus far, in the sense that a substantial change in the relationship between the human and the world could be observed today."[44] These interests brought Jung into contact with Wolfgang Pauli (1900–1958). Pauli, who was awarded the Nobel Prize in Physics in 1945, certainly holds a special position among the many renowned scientists who have contributed to the development of scientific worldviews and their philosophical implications in the twentieth century. His work at the confluence of physics, philosophy, and psychology deals with the problems of causality, determinacy, and the objectivity of science and reality.[45] Surprisingly, compared to Einstein, Heisenberg, and Bohr, Pauli's memory is far from being as ubiquitous as one might expect. Only toward the end of the twentieth century, when the holism debate once again began to shape discussions of physics, philosophy, and spirituality, do we see a renewed interest in Pauli's thinking.[46]

Pauli was familiar with the basic features of hermetic philosophy and its reception in mysticism, natural philosophy, and religion. In a lecture at the highly regarded International Scholars' Congress in Mainz (Germany) titled "Europe—Heritage and Task" (1955), Pauli spoke about the fundamental antagonisms of science in Europe, in which hermetic philosophy and the natural sciences, as determined by Newton and others, were in constant conflict. In Pauli's understanding, Kepler versus Fludd and Newton versus Goethe were examples of this tension, and the same antagonism was still palpable in the quantum mechanics of his day. He ended his lecture with the words: "Warned by the failure of all premature attempts at unity in intellectual history, I will not dare to predict the future. Contrary to the strict division of the activities of the human spirit into separate departments since the seventeenth century, I consider, however, the objective of overcoming the contradictions, which includes a synthesis that encompasses both rational understanding and the mystical experience of unity, to be the pronounced or unspoken mythos of our own time."[47]

For Pauli, metaphysical questions thus formed an integral part of physics itself. He described the emergence of nondeterministic physics as the return of the *anima mundi*, the "world soul," which had been banned in the seventeenth century. Pauli wrote about this in a book he published together with Jung in 1952.[48] *Naturerklärung und Psyche* (An Explanation of Nature and Psyche) contains Jung's essay "Synchronizität als ein Prinzip akausaler Zusammenhänge" (Synchronicity as a Principle of Acausal

Connections),[49] as well as Pauli's treatise "Der Einfluß archetypischer Vorstellungen auf die Bildung naturwissenschaftlicher Ideen bei Kepler" (The Influence of Archetypal Concepts on the Formation of Scientific Ideas in Kepler).[50] Jung understands the phenomenon of synchronicity as a "coincidence of meaning" among several events that are "acausally connected."[51] This shows that Jung's understanding of synchronicity is very close to the hermetic principle "as above, so below"—that is, to thinking in correspondences, which is also presupposed in astrology. It is therefore not surprising that Jung refers to astrology in the earlier-mentioned essay (a correlation that Pauli has never accepted). In this case, the emphasis is on the simultaneity of phenomena connected by similarities in meaning, but not by a causal relationship.[52]

Quantum mechanics offers interesting prospects for a physical interpretation of synchronicity, which led to an intense discussion over the course of the twentieth century, with direct recourse to Jung and Pauli (see chapters 6 and 7). At this point, it is important to stress that both Jung and Pauli regarded the *anima mundi* as a bridge between psychology and the natural sciences, especially quantum mechanics. Jung repeatedly used terms from alchemy to illustrate this, and even identified the world soul with the collective unconscious.[53] It is especially Mercury who embodies the world soul, as Jung explains in his treatise "Der Geist Mercurius" (The Mind Mercurius), which was originally a lecture at the Eranos conference in Ascona in 1942.[54] Thus, through alchemy, Jung ties a discursive knot that connects the soul to natural science, the cosmos, and hermetic philosophy, and at the same time presents complex psychology as the only science capable of overcoming the old tensions between the related disciplines. In his study of the tree symbol, Jung formulates this claim very clearly when he compares Robert Fludd's research to Johannes Kepler's:

> It is basically the old problem of universals, the contrast between realism and nominalism, which in our scientific age has practically been decided in a nominalistic direction. While the scientific point of view strives to explain nature on its own terms on the basis of careful empiricism, hermetic philosophy aims to create a description and an explanation that includes the psyche, that is, a holistic view of nature. The empiricist seeks,

> more or less successfully, to forget or suppress his archetypal principles of explanation, i.e., his psychological preconditions, which are indispensable for the process of cognition, in favor of his "scientific objectivity." Conversely, the hermetic philosopher considers the psychological preconditions, namely, the archetypes, as indispensable components of the empirical worldview. He is not yet so occupied by the object that he can disregard the tangible presence of his psychic preconditions in the form of eternal ideas that are perceived as real. The empirical nominalist, on the other hand, already has the modern attitude toward the psyche, that it must and can be eliminated as "subjective," in that its contents are nothing but retrospectively formulated concepts—*flatus vocis.* Therefore he hopes to be able to create a worldview that is independent of the observer in every respect. This hope has only partly been fulfilled in the course of history, as the results of modern physical research have shown: the observer cannot ultimately be switched off, i.e., the psychological precondition remains effective.[55]

When it comes to establishing complex psychology as a necessary link between the natural sciences and the humanities, another term is important to Jung: energy. As early as 1912, he had already dealt with the subject in a first draft of *Wandlungen und Symbole der Libido* (Transformations and Symbols of the Libido), but he continued to develop his reflections on the subject up to the publication of the treatise *Über die Energetik der Seele* (On the Energetics of the Soul) in 1928.[56] This study is also a reaction to misunderstandings caused by his earlier treatment of the subject of libido. Jung distinguishes a "mechanistic" from an "energetic" view of physical events. He also calls the energetic view "final," a term that implies directionality but not a teleological anticipation of the goal.[57] In this sense, Jung's concept resembles Henri Bergson's "creative evolution." "The energetic process," Jung maintains, "has a certain direction (goal) by unalterably (irreversibly) following the potential gradient. Energy is not a view of a substance moving in space, but a *concept* abstracted from the relationships of movement. Its basis is thus not the substances themselves, but their relations, while the basis of the mechanistic concept is the substance moving in space."[58] Both points of view are indispensable for the understanding of physical events.[59]

This raises the interesting question of how psychic energy is related to physical energy, which is basically a variation of the old mind-body problem. While Jung describes the soul as a "relatively closed system,"[60] which thus enables a quantification of energy, he also insists that psychology, just like physics, has the right to develop its own concepts and interpretation systems when it comes to energy.[61] In doing so, he refers to the preliminary work of Friedrich Schiller, Nicolas von Grot, Theodor Lipps, and William Stern, who introduced the concept of "psychic energy"; like Lipps, he distinguished it from the concept of "force" (*Kraft*). In order to arrive at a conceptual clarification, Jung suggests that the psychic process should simply be understood as a "life process. In this way we expand the narrower concept of a psychic energy to the broader concept of a *life energy*, which subsumes the so-called psychic energy as a specification."[62] Jung continues:

> *The concept of a life energy has nothing to do with a so-called life force*, because this force would be nothing more than a specification of a universal energy, which would remove the privilege of bioenergetics over physical energetics, bypassing the as-yet-unfilled gap between the physical process and the life process. I have proposed calling the hypothetically presumed life energy *libido*, with regard to the psychological use we intend to make of it, and thus to distinguish it from a universal concept of energy, while respecting the exclusive right of biology and psychology to define their own concepts. I do not intend to preempt the practitioner of bioenergetics, but to freely admit that I have intentionally applied the term *libido* to *our* use. He may suggest a "bioenergy" or "vital energy" for his own use.[63]

With these differentiations, Jung tries to distinguish his concept of libido from vitalist models. Like neovitalists such as Hans Driesch, Jung rejected a mechanistic model and saw the need for a final understanding of "becoming," but he wanted to avoid reducing psychology to biology. He did not want to get involved in the "question of psychophysical parallelism and interaction."[64] Jung "chose the alternatives favored by vitalism—an energic or final view of the psyche, a relatively closed system, and the possibility of a causal relationship between psyche and soma—for his concept of libido or psychic energy."[65] Jung admits that the proof of a causal relationship between psychic and physical energy processes has not yet been established. But "even the opponents of such a possibility have not succeeded in separating the mental process from the physical one with certainty."[66]

As I will show in the next chapter, the vitalist and monistic movements were extremely strong at the time when Jung developed his model of libido as mental energy. For Wilhelm Ostwald, the concept of energetics was the linchpin of both scientific and psychological-humanistic models. Jung was familiar with Ostwald's work on the type theory of humankind; in *Über die Energetik der Seele* he refers to Ostwald's hypostatic concept of energy,[67] so we can assume that he was also familiar with Ostwald's monistic views on energetics.

The works discussed in this chapter show the extent to which Carl Gustav Jung was involved in the discourse of his time, both in diverse psychological research perspectives and in the broader context of religious studies, philosophy, and the natural sciences. Although his teachings received little attention in academic psychology in the long run, his influence on the consolidation of a discourse that endowed the soul with metaphysical and religious properties and integrated it into a holistic understanding of science can hardly be overestimated. The discursive arrangement of soul–consciousness–cosmos–nature–energy–life force, which had already been established and which Jung developed further, was part of the intellectual discussion of the time and was a topic of keen public interest until the early 1930s. Monistic, vitalist, and occult readings of the soul were also booming at this time. I now turn to those debates.

5

OCCULTISM, THE NATURAL SCIENCES, AND SPIRITUALITY BEFORE 1930

Against the background of the intellectual, literary, and political discussions about the soul outlined earlier, I will now take a closer look at the scientific debates that have been interwoven with psychological and philosophical questions in many ways. Under the Weimar Republic, it is apparent that occultism played a key role in the discursive arrangements that had crystalized around the soul. Along with monism and vitalism, research into the occult forces of the soul forms an important starting point for the further development of the respective discourses. This is also the last phase, for the time being, in which academia seriously engaged with the soul. After 1930, the soul disappeared from academic psychology and science, only to be received all the more intensely outside the universities. How did this development come about?

The Soul in Monism and Vitalism

Biological explanations for psychological facts were already prominent in the nineteenth century.[1] In Britain, Alexander Bain and Herbert Spencer gave impetus to this trajectory, but Kurt Danziger reminds us that the movement was larger than most people acknowledge. "What was involved was a new recognition of the relevance of biological or physiological perspectives for psychology. Rather than constituting a world apart, the mind was now to be viewed in terms of its place in nature."[2] One reason this trajectory was disregarded in later retrospectives of the history of psychology was the fact that those who researched the psycho-physiological trajectory "completely missed the bus with regard to experimentation and quantification."[3] So while the biologistic form of psychology lagged behind the experimental as well as the metaphysical forms, at the turn of the century, interestingly enough, it was nonpsychologists who gave it a new boost. In Germany, this impetus is strongly linked to Ernst Haeckel (1834–1919).

Haeckel presented what was probably the most radical biologistic theory of the time.[4] In one of his most influential works, *The Riddle of the Universe*, known in German as *Die Welträthsel: Gemeinverständliche Studien über Monistische Philosophie* (first published in 1899, then in 1903 as the "people's edition," with a print run of 170,000 copies and an epilogue titled "The Creed of Pure Reason"), he dedicated an entire chapter to the soul. For him the soul is completely bound to its material existence.

> All the phenomena of the life of the soul are, without exception, connected to material processes in the living substance of the body, in the *plasma* or *protoplasm*. We have called that part of the latter, which appears as the indispensable carrier of the psyche, *psychoplasm* ("soul substance" in the monistic sense), i.e., we do not see it as a special "being," but we consider the *psyche as a collective term for all the psychic functions of the plasma*. In this sense, *soul* is as much a physiological abstraction as the terms *metabolism* or *procreation*.[5]

This complete biologization of the soul has enormous consequences, which Haeckel describes in detail.[6] Since the soul is regarded as part of evolutionary developments, the human soul is not fundamentally different from the souls of other beings, especially of evolutionarily related animals. In addition to the soul's "ontogenesis," it also has a "phylogenesis" as the development of the living soul in the evolutionary "ancestral line of the human." Thus character traits and soul traits are inheritable, a doctrine that would later underpin racist ideologies under National Socialism. Finally, Haeckel also devotes himself to religious-metaphysical views of the soul and explicitly rejects the idea of the immortality of the soul as completely unscientific.

By dissolving the soul into physicality and substance, Haeckel develops a discursive arrangement that manages without a traditional concept of religion on the one hand, but sacralizes the soul in the sense of monistic philosophy on the other. The universal law of substance that Haeckel develops leads him into cosmological contexts that assume metaphysical qualities. He even formulates this discursive knot very concretely: "World (= Nature = Substance = Cosmos = Universe = God)."[7] The soul is merely a subfunction in this larger scheme of cosmic evolution.

For Haeckel, these considerations are directly related to his interest in the link between the organic and the inorganic, and above all to the question of how the organic can arise from the inorganic. In his main early work, *Generelle Morphologie der Organismen* (General Morphology of Organisms), published in 1866 and subtitled *Allgemeine Grundzüge der organischen Formen-Wissenschaft, mechanisch begründet durch die von Charles Darwin reformirte Descendenz-Theorie* (General Characteristics of the Science of Organic Forms, Mechanistically Based on the Theory of Descent, as Reformed by Charles Darwin), Haeckel explicitly posed this question in the second volume, but it was only through the further development of biology and psychology that he felt he was in a position to provide a theoretically and empirically sound answer. In the preface to his last major work, published in 1917 under the title *Kristallseelen: Studien über das anorganische Leben* (Crystal Souls: Studies on Inorganic Life), Haeckel refers to several fundamental works that had appeared in 1904 and had massively altered understandings of the connections between organic and inorganic (soul) life. These were Otto Lehmann's discovery of "liquid, apparently *living* crystals"; Richard Semon's proof of "*mnemes* as a sustaining principle in the changing organic process"; experimental research on plants' sense organs and "soul life," conducted by Haberlandt, Nemec, Francé, and others; and finally proof of "coreless cells," which "reformed cell theory and replaced it with the *theory of plastides*," which Haeckel had also been working toward as early as 1866.[8] Only at this point did Haeckel feel he was in a position to draft a program for a new "biological philosophy" in his book on *Lebenswunder* (Miracles of Life, 1904), which at the same time complemented the statements he made in *Welträthsel.* He exclaims enthusiastically that this development has established the year 1904 as

> a milestone in the history of natural philosophy. As its most important achievement, we consider the definitive conviction of the fundamental *unity of all natural phenomena*, which finds its simplest and clearest expression in the concept of "monism." The artificial boundaries that had previously been established between inorganic and organic nature, between death and life, between natural science and the humanities, now fell away at a single stroke. *All substance contains life*, inorganic as well as organic; *all things are animate*, crystals as well as organisms. The old conviction of the inner, unified connection of all events, of the unlimited dominion of universal natural laws, rises unshakably anew.[9]

Haeckel himself makes clear the extent to which the genealogy of this discourse is connected with Goethe when he identifies the "landmark" year 1904 as the fulfillment of Goethe's natural philosophical project. No wonder then that he uses three quotations from Goethe as epigraphs for *Kristallseelen.* One of these is particularly apt for the discourse on the soul in the twentieth century: "Whoever does not want to get it into his head that spirit and matter, soul and body, thought and extension, will and motion, were, are, and will be the *necessary double ingredients of the universe*, which *both* demand *equal rights* for themselves, and therefore both together can probably be regarded as *God's representatives*—whoever cannot rise to this idea should have given up thinking long ago and spent his days on mean worldly gossip."[10]

The connection to Goethe is also clear in the role aesthetics plays in the process of understanding nature. The aesthetics of crystals and the *Art Forms of Nature* (one of Haeckel's most influential books)[11] as a whole offer direct empirical access to knowledge of nature. This creates cross-connections that were recognized in the Weimar Republic era. With reference to Haeckel, Arthur Titius notes: "If, however, lines connecting knowledge of nature to art and to speculation are recognized, then one will no longer be able to preemptively deny a connection between knowledge of nature and religion, as well as the justification of a religious view of nature."[12]

In *Kristallseelen*, Haeckel unfolds a broad theory of crystals, which he calls "Kristallotik" (crystallotics) or "Kristallkunde" (crystal science). On the basis of recent studies, he distinguishes four "orders" of crystals. While the "sterrocrystals" are what most people understand as "real," rigid crystals, the "collocrystals" are jelly crystals that swell in water and expand in volume without giving up their shape (for example, protein crystals in plant cells). "Biocrystals" are solid mixed crystals, created from living plasma and mineral substances (such as lime or pebbles), and "rheocrystals" are the "apparently living" crystals that Otto Lehmann had identified.[13] These distinctions are a prerequisite for Haeckel's belief that his *psychomatics* as "Fühlungskunde" (feeling-science, the science of the sensation of matter), outlined in chapter 4 of *Kristallseelen*, could overcome the unresolvable contradictions he identified between medical psychiatry and metaphysical psychology.

Under the keywords *Fühlung* (feeling) and *Ästhesis* (aesthesis), Haeckel also addresses the world soul:

> The "*world soul*" (psychoma), as a psycho-physical principle, is one of the three "essential attributes" of all substance; it is everywhere inseparably connected with the two other basic properties (energy and matter), both in organic ("animate") and in inorganic ("inanimate") nature. As *feeling*, or unconscious "sensation," it is the real "*interiorization*" of the substance, in contrast to its "exteriorization," which is energy. Feeling distinguishes the subject from the environment of the outside world (the object), while energy acts (expresses and exteriorizes itself) on it as a "force." In the aesthesis, two dynamic "original states" are opposed to each other, the positive *feeling of pleasure* as inclination or attraction, and the negative *feeling of unwillingness* [*Unlustgefühl*] as resistance or repulsion. The antagonism of positive and negative feeling corresponds to the old doctrine of the "loving and hating elements."[14]

In his attempt to establish the monistic worldview, Haeckel worked closely with Wilhelm Ostwald (1853–1932). They were united in their conviction that the development of the natural sciences meant that the philosophical and cultural interpretation of the relationship between nature and the human being had to be completely rethought. The strength with which each scientist supported the other in this intention can be seen from their correspondence, which was published in 2006, on the occasion of the hundredth anniversary of the founding of the *Deutscher Monistenbund* (German Monist League).[15] The German Monist League was founded in 1906 at Haeckel's suggestion, and it was Haeckel who persuaded Ostwald to take over the league presidency in 1911, which he then held until 1915.[16]

Ostwald, who was awarded the Nobel Prize in Chemistry in 1909, saw monism as a link between the natural sciences, the humanities, and religion, just as Haeckel did. He combined his election as president of the German Monist League with other activities—politically as a member of Berta von Suttner's peace movement, and artistically as a passionate painter. His ideas about color theory, referring back to Goethe, influenced artists such as the young Paul Klee and members of the Dutch artists' group De Stijl, including Piet Mondrian. Ostwald's work comprises more than forty thousand pages. As a representative of the monist movement, Ostwald propagated Social Darwinism, euthanasia, and eugenics, and after the war was lost in 1917, he combined monism with German-national revanchism.[17]

Ostwald's philosophy of "energetics" differed from Haeckel's monism in that Ostwald valued matter and substance less than Haeckel. He focused more on the cultural and spiritual aspects of "energy"—a critical response to Haeckel, and one that he shared with Hans Driesch (on whom more later). For his part, Ostwald saw the concept of energy, which he developed from the concept of "work," as overcoming the dualism between the natural sciences and the humanities. He demonstrated this theory in his book *Die Forderung des Tages* (The Call of the Day), published in 1910. In the chapter "General Energetics," he made it clear that even the concept of "matter," "in so far as such a concept should prove useful at all, needs to be defined on an energetic basis."[18] Haeckel had a completely different view on this question. Ostwald would later return to these differences between himself and Haeckel, namely, in his thirty-fifth Monist Sunday Sermon, titled "Haeckel and Ostwald." This controversy is also important for the discourse on the soul because the author repudiates Haeckel's conviction (which he had taken from Spinoza and Fechner) that matter could never exist without mind, and mind could never exist without matter, and that one could therefore even assume the existence of "atomic souls." According to Ostwald, Haeckel "regarded matter down to its last, smallest particles as connected with or animated by a soul."[19] However, this view had proven to be fundamentally wrong in the light of the latest scientific developments. Against the background of the laws of energy, the idea of a connection between matter and soul would make no sense. "Rather, the concept of energy is broad and comprehensive enough to also include psychic phenomena within its framework, which was not possible with all-too-narrow mechanics."[20]

We find similar statements in the chapter "Psychology and Biography" in *Die Forderung des Tages*. Ostwald clarifies: "The energetic conception of psychological phenomena is a particularly striking example of the already mentioned property of energetics to unconsciously and almost against one's will present itself as an explanatory principle for understanding areas that are seemingly quite far removed from on another. . . . Accordingly, physiology as well as psychology and cultural studies have their energetic foundations."[21] In the first part of the Monist Sunday Sermons, under the keyword "immortality," he notes:

> So overall, one result of contemporary science is *that the mind is a function of the body*. When the one value of the functional relationship, namely the body, or rather the life in it, becomes zero, then the value that depends on it, what we call *soul* or *life of the mind*, also disappears in all regards, as far as we are able to observe it. Because of the fundamental error *Plato* introduced into the entire observation of spiritual phenomena, as if the soul were an independent individual able to exist independently of the body and held together with the body only temporarily by certain unknown bonds, this simple fact has shifted and darkened in our consciousness in the most detrimental way. Our assessment of the relationship between soul and body has been further disturbed by the fact that Christianity later adopted this Platonism and enhanced it even further, to the extreme opposition between soul and body.[22]

A similar criticism of religion, especially of Christianity, is found in Ostwald's book *Religion und Monismus* (Religion and Monism), published in 1914, in which he describes monism as the overcoming of historical religions. Bit by bit, Ostwald disproves both Christianity's and the priestly caste's right to exist, and for every problem, monism turns out to be the modern solution. For instance, he asserts that it is much more pleasant to dive "into the flood of the undiscriminated [*Ununterschiedenen*]" at the end of one's life, with "the prospect of a deep and dreamless sleep," than it is to go through the "factor of uncertainty, yes, of horror" that Christianity brought to the end of life.[23] In the same year, in another book, he argues that there is a developmental relationship between Christianity and monism, "in that Christianity represents an earlier and therefore more imperfect stage of ethics. So we monists will look back on Christianity as we look back on our youth."[24]

Ostwald sticks to his guns in a consistent way; in his Sunday sermon "Energy," he had already emphasized that all human thoughts and mental functions must be derived from energy, and not from mystical or transcendental dimensions.

> Thus the whole circle of celestial bodies, on which a fantasy directed toward the magnificent is built, is a transformation of energy. And likewise, none of the thoughts that pass through my consciousness, sometimes clear, sometimes shadowy, originates . . . without the fact that every movement, even the slightest one, is based on a transformation of energy, at the cessation of which all thinking must cease as well. . . . Thus nothing can be called the greatest or the smallest that does not find its place within the framework of the concept of energy and is not subject to the law of the conservation of energy.[25]

In a unique way, Wilhelm Ostwald contributed to the scientification of religion and the religious-metaphysical transformation of science in the twentieth century. The discursive knot Ostwald and Haeckel provided—in which Haeckel places more emphasis on "soul," whereas Ostwald focuses more on "energy"—takes up explicitly religious, even Christian, semantics and concepts, combining them with psychological and scientific ones. In the second half of the twentieth century, ideas about "energy" would have a broad impact, as would spiritually and scientifically conceived ideas about "the soul."

Thus for Haeckel and Ostwald, the transcendental sources of humanity's special status had become obsolete. "Was there now no more hope that human values might have a transcendent source?" asks Marilyn Nagy. She answers: "There was, and this new hope came in the person of Hans Driesch, and the scientifically based doctrines of neo-vitalism which he developed."[26] Vitalism has a long history in European philosophy and science. Having been pushed into the background by the emphasis on materialistic scientific methods at the end of the nineteenth century, it was indeed primarily Hans Driesch (1867–1941) who reintroduced vitalist thinking. When he repeated the experiments with frog eggs that Wilhelm Roux had carried out in 1888, this time with sea urchin eggs, he found that only the first half of the experiment produced the same results; then a whole new sea urchin larvae formed—a result that ran contrary to Roux's mechanistic interpretation. This field of research, known as the morphogenesis of organisms, led Driesch to believe that there had to be a teleological, holistic construction principle that would provide all organisms with a developmental program from the outset—a factor in nature that generated the physicochemical processes in the organism as a whole. For Driesch, the term *entelechy*, which goes back to Aristotle, provided the most appropriate means of conceptualizing this. Entelechy denotes an immaterial factor, a "vital causality" that creates a complete whole. "Entelechial evolution" is the holistic-causal development of a system toward further diversity (for example, in embryology), in contrast to "machine development," which does not necessarily refer to the entirety of "becoming" (for example, when a machine develops into another machine that may be more complex but is not necessarily more diverse than the first).[27]

Driesch repeatedly turned against the doctrine of so-called psychophysical parallelism. This doctrine assumes a fundamental separation between a physical and a psychic world, whereby there are no psychic phenomena that do not have their counterparts in physical reality, which means they could be represented by mechanical natural processes.[28] However, if one turns the tables, then this parallelism would not apply in the same way, for the physical "in its entirety is definitely and merely a mechanical (or energetic or electrodynamic) system," as Driesch asserts.[29] Instead, Driesch tries to demonstrate that psychophysical parallelism does indeed concern two sides of a single reality. "We may refer to this parallelism as a whole by the moniker *My soulful body* or *The immediate psycho-physical person*."[30] For Driesch, the connection between the individual soul or person and the intersubjective, natural world is made through the concepts of "psychoid" and "soul." "Actually, there are many natural bodies," Driesch explains, "which behave in the same or similar ways according to their laws of becoming, like my body; namely the 'other people' and the animals. I may understand them *as if* a *soul* were assigned to their psychoid in a parallel fashion. This results in the term: *The other psycho-physical person*."[31] In his *Ordnungslehre*, Driesch also uses the term *das Seelische* (the soulful) instead of *soul*, since the soul could represent a connection with phenomena that are "foreign to the soul"; the "organization of the soul" ensures the order of the inner life and works outward into nature.[32]

These considerations belong to the discursive arrangement of occultism. In his well-known treatise *Der Vitalismus als Geschichte und als Lehre* (Vitalism as History and Doctrine, 1905), Driesch himself had already pointed out that so-called occult phenomena were also highly relevant to philosophy. He noted with surprise that psychology had not yet incorporated the insights of vitalism, although the mind-body problem, for which vitalism offered a solution, was also relevant to psychological phenomena. This brought Driesch close to Carl Gustav Jung's considerations; he met Jung in 1934 and appreciated his work, since both held similar views, especially in the field of parapsychology. "We agreed on many things, also about matters of parapsychology," Driesch writes in his autobiography.[33] The vitalist discourse should therefore be understood as a much broader field than vitalism in the narrower sense.[34]

In line with these considerations, in the 1920s Driesch increasingly engaged with paranormal phenomena and scientific investigations of such phenomena. He quickly became known as an authority in this field. From 1926 to 1927 he was president of the Society for Psychical Research, and in 1932 he published a book of methods for researching parapsychology, which had a significant impact and was reprinted several times. The third edition

(1952) contains a more than forty-page afterword by Hans Bender, "On the Development of Parapsychology from 1930 till 1950." In the subtitle of his book on parapsychology, Driesch puts the word *occult* in quotation marks. This is programmatic: "Precisely because parapsychology does real explanatory work, one should finally stop calling it 'occultism.'"[35] The distinction between occultism and parapsychology does not necessarily reflect different worldviews in the German-speaking world—in contrast to the French and English contexts. Parapsychological researchers such as Julian Ochorowicz, Albert von Schrenck-Notzing, or Enrico Agostino Morselli were positivists, if not materialists (as was Charles Richet in Paris), but nevertheless insisted on the reality of parapsychological phenomena.[36]

In his teaching, Driesch speaks of a "soul field" that connects the individual soul with other souls. This enables an exchange of knowledge between souls and persons, as regularly observed in parapsychological phenomena. Driesch goes even further and equips the higher "world consciousness" with agency. "The suprapersonal is not only an indeterminate framework connecting personal living souls and enabling paranormal direct knowledge transfer between them, but also a kind of suprapersonal *subject*. This subject, however, carries all the life plans of all human beings firmly formed within itself."[37]

Driesch also wanted to replace the term *Medium* (German for "psychic" or "medium") with a better one, since the word had a lingering spiritualist aftertaste. Thus he adopts the term *metagnome* from Eugène Osty, who was the director of the Institut Métapsychique International in Paris from 1924 until 1938, defining this "as a person with whom or in explicit reference to whom parapsychological phenomena are happening, a person who is thus indispensable for parapsychological phenomena."[38] Such attempts at scientific classification, which go along with the creation of a new language beyond occultism, reveal changes in discourses on the soul.

Thus the discourse on occult realities, which had significantly contributed to the emergence of academic psychology in the nineteenth century, was perpetuated and developed under the Weimar Republic. Egil Asprem rightly speaks of a lively debate conducted over three generations.[39] Haeckel and Ostwald also contributed to these discursive formations, although we should not file their work under "occultism"—their contribution consisted in strengthening and legitimizing the same discursive arrangement that was also a vehicle for occultism and vitalism in the narrower sense.

On the one hand, a kind of normalization of discourse took place during this period, because nineteenth-century scientific and technical innovations became more and more commonplace, while on the other hand there was a tendency to further professionalize the investigation of occult phenomena, either through scientific examination or with more precise psychological terminology. Hans Driesch is a good example of this, but he was by no means the only one.

Occultism in the 1920s

After completing his doctorate, Richard Baerwald (1867–1929) worked as a lecturer in "psychology and pathology of the soul" at the Humboldt University of Berlin. Baerwald is one of the authors who criticized experimental-reductionist psychology. As early as 1905, he lamented the fact that physiological psychology offered no solutions to philosophical and educational questions. In turn, "history and ethnography," Baerwald argued, "when they are based on psychological factors, often work with an ad hoc psychology that is far removed from the scientifically codified one."[40] In order to build a bridge between psychology and the humanities, Baerwald presents the "psychology of individual differences," which aims to show that the vocabulary of individual psychology can be used to depict the different dispositions and characteristics of cultural epochs. "There are zeitgeist individuals as well as personal individuals."[41] Particularly in German intellectual history, Baerwald finds extreme examples of a radically changing zeitgeist, and the "zigzag course of German intellectual life"[42] has produced sharp antitheses that clarify the connections between the soul and cultural epochs. As might be expected in this branch of German cultural hermeneutics, Baerwald refers to Goethe's era, which he then compares with the radically different experience of his own generation.

During his time in Berlin, Baerwald developed a growing interest in occultism, which he defined in 1920 as the "science of mediumistic phenomena."[43] In this overview—published by Teubner as the 560th volume in the series *From Nature and the Intellectual World: A Collection of Scientific Accounts for a General Audience*—Baerwald introduces readers to the field of occultism and at the same time shows that the previously highly popular field of "physical occultism," in which "physical mediums" pretend to help spirits appear and materialize, has been in decline since 1880 due to critical psychological research.[44] His overall verdict on spiritualism and occultism is unequivocal:

> Spiritualism has collapsed before our very eyes; the metaphysical belief in a higher existence beyond the tangible natural world of outward appearance has once again suffered defeat. But the human being's ineradicable longing for a mystical, an invisible beyond the indifferent world of perception does not remain unsatisfied; it simply finds what it is looking for in another place. A new "beyond of the soul" (Dessoir) opens up, a subconscious behind the normal, everyday consciousness, so full of foreboding knowledge and unknown forces that its wonders are hardly inferior to those of the dreamed heaven and the assumed spirit world. Within themselves, in the psychological and moral realms, humans regain what philosophical and scientific criticism has snatched from their faith out there in space—these words aptly express the law of the development of worldviews in the century after Kant.[45]

Consequently, for Baerwald, spiritualism and physical occultism have lost their right to exist. But beyond these views and practices, which have been exposed as unscientific and ethically dubious, Baerwald pleads for a critical occultism: "Today we have a better means of securing ourselves and keeping ourselves healthy: we can strip occult phenomena of what beguiles the senses by connecting them to their natural causes."[46] We may describe this as a kind of secularized occultism in which the discursive factor "science" becomes an important vehicle of meaning, as was the case with Ostwald and others.

Baerwald continued to pursue precisely this program. From 1926 to 1928 he was editor of the *Zeitschrift für kritischen Okkultismus* (Journal for Critical Occultism), which was dedicated to the scientific study of occult phenomena. In 1926 Baerwald published his *Okkultismus und Spiritismus und ihre weltanschaulichen Folgerungen* (Occultism, Spiritualism, and Their Ideological Implications). He outlines the subject area as follows:

> The area we want to enter here was called "secret sciences" in ancient times, but also "magic" or "spiritualism." . . . It was not until the nineteenth century that the term *occultism*, coined by Kiesewetter, came up, which in itself was simply a Latinization of the old word for secret sciences (occultus = hidden), but nevertheless it contained a new program. With this slogan, our field of science tried to catch up with the transformation astronomy and physics had undergone two to three centuries earlier; it tried to free itself from ghosts and demons, and to recognize forces in the world of experience, in this case psychological and physiological processes, as the cause of "occult phenomena." In many cases, although not consistently, the word *occultism* was used as a critique of spiritualism. People called themselves occultists if they wanted to suggest that they did not consider the dancing table or the emerging materialization to be an achievement or appearance of spirits, but realized that one was dealing exclusively with an effect of the medium or psychic. The new word thus became a banner and a symbol for the tendency to insert unexplainable and yet partly undeniable phenomena into the usual natural context.[47]

Consequently, he defines *occultism* as "the doctrine of mediumistic (psychic) phenomena," which is dedicated to the "scientific exploration of mediumistic (psychic) phenomena."[48] The book's table of contents can be understood as an attempt to structure and systematize the phenomena he mentions: "The Subconscious," "Mediumism" (including hysteria), "Riser Pipes of the Subconscious" (automatic writing, crystal visions, table turning and table rapping, the sidereal pendulum), "Telepathy," "Encapsulations of Hyperesthesia and Telepathy" (clairvoyance, psychometry, doppelganger, cross-correspondence, phantoms), "Prophecies," "The Physical Phenomena," and finally "Spiritualism and the Immortality Problem."

Traugott Konstantin Oesterreich (1880–1949) also belongs to the circle of influential German occultists of the time. After completing his doctorate in Berlin with the thesis *Kant and Metaphysics* (1906), Oesterreich worked for five years as an adjunct lecturer and an assistant at the Neurobiological Institute in Berlin before he completed his habilitation in philosophy at the University of Tübingen in 1910. It was not until twelve years later that he was appointed as a contracted associate professor of philosophy and psychology at the University of Tübingen. He would remain in this position until 1933. After the National Socialists came to power, his colleagues denounced him for his democratic, pacifist attitude. He was forced to retire and was only reinstated in 1945.

From the beginning, Oesterreich's interest went far beyond the field of philosophy. He dealt with psychology and psychopathology, working on questions of ego-identity and personality splitting in particular. These questions brought him to occultism and parapsychology. He took part in sessions with well-known psychics of the day, and his experiences in these sessions strengthened his conviction that parapsychology could provide important additional insights for psychology and philosophy. Together with Hans Driesch and Rudolf Tischner (on whom more later), he called for the founding of the German Central Institute for Parapsychology, modeled on the British Society for Psychical Research. In a lecture at the Second International Congress for Parapsychological Research, which took place in Warsaw in 1923, Oesterreich criticized the attitude of his philosophical colleagues who regarded parapsychological phenomena as relevant only for psychology, psychiatry, physics, and biology. "The truth is that the philosophical significance of psychic phenomena in particular cannot easily be overstated."[49]

In 1921 Oesterreich published his introductory work *Der Okkultismus im modernen Weltbild* (Occultism in the Modern Worldview), which was already in its third edition two years later. Let us take a quick look at this book. Similarly to Richard Baerwald, Oesterreich also describes occultism as a scientific tradition that has been the subject of critical research in England and France for several years, but has only recently become a major theme in Germany. In the introduction, Oesterreich addresses the fundamental crisis of humankind after World War I, and also the many serious crises in the natural sciences. His statement on psychology's dream of being recognized as a science is particularly interesting:

> This strange dream has come to an end. No serious researcher today can still believe that the role of experimental psychology within the humanities is even remotely equivalent to the role of mechanics within physics. All hope of finding laws of similar structure to the laws of mechanics in the life of the soul has remained unfulfilled. There is no permanent factor in the life of the soul apart from the ego, as the acts and states of which all psychological experiences are represented, whereas all mechanical physics presupposes the presence and existence of elementary physical components.[50]

But this was not all. Oesterreich explains that the position of psychology and the status of souls themselves are closely related to the physical world. "Physics is concerned with objects that represent an independent sphere of reality . . . the experiences of souls are partly determined by processes in the physical world. Every soul is thought to be connected with a physical organism."[51] This connection between material reality and the life of the soul had led to a situation in which "modern psychology and the new biology . . . have together uprooted the older materialistic worldview. . . . Nevertheless, they are far from putting a consistent worldview in its place."[52]

It is exactly such a coherent worldview that Oesterreich seeks to develop. But the term *occultism*, he notes, would be unfortunate as a designation for this project; while "occult," mysterious, and enigmatic phenomena such as X-rays, radioactivity, and Hertzian waves were new discoveries at the end of the nineteenth century, and as such were still surrounded by the "feeling of the consecrated, the mysterious," these phenomena had meanwhile been accepted as a matter of course. "It is no different with the 'occult' problems. As long as phenomena such as telepathy, clairvoyance, and materialization still appear unusual, they will be surrounded by the charm of the mysterious."[53] Nevertheless, he did not consider more recent, alternative terms—such as *scientific occultism*, *parapsychology*, or *metapsychology* (coined by Charles Richet, the physiologist and psychologist who received the Nobel Prize in 1913)—to be much better solutions. What mattered to him was the content; psychology must be the most important partner in this interdisciplinary cooperation.[54]

The remainder of Oesterreich's book is an attempt to systematize occult facts with detailed discussions of concrete "cases." The topics he covers include "states of incarnation," "clairvoyance and telepathy," "psychometry," "cross-correspondence," "physical mediumism, telekinesia, Eusapia Palladino," "materialization processes," and "my own parapsychophysical observations." The final chapter is titled "Theosophy—Rudolf Steiner"; he considers both Theosophy and Anthroposophy as questionable, deceptive practices, although he asserts that one must at least concede Steiner's "high moral tendencies."[55]

Baerwald's and Oesterreich's publications stand for many others. I will briefly mention Rudolf Tischner (1879–1961), who worked as an ophthalmologist in Munich and made his mark with publications on homeopathy and occultism. His *Einführung in den Okkultismus und Spiritismus* (Introduction to Occultism and Spiritualism), published in 1921 in the series *Questions at the Borders of the Life of Nerves and the Soul* and reprinted in a revised edition in 1923, basically follows the same program as Baerwald and Oesterreich (even if the author claims in his foreword that his book is the first overview of this kind).[56] Again, he describes spiritualism as an unproven interpretation of occult phenomena, while he defends occultism in its two forms—mental or parapsychological phenomena on the one hand, and material or paraphysical phenomena on the other—as an important part of the study of psychological and physical reality. Tischner demonstrates an understanding of people who hope spiritualism will provide them with answers, especially after the traumatic experiences of the World War. "One longs for a way out of the isolation in which modern naturalism has placed the soul; one does not want to be an atom in space, but a link in a meaningful event."[57] And in what almost seems like a reference to Max Weber's theory of disenchantment and reenchantment, Tischner—much like Baerwald—claims: "Seen in this light, the faith of the spiritualist is only a 'substitute,' but at the very least, its justification in the context of religion is not to be completely denied; for many people, the truly religious attitude is not possible; for others, spiritualism undoubtedly constitutes the bridge on which they return to religion. As one can see, occultism and, in a narrower sense, spiritualism are of great importance for religion, and everyone interested in religious questions should address it, whether as an opponent or as an ally."[58]

The restructuring of discursive arrangements in the first decades of the twentieth century, in which religious discourses were increasingly supplemented by and overlaid with discourses on the soul, is once again clearly visible here. Moreover, these contributions are evidence of a scientification of the concept of the soul in interdisciplinary research. Max Dessoir (1867–1947), whom Richard Baerwald has already mentioned, was yet another of Dilthey's students and also an important member of this larger discourse community. He addressed precisely this scientification in the foreword to the first edition of his book *Vom Jenseits der Seele* (The Soul's Beyond, 1917):

> On the other hand, there is the fact that reputable representatives of German science have recently begun to pay attention to this disreputable borderland. It is not only the example of foreign scholars, not only the praiseworthy example of the few German pioneers that has led to this more friendly atmosphere, but the movement of scientific work itself, which has been driven toward our questions from various points. Refined studies of mental and nervous disorders, which are still within the scope of orthodox medicine, the new direction of psychoanalysis, the equally young academic study of religion, ethnology, folklore studies, the *Völkerpsychologie*, and development psychology—they all came into contact with the phenomena we have before us. In former times, when the mechanistic worldview ruled in our country, to be scientific meant to be blind to and ignorant of certain facts, and psychology in particular did not extend as far as the psychic processes, but only to the limits set by the dictates of its representatives. This seems to be changing now, and there is already the danger that, on the basis of mere book knowledge, the verdict will be too favorable and too hasty.[59]

It was Dessoir who had coined the term *parapsychology* in the late 1880s, "in an attempt to delineate the scientific study of a certain class of 'abnormal,' though not necessarily pathological mental phenomena."[60] Over the course of his career, Dessoir increasingly shifted his role from that of a scientist to that of a public intellectual. This reveals how large the discourse community actually was at that time. It also extended beyond interdisciplinary university research, as I now want to demonstrate with the example of Carl Ludwig Schleich.

The Soul in Carl Ludwig Schleich: Clinical Surgery Between Psychology, Spirituality, and Poetry

TO AN "EXACT" NATURALIST

What you don't see in the pipe,
Built close to the forehead,
Has never quite existed for you,
And so you never understood
A world of finer senses
Above us, around us, and inside.
Picking apart the organic
Means boldly cutting up a work of art.
But what's at stake is uniting the world of the small
With the highest!
Even the cell is in the end
Incomprehensible, transcendent,
And life's final unit
Sees only who created it, in purity!
Senses can only touch
The symbols, and understanding
That world with seven seals
Can only be accomplished with magic mirrors,
Quietly made with reverence,
Inside a wheel of light: poetry, rules.
What lifts the wave in the image,
Is not what's ultimately alive:
Only an inkling weaves a bond
To the island called Unknown.[61]

This poem was written by Carl Ludwig Schleich (1859–1922), a surgeon from Berlin who, as a medical doctor, made a name for himself primarily by developing new methods of infiltration anesthesia. To a broader public, however, he was also known as a writer, philosopher, and poet. Schleich reached an audience of millions with his works, published by Rowohlt and Fischer presses. His book of memoirs, titled *Besonnte Vergangenheit* (A Sunny Past), became the first best seller for the young Rowohlt press and is one of the most successful memoirs ever published in the German language. His work closely linked scientific, medical, psychological, religious, and metaphysical topics, thus contributing to the consolidation of a discourse that would influence the entire twentieth century. Schleich is representative of an intellectual and cultural movement that, as we have already seen, reached a broad audience in Germany. Since his life and work have received surprisingly little attention in historical analysis, and since the metaphysical turn of the natural sciences as well as the scientific conception of metaphysics had such a decisive impact on the discursive history of the soul, I want to discuss Schleich in more detail.

Carl Ludwig Schleich was born in Stettin in 1859. Both of his parents brought him into contact with medicine at an early age: the surgeon Ernst Küster and the Berlin doctor Konrad Küster were his mother Konstanze's brothers. His father, Carl Ludwig, was an ophthalmologist and privy medical officer in Stettin, where he headed the Pomeranian Medical Association and the Stettin Medical Association for thirty-five years. So it was no wonder that Schleich studied medicine after graduating from high school in 1879, first at the University of Zurich—where he also studied music and became friends with the poet Gottfried Keller—and then at the University of Greifswald. Schleich almost changed his mind about his studies, for "entering the atriums of medical science" had made "an almost eerie and repulsive impression" on him, as he writes in his memoirs.[62] Not only the lack of cleanliness in the anatomy room, the dissected corpses and body parts lying around everywhere, but above all the horror of animal experiments filled him with disgust. "When I . . . as an entree act, had to witness the decapitation of six frogs by means of a smooth paper cut and the incredibly quick cerebral spinal cord sting (*Noeud vital*) in some poor cooing pigeons, my enthusiasm for medicine was over. I was filled with anger, and

I was determined to say goodbye to medicine forever. It seemed impossible for me to take part in these senseless cruelties."[63] His father was able to calm him down and make him continue his studies. But this small detail of his first experience with medical research says something about Schleich's holistic approach, which he would subsequently develop further.

After completing his basic studies in Greifswald, Schleich passed his first state examination in 1886 at the Charité in Berlin. One of his teachers in Berlin was the well-known doctor Rudolf Virchow. In 1887 Schleich received his doctorate at Greifswald under the supervision of the surgeon Heinrich Helferich. He initially worked as Helferich's assistant before opening a private clinic for gynecology and surgery in Berlin-Kreuzberg in 1889. He operated this clinic, with fifteen beds in the end, until 1901, when he was appointed professor and honored with the title of privy councilor. In 1900 he became head of the surgical department at the community hospital in Groß-Lichterfelde (which is today in the Berlin district of Steglitz-Zehlendorf).

Early on, Schleich also became known as a writer and philosopher. While he first published small books and articles in magazines such as Maximilian Harden's *Zukunft* or the *Neue Rundschau*, edited by Samuel Fischer, his book *Es läuten die Glocken: Fantasien über den Sinn des Lebens* (The Bells Are Ringing: Fantasies About the Meaning of Life) reached a larger audience for the first time. During and after World War I, he wrote for magazines such as *Arena*, *Über Land und Meer*, and *Gartenlaube*. By then he was a nationally known author.

An example of this publishing activity is the volume *Zwei Jahre kriegschirurgischer Erfahrungen aus einem Berliner Lazarett* (Two Years of Military Surgery Experience at a Berlin Hospital), published in 1916. The book brings together a series of short contributions that had previously appeared in the *B. Z.* [*Berliner Zeitung*] *am Mittag*. In a strange mixture of sensitive war journalism, medical details, and philosophical-religious-psychological reflections, the physician addresses the Berlin public and gives the following reasons for writing his book:

> [Our military hospitals] are the places where one learns to admire with astonishment the soul of our glorious people in its plain greatness,

> overwhelmingly simple in its intimate depth. The physician is granted the deepest insights into the soul of humankind; the hour of suffering, pain, danger, even death opens up to him the most remote corners of the emotional worlds of his patients, more so and more often than to the representatives of other professions. And so it is perhaps not uninteresting, even for a larger audience, to link the report on predominantly surgical matters in one of our military hospitals with an attempt to describe the purely psychological impressions that a whole flock of doctors working daily for the well-being of those affected have received time and again, and which in our private exchange of experiences always leap out as the most astonishing: the discovery of the soul of our people.[64]

In addition to contributions such as "The Technique of Nerve Sutures," "The Path of the Bullet," or "The Healing of Broken Bones," Schleich repeatedly brings psychological and philosophical considerations to bear—for example, in "Brain Shots and Brain Work." In his column "The Riddle of Hysteria," he addresses a topic that repeatedly preoccupied him in his work—namely, those cases "in which the disorders seem to be generated, as it were, purely by imaginative intervention in the organic functions."[65] He continues: "It remains an almost metaphysical mystery that these sick people, as in a clairvoyant imitation of real clinical scenes, compulsively reveal states about the course of which they cannot actually have the slightest idea."[66]

In his book *Vom Schaltwerk der Gedanken: Neue Einsichten und Betrachtungen über die Seele* (On the Thought Switchboard: New Insights and Reflections About the Soul, 1917), Schleich dedicates a whole chapter to hysteria as a "metaphysical problem." In doing so, he first dispels the prejudice that the clinical picture of "hysteria" is gender-specific. Instead, we must understand

> that deriving the name for hysteria from hystera = the uterus is an almost appalling error, the consequences of which still have an after-effect. For hysteria could just as well (or just as doubtfully) be called "spermeria," because occasionally the defective inner secretion of a man's sexual glands can also cause fluctuations in the mental sphere. Not only are many men

> hysterical, but also children of both sexes. Hysteria is therefore genderless, and it is finally time to free women from the spell of being the sole formers and bearers of hysteria, which men have probably only invented to make themselves believe that they are the more reasonable ones.[67]

Here we can already see that Schleich regarded hysteria—in his time a generic term for all possible forms of mental "disorder"—as a failure and inhibition of the function of the nerve system. It becomes a "metaphysical problem" because the somatic explanation of these phenomena is not sufficient to explain patients' sudden knowledge about symptoms of illness or the other forms of occult understanding they reveal. Schleich calls this the phenomenon of "mediumistic seeing, a kind of clairvoyance about disease prospects."[68] This certainly goes beyond what we would call psychosomatic phenomena today.

Three years later, Schleich published *Gedankenmacht und Hysterie* (The Power of Thought and Hysteria), an extended version of a lecture he gave in Berlin. Here the bridge he builds between medical-empirical phenomena and a spiritual-occult reality is even more evident. He refers to recent attempts "to draw compelling conclusions from the processes of religious raptures, dances, and convulsions about the actual nature of the basic religious moods of the soul."[69] Schleich contributes to these explanatory approaches and supplies medical arguments for this field of research, because "in a certain sense it is only hysterical phenomena that are suited to pouring the blazing light of pure knowledge, even about the entire world process, about the nature of creation, over the constitution of force and matter, of the animate and the inanimate."[70] In countless examples from his medical practice he tries to show that the power of thought can achieve undreamt-of material effects. With satisfaction he sees "the confirmation of the old Indian and philosophical idea . . . that nothing can have arisen that was not previously thought, that nothing exists in the sensual world that was not previously part of creative reason."[71]

In the last years of his life, Schleich devoted himself almost exclusively to research into the connections between physical, mental, and cosmic phenomena and forces. Two books in particular should be mentioned here: *Von der Seele* (On the Soul), first published in 1910 and later expanded, and the highly successful *Das Ich und die Dämonien* (The Ego and the Demons, 1920), in which the author "attempts to carry the methods of physiological analysis of mental functions through to their most extreme consequences—methods that had previously been used in earlier works (*Von der Seele* and *Vom Schaltwerk der Gedanken*)."[72] What does this mean concretely? It is no less than an attempt to synthesize natural-philosophical and artistic considerations on the soul (which Schleich found above all in Goethe), a medical analysis of bodily and nerve functions, and finally a religious-spiritual interpretation of the world in its entirety. This leads to passages like the following:

> Wherever one speaks of the soul, it would be much more appropriate to speak of mind, heart, and inner feeling in the usual sense. For the vulgar term *soul* does not cover the full concept of what we call a combination of rational mind, consciousness, and ego with basic temperamental moods. Functionally, according to our method of physiological analysis of the brain's activities, matters of the "soul" provide the keyboard of the ganglions with something like a pendulum swing, which is not expressed here in the forte or piano, but rather allows the purely mental mechanism to be impregnated with emotional motifs, of a joyful and melancholy nature. While we know that everything rational takes place within the ivory shell of the skull, a connection with the universe already occurs in the rational process ("Let one come into being that also connects me with you, O God!"), in that all the egoistic thinking of the forebrain can be more or less toned and rhythmically structured by rhythm and direction, the will and goal of the universe, the All-Spirit of nature, from which neither the desire nor the turning away of any living being can completely escape.[73]

For Schleich, the rhythmization of life is the linchpin of the attempt "to reach the mothers of knowledge, as it were," as he formulates it in *Von der Seele*. "*This is because rhythm is a kind of compromise between force and resistance*, a mutual clashing, dodging, fleeing, and finding one another, a harmonious play of the unfolding of energy and its inhibition, the circling and bubbling around each other of two opposites that are never quite compatible."[74]

In the chapter titled "Mother Earth," he talks about the web of life: "The life of the cosmos, the shining breath of the world, is transferred to matter in the form of rolling waves of radiation. In particularly fine power transformers, in small storage machines, organic matter has learned to accumulate the working capital of such waves of light, so that even at night and in the darkness of a winter day the machine does not stand still: in the green of the plants, in the red of the blood."[75] For Schleich, the power of the cosmos that permeates all dimensions of life and integrates the human into the rhythms and processes of nature is a spiritual fact. He exclaims almost euphorically: "It is she, our All-Mother, who according to Fechner is very much alive, breathing, moving, showing the pulses and circulation of the waters, who in each of her top soils, on rocky and sandy ground, even in her atmospheric veils of mist, everywhere carries cradles and breeding grounds for countless creatures, of which the smallest are no less carriers of wonder than the largest. Mother Earth!"[76]

Thus Carl Ludwig Schleich is a prominent example of the establishment of a discourse on the soul, which—in the sense of a monistic and holistic view of reality—entangles scientific explanations with religious and spiritual discourse strands. In his hugely successful publications, we can also see the integration of nature as a living being and as "Mother Earth," a discursive figure that was to become extremely influential toward the end of the twentieth century (I will come back to this topic in part 2). Schleich writes with the authority of a medical doctor, which adds to the public impact of his philosophical-religious writings. This even applies to his lyrical publications, which received further inspiration from his friendships with Gottfried Keller, August Strindberg, Richard Dehmel, and other artists. I already mentioned the success of Schleich's memoirs, but there is further evidence of his relevance to the themes that interest us here: when a collection of essays from Schleich's most important books appeared in 1951 under the title *Die Wunder der Seele* (Wonders of the Soul), Carl Gustav Jung wrote a long foreword and compared Schleich to Paracelsus—two completely different characters, and yet both revolutionaries "who represent a transitional period as characteristic exponents."[77] Both were, according to Jung, "carried and inspired by the effervescent surge of a new era," and both were strangers in their time and outsiders whose influence would only become evident later. Jung acknowledges that Schleich was driven by the same attempt to elucidate a nonreductionist science of the soul that is also the underlying intention of his own work:

> Today we already know that his path aims at that wholeness of mental and physical events which the medical and biological research of our times is making the strongest effort to achieve. While he himself is still caught up in a scientific language of concepts originating in the materialistic age, Schleich breaks through the narrow limits of a soulless materiality and crosses that threshold, barricaded with the most prickly prejudices, which until now has separated the soul from the body and has nipped in the bud any attempt to redeem it. Without knowing of my efforts, which for dark reasons remained unknown to the scientific public in Germany for a long time, he fought, in his own way, shoulder to shoulder with me for the recognition of the soul as a factor "sui generis" and thus broke new ground for psychology, which until then had been condemned to get along without a soul.[78]

Jung assessed Schleich's works as "groundbreaking in the sense of liberation from the narrow-mindedness of mere professorial expertise";[79] this can also be read as a prediction of the scientific (non)reception of his own work after the end of World War II, although his ideas nevertheless exerted a strong influence outside academic psychology.

Now that we have seen how the soul left the universities, it is time for an intermediate reflection. Which major trajectories have emerged in the cultural history of the soul up to the 1930s? How did the arrangement of discourses on the soul develop historically? One of the major trajectories we can identify is the scientification of the soul, which went hand in hand with the elimination of the concept of the soul in empirical psychology. In its attempt to be recognized as a (natural) science, professional psychology has committed itself to an empirical—which often means a physiological-medical—interpretation of the inner processes of human beings. The concept of the soul is too vague for such an approach, and it is also superfluous. What one sees instead is the propagation of new concepts, above all the concept of the "self"—that successive model of the concept of the "inner person," which had been so central in Europe.[80] The concept of the soul also became too vague for parapsychology as it had developed since the 1920s. After World War II, the concept of the soul was more or less eliminated from parapsychological research as well. Parapsychology was able to hold its ground primarily where it strictly adhered to the experimental method. In Germany, this applies to the Institute for Frontier Areas of Psychology and Mental Health in Freiburg (founded in 1950), as well as to the scientific associations founded after World War II.[81]

The scientification of the soul has also produced a second major trajectory of discursive arrangements, which stands in interesting tension with the elimination of the soul from academic psychology. Scientification here means the elaboration of concepts of the soul in disciplines such as biology and physics, which are the successors of nineteenth-century natural philosophy (biology for the organic, and physics for the theoretical aspect of the study of nature). In monism and vitalism, but also in Neoromantic philosophy, discursive arrangements were developed in which the soul was closely connected with concepts such as matter, cosmos, nature, life force, energy, and consciousness. If we add "people," "nation," or "race" to this arrangement, we get precisely that nationalistic mélange that became a dominant phenomenon in Europe, and especially in Germany.

The third trajectory cannot be limited to concrete sciences, but can be found in the establishment of an order of knowledge about the soul, which becomes visible both in the literary discourse of a poetic or Orphic science and in interdisciplinary contributions that combine religious-historical, philosophical, and psychological stores of knowledge. This discursive knot is also characterized by terms such as *soul*, *nature*, *knowledge*, *cosmos*, and *consciousness*, but at the same time, the trajectory clearly extends toward *art*, *ecstasy*, and *mysticism*.

Even if these trajectories can be distinguished in concrete individual cases, they form an overall structure that has had a significant social impact. Together they constitute the soul discourse of the first half of the twentieth century in Europe. The slide into European fascism, the rise of National Socialism in Germany, and finally the catastrophe of World War II were decisive cultural caesurae, and the discourse on the soul is no exception. Due to the racist twist given to the concept of the soul under National Socialism, it was hardly possible to use terms such as *Volksseele* (the people's soul) in Germany after the war. This also reinforced the tendency to ban the term *soul* from scientific vocabulary, and thus the standardization of psychological language made use of other terms. As Kurt Danziger writes: "Until the second half of the twentieth century there was not one but several disciplinary languages of psychology, and each of them had its own historical trajectory. In the aftermath of World War II, however, the language of American Psychology was adopted virtually everywhere, a situation that has only begun to change relatively recently."[82]

The significance of North America for the second half of the twentieth century applies not only to psychology, but to the cultural and discursive history of the soul as a whole. On the one hand, during the period when fascism dominated Europe, emigrants brought European conversations to America and continued them there in their own way; on the other hand, American culture took up these debates and linked them to its own scientific, philosophical, and literary traditions.

Even if the soul was banned from the universities, this did not spell the end of discourses on the soul. The soul may have been "extinguished" in this milieu, but—as Kamper and Wulf argue in their volume under the title *Die erloschene Seele*—this is only part of the story: "Within the framework of historical-anthropological work, it is necessary to reconstruct the flare, the glow, and the extinction of the soul in the course of Western history without falling prey to nostalgia."[83] As I will explain in the second part of this book, the decisive vehicles of discourses on the soul—above all the concepts of science, nature, cosmos, life, and consciousness—were taken up and further developed as part of a broad cultural reception. Holistic-spiritual-metaphysical psychology, above all Carl Gustav Jung's complex psychology, also endured: in the United States through the activities of the transpersonal movement, among other channels; in Europe through initiatives such as the Eranos conferences situated in a theosophical milieu. Many representatives of the discursive history of the soul have made contributions to these conferences, from Buber and Scholem, to van der Leeuw and Eliade, to Jung and Pauli. Jung played a central role in the Eranos conferences, and Thomas Hakl describes the appearances of Gershom Scholem and Henry Corbin from 1949 onward as "The Heyday Begins."[84] A look at the topics of the Eranos lectures shows the ubiquity of the concept of the soul and the continuity with which prewar discourses were carried on in this circle after 1945.

In short, the soul had served its time as a concept in empirical psychology, and yet it retained its importance as a vehicle for meaning when it came to questions about the human, nature, consciousness, and the cosmos. These discourses also returned to Europe via America and were extended to encompass global issues at the end of the twentieth century. In the second part of *A Cultural History of the Soul*, I reconstruct these developments.

PART II

FROM EUROPE TO AMERICA AND BACK

The Soul Goes Mainstream

6

TRANSPERSONAL PSYCHOLOGY

The Soul's Cosmic Potential

The search for suprapersonal and collective structures of the soul had, as described earlier, led to a number of considerations at the beginning of the twentieth century, which were taken up both within psychology and in the broader cultural discourse. Carl Gustav Jung's interpretative approaches were particularly influential (although not within the academy, as he complains repeatedly), and his theories of archetypes and the collective unconscious were often taken up in the subsequent period.

The National Socialist dictatorship and the disastrous war led to the decline of the German intellectual scene. Many intellectuals and artists, as well as psychologists, immigrated to the United States. This is one reason why German-language psychology lost influence after 1945 and American psychology played a decisive role in shaping the discourse from then on. The empirical-experimental psychology that followed the path laid out by Wilhelm Wundt and others remained one of the most influential currents, both in its institutional history and in the effects of its basic assumption that psychological theories must stand up to empirical testing. This line is most evident in postwar behaviorism and positivism. A second psychological current is psychoanalysis in the tradition of Sigmund Freud, which departs from the individual's soul and strives to make conscious what is hidden in unconscious processes, especially the dark drives within them.

A third current developed in direct engagement with Carl Gustav Jung. At first this current primarily impacted the United States, although it referred back to theories that were popular in Europe at the beginning of the twentieth century. A number of new approaches emerged in this alternative spectrum—from holistic and Gestalt therapy to existentialist psychology and Carl R. Rogers's person-centered therapy. These approaches further developed and critically engaged with psychoanalysis and complex psychology as Jung had pursued them and were enriched by the contributions of Roberto Assagioli, Wilhelm Reich, Karen Horney, Otto Rank, Erich Fromm, and others. Despite great differences in detail, these new approaches are characterized by the fact that they are based on a positive image of the human and that they place human self-realization within a supraindividual, even cosmic framework of interpretation. "Dissatisfied with a 'psychology without soul,'" Erhardt Hanefeld notes, "here the human being as a whole takes center stage again."[1] In 1957 Abraham H. Maslow (1908–1970) coined the term *humanistic psychology* for this movement, and in 1961 Anthony J. Sutich (1907–1976) founded the *Journal of Humanistic Psychology*, which became a visible platform for these new approaches. Over time, schools such as Fritz Perls's (1893–1970) Gestalt therapy, Jakob L. Moreno's (1889–1974) psychodrama, and various body therapies—such as the Alexander Technique, Feldenkrais, and bioenergetics—were established, and these still represent important directions in the psychotherapeutic field today.

Discussions about the advantages and disadvantages of the name *humanistic psychology* had taken place since the beginning of the movement, because many of its representatives were convinced that a fully developed personality actually transcends the boundaries of traditional human consciousness. The term *transhumanistic* came up for discussion, but in the 1960s the name *transpersonal psychology* was widely accepted and came to be understood as a "fourth force" in the spectrum of psychological research and therapy. Anthony J. Sutich expressed this programmatic view in the first issue of the *Journal of Transpersonal Psychology* in 1969.[2]

This is not the place to trace the history of transpersonal psychology in detail. Instead, I will discuss core representatives of this movement to show how existing discourses on the soul were further developed after World War

II and how new discursive arrangements emerged, which in turn heavily influenced North American and European culture.

Roberto Assagioli and Abraham H. Maslow: Psychosynthesis and Transpersonal Psychology

Many representatives of the early transpersonal movement took part in the psychological and cultural debates at the beginning of the twentieth century and continued them in new constellations after World War II. Their biographies often reveal continuities and discontinuities in the European and North American discourses on the soul. Roberto Assagioli is a good example of this.[3] Born in 1888 to Jewish parents, only thirteen years younger than Carl Gustav Jung, Assagioli was the first to make Freudian psychoanalysis known in Italy. In 1905, Assagioli began his medical studies at the famous Istituto di Studi Superiori in Florence and soon switched to psychiatry. At the same time he became interested in psychology and cultural history, and from 1906 he worked for the Florentine newspaper *Leonardo*. During a visit to Vienna in 1905, he made contacts with Freud's circles (according to Assagioli himself, he never met Freud in person), which he supplemented over the next two years with contacts with the Geneva circle around Edouard Claparède and Théodore Flournoy. Assagioli also made the acquaintance of theosophists in Rome, a contact that was to become as important for his work as his psychological network: he became a member of Alice A. Bailey's (1880–1949) Arcane School, worked as Bailey's translator at lectures in Italy, and became the Italian representative of the Arcane School.

In 1907 Assagioli also met Carl Gustav Jung for the first time. During his research at the Burghölzli, the psychiatric university hospital in Zurich, Assagioli decided to make psychoanalysis the subject of his doctoral thesis. He defended his thesis in Florence in 1910 under the title *La Psicoanalisi* (unfortunately no copy of his doctoral thesis has survived).

In 1909 Assagioli attended the Sixth International Psychological Congress in Geneva and was involved in the founding of the Italian

Psychological Society. As part of his dissertation, but also more generally, Assagioli was interested in psychology of religion, mysticism, and the study of what would later be called "altered states of consciousness." Jung had left the Burghölzli in 1909 to devote himself entirely to his practice in Küsnacht, but Assagioli visited him at home several times, as he found exchanging ideas with Jung extremely stimulating. It was probably during one of these visits in 1909 that the term *psychosynthesis* came up, for Jung mentions this in a letter to Freud. In their detailed analysis of the relationship between Jung and Assagioli, Massimo Rosselli and Duccio Vanni also state that "the communication between Jung and Assagioli at this time included not only their psychoanalytic interests, but also their mutual interest in paranormal phenomena, occultism, and Asian mysticism."[4]

After his doctorate, Assagioli first worked as an assistant physician to Eugen Bleuler at the Burghölzli before opening his own psychological practice in Florence. He shared with Bleuler and Jung an extremely critical attitude toward Freudian psychoanalysis, which he considered too limited. In the journal *Psiche* (Psyche), founded in 1912—for which Assagioli served as editor-in-chief until he was called up for military service in World War I and the journal was discontinued—we can clearly see an increasing alienation from Freud and a close proximity to Jung's ideas.[5]

Between the world wars Assagioli's life was in turmoil, but the basic principles of what was to become psychosynthesis were worked out during this period and were first made known to a wider public in 1927, under the title *A New Method of Healing: Psychosynthesis.* In 1940 Assagioli was arrested by the Italian fascists and later forced underground. After the end of World War II, Assagioli became one of the most important representatives of the new movement of transpersonal psychology. His position was determined by criticizing Freud and experimental psychology, but also by differentiating himself from Jung:[6] Assagioli agreed with Jung that there is a collective unconscious constituted by archetypes, but he differentiated several levels of this unconscious and was interested in the expansion of consciousness at the level of the transpersonal self. On this level the archetype itself can be experienced, while for Jung the archetype always remains unconscious. What Jung calls the process of individuation, Assagioli sees as the work of psychosynthesis. The integration of the transpersonal self through a connection between the personal and the transpersonal is both the means and the goal of this process. For Assagioli, the role of the will and the active work of the person to achieve this goal are more important than they are in Jung's reflections on individuation. And finally, their mutual fascination with Asian wisdom traditions and mysticism is worth mentioning—both Jung and Assagioli regarded these traditions as important alternatives to the "Western" tradition that would have to be integrated into complex psychology. The same was true for European philosophy and spirituality. "As Jung drew inspiration from physicists, Assagioli drew inspiration from Eastern teachings, especially teachings on energy systems and energetic fields. He named psycho-energetics a fifth force of psychology after the fourth (transpersonal), and he explored its potential for future development."[7]

Assagioli developed his theory and its practical therapeutic application in a work that spans more than sixty years. Some of his most influential, fundamental works on psychosynthesis were only published after his death in 1974, by which time psychosynthesis was also firmly established institutionally (beyond the Istituto di Psicosintesi, which Assagioli had founded in Rome as early as 1926). Those of Assagioli's contributions that build a bridge between the psychological discussions of the early twentieth century and the transpersonal movement of the postwar period are particularly important for the discursive history of the soul. This bridge-building often happens explicitly, for instance, when Assagioli refers back to William James, who represented "a prime example of an unbiased and scientific discussion of this topic," and who "strongly indicated the reality and meaning of the transcendental world."[8] It was important to him to take the reality of higher levels of consciousness and mystical experiences seriously and not to pathologize them as "hysteria" or some sort of disorder. Assagioli also quotes his own early writings, for instance, a contribution in *Psiche* 3 (1913), which states: "The intellectual and moral value of a personality is completely independent of the symptoms of illness that it may display and that it may have in common with other more primitive or truly degenerate personalities. If it is true that St. Theresa, St. Catherine of Genoa, and many other noble religious figures were struck by hysteria, this should in no way diminish our admiration for their spiritual gifts; rather, it should give us pause for thought regarding our view of the character of hysterical women in general."[9]

Rather, as Assagioli explains in his chapter "Mysticism and Medicine," these examples make clear that true mystics, by reaching the transpersonal levels, often fell into a state of physical exhaustion, which is by no means pathological, but a possible side effect of spiritual work. "The awakening and enlightenment of the soul, which from a psychological point of view can be understood as the bursting of a powerful surge of spiritual life into the ordinary personality, can cause temporary nervous disorders."[10] The process of psychosynthesis aims at integrating these aspects and experiences.

Assagioli dedicates a whole chapter to the "awakening of the soul," because for him this awakening is "the first bright flash of spiritual awareness that transforms and renews the whole being"; it is "an event of fundamental importance and incomparable value for the inner life of the human being."[11] Very much in the style of William James, Martin Buber, and Rudolf Otto, Assagioli provides examples of "awakened" people from the history of religion, mysticism, and the arts, including Leo Tolstoy and Walt Whitman. Assagioli thereby weaves the same discursive knot that we have encountered time and again:

> Just as the outer nature is permeated by light, so too—and this is often the main focus—there is an inner enlightenment, which lets the soul discover new, wonderful truths and enables it to solve, in a flash of inspiration, the problems that have tormented it up to now. It then sees the universe as a living whole and recognizes itself as an indestructible particle of it, tiny but necessary—a sound that is indissolubly connected with all the others and that together with them creates cosmic harmony. The soul feels how in this highest unity every opposition disappears, every disharmony is balanced.[12]

After a discussion of the "Eastern" wisdom tradition, using the example of Rabindranath Tagore and a comparison with European Christian mysticism, Assagioli concludes: "These are the great stages of the pilgrimage of the soul. The path is long, and only few are capable of completing it in this life. But the mere insight and knowledge that there are people who have succeeded in making it a reality is a great consolation and should be a precious incentive for us to shake off our own inertia and let our soul awaken."[13]

Psychosynthesis offers concrete techniques and practices to help unfold the soul's cosmic potential—from Jungian dream interpretation, to active imagination techniques (visualization, auditory evocation, and imaginative evocation of other senses), to meditation and techniques for the development of the will.[14]

In considering these practices and their theoretical foundations, it is easy to recognize the discursive connection between psychology, philosophy, and theosophy, which Assagioli also embodies biographically. The influences of this discourse can be seen in various elements of the twentieth-century spiritual scene. Besides transpersonal work in the narrower sense, this also applies to astrology, which Assagioli, like Jung, regarded as a legitimate interpretation of "synchronicity."[15] This fostered new astrological approaches, such as those developed in the so-called Huber School. Louise Huber (1924–2016) and her husband Bruno (1930–1999) came from a theosophical background. After three years helping to build up Bailey's Arcane School in Geneva, the two of them underwent psychological training with Roberto Assagioli. These educational experiences constituted the starting point for what they henceforth regarded as the most important task of astrology: psychological life support and spiritual orientation. This "new direction in astrology aims at the inclusion of spiritual laws of growth, which have far more to do with the idea of evolution, religion, and meditation than was originally assumed."[16] Therefore, in addition to cognitive-analytical approaches, their training programs also comprise meditative approaches to the horoscope—such as zodiac meditations or the observation of aspect figures as "cosmic images"—and ritual work, for example, in the execution of Alice A. Bailey's "Great Invocation."[17]

This brings us to Abraham H. Maslow, who is regarded as the second important pioneer of the transpersonal movement after Assagioli. Maslow also grew up in a Jewish home; at the beginning of the twentieth century, his parents had fled to New York to escape the anti-Semitic pogroms in Tsarist Russia. He studied psychology at the University of Wisconsin, where he mainly came into contact with experimental-behavioral psychology.

Later he continued his research at Columbia University in New York, where he worked with Alfred Adler, a former colleague of Sigmund Freud. During his tenure at Brooklyn College (1937–1951), where he worked with anthropologist Ruth Benedict and Gestalt therapist Max Wertheimer, and also afterward as a professor at Brandeis University (1951–1967), Maslow became increasingly critical of behaviorist psychology. Moreover, the horrors of World War II led him to explore new avenues that addressed the positive aspects of the human psyche, focusing on mental health and the hidden potential for human development.

In 1954, his book *Motivation and Personality* was published, which presented these considerations to a broad public and made an important contribution to what soon came to be called "humanistic psychology." In the foreword, Maslow states that the book was modestly conceived as a "supplement" to existing theories, with the working title *Higher Ceilings for Human Nature*, but it soon became clear that it was about more than supplementation. Instead, it was about "the profoundly holistic nature of human nature in contradiction to the analytic-dissecting-atomistic-Newtonian approach of the behaviorisms and of Freudian psychoanalysis."[18] He considered this new program part of a "humanistic" worldview that encompasses not only psychology, but also economics, sociology, biology, law, politics, and medicine.[19] The book unpacks the basic philosophical and psychological ideas of humanistic psychology, with special emphasis on the process of self-actualization.

Toward a Psychology of Being, first published in 1962, is a continuation of *Motivation and Personality* and is similar in structure to its predecessor. In the foreword to the second edition in 1968, Maslow is enthusiastic about the enormous development psychology has undergone in recent years. Humanistic psychology, as it was then commonly called, had established itself as a "third force" alongside and as an alternative to "objectivistic, behavioristic (mechanomorphic) psychology and to orthodox Freudianism."[20] This third psychology, Maslow continues, is clearly more than just psychology; in fact, it is "one facet of a general *Weltanschauung*, a new philosophy of life, a new conception of man, the beginning of a new century of work (that is, of course, if we can meanwhile manage to hold off a holocaust)."[21] But as pleasant as this development was, in his opinion it was only the prelude to even greater leaps of consciousness: "I consider Humanistic, Third Force Psychology to be transitional, a preparation for a still 'higher' Fourth Psychology, transpersonal, transhuman, centered in the cosmos rather than in human needs and interest, going beyond humanness, identity, self-actualization, and the like."[22] Here we already see the same line of discourse that would lead to animistic and object-oriented ontologies at the end of the twentieth century—ontologies in which the human being is only a small part of an organic, living cosmos. Maslow's analysis goes even further, however, placing this development in the context of secularism and disenchantment:

> These new developments may very well offer a tangible, usable, effective satisfaction of the "frustrated idealism" of many quietly desperate people, especially young people. These psychologies give promise of developing into the life-philosophy, the religion-surrogate, the value-system, the life-program that these people have been missing. Without the transcendent and the transpersonal, we get sick, violent, and nihilistic, or else hopeless and apathetic. We need something "bigger than we are" to be awed by and to commit ourselves to in a new, naturalistic, empirical, non-churchly sense, perhaps as Thoreau and Whitman, William James and John Dewey did.[23]

It is interesting to see how the concept of the soul (which Assagioli still used without hesitation) in *Toward a Psychology of Being* is replaced with transpersonal psychological concepts and at the same time discursively continued. Maslow summarizes the basic assumptions of this psychology to the effect that there is "an essential biologically based inner nature" in human beings, a nature that is ultimately unchangeable. "Each person's inner nature is in part unique to itself and in part species-wide."[24] The inner nature of the human is at the same time the "essential core of the person,"[25] which cannot be suppressed in the long run, and which urges one to actualization.

For Maslow, the goal of healing and becoming whole is to establish the connection between the collective person and the individual self. However, this is much more difficult today than it was in the past: "Every age but ours has had its model, its ideal. All of these have been given up by our culture; the saint, the hero, the gentleman, the knight, the mystic. About all we have left is the well-adjusted man without problems, a very pale and doubtful substitute."[26] One could only hope that there would soon be a new role model, based on the ideal of the fully integrated human being. By weaving together religious, philosophical, and psychological discourse strands, Maslow comes to a more precise description of this new ideal:

> That serious concern with this discrepancy could revolutionize psychology, there is no doubt in my mind. Various literatures already support such a conclusion, *e.g.*, projective testing, self-actualization, the various peak-experiences (in which this gap is bridged), the Jungian psychologies, various theological thinkers, etc.
>
> Not only this, but they raise also the problems and techniques of integration of this twofold nature of man, his lower and his higher, his creatureliness and his god-likeness. On the whole, most philosophies and religions, Eastern as well as Western, have dichotomized them, teaching that the way to become "higher" is to renounce and master "the lower." The existentialists, however, teach that *both* are simultaneously defining characteristics of human nature. Neither can be repudiated; they can only be integrated.[27]

Roberto Assagioli and Abraham H. Maslow thus continued a discussion that had been interrupted by European fascism and World War II. By emphasizing the psychological and psychic potential for the human being to participate in suprapersonal and cosmic energies, and by combining the concepts of wholeness and health with the concepts of soul, psyche, and spirituality, they made an important contribution to the emergence of a discursive web that would prove influential in the second half of the twentieth century, first in the United States, and then in Europe. It is also important to note that Assagioli and Maslow were not operating in isolation, and I could mention other biographies that illustrate the same dynamic, for instance, the life work of Franklin Merrell-Wolff (1887–1985), which Dave Vliegenthart has studied and masterfully interpreted.[28]

The term *New Age* is often used to refer to these phenomena, but the long-running lines of discourse in the arrangement that governs these orders of knowledge make it clear that this is only one chapter in a much longer historical process. The same is true of the core events of the "New Age" that took place in California in the 1960s and 1970s.

Consolidating the Discourse: Esalen and the Human Potential Movement

In 1980 Roger N. Walsh and Frances Vaughan published the anthology *Beyond Ego: Transpersonal Dimensions in Psychology*.[29] This volume can be seen as a kind of handbook of transpersonal psychology and as evidence that by the end of the 1970s, the transpersonal movement was already well established and had developed various branches. The list of authors includes important personalities who were active and influential in the early days of the transpersonal movement: In addition to the two editors themselves and Abraham H. Maslow, whom I have already introduced, among the relevant names are Ken Wilber, Fritjof Capra, Stanislav Grof, Ram Dass, Daniel Goleman, Jack Kornfield, Charles Tart, and Willis Harman. It is no accident that there is not a single woman on this list of authors—the transpersonal movement was no less androcentric than the psychology of the time as a whole.

If one reads the introduction by Roger N. Walsh and Frances Vaughan, as well as the volume's twenty-two chapters, one also notes that the prehistory of the transpersonal movement is almost completely ignored. Although there are references to Carl Gustav Jung, William James, and the holistically oriented European philosophy of nature, the genealogy of the transpersonal discourse as I have reconstructed it seems to be unimportant for the authors' self-understanding; the transpersonal movement is rather described as a revolutionary force that combines Western and Eastern wisdom traditions for the first time and opens up the transpersonal dimensions of the soul. The first part of the volume is therefore titled "Paradigm Shift," while the second part deals with "The Nature of Consciousness," thus marking the increasing importance of the term *consciousness*, which would soon replace the term *soul* in many ways. The third part on "Mental Health—East and West" can also be read as a programmatic new discursive arrangement, in that here we see not only the return of the long-running reception (and construction) of "Eastern" wisdom teachings, but also a stronger focus on "health" and "wholeness," which was to gain further importance in the subsequent period. Finally, parts 4 and 5 address the therapeutic implementation of these approaches in concrete practice as well as the interdisciplinary implications of transpersonal psychology.

We can compare this grouping of themes and discourse strands with publications by Jung, who repeatedly commented on the comparison of Western and Eastern mystical traditions and therapeutic practice.[30] Let me mention just one example here, namely, Jung's preface to D. T. Suzuki's *An Introduction to Zen Buddhism* in 1934 (a new German edition was published in 1958), as it concerns both the comparison between "East" and "West" and the aspect of healing and becoming whole. The ironic reference to European wishful thinking is also very well expressed here.

> Zen shows how much "becoming whole" means to the East. The preoccupation with Zen riddles may perhaps strengthen the small-minded European's back or give him glasses for his soul's shortsightedness, so that he can at least enjoy the view from his "dull hole in the wall" onto a world of mental experience that was previously obscured. Things will not turn out badly, because the overly frightened will be effectively protected from further ruin, as well as from any significance, by the helpful idea of "autosuggestion." But I would like to warn the attentive and sympathetic reader not to underestimate the intellectuality of the East or to suspect something cheap behind Zen. In this case, the eagerly cultivated Western belief in words, as applied to Eastern ideas, is a lesser danger, since fortunately the words in Zen are not so miraculously incomprehensible as they are in the Indian language. Nor does Zen play with complicated hata yoga techniques, which offer the physiologically minded European the deceptive hope that in the end, one can simply sit and breathe the spirit. In contrast, Zen demands intelligence and willpower, like all greater things that truly desire to become.[31]

The transpersonal movement has produced a large number of publications since the 1960s, including professional journals and book series. The creation of corresponding university programs (especially in California) and international societies, as well as training and seminar centers, has further contributed to the consolidation of these discursive structures. Perhaps the most influential center in this regard is the Esalen Institute in Big Sur, California. Founded in 1962 by Michael Murphy (born 1930) and Richard "Dick" Price (1930–1985), the Esalen Institute quickly became a major hub for the new movement. Virtually everyone who had a name in the American countermovement, in experimentation with mind-altering substances, and in the rapidly changing spiritual scene in the United States spent time at Esalen and left their mark there. In his detailed history of the Esalen Institute, Jeffrey J. Kripal rightly calls this spirituality "the religion of no religion."[32] And Marion Goldman argues that Esalen served to democratize the "spiritual privilege" of personal growth and transformation through psychological and religious exploration for middle-class seekers—a "democratization" that still targeted elite networks, however.[33]

The so-called Human Potential Movement, which was created in this context, encapsulates this research very well. Following Maslow, Murphy, and Price, but also in direct exchange with Aldous Huxley (who in the early 1960s gave seminars on "human potential" at Esalen) and others, this research aimed at the overall design of a "new human being" and a "new society" that opens up and develops the spiritual, transpersonal potential of the individual in social interaction and ultimately in planetary-cosmic consciousness. For the representatives of this movement, theory and practice are closely intertwined, so that all theoretical considerations always have implications for therapeutic work and spiritual practice—which also means that transpersonal theory can be tested and adapted through concrete experience.

Let us look at some representative examples. First there is Stanislav Grof, who together with Christina Grof (1941–2014) and Joan Halifax (born 1942) advanced research on LSD and extraordinary states of consciousness, and tried to identify basic patterns of such extraordinary states. The "pioneers of the transpersonal movement," as Roger N. Walsh calls them, discovered "that there are whole families of potential transpersonal states of consciousness, that these states were known and appreciated at all times and in all cultures, but that they have been largely denied and rejected in Western culture and society."[34] Grof, who is known especially through his research on what he calls "holotropic states of consciousness" as a subgroup of extraordinary states of consciousness, stresses that this is something other than "altered states of consciousness." In a summary of his work, published in 2012, he says: "From this perspective, the term 'altered states of consciousness' commonly used by mainstream clinicians and theoreticians is not appropriate, because of its one-sided emphasis on the distortion or impairment of the 'correct way' of experiencing oneself and the world."[35]

In *Psychology for the Future: Lessons from Modern Consciousness Research* (2000), also intended as an introduction to his decades of research on the subject, Grof explains that it was only with the emergence of a modern understanding of science that the separation between material and transcendent realms of reality was implemented. "Preindustrial cultures had a rich ritual and spiritual life that revolved around the possibility of achieving direct experiential contact with these ordinarily hidden domains and beings and to receive from them important information or assistance. They believed that it was an important and useful way to influence the course of material events."[36] In contrast to the more official opinion in psychology and especially psychiatry, Grof insists on human consciousness' independence from neurological processes:

> According to Western neuroscience, consciousness is a product of the physiological processes in the brain, and thus critically dependent on the body. Very few people, including most scientists, realize that we have absolutely no proof that consciousness is actually produced by the brain and that we do not have even a remote notion how something like that could possibly happen. In spite of it, this basic metaphysical assumption remains one of the leading myths of Western materialistic science and has profound influence on our entire society.[37]

Here Grof turns the tables, so to speak, and accuses the neurosciences of precisely the same unreflected metaphysics that they diagnose in the transpersonal movement. For Grof, the concept of "holotropic states" was a confirmation of what Carl Gustav Jung and Rudolf Otto intended with their idea of the "numinous."

> In light of the observations from the study of holotropic states, the current contemptuous dismissal and pathologization of spirituality characteristic of monistic materialism appears untenable. In holotropic states, the spiritual dimensions of reality can be directly experienced in a way that is as convincing as our daily experience of the material world. It is also possible to describe step by step procedures that facilitate access to these experiences. Careful study of transpersonal experiences shows that they are ontologically real and inform us about important aspects of existence that are ordinarily hidden.[38]

What for Jung was the mystical initiation of the soul into collective unconscious levels of reality thus becomes the experience of spiritual dimensions of reality and the achievement of a higher level of consciousness. Grof distinguishes between various forms of spiritual experience. The first, the form "of *the immanent divine*, involves subtly, but profoundly transformed perception of the everyday reality." The second form of spiritual experience, "that of *the transcendent divine*, involves manifestation of archetypal beings and realms of reality that are ordinarily transphenomenal, unavailable to perception in the everyday state of consciousness."[39] He then explains both forms by means of historical examples, drawing on the same list of spiritual teachers that we know from other contexts—for instance, Carl Gustav Jung, Martin Buber, and Rudolf Otto—such as Hildegard of Bingen, Meister Eckhart, Sufi masters, and kabbalistic sages. According to Grof, today's forms of religion—above all Christianity, Judaism, and Islam—have lost touch with mystical, "authentic" spirituality, as can be seen in the religious conflicts of the time as well as in terrorist and fundamentalist movements. It is interesting to see how Grof differentiates spirituality and religion in their respective connections to science, thereby marking a discursive knot that had taken root in many parts of the spiritual scene at the end of the twentieth century, particularly the inscription of "authenticity" as a feature of differentiation:

> There is no doubt that the dogmas of organized religions are generally in fundamental conflict with science, whether this science uses the mechanistic-materialistic model or is anchored in the emerging paradigm. However, the situation is very different in regard to authentic mysticism based on spiritual experiences. The great mystical traditions have amassed extensive knowledge about human consciousness and about the spiritual realms in a way that is similar to the method that scientists use in acquiring knowledge about the material world. It involves methodology for inducing transpersonal experiences, systematic collection of data, and intersubjective validation.[40]

Under the heading "Consciousness Evolution and Human Survival: Transpersonal Perspective on the Global Crisis," Grof turns to the ecological crisis, which he ultimately interprets as a spiritual crisis. "The research of holotropic states of consciousness," Grof notes, "has important implications not only for each of us individually, but also for the future of humanity and survival of life on this planet."[41] In almost apocalyptic tones, Grof names what he considers to be demonic forces at work in the world, among which he also counts—in stark contrast to transpersonal views in the 1960s—adolescent sexual freedom, "gay liberation, general promiscuity, open marriages, high divorce rate, overtly sexual books, plays and movies, sadomasochistic experimentation, and many others." But there is more:

> The demonic element is also becoming increasingly manifest in the modern world. Renaissance of satanic cults and witchcraft, popularity of books and horror movies with occult themes, and crimes with satanic motivations attest to that fact. The scatological dimension is evident in the progressive industrial pollution, accumulation of waste products on a global scale, and rapidly deteriorating hygienic conditions in large cities. . . . Many of the people with whom we have worked saw humanity at a critical crossroad facing either collective annihilation or an evolutionary jump in consciousness of unprecedented proportions.[42]

Hence Grof is convinced that only a fundamental transformation of human consciousness can save humanity—and the planet—from ruin.[43]

Another pioneer of the transpersonal movement is Ken Wilber (born 1949). In his research, Wilber distinguishes between the deep structure and the surface structure of mystical-religious experiences, thereby attempting to identify commonalities between phenomena as diverse as Christian mystics' encounters with angelic beings, Hindus merging with their *Ishta deva*, and shamanic journeys to other levels of reality. This is a phenomenological approach to hermeneutics, which is also familiar from the study of religion, and which has been criticized for omitting historical contexts and for issues with defining concrete categories of comparison. Working from this approach, Wilber constructs a developmental model that relates the different states of consciousness to the transpersonal depth structure.[44] He distinguishes between recognizing increasingly subtle areas of mind ("subtle states"), going beyond all objects and phenomena to "pure consciousness" ("causal states"), and finally recognizing all objects and phenomena as projections of consciousness ("absolute states"). This evolutionary model leads to clear evaluations of a phenomenon in terms of its transpersonal stage of development, for which Wilber has sometimes been criticized. He counters such criticisms by polemically distancing himself from any cultural relativist position and also by resisting "New Age" followers who invoke his theory: Wilber calls them naïve dreamers, pointing out that not every spiritual experience is transpersonal; such experiences are often confused with a prepersonal experience, i.e., a psychological regression into early childhood fantasies of omnipotence, which are the opposite of a transpersonal overcoming of the self. Wilber calls this the "pre/trans fallacy."[45]

Ultimately, however, Wilber is concerned not with playing off different explanatory approaches to reality against one another, but with integrating Western, Eastern, and other methods into a comprehensive model. For him, the differences simply consist in the fact that individual perspectives are located at a different point on the "spectrum of consciousness," and gross distortions would only arise if the approaches were applied to other areas of the spectrum.[46]

The interest in comparative studies of "Eastern" and "Western," Indigenous and mystical traditions and practices that extend the potential of human consciousness to transpersonal realms, also brought with it an increased interest in shamanic journeys of the soul and so-called shamanic states of consciousness. In chapter 8 I will address this topic in more detail, but at this point I want to refer to Roger Walsh's study on the transpersonal potential of shamanism, as Walsh's book clearly shows the connection between discourses on consciousness and the soul on the one hand, and spiritual practices on the other. With this study, Walsh aims to initiate "new psychological explorations of shamanism."[47] Without recourse to the scientific framework within which shamanism is interpreted, Walsh tries to create a typology of shamanic states of consciousness with direct reference to Ken Wilber—who in turn says that *The Spirit of Shamanism* is "the only book I can unreservedly recommend" when it comes to "the nature of the shamanic vision"[48]—and to interpret shamanic theory and practice with the tools of transpersonal analysis. He concludes that during their journeys, shamans would certainly have reached the subtle states of consciousness. One would also have to assume that some particularly advanced shamans had experienced causal and even absolute states.

As for the *unio mystica*, Walsh explains that shamans, even if they normally experience themselves as "free souls" separated from other worlds and beings, can at times unite with other spirits. In some religious traditions, this is expressed in terms of merging not only with other beings or spirits, but with the whole universe and with God. In the high regions of the subtle realms, certain forms of *unio mystica* enable mystics to gather information and power for other people to use.[49] Walsh deems it probable that some shamans have indeed reached a stage similar to *unio mystica*. What is more, shamanic practitioners in the West also report corresponding experiences. It seems, Walsh concludes, "that shamans may have been humankind's first transpersonal heroes—the first to systematically break their identification with the body and the world; the first to systematically enter transpersonal domains."[50]

Christina and Stanislav Grof also integrate shamanism into a typology of transpersonal experiences, and they do so with regard to the spiritual crisis. They distinguish ten types: (1) the shamanic crisis; (2) the Kundalini awakening; (3) the experience of unity ("peak experiences"); (4) psychological renewal by returning to the center; (5) the crisis of sensitive opening; (6) experiences from past lives; (7) communication with spiritual guides and "channeling"; (8) near-death experiences; (9) experiences with UFOs; and (10) states of possession.[51]

Based on their respective research, Wilber, Walsh, the Grofs, and others emphasize that the shamanic journey is closely related to extraordinary states of consciousness, out-of-body experiences, and transpersonal encounters, as these are also documented in other cultural contexts. The comparative view of states of consciousness allows the authors to describe shamanism as an anthropological constant, which—although reserved for the particularly gifted—does not appear to be culturally bound.

Needless to say, shamanic states of consciousness are only one among many materializations of the soul's cosmic potential. We can see the extent to which transpersonal psychology both draws on existing discourse on the soul and develops new discursive formations in the work of Charles T. Tart (born 1937). His programmatic survey *Transpersonal Psychologies* (1975) expresses all the discursive attributes relevant to our analysis. This is already evident in his introduction, which begins with a long quotation from Robert Ornstein's *The Nature of Human Consciousness: A Book of Readings* (1973). The quotation reads:

> Psychology is, primarily, the science of consciousness. Its researchers deal with consciousness directly when possible, and indirectly, through the study of physiology and behavior, when necessary. Psychologists are now returning to the essential questions of our discipline: How does the mind work? What are the major dimensions of human consciousness? Is consciousness individual or cosmic? What means are there to extend human consciousness? These questions have not yet had a full treatment within academic science, having been ruled out of inquiry by the dominant paradigm of the past 60 or so years.
>
> Yet there is a cultural and scientific evolution, if not revolution, in process. Academic people, being members of their culture, reflect the general interest in "Altered States" of consciousness, meditation, drug states, and new and old religions. The intent of this book is to assist in a small way in regaining a lost perspective in psychology. . . . There is, therefore, a continuing need to reestablish the basis of psychology and to link current research with that of other students of consciousness, such

> as William James and Carl Jung, and with the "esoteric" psychologies of other cultures, such as Sufism, Yoga, and Buddhism.[52]

Tart fully agrees with these programmatic claims. To Ornstein's diagnosis he adds that transpersonal research is not only interested in psychological and academic questions; it is also invested in global responsibility:

> The call to link our psychology with other psychologies, to understand our minds, is not simply of academic interest: our culture is in the midst of a crisis that may be resolved by nuclear annihilation, mass starvation, and the partial or total collapse of civilization. We look at economics, politics, ecology, crime, and so on to find the villains, but *we* are the villains. Ordinary man, man who does not know himself, neurotic man, psychotic man—all project their psychological inadequacies and conflicts out on the world, finding the villains out there and retaliating against them. Economics, politics, ecology, crime—these are all manifestations of how *we* behave, how *we* (mis)perceive, how *we* distort. Psychology is not merely an interesting academic study: it is the ultimate key to understanding ourselves, and, hopefully, saving ourselves.[53]

This passage illuminates the extent to which the political and ecological factors of the time challenged and changed psychological and philosophical interpretations. The twentieth-century wars of annihilation, the nuclear crisis, the Cold War, the Vietnam War, and also the ecological crisis, which was causing increasing concern toward the end of the twentieth century, were all part of the transpersonal movement, as well as of cultural changes more generally. Charles T. Tart and other representatives of transpersonal psychology regard a stronger awareness of these processes, which is also accompanied by a new understanding of the concept of "consciousness" itself, as a necessary response to these global challenges.

I would be going too far—and creating many redundancies—if I went into all the aspects of this approach here. From a discourse-analytical point of view, it may be sufficient to list the titles of the individual chapters in *Transpersonal Psychologies*, because the central discourse strands are clearly identified there, before they are further explained in the chapters themselves. Most of the chapters were written by Charles T. Tart, although a few were written by his colleagues (as indicated in parentheses): 1. Science, States of Consciousness, and Spiritual Experiences: The Need for State-Specific Sciences (Charles T. Tart); 2. Some Assumptions of Orthodox, Western Psychology (Charles T. Tart); 3. The Physical Universe, the Spiritual Universe, and the Paranormal (Charles T. Tart); 4. Zen Buddhism (Claire Myers Owens); 5. The Buddha on Meditation and States of Consciousness (Daniel Goleman); 6. Yoga Psychology (Haridas Chaudhuri); 7. Gurdjieff (Kathleen Riordan); 8. The Arica Training (John C. Lilly and Joseph E. Hart); 9. Contemporary Sufism (Robert E. Ornstein); 10. Psychology and the Christian Mystical Tradition (William McNamara); 11. Patterns of Western Magic (William G. Gray).

In his introduction, Tart explains: "This sampling of eight spiritual psychologies is far from complete, as space has precluded dealing with such important ones as Taoism, Alchemy, the Cabalistic Tradition, Tibetan Buddhism, and so on. I hope to organize a second volume to rectify these omissions."[54] In a number of subsequent publications, he did exactly this; his most recent monograph is *The End of Materialism: How Evidence of the Paranormal Is Bringing Science and Spirit Together*, published in 2009.[55]

Tart's earlier work is relevant for our analysis for another reason, too. It displays the transition from "religion" to "spirituality" that took place over the course of the twentieth century, which is particularly notable in self-descriptions. In a footnote to his introduction, Tart explains:

> I use the term "spiritual" in preference to "religious" because I feel the former term implies more directly the *experiences* that people have about the meaning of life, God, ways to live, etc., while "religious" implies too strongly the enormous social structures that embrace so many more things than direct spiritual experience, and which have often become hostile to and inhibiting of direct experience. When I hear "religious," I get all sorts of associations of priests, dogmas, doctrines, churches, institutions, political meddling, and social organizations.[56]

In Tart's "associations" with the concept of the religious we find exactly those discourse strands that define the discourse on "religion" toward the end of the twentieth century (though also in part much earlier, as we have seen), while "spirituality" is embedded in a new arrangement in which the concept can easily be combined with discourses on the soul, nature, and science.

Cosmos and Soul in Richard Tarnas

In its mixture of academic research, psychotherapy, and work in spiritually oriented networks, the transpersonal movement has made an unmistakable contribution to the establishment of an order of knowledge that sees itself as an alternative to reductionist materialistic approaches and formulates the necessity for a transformation of consciousness on individual, collective, and planetary levels. The transpersonal criticism of materialism (in Tart, Grof, and others) reminds us that, from the point of view of the history of science, naturalism is distinct from materialism. Wilhelm Wundt and others of his generation justified their fierce attacks on spiritualism by arguing that, in their eyes, it was a particularly horrible manifestation of materialism. The transpersonal movement stands in this line of interpretation. It often goes hand in hand with the presentation of grand narratives on the genesis of the modern world, reconstructing the intellectual, philosophical, and spiritual lines that, from the perspective of transpersonal authors, have led to the present situation. Ken Wilber is an important part of this conversation, as is Richard Tarnas (born 1950), whose *The Passion of the Western Mind: Understanding the Ideas That Have Shaped Our World View* (1991) and *Cosmos and Psyche: Intimations of a New World View* (2006) have found a broad readership and clearly illustrate the development of the discursive arrangement in the transition from Carl Gustav Jung to the transpersonal perspective.

After studying at Harvard University, Richard Tarnas came to Esalen in 1974 to study psychotherapy with Stanislav Grof and to work with Joseph Campbell, Gregory Bateson, Huston Smith, Elisabeth Kübler-Ross, and James Hillman. In 1976 he received his doctorate from Saybrook Institute with his thesis *Psychedelic Therapy*. He remained at Esalen until 1984.

Jeffrey J. Kripal notes: "For the first five years, he worked primarily as a gate guard. For the last five years, he worked as Esalen's program manager. Tarnas, in other words, was Esalen's 'gate-keeper' in both the literal and intellectual senses of the term."[57] After his time at Esalen—but still closely connected to the activities of the Institute—Tarnas became professor of philosophy and psychology at the California Institute of Integral Studies, where he established the graduate program in Philosophy, Cosmology, and Consciousness.

The Passion of the Western Mind treats the cultural history of Europe as a history containing all the aspects of a "great epic drama: ancient and classical Greece, the Hellenistic era and imperial Rome, Judaism and the rise of Christianity, the Catholic Church and the Middle Ages, the Renaissance, Reformation and Scientific Revolution, the Enlightenment and Romanticism and onward to our own compelling time."[58] Especially in the chapter "The Transformation of the Modern Era" and in the epilogue, Tarnas draws together the threads of intellectual history and describes the incipient transformation of the world as a necessary development of consciousness. He seeks to incorporate approaches to a synthesis of empirical and metaphysical worldviews, as they were developed by Goethe and Jung, into a new consciousness.

> Our moment in history is indeed a pregnant one. As a civilization and as a species we have come to a moment of truth, with the future of the human spirit, and the future of the planet, hanging in the balance. If ever boldness, depth, and clarity of vision were called for, from many, it is now. Yet perhaps it is this very necessity that could summon forth from us the courage and imagination we now require. Let us give the last words of this unfinished epic to Nietzsche's Zarathustra:
>
> And how could I endure to be a man, if man were not also poet and reader of riddles and . . . a way to new dawns.[59]

To give concrete form to these "new dawns," Tarnas sketches the contemporary situation in his epilogue, which is a continuation of Jung's studies of the collective unconscious and the archetypal structure of soul and consciousness (Tarnas, like other transpersonal authors, usually translates

Jung's *Seele*, or "soul," as "psyche"). Tarnas mentions Stanislav Grof's studies in particular as major contributions to shaping the new paradigm. Referring to his work as program manager at the Esalen Institute, he points out that

> in the course of those years virtually every conceivable form of therapy and personal transformation, great and small, came through Esalen. In terms of therapeutic effectiveness, Grof's was by far the most powerful; there was no comparison. Yet the price was dear—in a sense the price was absolute: the reliving of one's birth was experienced in a context of profound existential and spiritual crisis, with great physical agony, unbearable constriction and pressure, extreme narrowing of mental horizons, a sense of hopeless alienation and the ultimate meaninglessness of life, a feeling of going irrevocably insane, and finally a shattering experiential encounter with death—with losing everything, physically, psychologically, intellectually, spiritually. Yet after integrating this long experiential sequence, subjects regularly reported experiencing a dramatic expansion of horizons, a radical change of perspective as to the nature of reality, a sense of sudden awakening, a feeling of being fundamentally reconnected to the universe, all accompanied by a profound sense of psychological healing and spiritual liberation.[60]

The awakening of the transpersonal potential of the soul, Tarnas continues, can only be realized if the repressed feminine is fully integrated into modern consciousness. As Carl Jung "prophesied, an epochal shift is taking place in the contemporary psyche, a reconciliation between the two great polarities, a union of opposites: a hieros gamos (sacred marriage) between the long-dominant but now alienated masculine and the long-suppressed but now ascending feminine."[61] Tarnas turns Jung's archetypal doctrine of the soul into an epic drama of human existence:

> This is the great challenge, yet I believe it is one the Western mind has been slowly preparing itself to meet for its entire existence. I believe that the West's restless inner development and incessantly innovative masculine ordering of reality has been gradually leading, in an immensely

> long dialectical movement, toward a reconciliation with the lost feminine unity, toward a profound and many-leveled marriage of the masculine and feminine, a triumphant and healing reunion. And I consider that much of the conflict and confusion of our own era reflects the fact that this evolutionary drama may now be reaching its climactic stages. For our time is struggling to bring forth something fundamentally new in human history: We seem to be witnessing, suffering, the birth labor of a new reality, a new form of human existence, a "child" that would be the fruit of this great archetypal marriage, and that would bear within itself all its antecedents in a new form. I therefore would affirm those indispensable ideals expressed by the supporters of feminist, ecological, archaic, and other countercultural and multicultural perspectives.[62]

The gender constructions that characterize Jung's ideas about the female archetype and the "Anima"—conveyed by authors such as Tarnas—are found across a whole range of contemporary spiritual discourses, especially in nature-based spiritualities, astrology, paganism, and spiritually oriented therapies. Their androcentric perspective often goes unchallenged. With Tarnas, they even become the key to diagnosing the present age, as the concluding sentences of his book make clear: "Today we are experiencing something that looks very much like the death of modern man, indeed that looks very much like the death of Western man. Perhaps the end of 'man' himself is at hand. But man is not a goal. Man is something that must be overcome—and fulfilled, in the embrace of the feminine."[63]

As important as *The Passion of the Western Mind* may have been for understanding Europe's long cultural history, for Tarnas the study simply prepared the ground—both for himself and for his readers—for *Cosmos and Psyche*, which appeared fifteen years later. "*Cosmos and Psyche* addresses more precisely the crisis of the modern self and modern world view, and then introduces a body of evidence, a method of inquiry, and an emerging cosmological perspective that I believe could help us creatively engage that crisis, and our history itself, within a new horizon of possibility. I hope this book will point towards an enlarged understanding of our evolving universe, and of our own still-unfolding role within it."[64] Like its predecessor, this book is again a grand narrative, but now the topic is the most recent history and the solutions Tarnas offers for the current crises. Again, Jung's archetypes play a central role. For Tarnas, the planetary archetypes in particular can be used to explain cultural phenomena. In a long historical line, Tarnas locates the origin of the astrological, sacred interpretation of the archetypes in Greek antiquity.

> The earliest form of the archetypal perspective, and in certain respects its deepest ground, is the primordial experience of the great gods and goddesses of the ancient mythic imagination. In this once universal mode of consciousness, memorably embodied at the dawn of Western culture in the Homeric epics and later in classical Greek drama, reality is understood to be pervaded and structured by powerful numinous forces and presences that are rendered to the human imagination as the divinized figures and narratives of ancient myth, often closely associated with the celestial bodies.[65]

The understanding of archetypes, Tarnas argues, went through several transformations in Europe's intellectual history but reached its fullest development only in the twentieth century: "It was not until the turn of the twentieth century that the concept of archetypes, foreshadowed by Nietzsche's vision of the Dionysian and Apollonian principles shaping human culture, underwent an unexpected renascence."[66] In its most elaborate form, however, this doctrine was only to be found in the work of Carl Gustav Jung. "In his last formulations influenced by his research on synchronicities, Jung came to regard archetypes as expressions not only of a collective unconscious shared by all human beings but also of a larger matrix of being and meaning that informs and encompasses both the physical world and the human psyche."[67]

Tarnas builds on Jung's concepts, going beyond Jung's original considerations by including astrological hermeneutics: "The astrological thesis as developed within the Platonic/Jungian lineage holds that these complex, multidimensional archetypes governing the forms of human experience are intelligibly connected with the planets and their movements in the heavens. This association is observable in a constant coincidence between specific planetary alignments and specific archetypally patterned phenomena in human affairs."[68]

Over the course of the book, Tarnas applies the astrological theory of archetypes to important events in world history—from the French Revolution to the upheavals of the 1960s—but also to individual occurrences, for example, in Jung's life. For Tarnas, as for most contemporary astrologers, the discoveries of the trans-Saturnian planets Uranus, Neptune, and Pluto, as well as the great cycles of the planets in their relations to one another, are blueprints for parallel processes that run on the individual, collective, and planetary levels. Tarnas clearly belongs among those cultural interpreters who regard "modernity" as a major crisis in human development. "From seventeenth-century rationalism and empiricism to twentieth-century existentialism and astrophysics, human consciousness has found itself progressively emancipated yet also progressively relativized, unrooted, inwardly isolated from the spiritually opaque world it seeks to comprehend. The soul knows no home in the modern cosmos."[69] And elsewhere he notes: "It was Friedrich Nietzsche who seems to have recognized most intensely the full implications of the modern development, and experienced in his own being the inescapable plight of the modern sensibility: the Romantic soul at once liberated, displaced, and entrapped within the vast cosmic void of the scientific universe."[70] Humanity lost its understanding of the world as "a deep-souled, subtly mysterious cosmos of great spiritual beauty and creative intelligence."[71]

This talk of the "homelessness" of the soul in the modern cosmos and the "cosmic void of the scientific universe" on the one hand and the search for "a deep-souled, subtly mysterious cosmos" full of "spiritual beauty and creative intelligence" on the other hand marks exactly the discursive knot that is important for our analysis. Tarnas—who stands as a representative example of many other authors in the transpersonal movement—weaves further strands of discourse into this arrangement, intending to offer a solution to the planetary crisis of consciousness. His solution lies in becoming aware of archetypal dynamics and in the continued creative development of holistic understandings of nature in science, which regard the cosmos as sacred and animated. Quantum physics and other physical and biological models that point to the deep structure of reality and the evolution of consciousness are, for Tarnas as for countless others (as we will see in the following chapters), indications of a fundamental change, which he describes as "Awakenings of Spirit and Soul."[72]

Pulling religious discourse strands into the arrangement, Tarnas formulates the ultimate goal of this development in the last chapter of the book as "Towards a New Heaven and a New Earth."[73] This goal can only be achieved by changing what is considered generally accepted knowledge. "It will demand an initial act of trust in the possible reality of an ensouled cosmos of transformative beauty and purposeful intelligence."[74] Referring to Goethe's research on nature, Tarnas states that we can only share this knowledge through "receptive engagement with what we wish to comprehend, which transforms us in the very process of our inquiry. Thus the study of archetypal forms opens the archetypal eye. And thus the open encounter with the potential reality of an *anima mundi* makes possible its actual discernment."[75]

Tarnas ties together the discourse strands of soul–cosmos–consciousness–spirit–reality–science in a way that clearly follows the line of tradition extending from Goethe and the Romantic philosophy of nature; through Jung, Assagioli, and others; to the metaphysical exploration of the cosmos in biology and physics in the second half of the twentieth century. By including the discourse strands of the archetypes and the astrological interpretation of cosmic dynamics, he adds further momentum to the plausibility and legitimacy of a sacral-metaphysical understanding of the cosmos and the expectation of a fundamental change in human consciousness.

My investigation of the transpersonal movement has shown how discourses on the soul retained certain older features and also developed new characteristics when they traveled from Europe to North America. The concept of the soul was incorporated into the concepts of "psyche" and "consciousness," often in the same discursive arrangement as before—for example, in the transformation from "world soul" (*anima mundi*) to "cosmic consciousness." The continuities particularly related to Carl Gustav Jung's psychological terminology unmistakably reveal this dynamic. There are also clear continuities with regard to the discursive knot of cosmos–universe–nature. Two themes in particular have been further expended through their reception in the transpersonal movement: While the comparison between "East" and "West" had been an integral part of cultural discourses since the early twentieth century—especially visible in Jung's work, in theosophical contributions, and in learned events such as the Eranos conferences—the view that the West could profit from Eastern wisdom teachings and that these should be integrated into science and spirituality subsequently became a central theme. Another discourse strand that was added to the overall arrangement from the 1970s onward is the ecological crisis. The sense of urgency around political, ecological, and social action had an impact on discursive arrangements of nature and soul. Processes of sacralizing nature were accompanied by discussions on the transformation of individual and planetary consciousness. Following Jung's lead, the transpersonal movement regarded psychology as a fundamental science that could make necessary contributions to social science as well as to issues of philosophy and natural science.

To some extent, what we see in the transpersonal movement is evidence of natural philosophy's renaissance. This development, which is highly important for discourses on the soul, is the subject of the following chapter.

7

THE RENAISSANCE OF *NATURPHILOSOPHIE*

Quantum Mysticism, Cosmic Consciousness, and the Planetary Soul

Since the nineteenth century, the soul had been an integral part of the discursive arrangements of natural philosophy, occultism, and those areas of psychology and the natural sciences that regarded themselves as open to metaphysics. While the soul was more or less discarded in academic psychology, which from the 1930s onward was characterized by a strongly behaviorist and materialistic-empirical bent, it was Carl Gustav Jung's psychology and the newly emerging transpersonal movement that further consolidated these metaphysical arrangements of discourses on the soul, both outside the universities and in academic centers aligned with the American countermovement. This fostered interesting cross-references between the transpersonal movement, theosophical-humanistic discussions as they were conducted at the Eranos conferences, philosophical questions of theoretical physics, and new interpretative approaches in biology and ecology. These discursive entanglements—which were particularly concerned with questions of the nature of reality, the position of the human in the dynamic planetary system, and the metaphysical potential of science—gave rise to new ethical discussions and spiritual practices. I interpret this development as a renaissance of natural philosophy, in which theoretical and practical aspects of natural science and the experience of nature merge to form the framework for a religious-spiritual attitude that grew into a broad cultural phenomenon toward the end of the twentieth century.

The analysis of discursive arrangements can help to visualize the explicit and implicit references and entanglements across these different fields. In working out the structures supporting such a discourse, in this chapter I will concentrate on those elements that have a direct connection to "soul," "psyche," and "consciousness."

How the Hippies Saved Theoretical Physics

In his book *How the Hippies Saved Physics: Science, Counterculture, and the Quantum Revival*, David Kaiser describes the story of a small group of young physicists who dedicated themselves to the philosophical questions of quantum mechanics. In May 1975, Elizabeth Rauscher and George Weissmann, at the time doctoral students at Berkeley in California, founded an informal discussion group that soon became known as the Fundamental Fysiks Group, attracting like-minded people from across America and Europe. The members of this group shared a frustration over the fact that fundamental discussions of physics in the United States had been tamped down due to the Cold War ideological sentiment, which allowed for only pragmatic-calculative research. When Kaiser writes that these hippies "saved" theoretical physics, this is precisely one of the reasons: "They self-consciously opened up space again for freewheeling speculation, for the kind of spirited philosophical engagement with fundamental physics that the Cold War decades had dampened."[1] They wanted to revive the culture of discussion that had characterized the conversations between the heroes of theoretical physics in the 1920s—above all Einstein, Bohr, Heisenberg, and Schrödinger. The second reason for Kaiser's thesis is the fact that "members of the Fundamental Fysiks Group latched onto a topic, known as 'Bell's theorem,' and rescued it from a decade of unrelenting obscurity."[2] This refers to the theorem named after the Irish physicist John S. Bell, which I will address in more detail in a moment. The discussion of Bell's theorem then led—and this is Kaiser's third level of "salvation"—to groundbreaking new discoveries in theoretical and applied physics, such as the "no-cloning theorem": "Akin to Heisenberg's famous uncertainty principle, the no-cloning theorem stipulates that it is impossible to produce perfect copies (or 'clones') of an unknown or arbitrary quantum state. Efforts to copy the fragile quantum state necessarily alter it."[3] At the beginning of the twenty-first century, this discovery led to the development of tap-proof communication systems based on quantum theory. This historical connection is generally accepted today. Less well known, according to Kaiser, is "that the no-cloning theorem emerged directly from the Fundamental Fysiks Group's tireless efforts—at once earnest and zany—to explore whether Bell's theorem and quantum entanglement might unlock the secrets of mental telepathy and extra-sensory perception, or even enable contact with spirits of the dead."[4]

In addition to the reasons Kaiser mentions, we can refer to other developments in the sciences that opened up metaphysical speculation. As Mary-Jane Rubenstein argues, around 1950 the big bang hypothesis in particular turned the natural sciences into natural philosophy or—even worse for many involved—into theology. "The problem is that if we assume that the universe had a beginning, we are almost forced to appeal to some kind of supernatural force to get it going." She concludes: "The rise of the big bang hypothesis thus staged a return of the mythological at the heart of modern science. To the horror of many midcentury physicists, positing a beginning to the universe seemed to open their discipline constitutively to something beyond it."[5]

In any case, the Fundamental Fysiks Group soon developed into a kind of media event, and the "new physics" it represented influenced the scientific as well as the spiritual scene. Members of the group included Fritjof Capra (born 1939), whose *The Tao of Physics* (1975) became a milestone in "New Age" literature; Gary Zukav (born 1942), who reached a wide audience with *The Dancing Wu Li Masters* in 1979; and Nick Herbert (born 1937), who made significant contributions to "new physics" and also made these discussions accessible to a large audience, for example, in his best seller *Quantum Reality: Beyond the New Physics: An Excursion Into Metaphysics and the Meaning of Reality*, published in 1985. This remarkable mixture of theoretical physics, the Esalen branch of the Human Potential Movement, the exploration of human consciousness in a spiritual dimension (including experiments with mind-altering substances and practices), and a sociopolitical as well as an armament protest movement unfolded a field of discourse that also encompassed the orders of knowledge on the "soul."

Indeed, the quantum theoretical considerations that had fascinated Carl Gustav Jung and Wolfgang Pauli offer previously unimaginable possibilities for philosophical and metaphysical speculation, or in David Kaiser's words, "quantum mechanics is a science of the bizarre. Particles tunnel through walls. Cats become trapped, half dead and half alive. Objects separated light-years apart retain telepathic links with one another. The seaming solidity of the world evaporates into a cloud of likelihoods."[6] A much-discussed example of this is the principle of the Einstein-Podolsky-Rosen experiment, which refers to two "quantum dice." One dice is located in Vienna, the other in Budapest. Whenever both quantum dice are thrown simultaneously, the result is completely random—but they each show the same number. Moreover, there is no time lag between the results; even if a third dice were thousands of light years away, it would show the same result at the same time. There is a connection between the dice, but this connection cannot be explained by causality, such as in the billiard ball model.

Wolfgang Pauli depicted such an acausal relationship in what become known as the Pauli exclusion principle, which states that it is impossible for any two of the electrons in a polyelectron atom to have an identical set or the same four quantum numbers. Put differently, two or more identical fermions (particles with half-integer spin) cannot simultaneously occupy the same quantum state within a quantum system. Only as a result of this precondition can different elements emerge. An implication of the Pauli exclusion principle is that the mutual exclusion of the electrons is acausal, because the internal interrelations of the electron's movements are not controlled by a physical force or a transfer of energy, but—as F. David Peat explains—by "the direct manifestation of the overall form of the wave function in the whole system. . . . One could therefore say that the electron movements are the manifestation of a global pattern or an overall form, which cannot be locally limited—a true expression of synchronicity."[7]

The so-called EPR correlations (named after the Einstein-Podolsky-Rosen paradox), which were demonstrated in Bell's theorem and particularly in the Bell inequalities, are also connected to the Pauli exclusion principle and were demonstrated in the Einstein-Podolsky-Rosen experiment.[8] These "nonclassical correlations" were experimentally confirmed about twenty years later, between quantum particles located far from one another. Their relationship is not a causal connection; rather, all the particles in every location manifest a wave characteristic at the same time. According to Steven Weinberg, who received the Nobel Prize in Physics in 1979, this wave function can still be considered real; "it just behaves in ways that we are not used to, including instantaneous changes affecting the wave function of the whole universe."[9] The Fundamental Fysiks Group intensively discussed the same question.[10] These discussions led Nick Herbert to the conclusion that "the world's deep reality is maintained by an invisible quantum connection whose ubiquitous influence is unmediated, unmitigated, and immediate."[11] Furthermore, Herbert states, "Religions assure us that we are all brothers and sisters, children of the same deity; biologists say that we are entwined with all life-forms on this planet: our fortunes rise or fall with theirs. Now, physicists have discovered that the very atoms of our bodies are woven out of a common superluminal fabric."[12] This reads like a continuation of Wilhelm Ostwald's views.

These discussions on the philosophical implications of quantum mechanics—which had already captivated Einstein, Heisenberg, Bohr, and others[13]—underwent a powerful renaissance thanks to cross-connections with the American countermovement in the 1970s. Apart from Nick Herbert, Fritjof Capra deserves special mention here because he wrote one of the most successful books on the subject: *The Tao of Physics*. As David Kaiser explains: "With the New Age rage in full force by the mid-1970s, conditions were ripe for a book like *The Tao of Physics*. Capra's book capitalized on a tremendous, diffuse, untapped thirst, a widely shared striving to find some meaning in the universe that might transcend the mundane affairs of the here and now. The market for Capra's book had been teeming like a huge pot of water just on the verge of boiling. *The Tao of Physics* became a catalyst, triggering an enormous reaction."[14] As part of his preparatory research for the book, Capra studied Buddhist mysticism and philosophy in depth, from specialist literature in religious studies to the works of D. T. Suzuki and others, which had long been very successful in the United States and Europe. This construction of the "Eastern wisdom teachings" fit perfectly with the formulations and questions arising from the philosophical implications of quantum mechanics. In terms of discourse analysis, I am less interested in whether *The Tao of Physics* represents Buddhist meditation and mysticism "correctly" than I am in looking at the order of knowledge that results from the intertwining of the discourse strands of "Eastern" and "Western" traditions.

A closer look at Capra's book reveals precisely those views of the "mysticism of the East" that we have encountered time and again, from the works of William James and Martin Buber to those of Carl Gustav Jung, Mircea Eliade, and others. Furthermore, it is easy to see how the term *consciousness* serves as a bridge between psychological, religious, and scientific discourse strands. "Throughout history," Capra maintains, "it has been recognized that the human mind is capable of two kinds of knowledge, or two modes of consciousness, which have often been termed the rational and the intuitive, and have traditionally been associated with science and religion, respectively."[15] Rational, linear thinking, which Capra describes as the "Western" mode, is opposed to the intuitive "Eastern" mode. The remarkable thing about the "new physics," according to Capra, is that the natural world does not seem to follow the rational, linear mode: "The natural world . . . is one of infinite varieties and complexities, a multidimensional world which contains no straight lines or completely regular shapes, where things do not happen in sequences, but all together; a world where—as modern physics tells us—even empty space is curved. It is clear that our abstract system of conceptual thinking can never describe or understand this reality completely."[16] That is why Capra argues for taking Eastern philosophy and mysticism seriously as an orientation: "Absolute knowledge is thus an entirely non-intellectual experience of reality, an experience arising in a non-ordinary state of consciousness which may be called a 'meditative' or mystical state. That such a state exists has not only been testified by numerous mystics in the East and West but is also indicated by psychological research."[17]

Consciousness is the term that carries significant meaning for both Buddhist mysticism and theoretical physics, which Capra stresses with reference to Heisenberg's uncertainty principle.

> In Eastern mysticism, this universal interwovenness always includes the human observer and his or her consciousness, and this is also true in atomic physics. At the atomic level, "objects" can only be understood in terms of the interaction between the processes of preparation and measurement. The end of this chain of processes lies always in the consciousness of the human observer. Measurements are interactions which create "sensations" in our consciousness—for example, the visual sensation of a flash of light, or of a dark spot on a photographic plate—and the laws of atomic physics tell us with what probability an atomic object will give rise to a certain sensation if we let it interact with us. "Natural science," says Heisenberg, "does not simply describe and explain nature; it is part of the interplay between nature and ourselves."[18]

This brings Capra to the conclusion that "quantum theory has abolished the notion of fundamentally separated objects, has introduced the concept of the participator to replace that of the observer, and may even find it necessary to include the human consciousness in its description of the world. It has come to see the universe as an interconnected web of physical and mental relations whose parts are only defined through their connections to the whole."[19]

The entanglement of the discourse strands of consciousness–quantum mechanics–mysticism–nature–universe–knowledge–web, as Capra bears it out here, lends plausibility to an order of knowledge in which natural science and spirituality do not represent a contradiction. Quite the contrary: it is only in their mutual interference that the whole potential of human knowledge and experience is opened up. What for Jung, Pauli, and others was the "world soul"—which is described in both mysticism and physics, and which, as the driving force of the cosmos, codetermines the fate of the universe as well as the personal spiritual experiences of human beings—in Capra's mystically turned quantum mechanics becomes an instance that enables the individual human consciousness to merge with the cosmic consciousness by means of mystical experiences. I will discuss a very similar discourse formation later using the example of the mythopoetic narrative of the "Epic of Evolution" (chapter 10)—which, however, does not necessarily include the elements of mystical experience and extraordinary states of consciousness.

We can find the same argumentation in the theoretical physicist David Bohm's (1917–1992) work. Here too, the term *consciousness* constitutes the connection between East and West. Throughout his life, Bohm was interested in the limits of what people can recognize and experience, an interest that brought him to mystical and metaphysical questions early on. Toward the end of the 1950s this fascination grew steadily, which irritated some of his scientist friends. I have already briefly mentioned F. David Peat (1938–2017), himself a highly respected physicist and one of the most important interpreters of synchronicity in the Jungian line. In his friend Bohm's biography, he writes: "Some lamented that Bohm had gone 'off the rails,' that a great mind had been sidetracked, and the work of an exceptional physicist was being lost to science. Yet in the context of Bohm's childhood dreams and visions of light and of vast energies, his fascination with the 'ultimate,' and his stories of highly evolved consciousnesses living on distant planets, his new path was consistent with everything that had gone before."[20] But it was not until he accidentally came across Jiddu Krishnamurti's *The First and Last Freedom* at a public library that his thinking truly began to transform. Bohm listened to Krishnamurti's lectures in London and also met him for a personal conversation—a meeting he experienced as particularly healing and powerful. As Peat explains:

> Into this heady and esoteric world, Bohm entered passionately and wholeheartedly. In Krishnamurti's books he found a clear analysis of the nature of consciousness and the mechanism whereby the thinker separates him- or herself from the thought and the action of thinking, by positing him- or herself as a separate, independent entity. In this act of separation, and in the subsequent reification of the thinker and the thought, lie the origins of human problems. Krishnamurti's observations that "the thinker is the thought" and "the observer is the observed" struck Bohm as resembling his own—and Niels Bohr's—meditations on the role of the observer in

> quantum theory. Bohm had personally experienced the way in which the observation of a particular thought changes the movement of thought itself. His study of Hegel had led him to similar conclusions about the movement of thought. The physicist was well prepared for his engagement with Jiddu Krishnamurti.[21]

Against this background, it is no wonder that the concept of consciousness and the comparison of Eastern and Western approaches to it is a central building block of Bohm's theoretical physics, not least in the influential *Wholeness and the Implicate Order*, in which he extended the comparison to include the concept of "wholeness."[22]

The discussions that appear in these works are still very much alive in the twenty-first century. Perhaps the most fascinating follow-up to Niels Bohr's interpretation of quantum physics is Karen Barad's theory of "agential realism," which she presents as a new epistemology, ontology, and ethics. In such an agential realist account, the world is made up of entanglements of "social" and "natural" agencies, where the distinction between the two emerges out of specific "intra-actions."[23] As I will discuss in chapter 10, these "entanglement" theories are part and parcel of a new approach to nonreductionist theories of culture and science, and Barad can be seen as a link between those discourses. But the field is larger than this. By way of example, in his book *Consciousness and Quantum Mechanics*, Michael B. Mensky concludes that the Jung-Pauli dialogue and the resulting quantum mysticism, in combination with the EPR correlations and Bell's theorem, have proven the existence of parallel worlds. His final chapter concisely summarizes the discursive knot that interests us here: "Conclusion: Science, philosophy and religion meet together in theory of consciousness."[24]

In an article for *Behavioral Sciences*, Lothar Schäfer and Diogo Valadas Ponte also explore the connections between Jung's psychology and the mystical dimensions of quantum physics. They are convinced that both quantum physics and psychology have demonstrated a nonempirical dimension of reality consisting of original forms. These forms, though invisible, are real because their active influence becomes tangible in the empirical world. The authors thus regard the empirical world as an emanation from the cosmic realm of potentiality, with the basic forms of the universe appearing both as physical structures and as archetypes of the soul. Evolution is therefore the process not of a species adapting to its environment, but of the mind adapting to increasingly complex forms existing in cosmic potentiality. In the last instance, therefore, the human mind is of a mystical nature.[25]

One can see from such publications that the mystical understanding of quantum mechanics is by no means a "forgotten controversy," as Juan Miguel Marin claims.[26] Rather, it forms a discursive arrangement, the influence of which is still visible after more than fifty years. We can easily combine this observation with Mary-Jane Rubenstein's analysis of the multiverse discussion. Coming from a different direction, she arrives at a similar conclusion: "By the turn of the millennium . . . quantum mechanics, modern cosmology, and string theory had independently collided with one or another version of the multiverse. It is here that we begin to see the merging of scientific developments and philosophical expedience."[27]

Deep Ecology and the Spiritualization of *Naturphilosophie*

The term *deep ecology*, coined in 1973 by the Norwegian analytical philosopher Arne Naess (1912–2009), refers to a radical challenge to the anthropocentric orientations of contemporary ethics and politics.[28] From the very beginning, deep ecology was understood as an approach that integrated ethics, politics, biology, and spirituality into one overall design—an undertaking that naturally attracted harsh criticism from philosophical and scientific circles. This criticism is not entirely unjustified in view of the fact that some contributions to the deep ecological discussion refer less to "rational" argumentation (which is ultimately considered only one aspect of our grasp on reality) than to empathy and a priori decisions. An example of this is the scholar of religion Roger S. Gottlieb, who wants to take philosophically oriented deep ecology a step further:

> The Deep Ecology of which I speak here is not the version presented in the technical language of philosophical ethics. . . . Rather, I speak of a

> passionate, spiritually oriented, mystical communion with the earth and its many beings, a recognition of kinship with those beings that no more requires philosophical justification than does the connection we feel with our parents, pets, or lovers. As such, "Deep Ecology" is a spiritual philosophy; and the deepest experiences that animate its adherents are profoundly mystical.[29]

Deep ecological philosophy is characterized by a biocentric view of nature and the human. The absolutist view of the human approach is recanted, and each entity is given its own place and nonnegotiable value. Deep ecology authors often refer to recent findings in the field of biology, which is increasingly investigating the extremely diverse interconnections of ecosystems. A biocentric view therefore means perceiving "the entire order of the earth's biosphere as a complex but unified web of interlinked organisms, objects, and events."[30]

Deep ecology models and approaches offered significant plausibility to nature-based spiritualities as they developed in the second half of the twentieth century, especially since the celebration of the first Earth Day in 1970.[31] They express on a philosophical level that which in spiritual terms is the result of ritualized experiences of nature. This is why deep ecological philosophy often includes spiritual concerns, which also aligns with the self-understanding of leading deep ecology representatives. At stake is not only the recognition of the interconnectedness of all levels of being, but also the ways in which they are experienced and sensually communicated. Therefore Dieter Birnbacher states: "In the philosophical contributions of 'deep ecology' the discursive and argumentative part is largely pushed back by the expressive-poetic one. The awe-inspiring astonishment before nature is no longer merely described but conjured up and visualized. Similar to Romantic philosophy of nature, philosophy itself becomes part of the required process of the holistic, i.e., no longer exclusively rational, realization of the individual self."[32] This means that theory and practice are seen as two sides of the same coin, which in turn implies that many publications in the field of deep ecology comprise not only theoretical reflection, but also invocations, meditations, and spiritual exercises.[33]

I will discuss animistic and shamanic practices in more detail in the next chapter. But in order to visualize the discursive connections between deep ecology, metaphysically oriented psychology, and natural philosophy on the one hand and shamanic practices on the other, I want to point out the mutual references between deep ecology and shamanism. An example of this is the volume *Schamanische Wissenschaften: Ökologie, Naturwissenschaft und Kunst* (Shamanic Sciences: Ecology, Natural Science, and Art), published by Diederichs press. In their foreword, the editors—Franz-Theo Gottwald and Christian Rätsch—state that the volume is an attempt to explore new perspectives for the Western natural sciences. "Shamans usually proceed systematically and structurally. They teach us the other side of the 'reality' coin and are often more empirical, exact, and honest than the formation of modern scientific theory. Their model of (natural) science can therefore serve to question our own model of science, perhaps even to complement it, perhaps even to be a model for it."[34]

Jonathan Horwitz of the Scandinavian Center for Shamanic Studies in Copenhagen is also convinced that "in fact, it can be said that the shaman was the first scientist."[35] Operating on the holistic assumption that the Earth and the cosmos are a living structure of interconnected parts, and taking into account the scientific impression that the Earth's ecosystems are interconnected in a way that transcends purely causal levels and lends itself to metaphysical patterns of explanation, the shamanic model of interpreting reality—according to these authors—reveals potential explanations for the initially paradoxical findings of ecological research that are both thoughtful and satisfying. With reference to Willis Harman, a representative of the Human Potential Movement, Franz-Theo Gottwald writes: "Up to the present day, the empirical basis consisted merely of information about reality, which was in accordance with the classical scientific model of empiricism. Now the comparative view of shamanism in the deep ecological approach wants to access the whole spectrum of human forms of perception and cognition, to arrive at a holistic understanding of reality."[36]

If shamanic practices influence natural philosophical considerations, then deep ecological discourses conversely and even more commonly have an impact on shamanic self-understanding. We may think, for example, of

Jonathan Horwitz's description of his course "Shamanic Healing and Spiritual Ecology" (summer 1998): "Much of the course time will be spent connecting with the spirits of the stones and trees, the Moon and Sun, the wind and the rivers, and the creatures of the Earth. We will learn again from them to respect and work together with the Earth on a deep spiritual—and practical—level for our common continuation and growth."[37] On a more abstract level, Joan Halifax's conclusion points in the same direction: "Like Buddhism and shamanism, deep ecology is centered on questioning and directly understanding our place from within the web of creation. All three of these practices—Buddhism, shamanism, and deep ecology—are based on the experience of engagement and the mystery of participation. Rooted in the practice and art of compassion, they move from speculation to revelation through the body of actual experience."[38] The work and biography of Joan Halifax (born 1942) are themselves good examples of the interweaving of transpersonal, shamanic, Buddhist, and natural-philosophical discourse strands. In the 1970s, Halifax was involved in the LSD research of her then-husband, Stanislav Grof, as well as in Joseph Campbell's and Alan Lomax's research. From 1979 to 1989 she directed the spiritual center she founded, the Ojai Foundation in California, before founding the Upaya Institute and Zen Center in Santa Fe, New Mexico, in 1990, which she still heads—now as roshi.[39]

There are countless instances of seamless transitions between natural-philosophical and spiritual discourses on transpersonal psychology and the Human Potential Movement, explicitly so in the case of Stanislav Grof, whom I have already introduced in the previous chapter. After referring to Ken Wilber, whose writings argued for the necessity of an "integral theory of everything" and also outlined a basic sketch of such a theory, Grof states: "However, the credit for actually creating such a theory goes to Ervin Laszlo, arguably the world's greatest system theorist and interdisciplinary scientist and philosopher."[40] Here Grof is referring to the "connectivity hypothesis," which Laszlo developed to postulate the existence of a "psi-field" and later of the "Akashic Field," i.e., a "subquantum field, which holds a holographic record of all the events that have happened in the phenomenal world."[41] Grof sees Laszlo's work as a key example of the broad field of new physical theories that take the connection between spirituality and natural science seriously. For him, these include Fritjof Capra, Fred Alan Wolf, Nick Herbert, Amit Goswami, Gregory Bateson, Ilya Prigogine, and above all David Bohm and Rupert Sheldrake.

> All these revolutionary advances in science have been welcomed by the transpersonal circles as significant conceptual support for transpersonal psychology. . . . However, what was still missing was a large integrative vision, the "conceptual glue" that would weave all these pieces into a comprehensive tapestry of ideas about consciousness, psyche, and human nature, one that could also be reconciled with the revolutionary findings of other scientific disciplines about the nature of reality. It was Ervin Laszlo's work that turned out to be the "Rosetta stone" that the pioneers of consciousness research and transpersonal psychology sought after.[42]

It is therefore worthwhile to take a brief look at the work of Ervin Laszlo (originally spelled László, born in Budapest in 1932). Trained as a classical pianist and a member of the World Academy of Arts and Sciences, Laszlo has built bridges between art and science and between the humanities and the natural sciences in a way few others have done. He was nominated for the Nobel Peace Prize in 2004 and 2005. He has become known to a broad audience, above all as a philosopher of science and a systems theoretician; he has written more than seventy books, which have been translated into twenty languages.

In his *The Systems View of the World* (1972), Laszlo introduces the basic features of systems theory, which interprets the natural world as interlocking, living, self-sustaining systems. The principles of his systems theory are (1) natural systems are wholes with irreducible properties; (2) natural systems maintain themselves in a changing environment; (3) natural systems create themselves in response to the challenges of the environment; and (4) natural systems are coordinating interfaces in nature's hierarchy.[43] When it comes to the human position within these systems, Laszlo sees no space in which the human species could maintain its special position. According to new scientific insights, "it became difficult to convince oneself that anything as *sui generis* as a soul could have been acquired in the process of evolution. Man had to accept being placed in the ranks of other species in the animal kingdom."[44] While this may be acceptable to many people today, "the ultimate blow to our anthropocentric pretensions will be dealt by the realization that humanlike qualities are not necessarily 'higher' achievements or signs of evolutionary progress." Instead of revealing a teleology that would lead to the emergence of the human species as a kind of goal, "it is more likely that the human pathway of development is one of those innumerable experiments which evolution tries, follows up if successful, and abandons if not."[45]

In formulations like these, we can already see that Laszlo thinks "evolution" and also "nature" are equipped with some kind of agency. This agency does not follow a predefined, teleological plan, but responds creatively and intelligently to changes in the systems. From this perspective, it can be said that nature has "consciousness." Indeed, for Laszlo, it is consciousness that is most relevant for the evolution of the human being and for nature as a whole—which again reveals the overlap between holistic philosophies of nature and transpersonal psychology.[46] One way to describe this process is that in human consciousness, nature arrives at an understanding of itself. To be human, Laszlo notes, means "to have the almost unique opportunity of getting to know oneself and the world in which one lives."[47] The special capacities the human being has developed have to be used consciously: "The worlds we build for ourselves can be manifold, but they must remain compatible with the structured hierarchy of terrestrial nature. We can build worlds beyond these limits only at our immediate peril."[48]

Laszlo's theory is reminiscent of discursive arrangements within monistic religion, for instance, in Haeckel's and Ostwald's arguments at the beginning of the twentieth century. He also anticipates scientific narratives that would become influential later—such as the "Epos of Evolution" that Richard Dawkins, Edward O. Wilson, and others project onto the evolving consciousness of the planet (which I will discuss in chapter 10). Laszlo is convinced that only if humans take their conscious understanding and self-reflection seriously will it be possible to "achieve a culture that is viable and humanistic." He concludes his book with an admonition: "Exploring such knowledge and applying it in determining our future is an opportunity we cannot afford to miss. For if we do, another chapter of terrestrial evolution will come to an end, and its unique experiment with rational consciousness will be written off as a failure."[49]

Interestingly enough, over the course of his long career, Laszlo has seen the links between the systems view he advances and an understanding of the planet Earth as "Gaia." In 2015, he wrote the preface for a publication of the Italian Gaia Project, a "new paradigm in education" described as a "Planetary Consciousness and Self Awareness Development Program and Psychosomatic Health Promotion in accordance with WHO guidelines."[50] Again, consciousness serves as the main link between the discourse strands of evolution, science, humanity, and nature. Laszlo is clearly participating in a discourse that has formed at the end of the twentieth century as a bridge between biology, natural philosophy, and spirituality, and which also gave important impetus to the discourse on the soul.

As a result of the discussion in this chapter, we can say that the more recent contributions of natural philosophy, in productive exchange with the transpersonal movement on the one hand and with the theories of religious studies and anthropology on the other, offer a blueprint for the spiritual integration of the human into the encompassing system of nature and the cosmos, which many people have received with interest. The entire field of nature-based spiritualities, in which animism has been rediscovered as a positive category, is a visible expression of this reception. I will examine what this means for discourses on the soul in the following chapter.

8

THE SOUL AS THE LODESTAR OF NEW SPIRITUAL PRACTICES

Looking at the genealogy of discourses on the soul reveals how closely scientific contributions are intertwined with broad-based movements outside academic institutions, as well as how the two discourse practices influence each other. Theories of the soul, as well as natural philosophical theories on the unity of all living things or the consciousness of nature and the cosmos, developed a great influence on spiritual practices in the second half of the twentieth century. Conversely, those spiritual practices led to the revision of older scientific theories—a clear example of mutual interference between science and cultural practice. At the beginning of the twenty-first century, the vast field of nature-based spirituality is one of the fastest growing religious-spiritual movements worldwide. Following Roderick Nash, Bron Taylor calls this "the global greening of religion."[1] In addition to the processes involved in the discursive entanglements of science and spiritual practice, of secularization and sacralization movements, which I have already addressed earlier, the global ecological crisis is another important factor in this upsurge of nature-based spiritualities. At this point, I want to provide a more detailed account of those areas of contemporary Euro-American spiritualities in which the connection between the soul and nature is most visible. Given the discursive entanglements operative since the end of the nineteenth century, it is not surprising that we find the clearest manifestations of these discourses in shamanic and pagan practices. In these contexts, and far beyond, the term *animism* has experienced a great boom in recent years. And this is anything but self-evident.

Animism: From Negative Stereotype to Positive Identity Marker

The academic term *animism* originated in the same cultural environment that also gave rise to other influential concepts at the end of the nineteenth century. The British anthropologist Edward B. Tylor (1832–1917), in his book *Primitive Culture* (1871), defined *animism* as the belief in the animation of nature and the existence of spirits. Tylor, like Rohde and other scholars of his generation, was concerned with the question of the historical development of the concept of the soul. In keeping with the evolutionary view of cultural development, Tylor assumed that precursors of what would later become "religion" were created in "primitive cultures" from dreams and hallucinations, from which these early cultures derived the conviction that there was something like a soul that constituted a person's alter ego. This "second ego" can leave the body during sleep, during illness, or under special conditions. With the death of the body, this entity leaves the person and lives on as an independent soul spirit. Animals and plants also have a soul, as they also live and die. But even certain objects that appear in dreams—such as stones, weapons, or clothes—are animated according to this understanding. There has never been any clear archaeological evidence for such an interpretation, but this did not prevent Tylor from associating the first level of "religion" with soul spirits. Subsequently the soul spirits would become gods, and still later the idea of a single god emerged. Despite the highly precarious colonial setting of this construction, it was not Tylor's main intention to suggest a hierarchy or valuation on the basis of such a reconstruction. We must not forget that Tylor's concept of animism was intended to show the *simultaneous* existence of archaic ("simple") and developed forms of religion in modern society.[2] In contemporary spiritualism, for example, which Tylor followed with keen interest in England (he also took part in séances), he found a connection between "wild thinking" and Christian theology, so that animism could basically still be considered a part of modern culture, even if a suppressed one. Thus, Jason Ā. Josephson-Storm aptly describes E. B. Tylor as "the haunted anthropologist."[3]

Nevertheless, assessments of animism as a "preliminary stage" of religion, similar to considerations on "magic," led to a problematic constellation in the academic study of religion and in twentieth-century anthropology, which made use of academic categories in their colonial move to underpin the leading place of monotheism as well as European "rationality" and "science."[4] This move was repeatedly criticized over the course of many academic debates, so that the concept of animism was disavowed in the academic study of religion. As Gerhard Schlatter apodictically stated in the *Brill Dictionary of Religion*, summarizing a position that represents many others: "Animism no longer plays an important role in the literature or debates of religious studies." Unfortunately, not everyone seems to have noticed, so Schlatter continues: "To be sure, the concept repeatedly surfaces in popular scientific contexts, as well as in scholarly milieus that do not take into account advances in the study of religion. It is put forward as a name for tribal religions, or magical belief in spirits among 'nature peoples.' Nor has animism been expelled from an (in part trivial) connection in the art world or from writings inspired by missionary theory and practice."[5]

There is no reason for such a triumphal tone. Instead of attempting to drive the term away with claims of hegemony within the study of religion, one could also take seriously the apparent attractiveness of the concept, asking oneself where this comes from and why the term is so popular, especially in the field of art, in new forms of spirituality, and in the colonial contact zone. Moreover, anthropologists made early attempts to develop Tylor's concept further and thereby overcome colonialist undertones (for example, in Robin Horton's work). More recent research in the study of religion and anthropology attempts similar moves against the background of ontologies that place the agency of nonhuman animals and even of seemingly "inanimate objects" in a relational context with human perception and ritual action.

In 1999, Nurit Bird-David proposed a reassessment of the anthropological concept of animism.[6] This thread was taken up by other researchers, such as Anne-Christine Hornborg in her exploration of "other ways of understanding indigenous peoples' cosmologies than 'primitive'" and her question of "whether these ways might allow us to understand animism, not as a failed epistemology but a relational one."[7] This research provides new perspectives on nature-based spirituality, as expressed in religious practices such as paganism and shamanism, but also influences cultural milieus and lifestyles such as vegetarianism and veganism. These worldviews attribute intrinsic value to nature, often with religious connotations that sacralize nature and conceive of it as animated or ensouled. Today the term *animism* is also used as a self-designation for such spiritual orientations. Graham Harvey defines animists as "people who recognize that the world is full of persons, only some of whom are human, and that life is always lived in relationship to others. Animism is lived out in various ways that are all about learning to act respectfully (carefully and constructively) towards and among other persons."[8] In this field, also known as "new animism," the focus is on relationships—or, more abstractly, on relationality—as they address the relational meaning of persons and actions in a complex communicational space.

Looking at the discourses of nature-based spirituality, there is not much evidence of a negative connotation to the term *animism*. On the contrary, the term stands for the (positive) assumption that everything that exists is alive and animated—even supposedly lifeless things, such as stones or rivers. This is why Bron Taylor uses the term as a key concept to analyze "dark green religion," distinguishing a "spiritual animism" from a "naturalistic" one.[9]

When it comes to shamanism, Nevill Drury simply states: "Shamanism is really applied animism, or animism in practice."[10] In fact, the connection goes so deep that animism and shamanism can hardly be separated, as Jonathan Horwitz testifies: "The word shamanism has become over-used and really very over-worked. A lot of the time when people say 'shamanistic,' they actually mean animistic—a perception of the world as it truly is, with all things alive and in connection. 'Animism' is the awareness of our connection to the world that is the foundation of the practice of shamanism. These two things are inseparable."[11]

Michael Harner also calls animism "the 'bottom line' of any religion that considers the existence of spirits," and he draws attention to the fact—precisely in the sense of the discursive entanglements I explored in the previous chapter—that even modern physicists have often followed an animistic model of religion. "It is the sense of our unity with a living universe, the feeling that we are all just parts of that greater life, which is basic to animism."[12] For Horwitz it is also clear that because shamanism is a practice, animism should not be understood as mere belief: "Animism for the animist is not a belief: it is the way life is experienced. All objects do contain a life essence of their own, and as such do also contain power."[13] Following Carlos Castaneda, Horwitz thus introduces the term *power* (in the sense of "force" or "energy") into the overall discursive web: "One could even call it [the shamanic rite] making oneself accessible to power."[14]

These statements are reason enough to take a closer look at Euro-American shamanism.

Shamanism: Journeying Souls and Ritual Approaches to Nature

Despite the long history of fascination with shamanism in Europe, what is often called "neoshamanism" did not emerge until the 1970s.[15] The formation of this spiritual field in North America and Europe has to do with a whole range of factors, of which the following can be regarded as decisive.

Shamanism in its modern coinage is the result of a discourse community in which academic experts provided the blueprint for spiritual practice and often took on the role of spiritual teachers themselves. First we should mention Mircea Eliade, whose *Shamanism and Archaic Techniques of Ecstasy*, originally published in French in 1951, significantly contributed to the inspiration of later generations both inside and outside universities. This popularization of academic knowledge continued with the works of Carlos Castaneda (1925–1998), especially *The Teachings of Don Juan: A Yaqui*

Way of Knowledge, published by the University of California Press in 1971. His *Journey to Ixtlan: The Lessons of Don Juan* (1972) was also Castaneda's PhD dissertation in the field of anthropology at the University of California.

Michael Harner (1929–2018) must also be included in this list. Harner's *The Way of the Shaman: A Guide to Power and Healing* (1982) is one of the most influential publications in the field of contemporary Euro-American shamanism. Among other representatives of shamanic practice who have a master's degree or even a PhD in anthropology are Nevill Drury, Steven Foster, Jonathan Horwitz, Felicitas Goodman, Gala Naumova, and Hank Wesselman.

The constitution of this shamanic field has been nourished by the processes that have preoccupied us in the previous two chapters, from the spiritual awakening of the 1960s and 1970s, the Human Potential Movement, transpersonal psychology, and experimenting with extraordinary states of consciousness to the establishment of centers such as Esalen, which can be considered dispositives in the consolidation of shamanic discourse. Today a whole range of spiritual practices is identified as shamanic, mostly with recourse to animistic and nature-based perceptions.

The Center for Shamanic Studies, founded by Harner and others in 1979 and renamed the Foundation for Shamanic Studies in 1987, is one of the dispositives in the institutionalization of shamanism. This not-for-profit organization offers workshops, sells books and instruments, and ensures that the "Harner method" is followed by all participants (which in turn has produced orthodoxies and heterodoxies). The "Harner method" refers to the technique of so-called core shamanism, developed by Michael Harner and others, which is supposed to represent the lowest common denominator of all shamanic cultures. The transpersonal psychologist Roger Walsh, whom I have already introduced in chapter 6, presents a cross-cultural definition that matches this universal approach: "Shamanism can be defined as a family of traditions whose practitioners focus on voluntarily entering altered states of consciousness in which they experience themselves or their spirit(s), traveling to other realms at will and interact with other entities in order to serve their community."[16] In core shamanism, practitioners use music—usually a large frame drum or rattle—to induce a state of expanded perception (not necessarily a "trance") that allows them to send their consciousness—or soul—into the lower world or the upper world, where they interact with entities that are invisible to ordinary consciousness. The relationship between the practitioners and their helping spirits, who are teachers in the "other world," is maintained and intensified through further work, through dance and singing, and practitioners try to bring these experiences into everyday life. Such spiritual experiences are by no means reserved for specialists, but are described by most seminar participants as experiences they have had.

During the journeys to the upper and lower worlds, the practitioners get to know other personal helping spirits and teachers who will later be by their side when they perform shamanic journeys for other people. They may search for a "power animal" or a spiritual entity who can help with the problem in question. This entity is then blown into the client's chest and forehead.

Being familiar with the shamanic journey and having a close connection with helpers from the "other world" are prerequisites for more advanced shamanic work, which is essentially therapeutic. These shamanic activities also comprise accompanying dying people before and after death, for instance. Finally, deep ecological work has received increasing attention in recent years; this includes not only intensive conversation with plant spirits, stones, and other entities considered animate beings in an animistic worldview, but also healing work for energetically disturbed places or the planet as a whole.

Contemporary shamanism in a narrower sense also comprises adaptations of Indigenous traditions (which has repeatedly led to controversial discussions). Especially in the United States and Canada, the Vision Quest, the Sun Dance, and other Native American traditions are widely embraced. In parallel, there are efforts in Europe to link contemporary shamanism to ancient Celtic semantics.

Discourses on nature and the soul—directly intertwined via the concept of animism—form the center of these shamanic practices in North America and Europe. Even if the step from "soul" to "consciousness," as in transpersonal psychology, can also be seen in shamanic discourse, the concept of the soul has by no means been dropped. One example of this is

Paul Uccusic, a representative of the European section of the Foundation for Shamanic Studies. "A very handy formulation in its brevity," says Uccusic, "is that the soul is simply the essence of the human, the living part of ourselves. With this we follow a modern view, which is also widespread in the holistic psychology of the western hemisphere. Extensions can be made as soon as they are necessary for our considerations."[17] The soul is therefore not identical with the whole person, but it is a "part" (albeit an essential one) that, together with physical parts, forms the totality of a healthy person. Following these explanations, Uccusic refers back to the universal soul and the "earth soul" as Leibniz and Kepler would have defined it, which he describes as "a principle of existence or life" or "as the bearer of that never-ending life force" that is also so important in shamanism. Finally, Uccusic adds a third view, common in "traditional shamanism," which assumes "that several souls or parts of souls exist within the human being. They can be separated from each other, and the absence of such a part is usually not without consequences, the most important of which is that the person becomes ill."[18]

The contradictions of these views on the soul—for instance, the fact that the universal or world soul is defined precisely by its indivisibility—need not concern us here. What is decisive is the discursive intertwining of European cosmologies of the soul with psychotherapeutic and transpersonal interpretations. Sandra Ingerman's work shows how this can be translated into concrete shamanic practice. Ingerman is also an important representative of the Foundation for Shamanic Studies. Like Uccusic, she starts with a simple definition: "The word *soul* has taken on many meanings. Here I use it simply to mean our vital essence, or as the *Oxford English Dictionary* (second edition) says, 'the principle of life, commonly regarded as an entity distinct from the body; the spiritual parts in contrast to the purely physical.' According to this authority, our language also regards the soul as the seat of the emotions, feelings, or sentiments."[19] Thus the soul is ontologized as a separate entity and described as the (spatially understood) "seat" of emotions. It is astonishing how strongly Ingerman's (and others') approach reflects the dichotomous separation of body and soul in European cultural history, despite the emphasis on Indigenous and holistic models that characterizes much of the shamanic milieu. Entirely in keeping with

Neoplatonic tradition, Ingerman locates the vital essence and thus the actual "life core" of the human being in the soul.

Ingerman also assumes that the soul can be split and that in extreme cases people can lose (parts of) their soul. "The basic premise is that whenever we experience trauma, a part of our vital essence separates from us in order to survive the experience by escaping the full impact of the pain."[20] Soul loss can occur for several reasons. "The soul may leave a child who does not feel loved, or who feels abandoned, by his or her parents. In one of my clients, soul loss was caused by a parent's continual yelling, in another by the physical pain of falling off a bicycle. A soul might leave the body to survive physical or sexual abuse. . . . Being sickly as a child or suffering serious or chronic illness can often indicate soul loss."[21]

With these ideas about the world and the soul's connection with it, shamanic discourse participates in the larger milieu of nature-based spiritualities. In this field, it is not only "animism" that has enjoyed a more positive reception; "magic" has also been received more positively, although in a different way. Let us have a closer look at these differences.

Magic and Neopaganism

One reason why contemporary shamanism is a link to nature-based spiritualities is the fact that the term *shaman* has more positive connotations than, for example, the terms *witch* or *magician*, and consequently some practitioners in the field of paganism and magic fall back on shamanic terms and like to call specialists who work with natural forces *shamans*, even if the concrete practice differs from the techniques of (neo)shamanism described earlier.

But a look at the genealogy of today's discourses on neopaganism and magic also shows that these cross-connections to shamanism definitely have older origins. Gloria Flaherty is of the opinion that Goethe's *Faust* and Herder's reflections on natural magic can be regarded as manifestations of shamanic knowledge in the eighteenth century. For her, *Faust* is "a consummate masterpiece that incorporates into the very scheme of European cultural evolution nearly everything the eighteenth century had heard or thought about shamanism. . . . It also magnificently brings shamanism together with philosophy, specifically Renaissance Neoplatonism. Furthermore, it synthesizes the legendary German shaman of yore with the mythical magus, thereby creating a modern emblem for enlightenment in all the possible senses of the word."[22] Even if we need not go so far as to consider *Faust* or Goethe's *Werther* to be shamans, the close discursive intertwining of magic and shamanism—with natural philosophy providing a language to connect them—is beyond doubt. This applies not only to the German-speaking context, but also to British cultural history, as Ronald Hutton has pointed out in relevant works on paganism, shamanism, and the druidic reception.[23]

In the nineteenth century, as we have seen, occultism also brought psychology into this web, which became stronger over the course of the twentieth century. The hidden forces of the soul became a crystallization point to which psychological and magical theories and practices adhered. Let me explain these connections with reference to Israel Regardie's (1907–1985) biography. Similarly to other biographies of his generation (for example, that of Abraham H. Maslow), Regardie's life and work illustrate the interweaving of discourse strands about the soul as well as the shift from Europe to North America in the second half of the twentieth century.

Israel Regardie was born in London, the son of Jewish Orthodox immigrants from the Ukraine. In 1921 the family immigrated to the United States, and Regardie studied art in Washington and Philadelphia. A thorough study of Hebrew gave him access to kabbalistic sources that would become important for his later work. In addition, he read a lot about theosophy, Hindu philosophy, and yoga. During this time, he also became a member of the Societas Rosicruciana in America.

His reading of occult works also brought him to the writings of Aleister Crowley (1875–1947). He read the first part of Crowley's *Book 4* and decided to contact the author. Crowley then invited him to Britain, and in 1928 Regardie became Crowley's personal secretary. Four years later the two went their separate ways. Although Regardie distanced himself from Crowley personally, he remained convinced of the importance of the latter's teachings. As early as 1931, Regardie wrote *A Garden of Pomegranates*, which can be considered a preliminary study for his later work *Qabalah*, and in which he processed his experiences with Crowley.

This was followed in 1932 by *The Tree of Life: A Study of Magic*, which reached a wide audience and brought Regardie fame as an author. In this book Regardie describes the soul and its hidden powers as the central "switchboard" of magical philosophy and practice.

> According to the traditional philosophy of the Magicians, every man is a unique autonomous center of individual consciousness, energy and will—a soul, in a word. Like a star shining and existing by its own inward light it pursues its way in the star-spangled heavens, solitary, uninterfered with, except insofar as its heavenly course is gravitationally modified by the presence, near or far, of other stars. Since in the vast stellar spaces seldom are there conflicts between the celestial bodies, unless one happens to stray from its appointed course—a very rare occurrence—so in the realms of humankind there would be no chaos, little conflict and no mutual disturbance were each individual content to be grounded in the reality of his own high consciousness, aware of his ideal nature and his true purpose in life, and eager to pursue the road which he must follow.[24]

The soul as the center of personal consciousness, energy, and will; a connection between individual personality and cosmic consciousness, which recognizes the whole of nature and connects the human with the starry world: all of the discourse strands I have already identified come together here in a larger web and are integrated into a magical worldview.

Regardie's position comes very close to Aleister Crowley's views. Crowley also sees magic as a central link between consciousness, will, and science. In this he follows James George Frazer's definitions. At the beginning of *Magick in Theory and Practice*, Crowley approvingly quotes Frazer's *The Golden Bough*:

> Wherever sympathetic magic occurs in its pure unadulterated form, it is assumed that in nature one event follows another necessarily and invariably without the intervention of any spiritual or personal agency. *Thus*

> *its fundamental conception is identical with that of modern science; underlying the whole system is a faith, implicit but real and firm, in the order and uniformity of nature. . . . Thus the analogy between the magical and the scientific conceptions of the world is close. In both of them the succession of events is perfectly regular and certain, being determined by immutable laws, the operation of which can be foreseen and calculated precisely*; the elements of caprice, of chance, and of accident are banished from the course of nature.[25]

This leads Crowley to his famous definition of magic: "*MAGICK is the Science and Art of causing Change to occur in conformity with Will.*"[26] Bernd-Christian Otto is therefore right when he emphasizes how strongly Crowley's views on magic reflect the religious-scientific convictions of the time—especially those of James George Frazer—positively transformed and presented with confidence.[27] Jason Ā Josephson-Storm argues in a very similar way, stressing Frazer's importance for both disenchantment theories and occult practice: "Freud and Weber would read Frazer, and out of his work they would fashion streamlined versions of the disenchantment thesis, stripped of its engagement with 'survivals' and 'reinventions.' But Aleister Crowley and company would read the same author—and even the same text—and from it, stage the revival of modern magic."[28] The discursive approach I am advocating in this book also confirms Josephson-Storm's observation that Crowley was

> effortlessly . . . able to combine Frazer's folklore studies with William James's pragmatic mysticism and Müller's sacred books, and make them the basis for his own magical and religious projects. He was able to do so in part because the works themselves shared habits of thought that were common to the esoteric movements of the period. A perennial mysticism appeared just below the surface in James's and Müller's writings, while Frazer had (perhaps inadvertently) placed magic on a level with science. The most important thing this shows is that religious studies has had ramifications and influences on the religious field, and it was far from disenchanting. If anything, it contributed to the birth of new religious movements and re-enchantment projects.[29]

This is exactly what I refer to as the discourse community that fostered the scientification of religion in the twentieth century. Moreover, I would like to add that the discourse strands of will–art–energy–science, prominent in Crowley and Regardie, were also strongly represented in the discourses of natural philosophy and natural science at the time (for instance, in the works of Haeckel, Ostwald, and Driesch). Thus Crowley and Regardie operated in a field of discourse that was much broader than the discourse on "magic" would suggest.

The Welsh occultist, Rosicrucian, theosophist, and writer Dion Fortune (1890–1946) proposed a definition similar to Crowley's and Regardie's: "Magic is the art and science of changing consciousness according to the Will." As Graham Harvey notes: "These definitions, but not necessarily their creators, remain popular among Pagan and other magicians. They suggest two facets of magic: attempts to change things or situations and attempts to change the practitioner. Some magicians stress one of these approaches over the other but rarely deny the value of either."[30]

One year after the release of *The Tree of Life*, Regardie became a member of Stella Matutina, a successor organization to the Hermetic Order of the Golden Dawn, thanks to Dion Fortune's mediation. He was initiated into the Hermes Temple in Bristol and quickly passed through the order's degree system to the rank of Adeptus Minor. But he left the order in 1934, again due to conflicts with its leadership. Regardie caused a scandal when he collected the order's confidential documents and made them available to the public in a large-scale publication. From 1937 to 1940, he worked on the four-volume work *The Golden Dawn*, which was intended as a complete representation of contemporary Euro-American magic (and which is available in several reprints and translations today). Regardie explained the breach of his vow of silence by saying that the Golden Dawn's magical system should be regarded as the cultural heritage of human history and should therefore be widely publicized.

At the age of thirty, Regardie returned to the United States and began studying psychology. He engaged extensively with psychoanalysis, psychotherapy, and psychiatry, with special emphasis on the teachings of Sigmund Freud, Carl Gustav Jung, and Wilhelm Reich. After several years of chiropractic work, he moved to Studio City, California, before retiring to

Sedona, Arizona, in 1981—one of the focal points of the so-called New Age movement.

In many of his works, Regardie tried to strengthen the connection between magic and psychology in two directions. On the one hand, he demanded a solid knowledge of psychology from magical practitioners; on the other hand, he recommended rituals from the magical tradition for use in psychotherapy.

Israel Regardie is a good example of a widespread conception of magic that sees the human soul and human consciousness as the center of the knowledge and willpower that magical practice aims to develop. I will demonstrate just how strong this discursive arrangement is with a perhaps counterintuitive comparison—a deliberate "grouping" in Foucault's sense—namely, with reference to a process theologian who writes at the turn of the twenty-first century. Arguing that there is factual evidence for parapsychological phenomena, David Ray Griffin reintroduces, as it were, the concept of the soul into theistic Christian spirituality. What Regardie views as willpower, Griffin sees as the freedom of the soul. "The idea of the soul's existence and freedom," he argues, "would not suffice to support spiritual discipline as very important if the soul's power were thought to be limited to its power to determine its own states, as some forms of epiphenomenalism have held." But this would be an underestimation of the soul's power. "While psychosomatic phenomena show that it has the power to influence much more of its body, and sometimes dramatically (as in stigmata and psychosomatic healing), thought-transference and psychokinesis show that the soul's power can be exerted directly on actualities beyond one's own body, both 'physical' things and other souls. This power can, in relation to living matter, either promote or discourage growth, either bless or curse." The energy "radiating from one's soul" embeds the soul in a large network of power. In this way, pious Christian spirituality presents the practitioner with the same responsibility as serious magical work: "For these reasons, the soul's self-discipline is extremely important."[31]

If we look at the broader context of nature-based spirituality, we find many variants of this arrangement, and the will—or the idea that one's will should change reality—is not always as much in the foreground as it is in magic. I have already pointed out that shamanism, in contrast, assumes that nature is animated and other beings have agency, or that communication with and respect for other entities is more important than bending them to the human will. In fact, shamanism often foregrounds the adaptation of the human will to the structures of planetary communication. The result is a closer proximity to biocentric ethics—understood as an alternative to anthropocentric positions—than one typically finds in magic. This is reflected, for instance, in the title of Graham Harvey's book *Contemporary Paganism*, which is subtitled *Listening People, Speaking Earth*. Such forms of paganism take up holistic considerations from deep ecology and natural philosophy, translating human participation in overall ecological contexts into ritual practice.

What this means concretely is aptly demonstrated in the publications of the Wicca movement, which—despite its internal differentiation—is the strongest and most visible form of the branch of nature-based spirituality that focuses on the feminine aspects of the divine. Books by Starhawk, Vivianne Crowley, Caitlín Matthews, and others have made a significant contribution to the ideas of the twentieth-century witchcraft movement finding a broad audience in the United Kingdom and the United States, and are now being received in many parts of the world. The influence of Carl Gustav Jung, Joseph Campbell, and others can hardly be overlooked; this has had a strong—and certainly controversial—impact on the interpretation of the feminine in Wicca.[32] Vivianne Crowley, one of the leading personalities in the British Wicca movement, combines her spiritual work with a Jungian psychological interpretation and her academic research. Ronald Hutton calls Vivianne Crowley "the closest thing that Britain possessed to an informal successor to Alex Sanders," one of the founders of Wicca.[33]

Nature's sacredness and enlivenment are a common denominator in pagan spirituality, especially its Wicca-oriented and shamanic forms. Sometimes this is even expressed in "declarations." In the volume *Voices from the Circle: The Heritage of Western Paganism*, edited by Prudence Jones and Caitlín Matthews, we find the following "Declaration of Principles":

> The Pagan religions of Europe, including Druidism, Wicca and Asatrú, are not derived from Christianity and have nothing to do with Satanism,

which is a perversion of Christianity, but are an independent religious path, celebrating the Godhead, which all religions seek to contact, particularly in its feminine form of the Great Goddess, Mother of all things. Pagans recognize the divinity of Nature and of all living things. Accordingly, they do not condone blood sacrifice, rape, child abuse, substance abuse or any other activity which would violate the integrity of another living being, but on the contrary would seek to help and protect anyone who had been the victim of such practices.

In particular, black magicians, who wilfully inflict harm on others, are not Wiccans, whatever they may call themselves. Nor do pagans of any kind draw their power from the Christian Devil. Witches and other Pagans use the natural forces of the mind and the earth for healing and rebalancing, exactly as do Oriental practitioners of meditation, yoga and alternative medicine.

The ancient Nature religions of Europe and around the world have arisen once more in our day to help heal the rift between humankind and our planet. They are working for balance and for harmony, and it behoves us all to help bring the wisdom of the Old Ways into the light in a worthwhile and workable form for the New Age.[34]

That the authors distance themselves from "Satanism," "cults," and "black magicians" has everything to do with the media craze over 'cults and sects' that occupied the public in the United States and Europe in the 1980s and 1990s. But this declaration also shows the extraordinarily strong discursive connections between animism, reverence for nature, the healing of the individual as well as the planet, and finally the expectation of a New Age under the banner of female spirituality (very much reminiscent of Richard Tarnas, as discussed earlier).

Our look at nature-based forms of contemporary spirituality has illustrated the extent to which ideas from the study of religion and the transpersonal movement have been translated into newly emerging spiritual practice. The soul plays a bridging role in this process, combining nature experience, animism, and holistic experience of the living planet with deep ecological and scientific knowledge. In magical practices, discourses on energy, power, synchronicity (in Jung's sense), and human will also come into play—discourses that had already been firmly established in occult contexts in the first half of the twentieth century.

In order to explore the full breadth of this field of discourse, I now turn to a number of important testimonies from literature and film. Fiction, poetry, and film form another cornerstone of the cultural and discursive history of the soul in the twentieth century; they take up relevant discourse strands and develop them further in their own ways.

9

THE SOUL AS A CENTRAL MOTIF IN LITERATURE AND FILM

Orders of knowledge about the soul arise on all levels of cultural communication. It hardly matters whether this communication is conducted in the genre of scientific argumentation, political agitation, or artistic expression. It is the interaction of these different channels or dispositives that determines which forms societal knowledge and discourse structures take. My historical reconstruction in the previous chapters has repeatedly shown the importance of literary and artistic contributions for European and North American discourses on the soul. In this chapter, I want to pursue these contributions further. In doing so, I am not applying a distinction between "art" and "popular culture," since such a valuation has no relevance to the question of cultural influences. Rather, what is at stake is how arrangements of knowledge about the soul are anchored in the genres of literary and artistic production, and how these productions in turn confirm or change societal orders of knowledge.

The discourse strands relevant to the theme of this book are found in literature and film in a variety of ways. Here I would like to turn primarily to North American and British literature, since this represents a decisive link between the religious-spiritual, philosophical, and political realms. The soul also plays an important role in the genres of science fiction and fantasy. All of these examples show how social conceptions of the soul have connected with ideas of nature, cosmos, and transcendent reality.

The Soul in North American Nature Writing

Since its colonization by European settlers, the religious interpretation of landscape and nature has played a significant role in North America. In the construction of "wilderness," both pristine nature and the Indigenous cultures of America have become a projection screen for European Christian ideas. The biblical motif of the desert and the wasteland as places of probation formed an image of nature that oscillated between fearful reverence and fantasies of domination. In his study *Playing Indian*, Philip J. Deloria impressively demonstrates that the "Indians" have been a central reference point for American identity from the outset.[1]

Even though this feature has lost little of its influence today and is still found in the American form of civil religion, convictions other than Puritanism have also affected the American perception of nature. The deep ecological and nature-spiritual practices that were the subject of the last two chapters draw on Romantic and transcendentalist traditions not dissimilar to those of nineteenth-century Europe. To be sure, the direct influence of Schelling's natural philosophy is hardly identifiable at first glance—between 1817 and 1837, for example, none of Schelling's works appears in the curriculum at Harvard College. Joseph L. Esposito states: "the more they the American transcendentalists learned about German philosophy the more impatient they became with its complexities and abstractions."[2] But through the mediation of Samuel Taylor Coleridge, Victor Cousin, John Elliot Cabot (Emerson's biographer), William Ellery Channing, and others, German idealism was also received in the United States. An intellectual discourse on nature emerged—and this discourse always had a political and aesthetic dimension in addition to a natural-philosophical component. The environmental movement in the United States stands in this tradition, which has always been religiously influenced, as Evan Berry has pointed out: "I argue not only that the formation of the American environmental movement drew on religious sources but that these sources are its central conceptual ingredients, playing crucial roles in shaping ideas about the natural world, establishing practices of engaging with environments and landscapes, and generating modes of social and political interaction. Specifically, I argue that an explicitly Christian understanding of salvation grounded the environmental movement's orientation toward nature."[3] This marks a difference from environmental movements in Europe.

In the nineteenth century, the American discourse was very strongly connected with Ralph Waldo Emerson (1803–1882) and Henry David Thoreau (1817–1862), and then, at the beginning of the twentieth century, with John Muir (1838–1914) and Aldo Leopold (1887–1948). Since these authors lost little of their influence over the course of the twentieth century, I want to briefly identify those aspects of their work that are most important for our topic.[4]

Many historians regard Ralph Waldo Emerson as a founding figure of modern American nature discourse. Henry David Thoreau and John Muir sought contact with him, and Concord, Massachusetts, became a center of literary and transcendental philosophical activity at the time. Emerson, who was strongly influenced by Emanuel Swedenborg's Christian mysticism, provided a theoretical-philosophical framework that Thoreau and Muir subsequently expanded in their practical work and their orientation toward the concrete experience of nature.

As far as the conception of nature in this tradition is concerned, Emerson's *Nature* (1836), which built on the foundation of various previous essays, is of particular interest. In 1971 the editors of the book called it "some sort of new testament for a new age."[5] This resonates with Bron Taylor, who forty years later regards Emerson as one of the earliest representatives of what he calls "dark green religion"; the themes in this discursive arrangement include "a mystical/pantheistic sense of belonging to nature, animistic perceptions, an epistemological call to experience nature directly, a belief that all natural objects can awaken reverence, a critique of the shallow and myopic human cultures that do not have such understandings, and a claim that spiritual understanding in nature comes more easily to children than adults."[6] Let us have a look at a few commonly quoted passages from *Nature*.

After Emerson's introduction made it clear that he understands "nature" as everything that is "not me," the first chapter—titled "Nature"—leads him straight to the point. It begins with the sentences: "To go into solitude, a man needs to retire as much from his chamber as from society. I am not solitary whilst I read and write, though nobody is with me. But if a man would be alone, let him look at the stars. The rays that come from those heavenly worlds, will separate between him and vulgar things. One might think the atmosphere was made transparent with this design, to give man, in the heavenly bodies, the perpetual presence of the sublime."[7]

The connection between solitude in nature, in wilderness, and the experience of absolute reality is a fundamental tone that can be heard throughout North American nature writing. Emerson's work ties in with the poetic and aestheticizing attitudes of European Romanticism as well as with the Orphic discourse on nature and art. According to Emerson, poetry's ability to depict the hidden forces of nature can only be fully developed in the immediate vicinity of nature, not in the big city. "At the call of a noble sentiment, again the woods wave, the pines murmur, the river rolls and shines, and the cattle low upon the mountains, as he saw and heard them in his infancy."[8]

Emerson thus regards nature as animated and also as a source of deep spiritual experiences that can be depicted in poetry and art. But he does not go so far as to take the step Thoreau and Muir were to take after him: sacralizing nature itself as a divine being. Rather, he remains in the Christian-Calvinist tradition, which subordinates nature as God's creation to the human being. This is in contrast to Thoreau, for "while Emerson's eye seeks to dominate or devour nature, Thoreau—reminiscent of Addison in this—seeks a pleasure that leaves both the eye and nature intact."[9]

With such a shift in emphasis, it is not surprising that Thoreau became the central reference point for the twentieth-century environmental-ethical movements. "Thoreau," as Lawrence Buell puts it, "is the patron saint of American environmental writing." He continues: "It is especially in his partial odyssey from environmental naïveté to comparative enlightenment that he looks most representative of his culture and mirrors most closely today's environmental ferment."[10] Works such as *Walden*, *The Maine Woods*, and *Cape Cod*, all of them written with reference to excursions and journeys into New England's natural landscapes, enjoy almost canonical status in North American literature.

The extent to which Thoreau sacralizes and ontologizes nature is easily seen in *Walden*. The animals the narrator encounters are ambassadors of a transcendent nature that allows the observant, empathetically open-minded human access to the perfect natural order. A goose, for example, "groping about over the pond," cackles "as if lost, or like the spirit of the fog."[11] This motif recurs like the migrating geese the following year, when the first-person narrator observes "some solitary goose in the foggy mornings" who was "seeking its companion, and still peopling the woods with the sound of a larger life that they could sustain."[12] And finally, there is Walden Pond itself, which (or who?) becomes a place of power, a presence that transforms and sanctifies everything. Thoreau speaks of Walden as "character" and "neighbor," as "great bed-fellow," as "hermit,"[13] as an eye and iris that close when the lake freezes over.[14] And when the ice thaws again, he cries out: "Walden was dead and is alive again."[15] The mystical identity between human and lake becomes obvious when the narrator looks into the reflective water and asks: "Walden, is it you?"[16] Buell rightly says that such passages go beyond playful metaphors "toward an almost animistic evocation of Walden as a living presence, not merely a 'neighbor' but a mentor, a role model."[17]

While Emerson—despite all his admiration for nature—"envisaged" a visual appropriation and mastery of nature, Thoreau aims to deepen and intensify the senses. Patient observation leads almost automatically to nature opening to the observer. This motif, which is found again and again in Thoreau's work, anticipates later concepts that speak of wilderness revealing itself to human beings who willingly expose themselves to nature. "You only need sit still long enough in some attractive spot in the woods that all its inhabitants may exhibit themselves to you by turns."[18] With formulations such as these, Thoreau contributes to discourses that would materialize a hundred years later in shamanism and in animistic descriptions of nature, as well as in environmental self-understanding. No matter how we might imagine the "true" Thoreau, the discursive impact of his work is beyond doubt. "Thoreau," Bron Taylor notes, "has become something of a Rorschach test for people—he is taken as an exemplary social-justice advocate, antiwar crusader, abolitionist, conservationist, deep ecologist, radical environmentalist, and even as an anarchist."[19]

This brings us to John Muir, the founder of the Sierra Club and one of the major pioneers in the establishment of American national parks. Muir was a devoted environmentalist, taking his motivation from an animistic and pantheistic perspective: "Among all the great American nature writers, he was the most striking case of spontaneous pantheism. Muir was not only a notional pantheist; he felt it experientially."[20] This is why Muir still is a highly important point of reference for nature-spiritual milieus today. This is no surprise, given statements like the following, which has been quoted again and again: "When we try to pick out anything by itself we find that it is bound fast by a thousand invisible cords that cannot be broken to everything else in the universe. I fancy I can hear a heart beating in every crystal, in every grain of sand and see a wise plan in the making and shaping and placing of every one of them. All seems to be dancing to divine music. . . . The clearest way into the Universe is through a forest wilderness."[21] Muir developed a biocentric ethics early on, when he went on his famous thousand-mile walk from Indianapolis to Florida in 1867–1868. In his report on this trip, published only after his death, we find statements such as the following: "Well, I have precious little sympathy for the selfish propriety of civilized man, and if a war of races should occur between the wild beasts and Lord Man I would be tempted to sympathize with the bears."[22]

Such statements have retained their influence on the self-understanding of radical environmentalists until the present day. But this is only one side of the coin; the other side is Muir's spiritualization of experiences in nature. "As his pantheism deepened through a variety of wilderness epiphanies," Bron Taylor notes, "he articulated deep ecological sentiments long before the term was coined."[23] Again, *A Thousand-Mile Walk* is a clear expression of this, for instance, when Muir describes the Sierra Nevada with these words: "You bathe in these spirit-beams, turning round and round, as if warming at a camp-fire. Presently you lose consciousness of your own separate existence: you blend with the landscape, and become part and parcel of nature."[24] Here the interface between animism, pantheism, and a ritualized experience of nature becomes visible, enabling humans to communicate with more-than-human nature.

In addition to Emerson, Thoreau, and Muir, Aldo Leopold has had a lasting effect on America's environmentalism, ecological concerns, and nature ethics. While Leopold's work initially focused on the scientific dimension, philosophical and spiritual observations of nature took on significant importance in his later work. Leopold's guiding principle is expressed in the famous call to think "like a mountain." The underlying idea is that only a biocentric recognition of all forms of life can actually implement a program based on ecological talk of diversely networked ecosystems. But mystical approaches to nature were by no means alien to Leopold. He referred to the Russian philosopher Peter D. Ouspensky, who conceived of the Earth as a living being and presented a union of science and religion based on the Buddhist model as an antidote to European dualistic thinking.[25]

In the second half of the twentieth century, these discourses continued in various ways. I have already referred to Joan Halifax, whose combination of animism, shamanism, and Buddhism is a good example of the tradition we are dealing with here. On communication with nature, she writes: "The sacred languages used during ceremony or evoked in various states of consciousness outside culture (if we are Westerners) can move teller, singer, and listener out of the habitual patterns of perception. Indeed, speaking in the tongues of sea and stone, bird and beast, or moving beyond language itself is a form of perceptual healing."[26]

We find very similar statements in the work of Gary Snyder (born 1930). As a poet and an activist, Snyder was an important contributor to the foundation of the radical environmentalist group Earth First!, but he also exerted a strong influence on more moderate and spiritually oriented ecological groups in the United States. Bron Taylor notes: "For Gary Snyder, it was not only a sacred earth that the observant heart could discern. It was even possible to hear its sacred voices. Through his poetry and prose Snyder expresses an idea that has become increasingly widespread among radical environmentalists: the belief that animistic trans-species communication is possible and can even help foster proper nature-human relationships."[27]

Snyder, who lived and studied Buddhism in Kyoto, Japan, from 1956 until 1969, regards Buddhism as a bridge to a mystical experience of nature that is ultimately animistic. This is why he calls himself a "Buddhist–animist."[28] But shamanism is also a good example of such experiences of nature, and Snyder argues that poetry and song are among "the few modes of speech" that provide "access to that other yogic or shamanistic view (in which all is one and all is many, and many are all precious)."[29] For our discussion, it is also interesting to note how Snyder describes communication with non-human persons in nature: "They don't talk to you directly, but you hear a different song in your head."[30] These statements belong to the same Orphic web I have already retrieved from the works of Rilke, Hesse, Klages, and others.

Another artist who made important contributions to this Orphic web is Denise Levertov (1923–1997). Growing up as the daughter of a Hasidic-Jewish father and a Christian mother in England, and from 1948 in the United States, Levertov was very interested in religious and spiritual themes—themes that characterized her more than twenty volumes of poetry, for which she received numerous awards.[31] Her father, who worked as a lecturer at the University of Leipzig (Germany) before the family immigrated to England, gave her a bilingual edition of Rilke's poems in 1942. Rilke became one of her most important points of reference, as she explained in an essay on "Rilke as Mentor" in 1975.[32] Her intellectual background was characterized by an interest in religion and mysticism on the one hand (she read Martin Buber and others) and in philosophy and politics on the other (Hannah Arendt was an important influence in this respect). But she always came back to Rilke, to whom she dedicated a poem in 1989 ("To Rilke"). She was convinced "that Rilke, like the Hasidim, believes that the creative power of human beings lies in their receptivity of the divine spirit."[33]

Levertov also shared Rilke's fascination for the Dionysian and for Orpheus. From the mid-1960s onward, she identified her name (Denise) with Dionysus. Dionysus and Orpheus became her most important artistic heroes.[34] All the strands of the Orphic discourse web are expressed in the poem "A Tree Telling of Orpheus," which Levertov published along with her own illustrations in *Stonybrook* magazine in 1968.[35] This long poem is reminiscent of Rilke's art in many ways. It describes the encounter with Orpheus from the perspective of a tree. The leaves of the tree begin to tremble and a transformation takes place, through which the tree learns the language of the birds: "I seemed to be singing as he sang, I seemed to know / what the lark knows." Subsequently, a fundamental mystical experience takes place during which "language / came into my roots." Orpheus's mystical power is so great that he sets the trees in motion, and they follow the god, singing, laughing, and longing. After Orpheus triggers this transformation in the forest, he disappears, and the rumor is that he was killed and his wood was processed into firewood, but that his head floats in the water and his singing can still be heard. The trees remain forever transformed.

Levertov spent the last eight years of her life in Seattle. The landscape of the American northwest coast, especially the view of the impressive Mount Rainier (whose Indigenous name is Tacoma), inspired and shaped her. She dedicated numerous poems to Mount Rainier, and the mountain became the crystallization point of her nature mysticism—as was similarly the case for Gary Snyder.[36] In one of these poems ("Open Secret"), she describes Mount Rainier as a mountain she can only see from a distance, despite the "scarring roads / humans have carved in its flanks." Mount Rainier works from the transcendent realm; his "power / lies in the open secret of its remote / apparition."[37]

John Gatta notes that "the Rainier poems enact reverence for a physically embodied, transhuman presence that urges us to admit human limitation even if we live in a technologically advanced place like Seattle."[38] Levertov also shares this element with Snyder. And just as for Snyder, for Levertov it is true that "whatever Rainier finally means to her, theologically or otherwise, she understands to be the product of a phenomenological equation involving her inward soul as well as outward geography."[39] It is precisely this motif of the reflection of one's inner soul in the outer landscape that I will discuss in more detail in the next section.

But before I come to that, let me bring in an example from the twenty-first century. In *Becoming Animal: An Earthly Cosmology*, the American philosopher, cultural ecologist, and performance artist David Abram combines poetry, philosophy, and spirituality in an attempt to develop a new understanding of human perception. The language of nonhuman characters also plays an important role in this animistic design. "Obviously," Abram maintains, "these other beings do not speak with a human tongue; they do not speak in words. They may speak in song, like many birds, or in rhythm, like the crickets and the ocean waves. They may speak a language of movements and gestures, or articulate themselves in shifting shadows."[40]

As soon as humans become aware of their "animal bodies," they discover a long-forgotten way to use their senses.

> When we stumble outside in the morning, rubbing our eyes free of sleep and gazing toward the wooded hillside across the valley, our eyes cannot help but feel their own visibility and vulnerability; hence our animal body feels itself exposed to that hillside, feels itself seen by those forested slopes. Such reciprocity is the very structure of perception. We experience the sensuous world only by rendering ourselves vulnerable to that world. Sensory perception is this ongoing interweavement: the terrain enters into us only to the extent that we allow ourselves to be taken up within that terrain.[41]

These are all indicators of the world's "enchantment"—animated nature connects with the human soul through sensual experience and generates its own form of knowledge, which is contrasted with the reductionist form of scientific knowledge. I will discuss further examples of this in the next chapter—examples that are located at the crossroads of science, literature, and political activism.

The Soul's Inner and Outer Landscapes: From Romanticism to Science Fiction

Levertov's work already intimates the reflection of the inner soul in the outer landscape. It is worth pursuing this theme further because it is a motif that runs through the literature of the nineteenth and twentieth centuries.[42] Parallel to the idea that the soul is the "true core" of the personality—which is itself a spatializing metaphor—the influential motif of the "soul as landscape" developed in the European history of religion and culture.[43] Following Plato's model of the world soul, an independent discourse consolidated between the Enlightenment and Romanticism, which compared the journey into the soul's interior to an exploratory journey into the hidden regions of the world. Novalis's work was important in this regard, as was Karl

Philipp Moritz's "psychological novel" *Anton Reiser*, written between 1783 and 1790. In this novel there is no strict separation between material and spiritual reality, or between the sphere of the human and the sphere of nature. The poem "The Wise Man's Soul" also describes how the soul can approach the divine in flight:

> The wise man's soul upon its course
> Did swing above the clouds so high
> And boldly heeded the strong force
> That drew it upward in the sky.
>
> It strives to fill the void forsooth
> Within itself that it can see
> And tries to still the lust for truth
> Which always flees elusively. . . .
>
> And now it feels its inner void
> Begin to fill with ecstasy;
> It swims about quite overjoyed,
> Rejoicing in divinity.[44]

Anton Reiser is an example of early Romantic literature, which describes the expansion of the soul and its reflection in the outer landscape, but also its journey into realms of reality inaccessible to normal consciousness. This thread can be traced further, into the literature of the twentieth century. A look at science fiction literature is particularly interesting. Rilke had already spoken about the fact that the outer world corresponds to an "inner-world space" (*Weltinnenraum*) that extends through "all beings." In the poem "Es winkt zu Fühlung fast aus allen Dingen" (Almost All Things Beckon to Feeling), he writes:

> Through all beings extends the *one* space:
> Inner-world space. The birds fly quietly
> through us. O me, who wants to grow,
> I look outside, and *in* me grows the tree.[45]

A quick look at science fiction literature, especially from the second half of the twentieth century, reveals that a journey to remote, unknown cosmic worlds is in many cases a metaphor for the journey to the hidden worlds of one's own soul. However, the motif of the "inner space" is not primarily "a science fiction theme, but rather a whole direction of style, which in the mid-1960s, starting with the British SF magazine *New World*, changed the face of the genre for good."[46] As a logical counterpart to "outer space," J. G. Ballard introduced this concept into science fiction literature. Ballard implemented this in a whole series of literary works in which he referred to Sigmund Freud, Samuel Beckett, Carl Gustav Jung, and others. Later, the "New Wave" movement was taken up in the American science fiction scene, where Roger Zelazny's *Lord of Light* (1967) and Samuel R. Delany's *The Einstein Intersection* became influential representatives of this new direction, which tied in with Neoromantic ideas.

Following the motto "the myths of antiquity point the way inwards,"[47] science fiction literature stages cultural and religious traditions. Sometimes authors consult relevant research in the study of religion; Roger Zelazny, for example, adapted James George Frazer, Joseph Campbell, and others.[48] Samuel R. Delany even makes this dimension visible in the novel itself: "The central subject of the book is myth. This music is so appropriate for the world I float on. I was aware how well it fitted the capsulated life of New York. Its torn harmonies are even more congruent with the rest of the world. How can I take Lobey into the center of this bright chaos propelling these sounds? Drank late with the Greek sailors last night; in bad Italian and worse Greek we talked about myths. Taiki learned the story of Orpheus not from school or reading but from his aunt in Eleusis."[49]

Ursula K. Le Guin (1929–2018) takes up and processes mythological themes in her extensive oeuvre, which includes science fiction as well as poetry and literary-political contributions. Le Guin masterfully succeeds in exploring the boundaries of the "science fiction" genre and using it as a means of expression for cultural, political, psychological, and ecological reflections. According to Le Guin, good science fiction literature "deserves the title of a modern mythology."[50] In addition to the mythology known from ancient stories and religious traditions, science fiction offers access to elements that Le Guin calls "submyths," which are "those images, figures, and motifs which have no religious or moral resonance and no intellectual or aesthetic value, but which are vigorously alive and powerful, so that they cannot be dismissed as mere stereotypes."[51] Examples include Superman, blond heroes with swords and magic powers, mad scientists, benign dictators, capitalists who buy and sell whole galaxies, friendly aliens, but also "every pointy-breasted brainless young woman who was ever rescued from monsters, lectured to, patronized, or, in recent years, raped, by one of the aforementioned heroes."[52] Le Guin notes that even if it is painful to call these figures "mythological," they are alive in books, magazines, pictures, films, and advertisements—in short, in our consciousness. "Their roots are the roots of myth, are in our unconscious—that vast dim region of the psyche and perhaps beyond the psyche, which Jung called 'collective' because it is similar in all of us, just as our bodies are basically similar."[53] "Genuine mythology" survived for thousands of years, and rationality was not able to destroy its inherent mystery. In contrast to "fake" mythology—in which, as Le Guin puts it, the blond hero could just as easily be identified as a gerbil—a real mythological hero, such as Apollo, answers the gaze. This is what happened to Rilke, who looked at a statue of Apollo, "and Apollo spoke to him. 'You must change your life,' he said. When the genuine myth rises into consciousness, that is always its message. You must change your life."[54]

Thus the best science fiction literature tries to build a bridge between the conscious and the unconscious, "so that the readers can make the journey too."[55] And by applying Jung's theory of archetypes to science fiction literature, Le Guin explains: "The artist who works from the center of his own being will find archetypal images and release them into consciousness. The first science fiction writer to do so was Mary Shelley. She let Frankenstein's monster loose. Nobody has been able to shut him out again, either. There he is, sitting in the corner of our lovely modern glass and plastic living room, right on the tubular steel contour chair, big as life and twice as ugly."[56]

The fictional outer world thus becomes a metaphor for inner processes of consciousness, the collective unconscious in turn becoming the central authority for understanding the world beyond the merely rational. In many of her works, Le Guin combines this with cultural-critical, feminist, and ecological statements. In this interpretation, wars and ecological destruction almost become an indication of the loss of the soul's integrity and wholeness. One example of this is the novella *The Word for World Is Forest*, published in 1976, in which Le Guin tells the story of the planet Athshe, whose inhabitants live in peaceful coexistence and in harmony with nature until they encounter the colonial aspirations of the earth's inhabitants (called "Terrans" in the book). The Athsheans base their way of life on the active awareness of their dream worlds and their unconscious, while the Terrans act on the basis of their separation between unconscious drives and conscious rationality, and are therefore open to all forms of violence and destruction. The Athsheans can only interpret the Terrans' behavior as evidence of mental disorder. The difference between the two groups is outwardly visible in the fact that the Athsheans live deep in the forest, which the Terrans experience as threatening and systematically seek to destroy (a cross-reference to the Vietnam War, of which Le Guin was extremely critical). In the epilogue to the novella, Le Guin says she wrote the text almost as the dictation of a tree entity ("a boss with ulcers") who wanted to denounce ecological destruction. Ian Watson concludes: "Out of the original impetus to write about forest and dream, then, has come a world-forest that—while nonsentient itself—nevertheless functions metaphorically as mind: as the collective unconscious mind of the Athsheans."[57]

The theme of animated forests and plant worlds full of consciousness finds further expression in Le Guin's *Vaster Than Empires and More Slow* (1971). At the same time, it has a longer prehistory in science fiction literature. Above all, Watson refers to Olaf Stapledon's *Star Maker*, published in 1937, arguing that Stapledon, "that mystical atheist," is of all the "arboriculturists" in science fiction literature most closely related to Le Guin.[58] Today, of course, we must also mention James Cameron's *Avatar*, released in 2009, which is to date the most financially successful film of all time. Like *The Word for World is Forest*, *Avatar* is about overcoming human spiritual alienation from nature. The film weaves together several themes that crystallize around the idea that the world is animated and full of consciousness, which humans need to appreciate and experience again.[59]

All the works discussed in this chapter have played a significant role in stabilizing a discursive arrangement that entangles "soul" and "consciousness" with discourse strands on nature (or, more specifically, on forests), science, spirituality, and the role of humans in the overall cosmic context. The popularity of these works is not at all surprising, since they represent the continuation of an order of knowledge that runs throughout the twentieth century and that has only increased in importance in the twenty-first century, in the face of the worsening global ecological crisis. This is why I will engage with Ursula K. Le Guin once more in the next chapter, around questions of the so-called Anthropocene. At this point, however, I want to take a brief look at another momentous event in the history of discourse on the soul—J. K. Rowling's *Harry Potter.*

Harry Potter's Soul

When Joanne K. Rowling (born 1965) sold the manuscript *Harry Potter and the Philosopher's Stone* to the London publisher Bloomsbury in 1995, it was the beginning of a success story that would exceed all expectations. To date, more than five hundred million copies of the Harry Potter books have been sold—only the Bible sells more copies. The film adaptations of the adventures of this young wizard—who fights the dark forces with the help of his friends and has to learn to handle his magical powers—are also among the most successful productions of all time. Rowling's positive portrayal of magical practice has caused controversy, but this has not diminished her success. The magical world of Hogwarts, in which virtues such as friendship, trust, and courage are held up to the forces of evil, became a submyth in Ursula K. Le Guin's sense—not just a stereotype, but a living idea that changes imaginary worlds and therefore also perceptions of reality.

In terms of discourse theory, one could say that the Harry Potter novels and films represent a discursive event in which knowledge about magic and occultism is rearranged; discourses on magic, hidden dimensions of reality, the dissolution of the separation between the material and the spiritual, and animate nature, combined with discourses on friendship, courage, and mental power, have created a discursive knot with an impact that can hardly be overestimated. Of course, this does not mean that there are no precursors to this discursive arrangement. On the contrary: my reconstruction of the cultural history of the soul indicates that the ground was well prepared for Harry Potter's success. This is particularly true for the discursive arrangements around occultism, but by adding further discourse strands—above all the personal virtues of the hero and his friends—the story takes on a dynamic of its own, which in turn legitimizes and reinforces the discursive formation on magic and occultism.

A closer look at the plot of the narrative shows that the soul plays a pivotal role. Questions about the soul stand at the center of the story: What is the soul? How does the soul relate to the body? Can the soul be divided? Can the soul be lost, and what happens to the body if it is? Can the soul be "stored" in objects? Is the soul the stronghold of good, or can it fall prey to evil?[60]

Harry Potter and the Deathly Hallows is the seventh and last novel in the Harry Potter series. When it was published in 2007, the novel broke all of its predecessors' sales records. Over ten million copies were sold within twenty-four hours in the United States and the United Kingdom alone. This book is particularly interesting when it comes to questions about the soul, as J. K. Rowling's heroine Hermione Granger explains very vividly what the soul is all about:

> "Look, if I picked up a sword right now, Ron, and ran you through with it, I wouldn't damage your soul at all."
>
> "Which would be a real comfort to me, I'm sure," said Ron. Harry laughed.
>
> "It should be, actually! But my point is that whatever happens to your body, your soul will survive, untouched," said Hermione.[61]

So the soul exists independently of the body and can survive physical death. It can also remain in a kind of intermediate stage—this applies to Lord Voldemort (the antagonist), but also to the wizard Nick. When Voldemort first attacks Harry with the Avada Kedavra curse, which leads to the destruction of his own body, Voldemort himself remains alive, albeit in a weaker form—"less than spirit, less than the meanest ghost," as Rowling says in *Harry Potter and the Goblet of Fire.*[62]

As for the discourse on the soul in Harry Potter, two other aspects of the story are important—namely, the "dementor's kiss" and the so-called Horcruxes. Dementors are a separate category of evil magical beings, and their kiss is one of the worst things that can happen to a human being. As their name suggests, dementors suck positive feelings and memories out of people, and they can even snatch entire souls from their bodies. In *Harry Potter and the Prisoner of Azkaban,* Lupin tries to help Harry understand this:

> "They call it the Dementor's Kiss," said Lupin. . . . they clamp their jaws upon the mouth of the victim and—and suck out his soul."
>
> . . .
>
> "What—they kill—?"
>
> "Oh no," said Lupin. "Much worse than that. You can exist without your soul, you know, as long as your brain and heart are still working. But you'll have no sense of self anymore, no memory, no . . . anything. There's no chance at all of recovery. You'll just—exist. As an empty shell. And your soul is gone forever . . . lost."[63]

The Horcruxes, for their part, take on an important role in Harry Potter. Rowling links their story to Tom Riddle's (the future Lord Voldemort's) wish to overcome death with the help of a Horcrux. In *Harry Potter and the Half-Blood Prince,* Professor Horace Slughorn explains to the young Riddle how a Horcrux works. " 'Well, you split your soul, you see,' said Slughorn, 'and hide part of it in an object outside the body. Then, even if one's body is attacked or destroyed, one cannot die, for part of the soul remains earthbound and undamaged.' "[64] Riddle insists on knowing more and wonders how the soul can be split. Slughorn responds: "By an act of evil—the supreme act of evil. By committing murder. Killing rips the soul apart. The wizard intent upon creating a Horcrux would use the damage to his advantage: He would encase the torn portion." This, he warns, is extremely dangerous because "the soul is supposed to remain intact and whole," and splitting it is "an act of violation, it is against nature."[65]

Horcruxes support a magician's magical powers, but the soul of a powerful wizard such as Voldemort is extremely hard to control. Hence Albus Dumbledore warns Harry: "Never forget, though, that while his soul may be damaged beyond repair, his brain and his magical powers remain intact. It will take uncommon skill and power to kill a wizard like Voldemort even without his Horcruxes."[66]

When a sorcerer has created a Horcrux by committing the greatest crime—murder—the soul is split and damaged. The soul represents the deepest layer of one's humanity, and it is this humanity that is touched by evil. As Dumbledore explains in response to Harry's question: "Lord Voldemort has seemed to grow less human with the passing years, and the transformation he has undergone seemed to me to be only explicable if his soul was mutilated beyond the realms of what we might call 'usual evil.' "[67] Accordingly, Tom Riddle is initially described as a handsome young man, but through the loss of his soul and as a result of his crimes, he is transformed into a being (Voldemort) who has lost all humanity. In *Harry Potter and the Goblet of Fire*, when Voldemort fully regains his body in the graveyard, he is described as "whiter than a skull, with wide, livid scarlet eyes and a nose that was flat as a snake's with slits for nostrils."[68]

What does all this mean for the cultural history of the soul? Even though fantasy and science fiction are genres that describe fictional worlds, they nevertheless make a decisive contribution to the establishment, stabilization, and adaptation of discursive arrangements, which in turn carry orders of knowledge. In the end, religions are no less fictional than literature and myth, and nobody doubts the discursive impact of religious traditions. If "discourses determine the conditions of possibility of what (in a social group at a certain period of time) can be thought and said," to revisit Franz X. Eder's apt definition,[69] a far-reaching event such as this series of novels must certainly be taken into consideration. The idea that the inner and outer worlds of the soul reflect each other—a prominent theme we find in science fiction literature—gives the soul a transpersonal and ultimately even a cosmic dimension. We also find this theme of the soul's suprapersonal connection in Harry Potter, in the sense that the soul is a vehicle for a universal life force that can be lost through one's encounter with evil. The strict dualism between good and evil, as well as between the material body and the immaterial soul—both decisive characteristics of Harry Potter's anthropology—perpetuates a Platonic-Christian discourse formation that can be traced back to Augustine and early Christian theology.

Literary discourse as a whole, as I have argued both in this chapter and in previous ones, is an important infrastructure for discourses on the soul. Toward the end of the twentieth century, literary discourse was connected with scientific and ecological themes and discussions in many ways. As I will show in the final chapter of this book, discourses on animism and cosmic consciousness also affected political, ethical, and cultural spheres. Today one can almost speak of a global discourse on the soul, which is constituted by concepts such as nature, awe, consciousness, intelligence, and ecology.

10

ECOLOGICAL MOVEMENTS, SCIENTIFIC AESTHETICS, AND THE SACRALIZATION OF THE EARTH

We all know "Earthrise," the photo depicting the "rise" of the planet Earth, as seen from the moon. To date, only twenty-four people have seen this event live, and yet it has become a global cultural asset. The Earth as a fragile "blue planet" in the midst of the endless darkness of space has become an iconic motif at the interface between natural science, spirituality, and environmental protection. When NASA, founded in 1958, published the photo after the first Apollo expeditions in 1967 ("Apollo" being a submyth in Ursula K. Le Guin's sense), it was a historically significant event. From politics to science to California's counterculture movement—in which Steward Brand had been pushing for such a photo for years and immediately included it in his *Whole Earth Catalog*—many people agreed that a new era had begun, one that also placed the protection of this fragile planet in a new context.[1] The images of the Earth were "an opportunity to bring the sacred and secular together into some new kind of alliance suitable to the modern age. The photographs that came back from the Apollo missions immediately catalyzed the rapid growth of what where the nascent fields of ecology and environmentalism."[2] Madalyn Murray O'Hair, founder of the American Atheists and the most vehement advocate for the separation of state and religion in the 1960s, protested against the Christian message that the astronauts associated with the images. Later Apollo astronauts were therefore admonished to refrain from religious expressions during their missions. Nevertheless we may ask, in Christopher Potter's terms: "Was the opportunity to acknowledge the numinous in a secular way lost, or has the battle, even now, hardly yet begun?"[3]

The ongoing impact of this iconography today can be seen in a YouTube video published on August 12, 2014, under the title "The Earth—A Living Creature (The Amazing NASA Video)."[4] The film was created by NASA's Scientific Visualization Studio (SVS), an institution whose mission is "to promote a greater understanding of Earth and Space Science research activities at NASA and within the academic research community supported by NASA."[5] For the video, NASA SVS used real-time data to predict the movement of a category 4 typhoon off the coast of China in 2005. The film shows the Earth as a blue planet around which white clouds move at high speed. To underline the understanding of the Earth as a "living being" (as indicated in the title of the film), we hear the sounds of breathing and a heartbeat. Spectral music underlines the visualization and enhances the animistic representation of the planet.

I could mention hundreds of similar examples here. Together they represent an aestheticizing connection between scientific research and the religious-spiritual understanding of nature.[6] Lisa H. Sideris calls this "consecrated science."[7] Instead of adhering to an artificial separation between the natural sciences and metaphysics or spirituality, recent studies show the mutual dependency of these cultural systems. From a discourse-historical point of view, it is hardly possible to maintain the purity and objectivity of scientific knowledge of nature; much more interesting is the question of how allegedly secular systems have themselves contributed to generating new cosmological, metaphysical, and spiritual interpretations. We have already observed this process in many places, and in what follows I will extend these trajectories even further. Needless to say, I cannot address the broad field of natural sciences and spirituality in its entirety in this chapter; instead, I will focus on the role of the "soul" and related concepts in this interplay. In such an analysis, discourses of animism and theories of agency deserve special attention, as they regard nature as animated and equipped with the ability to act. Often these discourses are accompanied by terms such as *wonder*, *life force*, or *mystery*, but also—again—with *consciousness*.

Rachel Carson, Barry Lopez, and the Wonders of Nature

Scientific publications are often completely incomprehensible to laypersons. This is one reason why their influence is usually relatively limited. When it comes to the broad impact of scientific research, it is much more productive to look at publications written for a wider audience. Moreover, in such publications scientists can more easily and extensively incorporate their own interpretations, which go beyond purely scientific analysis and concern philosophical, political, or religious understandings.

In this hybrid field, we find books with an enormously broad impact. At the beginning of the twentieth century in Germany, authors such as Ernst Haeckel, Wilhelm Ostwald, Hans Driesch, or Carl Ludwig Schleich wrote works of this kind. In the United States we see a similar movement, but in this case the authors focused even more closely on religious and environmental ethics. Not infrequently, scientific authors and publications were instrumental in the founding of environmental protection organizations.[8] This was the case with Theodore Roosevelt (who also published as a naturalist during his lifetime) and the Boone and Crockett Club, and for John Muir (Sierra Club), Mable Osgood Wright (Audubon Society of Connecticut), Aldo Leopold (Wilderness Society), and Edward Abbey (EarthFirst!). Evan Berry points out that most influential environmentalist movements in the United States today originated during this period. "Early twentieth-century American environmental thought is at times kaleidoscopic in its wildly combinatory fusion of religious imagery, scientific data, bourgeois social norms, and allusions to romantic poetry, but a close analysis of sources from this era yields tangible insight into the cultural substrata of our environmental imagination."[9]

In the history of the twentieth century, Rachel Carson (1907–1964) uniquely embodies this combination of science, spirituality, and environmental responsibility. Her book *Silent Spring*, published in 1962, in which she denounced the devastating effects of the pesticide known as DDT, is often described as the real beginning of today's American environmental protection movement. In the words of her biographer, Linda Lear:

> Carson could not be silent. . . . She could not stand idly by and say nothing when all that was in jeopardy, when human existence itself was endangered. That was the message that brought her to the Senate hearing room. That was what had sustained her for the past five difficult years. Rachel Carson was an unlikely person to start any sort of popular movement. She treasured her solitude, defended her privacy, rarely joined any organization; but she meant to bear witness. She wrote a revolutionary book in terms that were acceptable to a middle class emerging from the lethargy of postwar affluence and woke them to their neglected responsibilities. It was a book in which she shared her vision of life one last time. In the sea and the bird's song she had discovered the wonder and mystery of life. Her witness for these, and the integrity of all life, would make a difference.[10]

Silent Spring has an almost canonical significance for environmentalist movements today. But Carson's spiritual and ethical convictions are much more strongly expressed in her other works.[11] She loved literature and was an extremely skillful writer, and thus her works are well known to millions of people. Her writing began early, when Carson worked for the US Fish and Wildlife Service (FWS). In 1943, the agency established the nearly sixty-square-kilometer (about twenty-three square miles) Chincoteague National Wildlife Refuge, and Carson was instrumental in this conservation project. In an official FWS publication, she poetically describes the significance of the conservation project, referring to the role human "civilization" plays in the devastation of biological diversity—a topic that appears in many contemporary discussions under the term *Anthropocene*, and to which I will return. "This is waterfowl country," she writes. "This is the kind of country the ducks knew in the old days, before the white man's civilization disturbed the face of the land. This is the kind of country that is rapidly disappearing except where it is preserved in wildlife sanctuaries."[12]

In 1955, what is probably Rachel Carson's most personal book—*The Edge of the Sea*—was published. Although this book is just as saturated with information and is written with as much biological expertise as her other publications, here she writes in a liberated style, taking her readers on a journey to explore the shore as a very special habitat.[13] The elements relevant to our analysis come up very clearly right away. In the foreword, she writes:

> Like the sea itself, the shore fascinates us who return to it, the place of our dim ancestral beginnings. In the recurrent rhythms of tides and surf and in the varied life of the tide lines there is the obvious attraction of movement and change and beauty. There is also, I am convinced, a deeper fascination born of inner meaning and significance. . . . For us as living creatures it has special meaning as an area in or near which some entity that could be distinguished as Life first drifted in shallow waters. . . . To understand the life of the shore, it is not enough to pick up an empty shell and say "This is a murex," or "That is an angel wing." True understanding demands intuitive comprehension of the whole life of the creature that once inhabited this empty shell: how it survived amid surf and storms, what were its enemies, how it found food and reproduced its kind, what were its relations to the particular sea world in which it lived.[14]

In the short first chapter, titled "The Marginal World," Carson relates a number of spiritual experiences that transform her scientific reflection into an animistic one. It is worth citing one of these in full:

> The shore at night is a different world, in which the very darkness that hides the distractions of daylight brings into sharper focus the elemental realities. Once, exploring the night beach, I surprised a small ghost crab in the searching beam of my torch. He was lying in a pit he had dug just above the surf, as though watching the sea and waiting. The blackness of the night possessed water, air, and beach. It was the darkness of an older world, before Man. There was no sound but the all-enveloping, primeval sounds of wind blowing over water and sand, and of waves crashing on the beach. There was no other visible life—just one small crab near the sea. I have seen hundreds of ghost crabs in other settings, but suddenly I was filled with the odd sensation that for the first time I knew the creature in its own world—that I understood, as never before, the essence of its being. In that moment time was suspended; the world to which I belonged did not exist and I might have been an onlooker from outer

> space. The little crab alone with the sea became a symbol that stood for life itself—for the delicate, destructible, yet incredibly vital force that somehow holds its place amid the harsh realities of the inorganic world.[15]

Put differently, this experience changes Carson's sensual perception; she grasps the essence of the ghost crab's inner being, and time seems to stand still—or perhaps she has access to transhistorical time, the time before humans appeared on this planet. All of these are characteristics of a mystical experience. At the end of the chapter, Carson summarizes:

> There is a common thread that links these scenes and memories—the spectacle of life in all its varied manifestations as it has appeared, evolved, and sometimes died out. Underlying the beauty of the spectacle there is meaning and significance. It is the elusiveness of that meaning that haunts us, that sends us again and again into the natural world where the key to the riddle is hidden. It sends us back to the edge of the sea, where the drama of life played its first scene on earth and perhaps even its prelude; where the forces of evolution are at work today, as they have been since the appearance of what we know as life; and where the spectacle of living creatures faced by the cosmic realities of their world is crystal clear.[16]

Carson's book describes the different types of beach, where life in the water and life on land meet and influence each other in many ways. The final chapter, titled "The Enduring Sea," contains some of the most famous passages in Carson's oeuvre. Once again she maintains: "Contemplating the teeming life of the shore, we have an uneasy sense of the communication of some universal truth that lies just beyond our grasp."[17] She is concerned with the deeper meaning of scientific observation, in which life's emotion, spirituality, and mysticism are united. "The meaning haunts and ever eludes us, and in its very pursuit we approach the ultimate mystery of Life itself."[18]

Shortly after publishing *The Edge of the Sea*, and before she began work on *Silent Spring*, Carson wrote an essay that appeared in *Woman's Home Companion* in 1956 under the title "Help Your Child to Wonder." Later reedited and published as *The Sense of Wonder*, which has been translated many times, this essay is another example of Carson's combination of scientific analysis, literary empathy, and feeling of responsibility for the future of the planet. The spiritual and mystical aspects of contemplating nature are also very clearly expressed here, as Linda Lear states in her introduction to the new edition: "Ultimately Carson believed that the value of contemplating the awe and beauty of nature was in the spiritual renewal, inner healing, and a new depth to the adventure of humanity."[19]

Carson's work weaves together several discourse strands that are vehicles of the spiritual contemplation of nature and express an animistic attitude toward nature. From these quotations we can distill the discursive elements of nature–evolution–beauty–contemplation–wonder–awe–spirituality–healing–meaning–significance–life–life force–mystery–cosmos–universal truth. With this arrangement, Carson demonstrates her close proximity to the literary discourse on nature in North America, which I sketched in the previous chapter. Carson's style is both scientific and literary. Discourse analysis indicates how artificial the separation between these cultural spheres and practices actually is.

This brings me to Barry Lopez (1945–2020), another influential author at the intersections of biology, literature, and environmental ethics. His early work *Of Wolves and Men* (1978) was very successful and was a finalist for the American National Book Award. Lopez had his breakthrough with *Arctic Dreams: Imagination and Desire in a Northern Landscape*, which won the National Book Award for Nonfiction in 1986 and became a best seller. Numerous awards followed, and in 2019 Lopez published *Horizon*, a long-term study and a reflection on his experiences and the state of the planet. *Horizon* was listed among the Best Books of the Year by both *The New York Times* and NPR. In March 2020, Lopez was elected to the American Academy of Arts and Letters. There can be no doubt that he is one of the most important American authors when it comes to ecology and the human relationship to nature.[20] Lopez is relevant to our topic because—like Rachel Carson—he crosses the boundaries of scientific analysis and exemplifies a spiritual attitude toward nature, which takes up discourses on the soul and brings them into environmental-ethical conversations. His work is a true example of Orphic science.

For Lopez, "landscape" is not merely a physical-material reality, but also a world of experience and a mirror for human desires and dreams (there are strong links here to the literature discussed in the previous chapter, which deals with parallelism between inner and outer landscapes). The Arctic landscape, which in its (supposed) barrenness runs counter to any romanticization of "lush nature" and seems pretty indifferent to the human visitor, is a particularly good example of landscape as a space of experience in which physical and mental levels of awareness merge. In *Arctic Dreams*, Lopez makes the invisible landscape visible and tangible. He refers to Euro-American cultural traditions and compares them with Indigenous experiences in the Arctic landscape.

> A Lakota woman named Elaine Jahner once wrote that what lies at the heart of the religion of hunting peoples is the notion that a spiritual landscape exists within the physical landscape. To put it another way, occasionally one sees something fleeting in the land, a moment when line, color, and movement intensify and something sacred is revealed, leading one to believe that there is another realm of reality corresponding to the physical one but different.
>
> In the face of a rational, scientific approach to the land, which is more widely sanctioned, esoteric insights and speculations are frequently overshadowed, and what is lost is profound. The land is like poetry: it is inexplicably coherent, it is transcendent in its meaning, and it has the power to elevate a consideration of human life.[21]

With this combination of poetry and scientific knowledge of nature, Lopez stands in the tradition of the Orphic web, which ranges from Goethe's "tender empiricism" to the work of Rilke, Levertov, and others. The landscape is simultaneously inaccessible and accessible. In order to experience its hidden dimensions, human observation must engage with the landscape emotionally. Lopez writes about this approach:

> Our perceptions are colored by preconception and desire. The physical landscape is an unstructured abode of space and time and is not entirely fathomable; but this does not necessarily put us at a disadvantage in seeking to know it. Believing them to be fundamentally mysterious in their form and color, in the varieties of life inherent in them, in the tactile

> qualities of their soils, the sound of the violent fall of rain upon them, the smell of their buds—believing landscapes to be mysterious aggregations, it becomes easier to approach them. One simply accords them the standing that one grants the other mysteries, as distinguished from the puzzles, of life.[22]

This idea of the landscape as mystery, as opposed to merely a puzzle, is reminiscent of Rachel Carson's description of "wonder." For Lopez, this wonder becomes accessible in a silent opening of the senses. He remembers a man in Anaktuvuk Pass who, when asked what he did when he first visited a new landscape, replied: "'I listen.' That's all. I listen, he meant, to what the land is saying. I walk around in it and strain my senses in appreciation of it for a long time before I, myself, ever speak a word. Entered in such a respectful manner, he believed, the land would open to him."[23] Respect, recognition, opening—these are the characteristics of a holistic knowledge of nature. For Lopez, humility is another necessary condition for grasping the landscape's spiritual dimensions. One of the most-cited passages in *Arctic Dreams* is the author's description of how he instinctively bows to a horned lark. This bow soon became a regular ritual: "I took to bowing on these evening walks. I would bow slightly with my hands in my pockets, toward the birds and the evidence of life in their nests—because of their fecundity, unexpected in this remote region, and because of the serene arctic light that came down over the land like breath, like breathing."[24] John Gatta states that this passage appears in retrospect as "the book's defining expression of environmental reverence."[25] I agree, also because the theme of bowing is taken up again at the very end of *Arctic Dreams*; looking at the Arctic coastal landscape, Lopez notes: "I bowed. I bowed to what knows no deliberating legislature or parliament, no religion, no competing theories of economics, an expression of allegiance with the mystery of life."[26] This sentence could have been taken from Rachel Carson's *The Edge of the Sea*. The same applies to Lopez's encounter with a collared lemming: "Whenever I met a collared lemming on a summer day and took its stare I would think: Here is a tough animal. Here is a valuable life. In a heedless moment, years from now, will I remember more machinery here than mind? If it could tell me of its will to survive, would I think of biochemistry, or would

I think of the analogous human desire? If it could speak of the time since the retreat of the ice, would I have the patience to listen?" He goes on: "I lay there knowing something eerie ties us to the world of animals. Sometimes the animals pull you backward into it. You share hunger and fear with them like salt in blood. . . . Few things provoke like the presence of wild animals. They pull at us like tidal currents with questions of volition, of ethical involvement, of ancestry."[27]

In *Horizon*, published thirty years later, Lopez expresses the same idea after encountering a mullet. In a "Carsonesque" way, he writes: "That minute and a half with the orange-eyed mullet was an experience my body as well as my mind continued to remember. Here, for me, was the edge of the miraculous. In every corner of the world there was such resplendent life, unexpected, integrated, anonymous."[28] We may compare these passages with Hermann Hesse's poem "Sometimes," which I quoted in chapter 2, ending with the words: "My soul turns into a tree / And an animal, and a cloud bank. / Then changed and odd it comes home / And asks me questions. What should I reply?"[29] We are dealing here with exactly the same discursive structure that was already fully developed at the beginning of the twentieth century, but that at the end of the century would be intertwined with new biological and ecological insights.

Lopez represents an idea of nature that regards the more-than-human world as animated, approaching it with the understanding that intelligence and consciousness are not limited to the human species. This leads to an attitude of humility and to the recognition of nature as something greater than the human.[30] In a passage in *Arctic Dreams*, Lopez describes this attitude in religious language:

> There is a word from the time of the cathedrals: agape, an expression of intense spiritual affinity with the mystery that is "to be sharing life with other life." Agape is love, and it can mean "the love of another for the sake of God." More broadly and essentially it is a humble, impassioned embrace of something outside the self, in the name of that which we refer to as *God*, but which also includes the self and *is* God. We are clearly indebted as a species to the play of our intelligence; we trust our future to it; but we do not know whether intelligence is reason or whether intelligence is

> this desire to embrace and be embraced in the pattern that both theologians and physicists call God. Whether intelligence, in other words, is love.[31]

The human self in this passage appears synonymous with what others call the human soul, which is mystically connected with the soul of the divine. Often the simple *presence of place* reveals the mystery, without the need for a cognitive understanding of it.[32] At the same time, Lopez by no means propagates a fusion of the human sphere with the world of animals and nature in general. Love of nature presupposes the distance between human beings and the nature they contemplate. For Lopez, anything else would amount to the colonization of the more-than-human world in an act of anthropocentric projection and appropriation. Horned lark and collared lemming are independent actors in an interplay of life and consciousness. This interplay opens up the sacral levels of landscape and nature. Becoming aware of this life and humbly opening up enable human actors to realize the mystery of life.

These opinions clearly come to the fore in *Horizon* as well. One example is Lopez's appreciation of the mysterious life of a stone. "Embedded in the system of belief that over the years came to replace (or perhaps augment) religion for me is a conviction that the numinous dimension of certain inanimate objects is substantial, as real as their texture or color. This is not, I think, an illusion. One might not be able to 'squeeze meaning' from a stone, but a stone, presented with an opportunity, with a certain kind of welcoming stillness, might reveal, easily and naturally, some part of its meaning."[33] Would Lopez endorse Haeckel's idea of the ensoulment of crystals? Probably not, but he is part of the same discourse community when it comes to the mysterious life of stones.

Mythopoetic Science and the "Epic of Evolution"

While Rachel Carson, Barry Lopez, and others—harking back to Neoromantic positions—promoted human modesty and admiration of nature and the cosmos, other scientists have created a large-scale narrative on the evolution of the cosmos and of humankind, which is almost religious in character. This tendency is particularly clear in the work of the evolutionary biologists Richard Dawkins (born 1941) and Edward O. Wilson (born 1929). Interesting for us here is the fact that these writers—particularly Dawkins—base their work on a radical criticism of all religious and creation-theological mythology but develop a scientific mythology that serves a function quite similar to old-time religion. Dawkins and Wilson are convinced that the emergence of the rationalistic natural sciences has put an end to the "grand narratives" of religious tradition. In keeping with Max Weber's disenchantment thesis, they maintain that "enlightened humans" still feel the need to connect their lives to larger frames of meaning in order to lend them importance and significance. One response to this demand is what Dawkins and Wilson call "mythopoetic science": a science that integrates scientific facts into a grand narrative. This narrative has been given different names, from the "Epic of Evolution" to the "Story (or Journey) of the Universe" to "Big History."[34] What they all have in common is what Martin Eger defines as "epic science"—namely, a narrative that begins with the big bang and then, in various stages, heads toward the arrival of human culture. An omniscient narrator thereby reveals the ultimate, authoritative story of human evolution.[35] In her study on mythopoetic science, Lisa H. Sideris argues: "These narratives define humans as the part of the universe that has become conscious of itself. Humans' dawning geological consciousness, combined with empirical knowledge of nature, will enable us to guide the future unfolding of the cosmic process, allowing our species to live in greater intimacy and harmony with the Earth."[36]

Besides Dawkins and Wilson, the theologian Michael Dowd and the ecologist and activist Connie Barlow are the primary representatives of this grand narrative. "Science banishes mystery and the miraculous, but the knowledge it returns is itself a thing of wonder and the stuff of magic. These claims receive enthusiastic support from some proponents of the Epic of Evolution. Self-styled 'evolutionary evangelists' Dowd and Barlow endorse the Epic as a 'religion of reality' and hail Dawkins as its courageous prophet. Converts to this religion of reality are not believers but 'knowers.' "[37] Questions of cosmos, nature, and consciousness are of particular importance for the cultural history of the soul, as they perpetuate discursive arrangements that were clearly expressed in the transpersonal movement and in the work of Ervin Laszlo, as described earlier.

The website the Epic of Evolution is proof of this interpretation. Its curator, the evolutionary biologist Cathy McGowan Russell, concisely summarizes what is at stake for Wilson and others.

> The Epic of Evolution is the emerging cosmology of the universe based on discoveries from all scientific disciplines. While many people think of evolution solely in terms of biological evolution, the Epic of Evolution also includes the evolution of matter, stars, galaxies, human culture and imagination. This story begins with the Great Radiance (a.k.a. Big Bang) and tells about the emergence of energy, matter, galaxies, stars, planets, chemicals, life, symbiosis, human culture, and our dreams for the future. A central idea of the Epic of Evolution is that evolution has a direction. This directionality is driven by the flow of energy and time. Paradoxically, this same energy flow that causes entropy of the universe is the same energy that drives the evolution of complexity. Energy flow drives parts of the universe toward greater complexity. On earth, energy flow drives life toward toward toward [*sic*!] greater cooperation and greater consciousness. Over time, human culture appears to be moving toward greater awareness and greater compassion.[38]

The basic components of this narrative are science–evolution–energy–matter–cosmos–life–consciousness (which replaces "soul" in this arrangement). Thus the representatives of mythopoetic science are doing something quite similar to what Wilhelm Ostwald was doing two generations before them: they conceive of "science" as the royal road to spiritual knowledge of the world, and "energy" as a universal pulsating force in matter and spirit.

In this context, it is also interesting to see how Loyal D. Rue presents the Epic of Evolution. Referring to E. O. Wilson, he argues that through the combination of materialistic science and higher knowledge of life's ultimate meaning, and due to recent breakthroughs in integrative science, it is possible "to construct a coherent narrative of the emergent properties of matter, life, and consciousness."[39] His book *Everybody's Story: Wising Up to the Epic of Evolution* (to which E. O. Wilson contributed a foreword) also programmatically states that now is the time to communicate the evolution of matter, life, and consciousness to a broad public.[40] This is a direct continuation of the discourse arrangements of monism and vitalism, as I have already analyzed them in previous chapters.

As a bridge between the monistic and vitalist discourses of the first half of the twentieth century and these new universal histories of science and consciousness, one can consider the work of the Jesuit and paleontologist Pierre Teilhard de Chardin (1881–1955), which is repeatedly conjured up in the Epic of Evolution. The other crucial reference point is the theologian and cultural historian Thomas Berry (1914–2009). Edward O. Wilson and Loyal D. Rue, Michael Dowd and Connie Barlow, as well as Brian Swimme and Mary Evelyn Tucker in their project Journey of the Universe, all take up these contributions; they describe the evolutionary process as the merging of matter and spirit, energy and consciousness in a great creative event, the goal of which is that humanity becomes aware of its role in the cosmos.[41]

As I have already mentioned, these discourse strands can be traced back to early twentieth-century debates. Genealogically and in terms of the history of ideas, however, their history goes back much further. That the divine order of creation is only completed in the salvific-historical process of human recognition of this same order—in other words, that God comes to full realization only in the human being—is an old idea in Jewish kabbalah. Hegel took this idea from kabbalistic thinking and proclaimed that the Absolute Spirit unfolds in the historical process, ultimately recognizing itself at the fulfillment of history. The Epic of Evolution stands in this kabbalistic-Hegelian tradition, but it presents the philosophical-religious history of salvation as the grand narrative of natural science, evolution, and cosmology.

The Globalization of Dark Green Religion

All the personalities described in this chapter—each in their own way—have contributed to the stabilization of an order of knowledge in which the human role is redefined in interaction with the more-than-human world and with the cosmos. Discourses on the soul enter this arrangement via concepts of animism and consciousness. Global ecological challenges make this redefinition more urgent than ever, and it is therefore not surprising that these scientific and literary contributions have been taken up across a large swathe of the public sphere. They have become part of worldwide political and cultural discourses. Bron Taylor describes these processes as the "global greening of religion" and the globalization of what he calls "dark green religion." In contrast to "green religion," which considers environmentally friendly behavior to be in harmony with religious duties, Taylor defines "dark green religion" as the conviction that nature is sacred, that it represents an intrinsic value, and that it therefore deserves reverence and protection.[42] Hence this is less a "religion" in the conservative sense of the term than it is a set of beliefs and corresponding actions, which derive from nature's intrinsic value and its spiritual significance for the human being. From the perspective of discourse theory, we could describe "dark green religion" as a discursive arrangement that generates meaning and orders of knowledge related to the more-than-human world; these orders of knowledge reach broad audiences in a wide variety of social circles and offer guidance for action on individual, cultural, and political levels.

Discourses on the soul play a considerable role in this arrangement, again especially when it comes to descriptions that conceive of nature as animate and endowed with consciousness. The link to the soul is often explicit, as in the surfing community that cultivated the concept of "soul surfing"—the idea that surfing "puts you one with nature, clears your soul of bad vibes, and can make you a more humble person."[43]

Since the 1980s, such arrangements have increasingly affected international politics. The work of the United Nations Educational, Scientific and Cultural Organization (UNESCO), founded in 1945, shows this very clearly. In 1988, for example, UNESCO published its report *Man Belongs to the Earth: International Cooperation in Environmental Research*, which was one outcome of the Man and the Biosphere program launched in 1971. The report not only describes worldwide ecological problems that require active political intervention, but also refers in a variety of ways to scientific, philosophical, and ethical positions that address humanity's place in the overall ecological process. The report celebrates Ernst Haeckel as the thinker who brought the concept of "ecology" into the discussion, even though it was only really embraced in the 1930s and 1940s, "with such landmarks as Lindeman's classic paper of 1942 on the hierarchical trophic (food chain) structures of ecosystems, which laid emphasis on the flow of energy through ecosystems and its links with ecological succession."[44] The other icon in this report is Rachel Carson, whose *Silent Spring* "was to become a watershed in the brief history of ecology."[45] The title of the report is a reference to a speech given by Chief Seattle, whose words, allegedly spoken in 1854, have had a huge impact to this day (even if the speech was never given in this form—an example of the difference between the discursive production of knowledge and historical facts): "The Earth does not belong to man; man belongs to the Earth."[46]

Man Belongs to the Earth goes far beyond political and scientific questions, propagating the veneration of what is considered sacred nature. In the chapter on threatened mountain ecosystems, we find the following:

> From Fujiyama to Olympus to Sinai, every high mountain has been looked upon with awe and reverence by those who live within its shadow. Indeed, so strong has been this instinctive sense of the sacred nature of mountains that even the plainsmen of Mesopotamia felt the need to construct artificial mountains, the "ziggurats," in an attempt to reach upwards to the gods.
>
> Perhaps this is because each one of us has his [*sic*!] own interior mountain to climb, to enjoy and to reverence. Even today, when men [*sic*!] have stood upon the summit of mount Everest, the challenge and the reverence remain. A mountain must be climbed, revered and preserved, in the famous mountaineering phrase, "because it's there."[47]

The report describes not only mountains, but also islands as "sacred," and refers to Christian pilgrims' search for paradise.[48] Ascending a mountain, venerating nature in the "outer" world as a reflection of processes within one's soul, or in an attempt to unite with the gods—the discursive entanglement of nature and the soul could hardly find clearer expression in a political document. Nevertheless, the language of the report is gendered in a highly problematic way. The aggressive description of male subjugation of the mountain ("A mountain must be climbed") blatantly contradicts the call to venerate nature and to critically assess the human factor in the destruction of global ecosystems.

One year before this report appeared, the United Nations had already published a report titled *Our Common Future*, better known as the "Brundtland Report" after the name of the commission's chairperson, the then-acting Norwegian prime minister Gro Harlem Brundtland. This report coined the term and defined the concept of "sustainable development" for subsequent discussions.

Under the headline "Survival," the report says nature is "bountiful" but also "fragile and finely balanced." It asserts that we have reached the limits of this balance in many places; "we must be ever mindful of the risk of endangering the survival of life on Earth."[49] According to the report, the issue goes beyond the protection of nature and touches on humanity's moral obligations. The report demands that "the case for the conservation of nature should not rest only with development goals. It is part of our moral obligation to other living beings and future generations."[50] Despite the otherwise careful diplomatic language of the report, Bron Taylor rightly interprets this as an example of dark green religion and notes that this is one of the first declarations of a biocentric attitude in an official UN document.[51] This is confirmed once again when the report reproduces an objection from the audience during a public reading in Jakarta on March 26, 1985:

> We in Asia, I feel, want to have an equilibrium between the spiritual and material life. I noticed that you have tried to separate religion from the technological side of life. Is that not exactly, the mistake in the West in developing technology, without ethics, without religion? If that is the case, and we have the chance to develop a new direction, should we not advise the group on technology to pursue a different kind of technology which has as its base not only the rationality, but also the spiritual aspect? Is this a dream or is this something we cannot avoid?[52]

The call to unite the spiritual and material dimensions of life and to connect technology with ethics or religion had an impact on many conferences and documents in the period following this report. That is particularly true of the United Nations Conference on Environment and Development (UNCED), held in Rio de Janeiro in 1992; the follow-up conference in New York in 1997; and the World Summit on Sustainable Development, held in Johannesburg in 2002. During the conference in Rio, the Earth Charter was conceived as a way of promoting and monitoring sustainability and environmental protection. Support came from influential representatives from the fields of science and politics—for example, from Russian president Michael Gorbachev, who in 1997 expressed himself as an outspoken advocate of nature religion. "It should not be surprising, therefore," Bron Taylor notes, that the Earth Charter, the final version of which was presented in Johannesburg in 2002, "was the most impressive international example yet of dark green religion."[53]

Parallel to these political initiatives, and often in direct engagement with them, many environmentalists also display a strong spiritual and animistic understanding of the more-than-human world. When it comes to the various forms of animism, we can find all the strands Taylor distinguishes in these descriptions. Some people give a more naturalistic explanation, starting from nature's "life force" without endowing it with religious concepts; others present a strongly spiritual description that sacralizes nature. What Taylor calls "Gaian earth religion" is also easy to substantiate—namely the view that the Earth is an animated, conscious system whose knowledge and vital energy comes into contact with human consciousness in many ways.[54] The term *Gaia* refers to the ancient Greek Earth goddess, who has been "resurrected," as it were, by James Lovelock's "Gaia Hypothesis." In conjunction with the "Earthrise" iconography, this results in a spiritual interpretation of earth's (or Earth's) intelligent system, which is clearly visible in the Wikipedia entry on the "Gaia hypothesis," where a photo of the blue planet is used for illustration.[55] But as influential as Lovelock's "hypothesis" is, it does not represent the central cord of the discursive knot. Others, such as the already-mentioned Ervin Laszlo, have made equally important contributions.[56]

As an instance of the concrete enactment of these ideas, we can look to the famous example of Julia Butterfly Hill, who on December 10, 1997, climbed a huge redwood tree called "Luna," which had previously been occupied by Earth First! activists. Julia Butterfly Hill, whose middle name refers to her childhood love for butterflies, would spend two full years in the tree—two years in which she developed an intense relationship with Luna. Hill became a worldwide phenomenon, as did the spiritual and animistic experiences she reported. Upon entering the redwoods, one of the most impressive forests on the planet, she had a metaphysical experience: "The first time I entered into the redwood forest . . . I dropped to my knees and began crying because the spirit of the forest just gripped me."[57]

Descriptions like these are a common thread running through environmental activists' accounts of their experiences. As another example, Graham Innes, an Australian activist who was buried up to his neck in the earth during a protest action, reports "a slow dawning of awareness of a hitherto unknown connection—Earth bonding [when the Earth's] pulse became mine, and the vessel, my body, became the vehicle for her expression . . . it was as though nature had overtaken my consciousness to speak on her behalf."[58] The example of "Reverend Fly," whom Bron Taylor interviewed during protest actions in the Redwood Forest in Northern California, is also very revealing in terms of the discourse structure that interests us here. "What we know about redwoods is that they sprout; they hold on to each other," explains Fly. The redwoods are part "of this continuous, sprouting, living being, or consciousness, that once covered millions of acres."[59] For Fly and his friend "Goat," this is the original meaning of spirituality. "It is honoring the universal power, the flow, the power far beyond me, [the power] that I exist in." Spirituality is "when I know what the trees are saying, when I know what my friends are thinking, [it's when] I and the people I'm with open ourselves to other energies or to a higher vibrational level. People call them all sorts of things, Ghosts. Fairies. Telepathy. It has [convinced me we are not] separate from each other, and from the rocks, and everything else."[60] Nature, energy, consciousness, universal force, life force—again, these are all terms that carry the discourse on the soul, and they are entangled with the concepts of spirit, spirituality, telepathy, and related terms.

One could object that Julia Butterfly Hill, Reverend Fly, and Goat are marginal examples and do not necessarily stand for a broader movement. But this is only partly true. Firstly, discourse analysis shows that the same orders of knowledge are evident in these extreme examples as in UN reports, which can hardly be described as marginal. Secondly, radical changes in cultures and orders of discourse often originate "on the margins"—namely, through actions the majority culture regards as extreme and considers difficult to integrate. Thirdly, my reconstruction shows that these positions are not as extreme as they might seem, but rather draw on and extrapolate from discursive arrangements that have a long history. In my line of argumentation, I would go even further and claim that what we are actually dealing with here is a profound cultural change that establishes an order of knowledge about the planet in which humans are seen as embedded in structures of nonhuman life, intelligence, and consciousness. Dark green religion and nature-based spirituality should therefore be considered an influential global phenomenon.

One indication of the broad acceptance of this order of knowledge is the fact that popular scientific and literary publications addressing precisely this discourse arrangement have become best sellers in recent years. Let me illustrate this with two examples.

Richard Powers's novel *The Overstory* was published in 2018 and immediately became a *New York Times* best seller. It was included in the list of the "10 Best Books of 2018" in the *Washington Post* and the *Chicago Tribune*. At the end of the year, the book was shortlisted for the 2018 Man Booker Prize. *The Overstory* is a novel about "reimagining our place in the living world," as a review in the *New York Times* put it.[61] The novel describes nature and especially the trees as powerful and animated. Much like in Levertov's "A Tree Telling of Orpheus," Powers's trees are integrated into a communicational space that encompasses nature and human beings, whereby the trees offer long-forgotten knowledge that is decisive for the future of the planet: "*A chorus of living wood sings to the woman*: if your mind were only a slightly greener thing, we'd drown you in meaning. *The pine she leans against says*: Listen. There's something you need to hear."[62]

Through at first inexplicable and sometimes mysterious coincidences, different characters in the novel come together to actively engage in saving endangered forests in California and other parts of the world. Only over the course of the narrative does it become clear that the trees themselves—and their intelligence—are responsible for these events. Despite their very different origins and personalities, the protagonists are initiated into an animistic world, and they sense the insignificance of the human species in comparison to nature as a whole, as well as nature's soul and consciousness. Thus the character Nicholas understands that "it's all encoded somehow in that animated tree," and while looking at an ant colony, Adam learns that "the colony possesses something; Adam doesn't know what to call it. Purpose. Will. A kind of awareness—something so different from human intelligence that intelligence thinks it's nothing."[63] The study of nature leads him to conclude that "humankind is deeply ill. The species won't last long. It was an aberrant experiment. Soon the world will be returned to the healthy intelligences, the collective ones. Colonies and hives."[64]

The character Neelay, on the other hand, who learns computer programming from his father, is pressed into service by the trees themselves, after an "accident" that leaves him a paraplegic for the rest of his life. "The whole wide universe waits to be animated," and so Neelay sets to work. "Vishnu has put all of living possibility into their little eight-bit microprocessor, and Neelay will sit in front of the screen until he sets creation free."[65] He designs a computer game that will make him one of the richest people in the industry. The program first appears to him in a vision in Stanford, California:

> The game will put its players smack in the middle of a living, breathing, seething, animist world filled with millions of different species, a world desperately in need of the players' help. And the goal of the game will be to figure out what the new and desperate world wants from you.
>
> The vision ends, depositing him again in Stanford's inner quad. The vision, religious and dark green, fades back into its Platonic shadow, wood.[66]

This passage reveals the academic concepts embedded in this literary document. Richard Powers acknowledges this explicitly when he says to Everett Hamner in an interview: "The book is indeed filled with what Bron Taylor would call *dark green religion*. But in most cases, it's a religion without metaphysics, which is something that even the religion of humanism can't always claim! Tree-consciousness is a religion of life, a kind of biopantheism. My characters are willing to entertain a *telos* in living things that scientific empiricism shies away from. *Life wants something from us.* The trees say to each of these people: *There's something you need to hear.*"[67]

One person in the novel who quite clearly represents this direction is Patty. As a child, her father told her: "We know so little about how trees grow. Almost nothing about how they bloom and branch and shed and heal themselves. We've learned a little about a few of them, in isolation. But nothing is less isolated or more social than a tree."[68] Later, after her father is killed in an accident, Patty keeps the things that characterized him most. "She preserves his precious library—Aldo Leopold, John Muir, his botany texts, the Ag Extension pamphlets he helped to write. She finds his copy of adult Ovid, marked all over, as people mark beeches. The underscores start, triple, on the very first line: Let me sing to you now, about how people turn into other things."[69] For Patty, as for her father, John Muir is a constant reference point in her scientific research. "Late at night, too tired from teaching and research to work more, she reads her beloved Muir. *A Thousand-Mile Walk to the Gulf* and *My First Summer in the Sierra* float her soul up to her room's ceiling and spin it like a Sufi."[70]

The interweaving of religious and scientific language, the overall arrangement of which always includes discourses on the soul, animation, and consciousness, is a basic element in *The Overstory*. Getting involved with the trees' intelligence and life energy generates a knowledge that extends beyond scientific-reductionist knowledge—"When her eyes open again, truths rush into her head. Like Enlightenment, but without the glow"—allowing both fictional characters and readers to sense the sacral dimension of nature, as in the description of a redwood giant as a "russet, leathery apotheosis."[71]

The Overstory is not an isolated case. At the interface of literature and science, several successful books that address these themes in a very similar way have been published in recent years.[72] One of these successful authors is Peter Wohlleben. His German book *Das geheime Leben der Bäume* (*The Secret Life of Trees*), published in 2015 and subtitled "What They Feel, How They Communicate—the Discovery of a Hidden World," made the German forester famous almost overnight. More books and publications in other media followed and have been translated into several languages.[73] Today Wohlleben is one of the internationally best-known representatives of "new forestry," an approach to forests and ecology that opposes reductionist models and propagates a holistic understanding of nature in which the more-than-human world is taken seriously as an actor in a living system—very much in the spirit of Richard Powers's novel. And indeed, with *The Secret Life of Trees*, it is hard to escape the impression that Powers used Wohlleben as inspiration for the character of the zoologist Patricia Westerford in his novel. Several reviewers in the German press have noted this, for example, Martin Ebel: "But isn't Richard Powers, especially in German translation, preaching to the converted? Hasn't *The [Secret] Life of Trees* by the forester Peter Wohlleben been on the best-seller list for three years and found many imitators?"[74]

Just like the fictional Patricia "Patty" Westerford, Peter Wohlleben describes how trees communicate with one another, how they care for one another, and how they warn one another when danger is imminent by means of messenger substances—all backed up by references to new research. According to Wohlleben, trees have emotions and memory, and the more one knows about the life of plants, the less the ethical and biological separation between the animal world and the plant world can be maintained. Similarly to Rachel Carson, Wohlleben uses terms such as *wonder* and *awe* when talking about protecting forests, and nature as a whole. "Our descendants should also be able to walk among the trees in awe. . . . It is also the little riddles and wonders that need to be preserved. . . . And who knows, perhaps one day the language of trees will actually be decoded and thus provide material for more incredible stories."[75]

In *Das Seelenleben der Tiere* (literally The Soul-Life of Animals), Wohlleben again presents himself as an "interpreter" of scientific research for "normal" people as he tries to express in everyday language the extent to which animal studies have already dissolved the artificial divisions between humans and animals when it comes to thinking and feeling (I will return to some of this research in the next section). In this process, we see the emergence of "an image of the animal world surrounding us that transforms the dull biorobots (as I called them above), driven by a fixed genetic code, into faithful souls and lovable goblins."[76] We find elements of dark green religion in Wohlleben's books, although he is less explicit in propagating the intrinsic values in nature. "My wish is . . . that we would learn a little more respect in dealing with our living environment, be it animals or plants."[77] Distancing himself from philosophical traditions that describe animals as machines, Wohlleben goes one step further and answers the question of whether animals possess a soul in the affirmative. "Squirrels, deer, or wild boars with souls—that is what it comes down to and what warms the heart when we observe such animals roaming freely."[78] In acknowledging that animals have souls, Wohlleben adds his voice to the choir of ecologists and scientists who have argued similarly. Perhaps the most famous voice in this group is Jane Goodall (born 1934), who clearly states: "Many theologians and philosophers argue that only humans have 'souls.' My years in the forest with the chimpanzees have led me to question this assumption."[79]

Ecological Crises and Cultural Studies, or: Paradoxes of the Anthropocene

Time and again we have seen how strongly the academic world is intertwined with the world outside academia. Scientific contributions are absorbed into literature, art, politics, and the media, and theories of religion and metaphysics are translated into spiritual practices in everyday life. Likewise, scientific theories are influenced by the themes of the day.[80] Scientists form a discourse community alongside and together with all other cultural producers. The fields of ecology and nature-based spirituality are not exempt from this. On the contrary: a look at the development of scientific theories over the last thirty years or so reveals an almost seamless connection between academic models of interpretation and political-cultural realities. This is not surprising, because how could scientists remain uninvolved in the global ecological catastrophes that challenge human life on the planet? We are in the middle of the so-called sixth period of mass extinction since life began on the planet 540 million years ago. The term *Sixth Extinction* was popularized by Elizabeth Kolbert.[81] The fact that she received the 2015 Pulitzer Prize for her nonfiction book on the topic proves the extent of public interest in this issue.

For the last several years, the term *Anthropocene* has been used to frame discussions of the mass extinction of species and the global ecological transformations caused by human activity. The term was coined in the early 1980s by Eugene F. Stoermer (1934–2012), who worked as a biologist and an expert on diatoms at the University of Michigan. Even the academic journal *Science* has adopted this vocabulary and published articles describing the decisive role of human activity in the ongoing mass extinction.[82] The concept of the Anthropocene goes far beyond scientific questions, however, because it concerns the connections between human and nonhuman life on the planet and questions about the meaning and significance of human history. Therefore the term plays a role in cultural studies and in philosophical as well as scientific contexts. With regard to our concerns here, these discussions are important insofar as they develop concepts of animism, consciousness, and agency with regard to the more-than-human world; in turn, these concepts organize societal knowledge about the soul, the human, and nature in a specific way. I want to outline some of the basic lines of these arguments here.

In general, one could say the boundaries that traditionally existed (at least in Europe and North America) between human and animal, between spirit and matter, and between the social and the natural have been blurred in recent decades. As Arianne Françoise Conty puts it: "Subjects and objects, the infatuation of modernity, have gone out of fashion. Scholars today see agency, events, lines of flight and entanglements where they used to see subjects and objects, often leading to an indiscretion between the two that is celebrated as having finally overcome the anthropocentrism responsible for justifying a human subject over and against a world of things."[83] As for the boundaries between humans and animals, my discussion of Peter Wohlleben and others has already indicated that the similarity between these two groups is much greater than is often assumed. This is repeatedly confirmed in more recent research, which has even led some authors to advance the "posthumanism" thesis.[84] One of the driving forces behind this change is the interdisciplinary field of animal studies. As Jonathan K. Crane explains, animal studies draws on history, anthropology, economics, philosophy, religious studies, political science, law, biology, psychology, and other disciplines, which indicates the complexity of the field.[85] Animal studies are part of a larger scientific and societal discussion in which the position of humans in a global ecological context is being redefined, often with religious connotations that link ecological questions to the veneration of nature as a living being.

Since the publication of Peter Singer's now-classic *Animal Liberation: A New Ethics for Our Treatment of Animals* (1975), bioethics and animal studies have gained increasing influence. As a critical reaction to Aristotle, Descartes, and Kant, who regarded animals as inanimate machines without personality or agency, the privileging of humans over other animals—a practice for which Singer coined the term *speciesism*—has come under pressure.[86] One after the other, the bastions supporting a belief in humans' privileged position have fallen. Today, the argument that there is a fundamental difference between humans and animals can hardly be upheld. Nonhuman animals have language, personality, agency, a theory of mind, and a rich social life with individual characters, rituals, and interspecies communication.[87] Paola Cavalieri has gone so far as to announce the "death of the animal"—namely, the end of the distinction between humans and other animals.[88] In a similar vein, Jonathan K. Crane argues that "the spiraling anthropocentrism that has long reigned in animal studies is increasingly found wanting, if not suffocating."[89] In an attempt to overcome this anthropocentrism, Crane and others regard animals not only as competent personalities, but also as independent ethical actors in an interspecies dialogue.

This discussion has long since ceased to be limited to the field of animal studies. Particularly with regard to agency, the primacy of the human being in the constitution of knowledge has been subjected to critical examination. In this context, some scholars even attribute agency to "things." From an archaeological perspective, for example, Ian Hodder describes human dependency on things, which leads him to a new understanding of agency:

> The study of agency contributes to the analysis of entanglement, but the emphasis in entanglement theory is less on the agent itself and more on the networks of entanglement that make possible and constrain certain forms of agency and certain forms of agent. There is not just a human subject creating agency but a distributive agency consisting of a "swarm

> of vitalities at play."[90] Agency is simply the ever-present force of things: the life force of humans and all organic things, and the forces of attraction, repulsion, etc. of all material things and their interactions.[91]

Here we see once again how the concepts of force, life force, and vitality are combined with the agency of immaterial and material actors.

In addition to entanglement, the concept of "relationality" has recently played a major role when it comes to the question of nonhuman agency, including "things." In this context, agency is not simply ascribed to other actors; it does not (necessarily) originate from the things themselves, but results from the encounter between actors, be they persons or other things. In the resulting relationship, mutual influence and dependency arise.[92] Bruno Latour's work has been an important catalyst in this discussion; forty years ago, Latour pointed out that even the "exact" natural sciences fall back on social structures in their production of knowledge, and thus social structures ultimately decide which knowledge is considered acceptable.[93] One result of this work was the removal of the distinction between the "natural" and the "social," which also led Latour to address the ambivalence of the "factual" in the production of knowledge. Factual knowledge is almost a fetish of what we consider "modern," and so Latour introduced the term *factish* into the discussion, at the same time claiming that we have never actually been modern.[94]

Latour's recent contributions to the discussion are especially important for our topic because they deal with discourses on nature and animism. In his Gifford Lectures, published under the title *Facing Gaia*, he details the artificial separation between the animate human world and the inanimate world of other things. He also takes up concepts of consciousness and the soul, and speaks of "metamorphic zones" in which the material and the immaterial merge into each other.

> When we claim that there is, on one side, a natural world and, on the other, a human world, we are simply proposing to say, after the fact, that an arbitrary portion of the actors will be *stripped of all action* and that another portion, equally arbitrary, will be *endowed with souls* (or consciousness). But these two secondary operations leave perfectly intact the

> only interesting phenomenon: the exchange of forms of action through the transactions between agencies of multiple origins and forms at the core of the metamorphic zones. This may appear paradoxical, but, to gain in realism, we have to leave aside the pseudo-realism that purports to be drawing the portrait of humans parading against a background of things.[95]

Latour discusses Lovelock's "Gaia hypothesis" in detail and opposes the interpretation which claims that Lovelock would have spoken out in favor of an animistic view of the planet. This is not the case, Latour maintains: "His problem is indeed to understand in what respect the Earth is active, *but without endowing it with a soul*; and to understand, too, what is the immediate consequence of the Earth's activity—in what respect can one say that it *retroacts to the collective actions of humans*?"[96] The basic problem, Latour says, is actually the "moderns'" assumption that their science is radically "de-animistic."

> Although the official philosophy of science takes the second movement of deanimation as the only important and rational one, the opposite is true: animation is the essential phenomenon; and deanimation is the superficial, auxiliary, polemical, and often defensive phenomenon. One of the great enigmas of Western history is not that "there are still people naïve enough to believe in animism," but that many people still hold the rather naïve belief in a supposedly deanimated "material world." And this is the case at the very moment when scientists are multiplying the agencies in which they—and we—are more and more implicated every day.[97]

Latour's troubling of the separation between human and nature and between the material and the spiritual is both an expression of the discursive change I am concerned with here and an attempt at its conscious theorization. We see something similar in the work of Donna J. Haraway, who, like Latour, is interested in science and technology studies, but combines that research in her own way with theories from feminist and cultural studies. Her books *When Species Meet* (2008) and *Staying with the*

Trouble: Making Kin in the Chthulucene (2016) are indispensable contributions to the discussion about anthropocentrism, the (fluid) boundaries between the genera, and the question of how to deal with the ecological transformation of the planet. In order to overcome the often judgmental distinctions between "human" and "animal," Haraway creates new expressions, speaking of "companion species" that are "becoming-with" one another in constant interaction: "Companion species are relentlessly becoming-with. The category companion species helps me refuse human exceptionalism without invoking posthumanism."[98] This is the basis on which she states elsewhere: "I am not a posthumanist; I am who I become with companion species, who and which make a mess out of categories in the making of kin and kind. Queer messmates in mortal play, indeed."[99] In this sense, the question whether nonhuman animals are animate does not even arise, because animistic qualities can only be attributed to all companion species or to no species at all.

In the same line of thought, Haraway can only describe the concept of the Anthropocene as anthropocentric hubris: "Species Man did not shape the conditions for the Third Carbon Age or the Nuclear Age. The story of Species Man as the agent of the Anthropocene is an almost laughable rerun of the great phallic humanizing and modernizing Adventure, where man, made in the image of a vanished god, takes on superpowers in his secular-sacred ascent, only to end in tragic detumescence, once again."[100] If one had to choose a term for this epoch, therefore, the only suitable one would be the Capitalocene.[101]

Haraway is not alone in this criticism. Marc Bekoff and Jessica Pierce also argue: "This epoch, which is being called the Anthropocene, or Age of Humanity, is anything but humane. It rightfully could be called the Rage of Humanity."[102] In 2019, Barry Lopez wrote: "The tendency of some to exaggerate our own importance as a species in the great theater of life on Earth is a sign of hubris."[103] And Bruno Latour comes from yet another direction: "If we were to try to separate Science and Religion today, from the vantage point of the Anthropocene, it would be a real massacre, given how much Science there is in Religion and how much Religion there is in Science."[104] It is noteworthy that many of these contributions include the dimension of the religious in their assessment of the Anthropocene, although the term itself is primarily aimed at the ecological and economic aspects of the phenomenon.

The emphasis on the fluid boundaries between the human and the natural world, between the social and the natural, is certainly an important feature of interdisciplinary research today. Cultural sciences, animal studies, and science and technology studies have provided the impetus to critically question the boundaries between the material and the spiritual. A whole field of research has developed in this area. Often referred to as "new materialism," this research addresses three levels, which Diana Coole and Samantha Frost describe as follows:

> First among them is an ontological reorientation that is resonant with, and to some extent informed by, developments in natural science: an orientation that is posthumanist in the sense that it conceives of matter itself as lively or as exhibiting agency. The second theme entails consideration of a raft of biopolitical and bioethical issues concerning the status of life and of the human. Third, new materialist scholarship testifies to a critical and nondogmatic reengagement with political economy, where the nature of, and relationship between, the material details of everyday life and broader geopolitical and socioeconomic structures is being explored afresh.[105]

Here one can see very clearly how the influential occultist discourses around 1900 continue to have an impact on today's orders of knowledge, which are even more strongly interlinked with economic and ecological questions. Research on new materialism sometimes attempts to leave behind precisely these occultist discourses and to grasp the vitality and spirituality of matter conceptually, "without relying upon mysticisms derived from animism, religion, or romanticism."[106] From the perspective of discourse history, however, the continuity of these orders of knowledge is particularly striking. The rhetorical demarcations of "mysticism," "animism," "religion," and even "romanticism" constitute an attempt to establish new materialisms as a 'secular' and scientifically serious field of research. In the sense of "nondogmatic" and "critical" analysis, one would conversely expect this research to critically examine these artificial and evaluative categorizations of mysticism, animism, and related concepts, rather than merely perpetuating these hegemonic orders of knowledge by enforcing a critical distance from concepts considered beyond the pale.

The newly emerging fields of biosemiotics and ecocriticism are probing the merging of the human and nonhuman realms, of the material and the immaterial at a high theoretical level. Extending animal studies research results, often with reference to semiological structuralism and the semiotics of Charles Sanders Peirce, biosemiotics deals with interaction and communication across species and beyond spoken language—a project that Wendy Wheeler, in a formulation that conjures up vitalist discourse, calls "a feeling for life."[107] This combination of semiotics with vitalist and animist discourses is also characteristic of ecocriticism or, as a recent volume has it, *Material Ecocriticism*:

> The conceptual argument of *Material Ecocriticism* is simple in its outlines: the world's material phenomena are knots in a vast network of agencies, which can be "read" and interpreted as forming narratives, stories. Developing in bodily forms and in discursive formulations, and arising in coevolutionary landscapes of natures and signs, the stories of matter are everywhere: in the air we breathe, the food we eat, in the things and beings of this world, within and beyond the human realm. All matter, in other words, is a "storied matter." It is a material "mesh" of meanings, properties, and processes, in which human and nonhuman players are interlocked in networks that produce undeniable signifying forces.[108]

Those "coevolutionary landscapes," in which meanings, materialities, and narratives merge, denote something similar to Haraway's "becoming-with." Such an approach includes all types of communication, both linguistic and nonlinguistic. Moreover, artistic and poetic expressions are also consciously taken seriously, in a way reminiscent of the poetic and Orphic science of the nineteenth century.[109] Such an approach implements the openness of these systems, both theoretically and practically.

Ursula K. Le Guin embodies this openness in a particularly interesting way. Le Guin, whom we have already encountered as a writer and thinker in chapter 9, has also commented on the subject of the Anthropocene. She did so as a keynote speaker at the "Anthropocene: Arts of Living on a Damaged Planet" congress, held at the University of California, Santa Cruz, in 2014. In her short lecture, titled "Deep in Admiration," entirely in the spirit of more recent cultural studies models, she first describes relationality as a central concept when it comes to the mutual dependency of species, but also of humans and other "things." "One way to stop seeing trees, or rivers, or hills only as 'natural resources,' is to class them as fellow being—kinfolk."[110] Attributing the status of animate and conscious subjects to the beings and things of the world—instead of objectifying them, as is often done—does not mean co-opting, colonizing, or exploiting them. "Rather, it may involve a great reach outward of the mind and imagination."[111] Poetry, for Le Guin, is the human language in which the knowledge of a tree, a river, or a stone can be made intelligible. Le Guin thus weaves herself into the Orphic web of knowledge, nature, and art, to which I have repeatedly referred. Science, Le Guin argues, is a description from outside, while poetry is a description from inside.[112] Both are important perspectives when it comes to an understanding of the world that seeks to go beyond the simple accumulation of information. A perfect example of how she translates these ideas into poetry is her poem "The Canada Lynx."[113] In this poem, Le Guin transmits a knowledge that a purely scientific-rational description cannot render accessible. The poem is therefore no less "true" than a scientific account—it is perhaps even "truer," since it seeks to take into account the lynx's life and emotional world, as well as the human perspective. In just nine lines, and in a way that is unsurpassed in its complexity and simplicity, Le Guin links topics such as overpopulation, reductionist philosophy and science, anthropocentrism, and species extinction.[114]

In this long chapter, we have seen that Rachel Carson and Barry Lopez connect naturalism and spirituality through concepts such as wonder; the "Epic of Evolution" brings human consciousness into connection with the unfolding universe; dark green religion makes the animation and spiritual meaning of the natural world tangible to human beings; and new interpretations in cultural studies try to keep pace with this discursive development and contribute to the strengthening of the underlying order of knowledge. Together, these diverse voices form a discourse community that works to establish and transform discourses on the soul, consciousness, animism, nature, and science. Ursula K. Le Guin takes up all of these aspects when she speaks of wonder, connectedness, and the sacred dimension of nature. The Orphic scientist should therefore have the last word: "By admiration, I understand reverence for the infinite connectedness, the naturally sacred order of things, and joy in it, delight. So we admit stones to our holy communion, so the stones may admit us to theirs."[115]

EPILOGUE

A Cultural Studies Soul Retrieval

Where do we stand at the end of this cultural and discursive history of the soul in the twentieth century? One thing should be clear: even today, the soul is still an important vehicle of meaning when it comes to determining the human place in the overall structure of nature, history, and the world. Many also see the soul as a bridge between the individual personality and a collective existence that connects a person with other humans and also fills the more-than-human world with life and consciousness. In view of this great significance, it is also clear that my historical reconstruction of the discourse on the soul in Europe and North America could only describe one part of an immense field. Nevertheless, in my opinion, this constitutes a part that is representative of a broad cultural development, and that moreover enables important insights into how societal debates about "modernity" and the search for the meaning of human existence have proceeded since the end of the nineteenth century.

Analyzing the concept of the soul in its discursive entanglement with other concepts has proven to be very helpful. Such an approach makes it clear that the concept of "soul," which has carried connotations of life, breath, and consciousness since antiquity, was integrated in the nineteenth and early twentieth centuries into a discursive formation that can be called both occult and Orphic: occult in the sense that the soul was entangled with concepts of spirit–matter–science–life force–energy–nature; and Orphic in the sense that the soul was entangled with ecstasy–art–music–literature–nature–empathy–knowledge.

In identifying the cultural locations in which these discourses formed—with many cross-connections among them—we first cite the universities, with newly created disciplines such as psychology, theoretical physics, or the academic study of religion, which still had to find their place in relation to the traditional faculties of medicine, philosophy, and theology. The determination of this relation often turned out to be work on what was henceforth to be considered "science" and, in turn, on those aspects and issues that were to be excluded from the canon of knowledge as not empirically verifiable—including the soul. A second location of discursive formation was the huge field of extremely influential nonfiction books on the subject; particularly between 1890 and 1930, experts from a wide variety of fields—including many scientists, who brought academic knowledge to a general and highly interested public—engaged with issues of the soul. The fields of literature and art constitute a third location for this discursive formation; what was negotiated in philosophy, psychology, natural science, and the history of religion was given literary and artistic form here. We can identify politics as a fourth location, one that took up impulses from science, philosophy, historiography, and literature to connect the soul with collective or ecological constructions.

Although each of these locations developed different emphases, discourse analysis shows that the relevant arrangements of discourse on the soul reveal considerable stability across cultural locations. A discourse community formed around questions of the soul—a community that, as a whole, created contexts of meaning with considerable impact. Sometimes we need to deliberately regroup such discourse strands in order to make these implicit collaborations visible. We can see just how strong this effect was when we consider the fact that these same discursive knots lost little of their significance in the second half of the twentieth century. After the catastrophe of World War II, the focus of intellectual and cultural developments shifted from Europe to North America, where European discourse structures—often in concrete biographies—were combined with already existing North American ideas about the soul. Above all, the connection with discourses on nature and with American transcendentalism was to have a great impact. Literary, scientific, and philosophical conversations in the United States, in which the transpersonal movement played a considerable role, developed a discourse on the soul that focused on the elements of consciousness–animism–nature–cosmos–spirituality, at times even replacing "soul" with "consciousness," while leaving the rest of the discursive arrangement intact. This discourse was further strengthened when, toward the end of the twentieth century, the ecological crisis raised fundamental questions about human life on the planet. Biocentric ethics and animistic spirituality connected the discourse on the soul with nature–ecology–awe–nonreductionist science, which also found expression in active environmental protection and political programs. Once again, we see a discourse community in which contributions from natural science, the humanities, literature, art, politics, and spiritual practice influenced and strengthened one another.

The analysis of these discursive arrangements and discourse communities shows how misleading the talk of secularization and of the supposed enmity between religion and science really is. Both turn out to be tropes that are themselves part of the work on "modernity," an act of self-assurance that can hardly be aligned with the historical sources. I do not mean to deny that it can be quite useful to speak of "secular reference systems" or similar approaches as they arose in connection with the criticism of religion and the creation of religiously independent (or at least formally independent) institutions and scientific disciplines in the nineteenth century. However, secularization—in the sense of finally suppressing the religious—has never occurred. Discourse analysis very clearly shows how previously "religious" elements of discourse became part of an arrangement in which they are effortlessly linked to 'secular' science—examples of this include elements such as wonder–awe–empathy–sacred–animism–divine order–cosmos–creation–nature. And as soon as the sources begin to speak of "spirituality" as distinct from traditional, institutionalized "religion," the remnants of the antagonism between religion and science evaporate from the picture almost completely. We can even identify a mechanism by which science, while regarding itself as secular, has brought forth new spiritual interpretations and practices—a process I describe as the scientification of religion.

Hence, from the perspective of discourse history, religion has never disappeared. This also means that what is sometimes grandiosely referred to as the "radical Enlightenment" is by no means the mode in which "modern" culture operates. In discourse analysis, secularism as an ideology—in contrast to secularity or secular systems of reference—is to be treated in the same way as religious, spiritual, or political interpretations of the world. If one then combines this with an analysis of the dynamic dispositives of "church" (or, more broadly, "institutionalized religion," which includes a hierarchical order and a canonical doctrine) and "science" (with institutions such as universities, scientific associations, Nobel Prizes, and specialist journals), one gets a fairly clear picture of how the perception and social significance of religion have changed since the nineteenth century.

This also means that research on the soul is very well suited to studying the changes in religious discourses. However, in order to do so, one must focus the analytical lens differently than the academic study of religion traditionally does. Large parts of this discipline are still obsessed with conceptual questions and are afraid that abandoning a definition of religion would be tantamount to abandoning the discipline. Thus they miss the fact that formerly "religious" discourses are now present in many forms in the natural sciences, literature, art, popular culture, politics, and new spiritual practices, even if these cultural forms no longer require the concept of religion (or merely retain it as a delimiting category).

An academic study of religion that insists on a definition of religion as a prerequisite for doing its "proper" work loses touch with its objects. This is why cultural studies, cultural history, anthropology, and the sociology of knowledge are much better equipped to analyze religious and spiritual fields of discourse today. Instead of asking how such changes can be brought into line with a—necessarily precarious—definition of religion, my research is simply interested in how people in different historical and cultural constellations negotiate their relationship to the more-than-human world. This can be accomplished with recourse to deities, but also to metaphysical interpretations of the cosmos, mythopoetic representations of the history of evolution, deep-ecological and biocentric descriptions of nature as animate and agentic, vitalist and monistic considerations of the unity of matter and spirit, rituals and spiritual practices, and much more. One of the most fascinating features of a cultural and discursive history of the soul is that it provides information on how discourse communities in Europe and North America have renegotiated the relationship between the human and the more-than-human world philosophically, scientifically, artistically, literarily, politically, and spiritually. It remains to be seen whether this will lead to the creation of a future planetary community in which there is still room for the human species.

NOTES

PROLOGUE

1. Andrew M. Colman, ed., *A Dictionary of Psychology* (Oxford: Oxford University Press, 2015), www.oxfordreference.com/view/10.1093/acref/9780199657681.001.0001/acref-9780199657681. As for the American Psychological Association (APA), the vision statement of this professional association is representative of the self-understanding of many psychologists today. Under the headline "Science of Psychology," the APA website states: "The science of psychology benefits society and enhances our lives. Psychologists examine the relationships between brain function and behavior, and the environment and behavior, applying what they learn to illuminate our understanding and improve the world around us. . . . Psychologists employ the scientific method—stating the question, offering a theory and then constructing rigorous laboratory or field experiments to test the hypothesis. Psychologists apply the understanding gleaned through research to create evidence-based strategies that solve problems and improve lives." See www.apa.org/action/science. In this approach, there is no place for the soul.
2. For a more comprehensive discussion of my understanding of the discursive study of religion, see Kocku von Stuckrad, *The Scientification of Religion: An Historical Study of Discursive Change, 1800–2000* (Berlin: De Gruyter, 2014), 1–18; Kocku von Stuckrad, "Historical Discourse Analysis: The Entanglement of Past and Present," in *Religion and Discourse Research: Disciplinary Use and Interdisciplinary Dialogues*, ed. Jay Johnston and Kocku von Stuckrad (Berlin: De Gruyter, 2021), 77–87.
3. Franz X. Eder, "Historische Diskurse und ihre Analyse—eine Einleitung," in *Historische Diskursanalysen: Genealogie, Theorien, Anwendungen*, ed. Franz X. Eder (Wiesbaden: VS Verlag für Sozialwissenschaft, 2006), 9–23, p. 13. If not indicated otherwise, all translations in this book are mine.
4. Michel Foucault, *The Archaeology of Knowledge: And The Discourse on Language*, trans. A. M. Sheridan Smith (1972; New York: Vintage, 2010), 29. He adds that it "is not therefore an interpretation of the facts of the statement that might reveal [the relations], but

the analysis of their coexistence, their succession, their mutual functioning, their reciprocal determination, and their independent or correlative transformations."

5. By way of example, the Sanskrit term *atman*, which is highly important for Hindu philosophy, derives from the same root as the Latin term for the soul (*anima*) and even the Germanic *Atem/Odem*, all of which are closely related to "breath," "air," and "life" itself (see chapter 1 for a more detailed discussion). However, my analysis does not cover the cultural history of the Indian subcontinent (which is far beyond my expertise). Nevertheless, I do pay attention to how Euro-American culture has addressed Hindu practices and theologies, and how it got entangled with the respective traditions. A masterful analysis of exactly these entanglements is now available in David L. Haberman, *Making the Impossible Possible in the Worship of Mount Govardhan* (London: Oxford University Press, 2020).
6. In this approach, I agree with Courtney Bender, who notes: "Locating the production of spirituality in so-called secular institutions unsettles the logics of institutional differentiation that continue to lie at the heart of our theories of secularization and, thereby, our projects of analyzing religion." Courtney Bender, *The New Metaphysicals: Spirituality and the American Religious Imagination* (Chicago: University of Chicago Press, 2010), 183.
7. Over the last couple of decades, Catholic theology has struggled enormously with the fact that modern culture no longer seems to provide a place for the soul, or at least not in the way Catholic tradition had understood "the soul" since the Middle Ages. The attempts Christian theologians have made to retain the traditional understanding of the soul are not the main focus of my analysis; when it comes to attempts to incorporate new approaches to spirituality, as well as nontheistic ideas about humankind's (and "God's") place in nature and the cosmos, I will address such attempts in this book because they are part of the grouping I am interested in here. One example is the field of "process theology," which aims to bridge the gap between ecological thinking, science, and nontheistic theologies. See particularly the work of David Ray Griffin, who applies the influential process philosophy of Alfred North Whitehead and Charles Hartshorne to theology and philosophy of religion. For the topic of the present book, the following contributions are particularly noteworthy: David Ray Griffin, *Parapsychology, Philosophy, and Spirituality: A Postmodern Exploration* (Albany: State University of New York Press, 1997); David Ray Griffin, *Unsnarling the World-Knot: Consciousness, Freedom, and the Mind-Body Problem* (Berkeley: University of California Press, 1998); David Ray Griffin, *Reenchantment Without Supernaturalism: A Process Philosophy of Religion* (Ithaca, NY: Cornell University Press, 2018). See also John B. Cobb and David Ray Griffin, eds., *Mind in Nature: Essays on the Interface of Science and Philosophy* (Washington: University Press of America, 1977). A more theistic approach is represented by Catherine Keller, *On the Mystery: Discerning Divinity in Process* (Minneapolis: Fortress, 2008).
8. Therefore it should be clear that I am interested in "hybrids," "entanglements," and the "messiness" of historical data, which I try to make sense of through a creative "regrouping." That is why I find it problematic to employ an approach that starts with clear demarcations between concepts, subsequently traces these predefined differences through the course of history, and thus—voilà!—finds confirmation of what was assumed in the beginning. An example of such an approach is Graham Richards, *Psychology, Religion, and the Nature of the Soul: A Historical Entanglement* (New York: Springer Science +

Business Media, 2011). Despite many highly interesting historical insights (which are relevant to my own study as well), Richards presents this history mainly as a conflict and a competition between psychology and Christianity, with a strong aversion to what he calls "postmodernism." On this basis, he feels confident making very clear demarcations right at the beginning, even though he intends to criticize the "secular" self-understanding of professional psychology: "Heterogeneous though it be, Psychology is, unambiguously, an academic discipline of a predominantly scientific character, albeit one with numerous wider social dimensions and in which the meaning of the injunction to be 'scientific' is perennially controversial. It is not a centre of economic or political power, nor is it a formally constituted social organisation or source of clear prescriptive rules and guidelines for the conduct of life. . . . Religions, by contrast, have typically been all these things. In offering transcendental frameworks within which all of human life should be conducted and construed, religions engage with it at all levels" (6). Discursive approaches, as I apply them in my analysis, certainly trouble these understandings of both "Psychology" (capital P) and "religion" (which in Richards's case seems to converge mainly with Christianity, or even Catholicism).

1. NATURE RESEARCH, PSYCHOLOGY, AND OCCULTISM

1. On these histories, see J. R. Kantor, *The Scientific Evolution of Psychology*, vol. 1 (Chicago: Principia, 1963), 61–293; Jan N. Bremmer, *The Early Greek Concept of the Soul* (Princeton: Princeton University Press, 1983); Gerd Jüttemann, Michael Sonntag, and Christoph Wulf, eds., *Die Seele: Ihre Geschichte im Abendland* (Weinheim: Psychologie Verlags Union, 1991), 15–93; Richard Sorabji, "Soul and Self in Ancient Philosophy," in *From Soul to Self*, ed. James C. Crabbe (London: Routledge, 1999), 8–32. For a useful overview of ancient concepts of the soul, see Hendrik Lorenz, "Ancient Theories of Soul," in *The Stanford Encyclopedia of Philosophy* (Summer 2009 edition), ed. Edward N. Zalta, https://plato.stanford.edu/archives/sum2009/entries/ancient-soul/.
2. Burkhard Gladigow, "'Tiefe der Seele' und 'inner space': Zur Geschichte eines Topos von Heraklit bis zur Science Fiction," in *Die Erfindung des inneren Menschen: Studien zur religiösen Anthropologie*, ed. Jan Assmann (Gütersloh: Gütersloher Verlagshaus Mohn, 1993), 114–132, p. 126.
3. See E. R. Dodds, *The Greeks and the Irrational* (Berkeley: University of California Press, 1963); Jan Assmann, ed., *Die Erfindung des inneren Menschen: Studien zur religiösen Anthropologie* (Gütersloh: Gütersloher Verlagshaus Mohn, 1993); Gladigow, "'Tiefe der Seele' und 'inner space'"; Albert I. Baumgarten, Jan Assmann, and Guy G. Stroumsa, eds., *Self, Soul and Body in Religious Experience* (Leiden: Brill, 1998); Helmut Zander, *Geschichte der Seelenwanderung in Europa: Alternative religiöse Traditionen von der Antike bis heute* (Darmstadt: Primus, 1999), 57–152; Jan N. Bremmer, *The Rise And Fall Of The Afterlife: The 1995 Read-Tuckwell Lectures at the University of Bristol* (London: Routledge, 2002). For a comparative perspective, see Hans G. Kippenberg, Yme B. Kuiper, and Andy F. Sanders, eds., *Concepts of Person in Religion and Thought* (Berlin: Mouton de Gruyter, 1990).
4. For a good overview, see Lloyd Gerson, "Plotinus," in *The Stanford Encyclopedia of Philosophy* (Fall 2018 edition), ed. Edward N. Zalta, https://plato.stanford.edu/archives/fall2018/entries/plotinus/. As Mary-Jane Rubenstein rightly points out, the Platonic

understanding of the world soul, including the puzzling relation between divisibility and indivisibility, stood at the beginning of a long and perplexing argument about the world itself/worlds themselves. See Mary-Jane Rubenstein, *Worlds Without End: The Many Lives of the Multiverse* (New York: Columbia University Press, 2014), 21–69.

5. Clemens Zintzen, "Bemerkungen zur neuplatonischen Seelenlehre," in *Die Seele: Ihre Geschichte im Abendland*, ed. Gerd Jüttemann, Michael Sonntag, and Christoph Wulf (Weinheim: Psychologie Verlags Union, 1991), 43–58, p. 46.
6. See Klaus Corcilius and Dominik Perler, eds., *Partitioning the Soul: Debates from Plato to Leibniz* (Berlin: De Gruyter, 2014).
7. See Gorgias 43a, Phaidrus 250c, Nomoi 958c.
8. See Wilhelm Schmidt-Biggemann, *Philosophia perennis: Historische Umrisse abendländischer Spiritualität in Antike, Mittelalter und Früher Neuzeit* (Frankfurt am Main: Suhrkamp, 1998).
9. For a nuanced discussion of the history of such theological reception (and the fact that there were discontinuities and breaks as well), see Louise Hickman, "The Nature of the Self and the Contemplation of Nature: Ecotheology and the History of the Soul," in *The Concept of the Soul: Scientific and Religious Perspectives* (Science and Religion Forum), ed. Michael Fuller (Newcastle Upon Tyne, UK: Cambridge Scholars, 2014), 5–28.
10. As an example of a recent defense of Aquinas, see Peter Hunter, who claims that "the Roman Catholic tradition, and especially the doctrine of the soul of Thomas Aquinas, could make sense in the modern world. 'Soul' isn't simply an out-dated concept from a past age. And Aquinas' thoughtful approach isn't simply dead science." Peter Hunter, "Catholicism, Materialism and the Soul," in Fuller, *The Concept of the Soul*, 29–37, pp. 36–37. For a Christian theological position that is critical of body-soul dualism, see Nancey Murphy, "What Happened to the Soul?: Theological Perspectives on Neuroscience and the Self," *Annals of the New York Academy of Sciences* 1001, no. 1 (2003): 51–64.
11. As a philosophical contribution to this discussion, see Richard Swinburne, *The Evolution of the Soul*, rev. ed., Gifford Lectures, 1983–1984 (Oxford: Clarendon, 1997). Swinburne argues that mental events should be distinguished from physical ones (such as brain events). Mental events consist in the instantiations of properties in immaterial substances, or souls. As in traditional Catholic thinking, Swinburne also thinks that the human being consists of two parts—the "essential part" being the soul, while the body is considered a contingent part. As further evidence of his traditional theological orientation, he singles out the human being as the only species with the ability to reason logically as well as the only one capable of having moral awareness, free will, and an integrated system of beliefs and desires.
12. Kocku von Stuckrad, *Locations of Knowledge in Medieval and Early Modern Europe: Esoteric Discourse and Western Identities* (Leiden: Brill, 2010), 100.
13. Gerd Jüttemann, ed., *Die Geschichtlichkeit des Seelischen: Der historische Zugang zum Gegenstand der Psychologie* (Weinheim: Psychologie Verlags Union / Beltz, 1986); Jüttemann, Sonntag, and Wulf, *Seele*.
14. Lorenz Oken, *Lehrbuch der Naturphilosophie*, 3rd, rev. ed. (Zurich: Friedrich Schultheß, 1843; reprint Hildesheim: Georg Olm, 1991), §15, p. 2; first edition published in 1809.
15. Oken, §38, p. 6.
16. Oken, §90, p. 19.
17. Oken, §162, p. 31 (both quotations).

18. Oken, §169, p. 32 (emphasis original).
19. Oken, §993, p. 161.
20. Oken, §1019, p. 165 (emphasis original).
21. As another example of this discourse, we may think of Gustav Theodor Fechner (1801–1887). On Fechner's "science as ontopoiesis" and its links to Oken and others, see Robert Matthias Erdbeer, *Die Signatur des Kosmos: Epistemische Poetik und die Genealogie der Esoterischen Moderne* (Berlin: De Gruyter, 2010), 433–506.
22. Odo Marquard, *Transzendentaler Idealismus—Romantische Naturphilosophie—Psychoanalyse* (Cologne: Verlag für Philosophie Jürgen Dinter, 1987), 56.
23. "Ainsi nous rendre comme maîtres et possesseurs de la nature": René Descartes, *Discours de la méthode: Texte et commentaire*, ed. Etienne Gilson, 5th ed. (1627; Paris: Vrin, 1976), 62.
24. The quotation is from Kant's "Prolegomena to Any Future Metaphysics That Can Present Itself as a Science" (1783), quoted in Marquard, *Transzendentaler Idealismus*, 56.
25. Marquard, *Transzendentaler Idealismus*, 57.
26. Gotthilf Heinrich von Schubert, *Die Symbolik des Traumes*, 2nd ed. (Bamberg: Carl Friedrich Kunz, 1821), 31; first edition published in 1814.
27. Amanda Jo Goldstein, *Sweet Science: Romantic Materialism and the New Logics of Life* (Chicago: University of Chicago Press, 2017), 8.
28. Johann Wolfgang von Goethe, *Wilhelm Meisters Wanderjahre* (Frankfurt am Main: Insel, 1982); first edition published in 1821, quoted from the online edition at www.projekt-gutenberg.org/goethe/meisterw/mstw212c.html.
29. Arthur Titius, *Natur und Gott: Ein Versuch zur Verständigung zwischen Naturwissenschaft und Theologie*, 2nd ed. (Göttingen: Vandenhoeck und Ruprecht, 1931), 266.
30. Novalis (Friedrich von Hardenberg), *Novalis: Werke, Tagebücher und Briefe Friedrich von Hardenbergs*, ed. Hans-Joachim Mähl and Richard Samuel, 3 vols. (Darmstadt: Wissenschaftliche Buchgesellschaft), 1:225 (emphasis added).
31. Goldstein, *Sweet Science*, 101; see also the chapter "Goethe's Scientific Revolution" in Robert J. Richards, *The Romantic Conception of Life: Science and Philosophy in the Age of Goethe* (Chicago: University of Chicago Press, 2002), 407–502.
32. Kate Rigby, *Reclaiming Romanticism: Towards an Ecopoetics of Decolonization* (London: Bloomsbury Academic, 2020), 2. And she goes on: "The flurry of exploration, experimentation, agitation, reflection and creation across diverse fields of activity that was going in northwestern Europe around 1800, fanning out to other parts of the world during the course of the nineteenth century and beyond, took diverse forms and had divergent tendencies."
33. Lorraine Daston and Peter Galison, *Objectivity* (New York: Zone, 2007), 28–29; see also Goldstein, *Sweet Science*, 13.
34. Gotthilf Heinrich von Schubert, *Die Geschichte der Seele*, 4th ed. (Stuttgart: J. G. Cotta, 1850), 80; first edition published in 1830.
35. Schubert, 84.
36. Schubert, 86.
37. Schubert, 87.
38. Schubert, 90.
39. See particularly Corinna Treitel, *A Science for the Soul: Occultism and the Genesis of the German Modern* (Baltimore: Johns Hopkins University Press, 2004); Alex Owen, *The Place of Enchantment: British Occultism and the Culture of the Modern* (Chicago:

University of Chicago Press, 2004); Andreas Sommer, "Crossing the Boundaries of Mind and Body: Psychical Research and the Origins of Modern Psychology," PhD diss., Science and Technology Studies, University College London, 2013; Egil Asprem, *The Problem of Disenchantment: Scientific Naturalism and Esoteric Discourse, 1900–1939* (Leiden: Brill, 2014); Tessel M. Bauduin and Henrik Johnsson, eds., *The Occult in Modernist Art, Literature, and Cinema* (Cham: Palgrave Macmillan / Springer, 2017); Jason Ā. Josephson-Storm, *The Myth of Disenchantment: Magic, Modernity, and the Birth of the Human Sciences* (Chicago: University of Chicago Press, 2017); Richard Noakes, *Physics and Psychics: The Occult and the Sciences in Modern Britain* (Cambridge: Cambridge University Press, 2019).

40. Ulrich Linse, *Geisterseher und Wunderwirker: Heilssuche im Industriezeitalter* (Frankfurt am Main: Fischer, 1996), 16. For the broader context, see also Marcus Hahn and Erhard Schüttpelz, eds., *Trancemedien und Neue Medien um 1900: Ein anderer Blick auf die Moderne* (Bielefeld: transcript, 2009).
41. See Sommer, "Crossing the Boundaries," 87–93; Josephson-Storm, *Myth of Disenchantment*, 184–191.
42. Carl du Prel, *The Philosophy of Mysticism*, trans. C. C. Massey, 2 vols. (London: George Redway, 1898); German original as *Die Philosophie der Mystik* (Leipzig: Günther, 1885); Carl du Prel, "Der Dämon des Sokrates," *Sphinx* 4 (1887): 217–227, 329–335, 391–400; Carl du Prel, "Moderner Tempelschlaf," *Sphinx* 9 (1890): 1–6, 105–111.
43. Karl Kiesewetter, *Geschichte des neueren Occultismus: Geheimwissenschaftliche Systeme von Agrippa von Nettesheim bis zu Karl du Prel*, 2nd, updated, and expanded ed., ed. Robert Blum (Leipzig: Max Altmann, 1909), preface to the first edition, p. vii.
44. Karl Kiesewetter, *Der Occultismus des Altertums* (Leipzig: Wilhelm Friedrich, 1896), 3 (emphasis original).
45. Antoine Faivre, "Occultism," in *The Encyclopedia of Religion*, ed. Mircea Eliade (editor in chief), 11:36–40 (New York: Macmillan, 1987), p. 36 (emphasis original).
46. Karl Hoheisel, "Okkultismus I," in *Religion in Geschichte und Gegenwart*, 4th, thoroughly revised edition, ed. Hans Dieter Betz et al. (Tübingen: Mohr Siebeck, 2003), 498–499, p. 498.
47. Kiesewetter, *Geschichte des neueren Occultismus*, 3.
48. Explicitly so in Karl Kiesewetter, *Die Geheimwissenschaften*, 2nd ed. (Leipzig: Wilhelm Friedrich, 1894), which has "secret sciences" in the title.
49. On the North American discourses, see Howard Kerr and Charles L. Crow, eds., *The Occult in America: New Historical Perspectives* (Urbana: University of Illinois Press, 1983).
50. Alex Owen, *The Place of Enchantment: British Occultism and the Culture of the Modern* (Chicago: University of Chicago Press, 2004), 7.
51. Owen, 4 (emphasis original).
52. Steven Shapin, *A Social History of Truth: Civility and Science in Seventeenth-Century England* (Chicago: University of Chicago Press, 1994), 412.
53. Kurt Danziger, *Constructing the Subject: Historical Origins of Psychological Research* (Cambridge: Cambridge University Press, 1990), 182.
54. Very good historical accounts can be found in Henri F. Ellenberger, *The Discovery of the Unconscious: The History and Evolution of Dynamic Psychiatry* (London: Allen Lane Penguin, 1970); Heinrich Balmer, ed., *Die Psychologie des 20. Jahrhunderts*, vol. 1, *Die europäische Tradition: Tendenzen, Schulen, Entwicklungslinien* (Zurich: Kindler, 1976);

Roger Smith, *The Fontana History of the Human Sciences* (London: Fontana, 1997), 492–529 and 575–870.

55. See Klaus-Jürgen Bruder, "Zwischen Kant und Freud: Die Institutionalisierung der Psychologie als selbständige Wissenschaft," in *Die Seele: Ihre Geschichte im Abendland*, ed. Gerd Jüttemann, Michael Sonntag, and Christoph Wulf (Weinheim: Psychologie Verlags Union, 1991), 319–339; Stephanie Gripentrog, *Anormalität und Religion: Zur Entstehung der Psychologie im Kontext der europäischen Religionsgeschichte des 19. und frühen 20. Jahrhunderts* (Würzburg: Ergon-Verlag, 2016), 250–255.
56. Zander, *Geschichte der Seelenwanderung*, 505–550.
57. Bruno Latour, "The Recall of Modernity: Anthropological Approaches," *Cultural Studies Review* 13 (2011): 11–30.
58. Joseph Beck, *Grundriß der Empirischen Psychologie und Logik*, 2nd ed. (Stuttgart: Verlag der J. B. Metzler'schen Buchhandlung, 1846), 16 (emphasis original). Later in this book, we will see that Ernst Haeckel developed quite a similar concept of the soul at the beginning of the twentieth century.
59. Johann Friedrich Herbart, *Lehrbuch zur Psychologie*, 2nd, improved ed. (Königsberg: August Wilhelm Unzer, 1834), 1 (emphasis original).
60. Herbart, 122–123.
61. Herbart, 123 (emphasis original).
62. Herbart, 3 (emphasis original).
63. Eduard Beneke, *Lehrbuch der pragmatischen Psychologie oder der Seelenlehre in der Anwendung auf das Leben* (Berlin: E. S. Mittler, 1853), 1.
64. Eduard Beneke, *Lehrbuch der Psychologie als Naturwissenschaft*, 4th ed. (Berlin: E. S. Mittler, 1877), 28; first edition published in 1833.
65. Bruder, "Zwischen Kant und Freud," 322–323.
66. Danziger, *Constucting the Subject*, 17–48; Sommer, "Crossing the Boundaries," 202–229.
67. Wilhelm Wundt, *Vorlesungen über die Menschen- und Thierseele*, 3rd ed. (Hamburg: Voss, 1897), 366.
68. Wundt, 379.
69. Wilhelm Wundt, *Der Spiritismus: Eine sogenannte wissenschaftliche Frage: Offener Brief an Herrn Prof. Dr. Hermann Ulrici in Halle* (Leipzig: Engelmann, 1879). See Andreas Sommer, "Normalizing the Supernormal: The Formation of the 'Gesellschaft für Psychologische Forschung' ('Society for Psychological Research'), c. 1886–1890," *Journal of the History of the Behavioral Sciences* 49 (2013): 18–44, p. 35.
70. Wundt, *Vorlesungen*, 380.
71. Another example, which I mention here only in passing, is Oswald Külpe, *Grundriss der Psychologie: Auf experimenteller Grundlage dargestellt* (Leipzig: Wilhelm Engelmann, 1893).
72. Wilhelm Jerusalem, *Lehrbuch der Psychologie*, 3rd, completely rev. ed. (Vienna: Wilhelm Braumüller, 1902), 206–213.
73. Jerusalem, 14 (emphasis original).
74. Jerusalem, 15 (emphasis original).
75. Bruder, "Zwischen Kant und Freud," 322.
76. Friedrich Jodl, *Lehrbuch der Psychologie*, 3rd ed. (Stuttgart: J. G. Cotta'sche Buchhandlung Nachfolger, 1908), 38; first edition published in 1896.
77. Jodl, 45–46.
78. Otto Klemm, *Geschichte der Psychologie* (Leipzig: B. G. Teubner, 1911), 175–221.

79. Klemm, 12–13 (emphasis original).
80. Jens Schlieter provides a detailed analysis of these discourses with reference to near-death experiences. When he addresses the "survival of the soul" after death, locating this discourse in the religious domain, he merges the strands of "soul" and "consciousness" in his analysis of the ontological, epistemic, intersubjective, and moral significance that these discussions reveal. See Jens Schlieter, *What Is It Like to Be Dead?: Near-Death Experiences, Christianity, and the Occult* (New York: Oxford University Press, 2018), 35–37.
81. K. O. Beetz, *Einführung in die moderne Psychologie*. Pt. 1, *Allgemeine Grundlegung* (Osterwieck: A. W. Zickfeldt, 1900), 40.
82. Wilhelm Dilthey, "Ideen über eine beschreibende und zergliedernde Psychologie," in *Gesammelte Schriften*, vol. 5, *139–240* (Stuttgart: Vandenhoeck und Ruprecht, 1894), 195.
83. Dilthey, 195.
84. Letter from December 31, 1893, ed. Le Clair, 31; quoted in Sonu Shamdasani, *Jung and the Making of Modern Psychology: The Dream of a Science* (Cambridge: Cambridge University Press, 2003), 3.
85. Shamdasani, *Jung and the Making of Modern Psychology*, 4.
86. Lorraine Daston, "The Theory of Will Versus the Science of Mind," in *The Problematic Science: Psychology in Nineteenth-Century Thought*, ed. William R. Woodward and Mitchell G. Ash (New York: Praeger, 1982), 88–115.
87. On the bitter German debate about Wundt's turn, see Sommer, "Crossing the Boundaries," 210–262.
88. Shamdasani, *Jung and the Making of Modern Psychology*, 4–11.
89. William James, "The Hidden Self," *Scribner's Magazine* 7 (1890): 361–373, p. 361.
90. Sommer, "Crossing the Boundaries," 118; see his detailed discussion on pp. 108–125.
91. Krister Dylan Knapp, *William James: Psychical Research and the Challenge of Modernity* (Chapel Hill: University of North Carolina Press, 2017).
92. With Knapp, it is important to note that "while James investigated and studied psychic phenomena, he was not a believer or a seeker. Nor was he a practitioner or an apologist for Spiritualism. . . . James was thus not a Spiritualist, though he did encourage his family members and friends to develop their potential mediumistic abilities." And Knapp goes on: "Similarly, James was neither a skeptic nor a debunker. He did not belong to an informal but growing network of self-proclaimed doubters and critics bent on proving Spiritualists' claims false and on exposing mediums as clever charlatans . . . His purpose, then, was neither to advance a religious cause nor to undermine one but rather to understand and hypostatize psychic phenomena." Knapp, 4.
93. William James, *The Principles of Psychology*, 2 vols. (New York: Dover, 1950), 1: 291–294, 296, 319, 343–344, 348, 350; first edition published in 1890; William James, *Psychology: Briefer Course* (New York: Henry Holt, 1910), pp. 176–181, 194, 196, 198, 200, 202–203, 215–216; first edition published in 1892. The amount of scholarly literature on William James is enormous. For an excellent intellectual biography, see Robert D. Richardson, *William James: In the Maelstrom of American Modernism* (Boston: Houghton Mifflin, 2006); see also Richard M. Gale, *The Philosophy of William James: An Introduction* (New York: Cambridge University Press, 2005). For a quick overview, see Wayne P. Pomerleau, "William James (1842–1910)," *Internet Encyclopedia of Philosophy*, www.iep.utm.edu/james-o/.
94. Sommer, "Crossing the Boundaries," 281.
95. Treitel, *A Science for the Soul*, 56–80.

2. FASCINATION WITH THE SOUL

1. Shirley Nicholson, ed., *Shamanism*, 5th ed. (Wheaton: Theosophical Publishing House, 1996), 6.
2. Piers Vitebsky, *The Shaman* (Boston: Little, Brown, 1995), 99. I will address such literary continuations of the Orphic discourse in chapter 9.
3. See Kocku von Stuckrad, *Schamanismus und Esoterik: Kultur- und wissenschaftsgeschichtliche Betrachtungen* (Leuven: Peeters, 2003), 84–88.
4. See Klaus Lichtblau, *Kulturkrise und Soziologie um die Jahrhundertwende: Zur Genealogie der Kultursoziologie in Deutschland* (Frankfurt am Main: Suhrkamp, 1996); Hans G. Kippenberg, *Discovering Religious History in the Modern Age*, trans. Barbara Harshav (Princeton: Princeton University Press, 2002), 98–112.
5. For more details on the following, see von Stuckrad, *Schamanismus und Esoterik*, 89–101.
6. See Max L. Bäumer, "Das moderne Phänomen des Dionysischen und seine 'Entdeckung' durch Nietzsche," *Nietzsche-Studien* 6 (1977): 123–153.
7. Friedrich Nietzsche, *Sämtliche Werke*, 15 vols., ed. Giorgio Colli and Mazzino Montinari (Munich: dtv, 1999), 1:554–555.
8. Nietzsche, 1:555.
9. Rüdiger Safranski, *Nietzsche: Biographie seines Denkens* (Munich: Hanser, 2000), 59.
10. Nietzsche, *Sämtliche Werke*, 1:135.
11. Friedrich Nietzsche, *Friedrich Nietzsches Briefwechsel mit Erwin Rohde*, ed. Elisabeth Förster-Nietzsche and Fritz Schöll (Leipzig: Insel, 1923), 2:332.
12. See von Stuckrad, *Schamanismus und Esoterik*, 96–101.
13. Nietzsche, *Sämtliche Werke*, 1:134.
14. Nietzsche, 1:135–136.
15. See Kocku von Stuckrad, "Utopian Landscapes and Ecstatic Journeys: Friedrich Nietzsche, Hermann Hesse, and Mircea Eliade on the Terror of Modernity," *Numen: International Review for the History of Religions* 57 (2010): 78–102.
16. Jürgen Habermas, *Der philosophische Diskurs der Moderne: Zwölf Vorlesungen*, 6th ed. (Frankfurt am Main: Suhrkamp, 1998), 117; first edition published in 1988.
17. Peter Sloterdijk and Thomas H. Macho, eds., *Weltrevolution der Seele: Ein Lese- und Arbeitsbuch der Gnosis von der Spätantike bis zur Gegenwart*, 2 vols. (Munich: Artemis & Winkler, 1991), 2:710–713.
18. Nietzsche, *Sämtliche Werke*, 1:456 (emphasis original).
19. Safranski, *Nietzsche*, 360.
20. Adam Lecznar, *Dionysus After Nietzsche:* The Birth of Tragedy *in Twentieth-Century Literature and Thought* (Cambridge: Cambridge University Press, 2020).
21. For a good introduction and overview of Rilke's work, context, and legacy in the English-speaking world, see Karen J. Leeder and Robert Vilain, eds., *The Cambridge Companion to Rilke* (Cambridge: Cambridge University Press, 2010).
22. Walter A. Strauss, *Descent and Return: The Orphic Theme in Modern Literature* (Cambridge, MA: Harvard University Press, 1971), 140.
23. See Dianna C. Niebylski, *The Poem on the Edge of the Word: The Limits of Language and the Uses of Silence in the Poetry of Mallarmé, Rilke, and Vallejo* (New York: P. Lang, 1993).
24. Ian R. Leslie, "Betrachtungen über Religion und Kunst in den Schriften von R. M. Rilke und D. H. Lawrence" (PhD diss., Freie Universität Berlin, 1990), 138; see also Winfried

Eckel, *Wendung: Zum Prozeß der poetischen Reflexion im Werk Rilkes* (Würzburg: Königshausen und Neumann, 1994), 175–204. As for the esoteric and occultist dimensions of Rilke's work (similar to my argument here), see Gísli Magnússon, *Dichtung als Erfahrungsmetaphysik—Esoterische und okkultistische Modernität bei R. M. Rilke* (Würzburg: Königshausen und Neumann, 2009).

25. See Strauss, *Descent and Return*, 172–175.
26. Rainer Maria Rilke, *The Selected Poetry of Rainer Maria Rilke*, ed. and trans. Stephen Mitchell (New York: Vintage International, 1989), 49.
27. Rilke, 49.
28. Rilke, 51.
29. Rainer Maria Rilke, *Selected Poems of Rainer Maria Rilke*, trans. Robert Bly (New York: Harper and Row, 1981), 105–107.
30. Letter from April 20, 1923; see Rainer Maria Rilke, *Briefe aus Muzot 1921 bis 1926*, vol. 6, *Briefe*, ed. Ruth Sieber-Rilke and Carl Sieber (Leipzig: Insel, 1935), 3:195.
31. Sonnet I, 1; from Rilke, *Selected Poetry*, trans. Mitchell, 227.
32. Sonnet I, 2; from Rilke, *Selected Poetry*, trans. Mitchell, 229 (also the following quotation).
33. Renate Breuninger, *Wirklichkeit in der Dichtung Rilkes* (Frankfurt am Main: Peter Lang, 1991), 295.
34. Sonnet I, 26; from Rainer Maria Rilke, *In Praise of Mortality: Selections from Rainer Maria Rilke's* Duino Elegies *and* Sonnets to Orpheus, trans. and ed. Anita Barrows and Joanna Macy (Brattleboro: Echo Point, 2005), 105. As further evidence of the discourse community and the discursive formations I am reconstructing here, one of the translators and editors of this edition of Rilke's poems is Joanna Macy, an American scholar and practitioner of Buddhism. Together with the Australian Buddhist John Seed, she developed the "Council of All Beings," a ritual process that invokes a connection with the planet and its inhabitants. This is a direct bridge between Rilke's contribution to the Orphic web and adaptations of the same discursive arrangement in nature-based and animistic spiritualities two generations later. On Joanna Macy and John Seed, see Bron Taylor, *Dark Green Religion: Nature Spirituality and the Planetary Future* (Berkeley: University of California Press, 2010), 21–22, where he subsumes the Council of All Beings under the rubric of "Naturalistic Animism or Gaian Naturalism" (p. 22).
35. Rilke, *In Praise of Mortality*, 105.
36. Sonnet I, 5; from Rilke, *In Praise of Mortality*, 75.
37. Sonnet II, 28; from Rilke, *Selected Poetry*, trans. Mitchell, 253.
38. Sonnet II, 17; from Rainer Maria Rilke, *Sonnets to Orpheus and Duino Elegies*, trans. Jessie Lemont (Newburyport: Dover, 2020), 49.
39. Sonnet II, 26; from Rilke, *Sonnets to Orpheus and Duino Elegies*, trans. Jessie Lemont, 58.
40. Sonnet II, 29; from Rilke, *Selected Poetry*, trans. Mitchell, 255.
41. Hermann Hesse, *News from the Universe*, trans. Robert Bly (San Francisco: Sierra Club Books, 1980), 86. For our discursive interpretation, it is noteworthy that this translation of Hesse's poems was published with Sierra Club Books, which is associated with the environmental organization cofounded by John Muir (more on this in chapter 9). The German version can be found in Hermann Hesse, *Die Gedichte*, ed. Volker Michels, 5th ed. (Frankfurt am Main: Suhrkamp, 1998), 231.
42. Joan Halifax, *The Fruitful Darkness: Reconnecting with the Body of the Earth* (San Francisco: HarperCollins, 1994), 91. Halifax also uses the Sierra Club Books edition of Robert Bly's translation.

43. Tracing the theme of "soul" and "ensoulment" in fin-de-siècle art would merit an entire chapter of its own. The influence of occultism—especially via the Theosophical Society and Steiner's Anthroposophy—was immense. In passing, I will simply mention the work of Hilma af Klint (1862–1944) and Franz Marc (1880–1916). Af Klint was the first to create abstract art after the turn of the century; deeply influenced by theosophical thinking and engaged in (disappointing) conversations with Rudolf Steiner, she wanted to express the "soul" and the metaphysical "essence" of being in her abstract forms and colors. Marc, as one of the first expressionistic painters and a cofounder of the Blaue Reiter, saw animals in particular as the expression of the soul of nature, and he tried to capture that "pureness" in his work. See Iris Müller-Westermann and Jo Widoff, eds., *Hilma af Klint: A Pioneer of Abstraction* (Ostfildern: Hatje Cantz, 2013); Anna Maria Bernitz, "Hilma af Klint and the New Art of Seeing," in *A Cultural History of the Avant-garde in the Nordic Countries, 1900–1925*, ed. Hubert van den Berg and Marianne Ølholm (Amsterdam: Brill / Rodopi, 2012), 587–597; John F. Moffitt, "'Fighting Forms: The Fate of the Animals': The Occultist Origins of Franz Marc's 'Farbentheorie,'" *Artibus et Historiae* 6 no. 12 (1985): 107–126; Cathrin Klingsöhr-Leroy and Andrea Firmenich, eds., *Franz Marc und Joseph Beuys: Im Einklang mit der Natur* (Munich: Schirmer/Mosel, Franz Marc Museum, 2011) (on Marc and Beuys, another Orphic artist whom space does not permit me to discuss further here). For the wider context, see also Tessel M. Bauduin and Henrik Johnsson, eds., *The Occult in Modernist Art, Literature, and Cinema* (Cham: Palgrave Macmillan / Springer), 2017.
44. Katharina and Anton Kippenberg were influential publishers (Insel Verlag) and supporters of contemporary art and literature. Katharina Kippenberg even wrote a biography of Rilke; see Katharina Kippenberg, *Rainer Maria Rilke: Ein Beitrag* (Leipzig: Insel Verlag, 1935).
45. On the link between occultism and the "new woman," see Barbara Hales, "Mediating Worlds: The Occult as Projection of the New Woman in Weimar Culture," *German Quarterly* 83, no. 3 (2010): 317–332.
46. Silke Kettelhake, *Renée Sintenis: Berlin, Boheme und Ringelnatz* (Berlin: Osburg, 2010), 63.
47. Paul Appel in Rudolf Hagelstange, Carl Georg Heise, and Paul Appel, eds., *Renée Sintenis*, with contributions from Rudolf Hagelstange, Carl Georg Heise, and Paul Appel (Berlin: Aufbau-Verlag, 1947), 31.
48. Hagelstange, Heise, and Appel, 25.
49. Hagelstange, Heise, and Appel, 26.
50. Hagelstange, Heise, and Appel, 28 (emphasis original). The following quotation is from p. 31.
51. For the larger context, see also Lutz Greisiger, Sebastian Schüler, and Alexander van der Haven, eds., *Religion und Wahnsinn um 1900: Zwischen Pathologisierung und Selbstermächtigung / Religion and Madness Around 1900: Between Pathology and Self-Empowerment* (Würzburg: Ergon, 2017). For the literary discourse, see also Lecznar, *Dionysus After Nietzsche*.
52. Lytton Naegele McDonnell, "Ecstatic Anthems" (PhD diss., Rutgers University, 2018), doi:10.7282/T3GF0XQH.
53. See von Stuckrad, *Schamanismus und Esoterik*, 96–101.
54. Erwin Rohde, *Psyche: Seelencult und Unsterblichkeitsglaube der Griechen*, 2 vols., 5th/6th eds. (Tübingen: Mohr-Siebeck, 1910), 2:19 (emphasis original); first edition published in 1894.

55. Rohde, 2:20.
56. Lecznar, *Dionysus After Nietzsche*, 34. See the entire chapter on Harrison, pp. 34–67.
57. Camille Paglia, *Sexual Personae: Art and Decadence from Nefertiti to Emily Dickinson* (New Haven, CT: Yale University Press, 1990), 84.
58. Ulrike Brunotte, *Dämonen des Wissens: Gender, Performativität und materielle Kultur im Werk von Jane Ellen Harrison* (Würzburg: Ergon, 2013), 214.
59. See Brunotte, *Dämonen des Wissens*.
60. Her reviews of the two parts of Rohde's book came out in *Classical Review* 4 (1890): 376–377 and no. 8 (1894): 165–166.
61. Annabel Robinson, *The Life and Work of Jane Ellen Harrison* (Oxford: Oxford University Press, 2002), 112. For Harrison's work on Rohde's ideas, see Jane Ellen Harrison, *Themis: A Study of the Social Origins of Greek Religion. With an Excursus on the Ritual Forms Preserved in Greek Tragedy by Gilbert Murray and a Chapter on the Origin of the Olympic Games by F. M. Cornford*. 2nd ed. (Cambridge: Cambridge University Press, 1927), for instance, at pp. 47–48; 1st published in 1912.
62. Kippenberg, *Discovering Religious History in the Modern Age*, 176.
63. Kippenberg, 176.
64. Martin Buber, *Ekstatische Konfessionen: Gesammelt von Martin Buber* (Berlin: Schocken, 1923), 22; first edition published in Jena by Diederichs in 1909.
65. See Nils Roemer, "Reading Nietzsche—Thinking About God: Martin Buber, Gershom Scholem, and Franz Rosenzweig," *American Catholic Philosophical Quarterly* 84 (2010): 427–441; Kocku von Stuckrad, *The Scientification of Religion: An Historical Study of Discursive Change, 1800–2000* (Berlin: De Gruyter, 2014), 117–124. I will come back to Buber in the next chapter.
66. Rudolf Otto, *Das Heilige: Über das Irrationale in der Idee des Göttlichen und sein Verhältnis zum Rationalen* (Munich: C. H. Beck, 2004); first edition published in 1917. English translation: *The Idea of the Holy*, trans J. W. Harvey (New York: Oxford University Press, 1923).
67. Kippenberg, *Discovering Religious History in the Modern Age*, 181–182. On Otto's importance, see also Jörg Lauster, Peter Schüz, Roderich Bart, and Christian Danz, eds., *Rudolf Otto: Theologie—Religionsphilosophie—Religionsgeschichte* (Berlin: De Gruyter, 2014.
68. See also von Stuckrad, *Scientification of Religion*, 126–129.
69. Gerardus van der Leeuw, *Mystiek* (Baarn: Hollandia-Drukkerij, 1924), 4.
70. Gerardus van der Leeuw, *Sacred and Profane Beauty: The Holy in Art*, trans. David E. Green, with a preface by Mircea Eliade and a new introduction and bibliography by Diane Apostolos-Capadona (New York: Oxford University Press, 2006), 34; first English translation published in1963; Dutch original published in 1932.
71. Van der Leeuw, 35.
72. Van der Leeuw, 70–71. On this topic, see also Kimerer Lewis LaMothe, *Nietzsche's Dancers: Isadora Duncan, Martha Graham, and the Revaluation of Christian Values* (New York: Palgrave-Macmillan, 2006).
73. Van der Leeuw, *Sacred and Profane Beauty*, 59, where he defines the "Dionysiac" as "ecstatic intoxication."
74. Van der Leeuw, 66 (both quotations).
75. Gerardus van der Leeuw, *Sakramentales Denken: Erscheinungsformen und Wesen der außerchristlichen und christlichen Sakramente* (Kassel: Johannes Stauda-Verlag, 1959), 151.

76. Van der Leeuw, 151.
77. Van der Leeuw, 152 (emphasis original).
78. See Gangolf Hübinger, ed., *Versammlungsort moderner Geister: Der Eugen Diederichs Verlag—Aufbruch ins Jahrhundert der Extreme* (Munich: Eugen Diederichs, 1996).
79. Karl Joël, *Der Ursprung der Naturphilosophie aus dem Geiste der Mystik* (Jena: Eugen Diederichs, 1906), 15.
80. Joël, 161; see also p. viii.
81. On the complex history of pantheism in European intellectual history, see Mary-Jane Rubenstein, *Pantheologies: Gods, Worlds, Monsters* (New York: Columbia University Press, 2018).
82. Joël, *Ursprung der Naturphilosophie*, 11.
83. Joël, 13.
84. Karl Joël, *Seele und Welt: Versuch einer organischen Auffassung* (Jena: Eugen Diederichs, 1912), 1–2.
85. Joël, 2.
86. Joël, 4–5.
87. See Barbara Beßlich, *Wege in den "Kulturkrieg": Zivilisationskritik in Deutschland, 1890–1914* (Darmstadt: Wissenschaftliche Buchgesellschaft, 2000).
88. Christoph Bernoulli and Hans Kern, eds., *Romantische Naturphilosophie* (Jena: Eugen Diederichs, 1926), v.
89. Bernoulli and Kern, viii (emphasis original).
90. Given the importance of Ludwig Klages for the development of philosophy and occultism in the twentieth century, it is astonishing how little has been published on him in English. As Jason Ā. Josephson-Storm notes: Klages "is found in many footnotes and is frequently referenced in works on Walter Benjamin or in the context of German irrationalism, or *Lebensphilosophie*, but Klages's major monographs have never been translated into English, and he is rarely studied on his own terms." Jason Ā. Josephson-Storm, *The Myth of Disenchantment: Magic, Modernity, and the Birth of the Human Sciences* (Chicago: University of Chicago Press, 2017), 215. See Josephson-Storm's discussion of Klages on pp. 210–225. Relevant scholarly works on Klages include: Michael Großheim, *Ludwig Klages und die Phänomenologie* (Berlin: Akademie-Verlag, 1994); Hans Kunz, *Martin Heidegger und Ludwig Klages: Daseinsanalytik und Metaphysik* (Munich: Kindler, 1976). See also the recent English study by Nitzan Lebovic, *The Philosophy of Life and Death: Ludwig Klages and the Rise of a Nazi Biopolitics* (New York: Palgrave Macmillan, 2013).
91. Ludwig Klages, *Der Mensch und das Leben*, edition of "Mensch und Erde" (1913) and "Bewußtsein und Leben" (1915) (Jena: Eugen Diederichs, 1937), 10. An English translation of this work is available as Ludwig Klages, *The Biocentric Worldview: Selected Essays and Poems of Ludwig Klages*, trans. Joseph Pryce (London: Arktos, 2013). See also Ludwig Klages, *Cosmogonic Reflections: Selected Aphorisms from Ludwig Klages*, trans. Joseph Pryce (London: Arktos, 2015).
92. Klages, *Der Mensch und das Leben*, 12.
93. Klages, 16.
94. Klages, 23 (emphasis original).
95. Klages, 29–30 (emphasis original).
96. See Todd LeVasseur and Anna Peterson, eds., *Religion and Ecological Crisis: The "Lynn White Thesis" at Fifty* (New York: Routledge, 2017); see also chapter 10.

97. Ludwig Klages, *Vom kosmogonischen Eros*, 6th, corrected ed. (Bonn: H. Bouvier u., 1963); first edition published in 1921.
98. See Josephson-Storm, *Myth of Disenchantment*, 210–221; 269–278; see also Jason Ā. Josephson-Storm, "Max Weber in the Realm of Enchantment," blog post for *Forbidden Histories*, April 4, 2018, www.forbiddenhistories.com/weber-josephson-storm/.

3. THE MOBILIZATION OF THE SOUL

1. Benedict Anderson, *Imagined Communities: Reflections on the Origin and Spread of Nationalism*, rev. ed. (London: Verso, 2006), 12.
2. See Gemma Blok, Vincent Kuitenbrouwer, and Claire Weeda, eds., *Imagining Communities: Historical Reflections on the Process of Community Formation* (Amsterdam: Amsterdam University Press, 2018). See also Anderson's afterword to the new 2006 edition in Anderson, *Imagined Communities*, 207–229.
3. François Millepierres, *La vie d'Ernest Renan, sage d'Occident* (Paris: Librairie Marcel Rivière et Cie, 1961), 10.
4. Eduard Platzhoff, *Ernest Renan: Ein Lebensbild* (Dresden: Carl Reißner, 1900), 112–113.
5. Walther Küchler, *Ernest Renan: Der Dichter und der Künstler* (Gotha: Friedrich Andreas Perthes, 1921), 123.
6. Küchler, 125.
7. Ernest Renan, *Qu'est-ce qu'une Nation? et autres écrits politiques*, ed. Raoul Girardet (Paris: Imprimerie nationale Éditions, 1996), from the introduction, p. 21.
8. I quote Martin Thom's translation of "What Is a Nation?," which is included in Homi K. Bhabha, ed., *Nation and Narration* (London: Routledge, 1990), 8–22. The quotation is from p. 12. The original French text of the speech can be found in Renan, *Qu'est-ce qu'une Nation?*, 223–243.
9. Bhabha, *Nation and Narration*, 14.
10. Bhabha, 15.
11. Bhabha, 19.
12. Bhabha, 19.
13. Bhabha, 20.
14. Brent Hayes Edwards, introduction to W. E. B. Du Bois, *The Souls of Black Folk*, ed. Brent Hayes Edwards (Oxford: Oxford University Press, 2007), xiv; first edition published in 1903.
15. David Levering Lewis, *W. E. B. Du Bois: Biography of a Race, 1868–1919* (New York: Henry Holt, 1993), 282.
16. Du Bois, *Souls of Black Folk*, 8.
17. Du Bois, 182.
18. Du Bois, 184.
19. Du Bois, 184–185.
20. Carol Wayne White, *Black Lives and Sacred Humanity: Toward an African American Religious Naturalism* (New York: Fordham University Press, 2016); on Du Bois, see pp. 75–92.
21. Dieter Borchmeyer, *Was ist deutsch?: Variationen eines Themas von Schiller über Wagner zu Thomas Mann* (Eichstätt: Katholische Universität Eichstätt-Ingolstadt, 2010), 3.

22. See Akademie der Künste, Berlin, *Waldungen: Die Deutschen und ihr Wald*, Ausstellung der Akademie der Künste vom 20. September bis 15. November 1987 (Berlin: Nicolaische Verlagsbuchhandlung, 1987).
23. German version in Johann Gottfried Herder, *Sämmtliche Werke: Zur schönen Literatur und Kunst*, vol. 3/1, *Gedichte* (Stuttgart: J. G. Cotta, 1827), 221; my translation.
24. Bernd Weyergraf, "Deutsche Wälder," in *Waldungen: Die Deutschen und ihr Wald*, ed. Akademie der Künste, Berlin (Berlin: Nicolaische Verlagsbuchhandlung, 1987), 6–12, p. 6.
25. Friedrich Rothe, "Deutscher Wald um 1900," in Akademie der Künste, Berlin, *Waldungen*, 69–73, p. 72.
26. Rothe, 72–73.
27. Ludwig Klages, *Vom kosmogonischen Eros*, 6th, corrected ed. (Bonn: H. Bouvier, 1963), 110 (emphasis original); first edition published in 1921.
28. See John Williams, "Giving Nature a Higher Purpose: Back-to-Nature Movements in Weimar Germany, 1918–1933" (PhD diss., University of Michigan, 1996), https://deepblue.lib.umich.edu/handle/2027.42/129825; John A. Williams, "'The Chords of the German Soul Are Tuned to Nature': The Movement to Preserve the Natural *Heimat* from the Kaiserreich to the Third Reich," *Central European History* 29 (1996): 339–384. See also Simon Schama, *Landscape and Memory* (New York: A. A. Knopf, 1995), 75–134.
29. Ernst Piper, *Alfred Rosenberg: Hitlers Chefideologe* (Munich: Karl Blessing, 2005).
30. Kurt Hutten, *Christus oder Deutschglaube? Ein Kampf um die deutsche Seele* (Stuttgart: J. F. Steinkopf, 1935).
31. Alfred Rosenberg, *Der Mythus des 20. Jahrhunderts: Eine Wertung der seelisch-geistigen Gestaltenkämpfe unserer Zeit*, 13th–16th ed. (first ed. 1930) (Munich: Hoheneichen-Verlag, 1933), 1.
32. Rosenberg, 22.
33. Rosenberg, 23.
34. Rosenberg, 140 (emphasis original).
35. Rosenberg, 141–142 (emphasis original).
36. Rosenberg, 622.
37. Rosenberg, 622.
38. Rosenberg, 623.
39. Rosenberg, 623.
40. On this theme, see also Rainer Guldin, *Politische Landschaften: Zum Verhältnis von Raum und nationaler Identität* (Bielefeld: transcript, 2014).
41. See Akademie der Künste, Berlin, *Waldungen*, 280–281.
42. Günther Müller, *Geschichte der deutschen Seele: Vom Faustbuch zu Goethes Faust* (Freiburg: Herder, 1939), 378.
43. Du Bois, *Souls of Black Folk*, 184.
44. Yaron Peleg, *Orientalism and the Hebrew Imagination* (Ithaca, NY: Cornell University Press, 2005), 3.
45. Klaus Holz, "Der Jude: Dritter der Nationen," in *Die Figur des Dritten: Ein kulturwissenschaftliches Paradigma*, ed. Eva Eßlinger et al. (Frankfurt am Main: Suhrkamp, 2010), 292–303. See also Peleg, *Orientalism and the Hebrew Imagination*, 5.
46. See Jonathan Boyarin and Daniel Boyarin, eds., *Jews and Other Differences: The New Jewish Cultural Studies* (Minneapolis: University of Minnesota Press, 1997); Ivan

Davidson Kalmar and Derek J. Penslar, eds., *Orientalism and the Jews* (Waltham, MA: Brandeis University Press, 2005).

47. On the following, see also Kocku von Stuckrad, *The Scientification of Religion: An Historical Study of Discursive Change, 1800–2000* (Berlin: De Gruyter, 2014), 117–124.
48. Jonathan Hess, "Sugar Island Jews?: Jewish Colonialism and the Rhetoric of 'Civic Improvement' in Eighteenth-Century Germany," *Eighteenth-Century Studies* 32 (1998): 92–100.
49. Michael Brenner, "Gnosis and History: Polemics of German-Jewish Identity from Graetz to Scholem," *New German Critique* 77 (1999): 45–60, p. 46.
50. See Steven E. Aschheim, *Brothers and Strangers: The East European Jew in German and German Jewish Consciousness, 1800–1932* (Madison: University of Wisconsin Press, 1982); Paul R. Mendes-Flohr, "Fin de Siècle Orientalism, the *Ostjuden*, and the Aesthetics of Jewish Self-Affirmation," in *Divided Passions: Jewish Intellectuals and the Experience of Modernity*, ed. Paul R. Mendes-Flohr (Detroit: Wayne State University Press, 1991), 77–132.
51. Arnold Zweig, *Das ostjüdische Antlitz: Zu fünfzig Steinzeichnungen von Hermann Struck* (Berlin: Welt-Verlag, 1920), 32.
52. Zweig, 34.
53. Handwritten manuscript found among Buber's notes for his dissertation, Martin Buber Archive, B/7. Quoted in Paul Mendes-Flohr, *From Mysticism to Dialogue: Martin Buber's Transformation of German Social Thought* (Detroit: Wayne State University Press, 1989), 61–62 (translations by Mendes-Flohr). In the subsequent passage of that same manuscript, Buber adds "cognition" (*Erkennen*) to the discursive knot of world–psyche–energy–existence–natural powers: For Buber, cognition "constitutes not an inner relation to the movements of world and psyche, but only one of classifying (*Einordnen*) perceptions" (p. 62).
54. Mendes-Flohr, *From Mysticism to Dialogue*, 66. On Nietzsche and "spiritual/religious Zionism," above all in Buber and Hillel Zeitlin, see also Jacob Golomb, *Nietzsche and Zion* (Ithaca, NY: Cornell University Press, 2004), 155–214.
55. Martin Buber, *Drei Reden über das Judentum* (Frankfurt am Main: Literarische Anstalt Rütten und Loening, 1919), 48–49.
56. See the speech "Die Erneuerung des Judentums" ("The Renewal of Judaism") in Buber, 82–85.
57. "Das Judentum und die Menschheit," in Buber, 55–56.
58. Buber, 79.
59. "Das Judentum und die Juden" ("Judaism and the Jews"), in Buber, 22.
60. "Das Judentum und die Menschheit," in Buber, 52.
61. "Das Judentum und die Menschheit," in Buber, 53.
62. "Die Erneuerung des Judentums," in Buber, 102.
63. See Klaus Samuel Davidowicz, *Gershom Scholem und Martin Buber: Die Geschichte eines Mißverständnisses* (Neukirchen-Vluyn: Neukirchener Verlag, 1995), 1–21.
64. David Biale, *Gershom Scholem: Kabbalah and Counter-History* (Cambridge, MA: Harvard University Press, 1979). On Buber and Scholem as part of a "Jewish Metagnosis," see also Peter Sloterdijk and Thomas H. Macho, eds., *Weltrevolution der Seele: Ein Lese- und Arbeitsbuch der Gnosis von der Spätantike bis zur Gegenwart*, 2 vols. (Munich: Artemis und Winkler, 1991), 1:249–255.

65. Gershom Scholem, *Tagebücher, nebst Aufsätzen und Entwürfen bis 1923*, vol. 1, ed. Karlfried Gründer and Friedrich Niewöhner, in collaboration with Herbert Kopp-Oberstebrink (Frankfurt am Main: Jüdischer Verlag, 1995), 226.
66. Scholem, 1:226 (emphasis original).
67. Davidowicz, *Gershom Scholem und Martin Buber*, 67.
68. Gershom Scholem, *Tagebücher, nebst Aufsätzen und Entwürfen bis 1923*, 2nd half binding 1917–1923, ed. Karlfried Gründer, Herbert Kopp-Oberstebrink, and Friedrich Niewöhner, in collaboration with Karl E. Grözinger (Frankfurt am Main: Jüdischer Verlag, 2000), 151 (*tikkun* in Hebrew letters in the original).
69. Hans Thomas Hakl, *Eranos: An Alternative Intellectual History of the Twentieth Century*, revised and expanded ed., trans. Christopher McIntosh with the collaboration of Hereward Tilton (Montréal: McGill-Queen's University Press, 2013), 33–42.
70. See Michael Gamper, "Charisma, Hypnose, Nachahmung. Massenpsychologie und Medientheorie," in *Trancemedien und Neue Medien um 1900: Ein anderer Blick auf die Moderne*, ed. Marcus Hahn and Erhard Schüttpelz (Bielefeld: transcript, 2009), 351–373.
71. Wilhelm Wundt, *Völkerpsychologie: Eine Untersuchung der Entwicklungsgesetze von Sprache, Mythus und Sitte*, 10 vols. (Leipzig: Engelmann [subsequently Kröner], 1900–1920).

4. CARL GUSTAV JUNG

1. "Allgemeine Gesichtspunkte zur Psychologie des Traumes," in Carl Gustav Jung, *Gesammelte Werke*, 18 vols. (Zurich: Rascher and Olten: Walter, 1958–1981), 8:§525; first published in English as "The Psychology of Dreams" in *Collected Papers on Analytical Psychology* (London, 1916); then, as a significantly expanded manuscript, included in *Über die Energetik der Seele* (Zurich: Rascher, 1928); as well as in a further developed version in *Über psychische Energetik und das Wesen der Träume* (Zurich: Rascher, 1948).
2. Sonu Shamdasani, *Jung and the Making of Modern Psychology: The Dream of a Science* (Cambridge: Cambridge University Press, 2003), 13–15; see also 344–348.
3. For relatively recent biographies, see Deirdre Bair, *Jung: A Biography* (London: Little, Brown, 2004); Sonu Shamdasani, *C. G. Jung: A Biography in Books* (New York: W. W. Norton, 2012); cf. also Sonu Shamdasani, *Jung Stripped Bare by His Biographers, Even* (London: Karnac, 2005).
4. Even Deirdre Bair's biography, which was published in the United States in 2003, could still only speculate about the *Red Book*; see Bair, *Jung*, 292–295, and especially 745–746n9.
5. Shamdasani, *Jung and the Making of Modern Psychology*, 3.
6. Shamdasani, 67.
7. Shamdasani, 63.
8. Bair, *Jung*, 46–52.
9. Shamdasani, *C. G. Jung*, 35–41.
10. Shamdasani, *Jung and the Making of Modern Psychology*, 92–93; on "Jung without Freud" see also 11–13.
11. Jung, *Gesammelte Werke*, 9/1:§113; on James and Jung, see Eugene Taylor, "Jung and William James," *Spring: A Journal for Archetypal Psychology and Jungian Thought* 20 (1980): 157–169.

12. Shamdasani, *Jung and the Making of Modern Psychology*, 91.
13. Jung, *Gesammelte Werke*, 18:§1740.
14. Jung, *Gesammelte Werke*, 9/1:§1–3 (emphasis original).
15. Marilyn Nagy, *Philosophical Issues in the Psychology of C. G. Jung* (Albany: State University of New York Press, 1991), 55.
16. Jung, *Gesammelte Werke* 10:§31.
17. Jung, 10:§31.
18. Jung, 10:§32.
19. Jung, 10:§32.
20. Jung, 7:§41.
21. *Die Schizophrenie*, first published in 1958, in *Gesammelte Werke* 3:§565 (emphasis original).
22. *Psychologie und Religion*, first published in 1939; see Jung, *Gesammelte Werke* 11:§5.
23. *Theoretische Überlegungen zum Wesen des Psychischen*, in Jung, *Gesammelte Werke* 8:§411 (emphasis original).
24. Jung, *Gesammelte Werke* 8:§412; in a footnote, Jung adds that "nature" here has "the meaning of the par excellence given and existing."
25. *Die Wandlung der Libido*, in Jung, *Gesammelte Werke*, 5:§224; "pattern of behaviour" is in English in the original, with British spelling.
26. *Die Struktur der Seele*, first version 1927, in Jung, *Gesammelte Werke*, 8:§342.
27. See Sonu Shamdasani, "Liber Novus: The 'Red Book' of C. G. Jung," in *The Red Book: Liber Novus*, ed. Sonu Shamdasani (New York: W. W. Norton, 2009), 193–221. For the psychoanalytic reception, see Thomas Arzt, ed., *Das Rote Buch: C. G. Jungs Reise zum "anderen Pol der Welt"* (Würzburg: Königshausen und Neumann, 2015).
28. See Wouter J. Hanegraaff, "The Great War of the Soul: Divine and Human Madness in Carl Gustav Jung's Liber Novus," in *Religion und Wahnsinn um 1900: Zwischen Pathologisierung und Selbstermächtigung / Religion and Madness Around 1900: Between Pathology and Self-Empowerment*, ed. Lutz Greisiger, Sebastian Schüler, and Alexander van der Haven (Würzburg: Ergon, 2017), 101–135.
29. Shamdasani, "Liber Novus," 204, with reference to Ludwig Staudenmaier's experiments with magic; on this further proof of the discursive entanglement of magic, science, occultism, and psychology, see Ludwig Staudenmaier, *Die Magie als experimentelle Naturwissenschaft* (Leipzig: Akademische Verlagsgesellschaft, 1912).
30. Aniela Jaffé, *Erinnerungen, Träume, Gedanken von C. G. Jung: Aufgezeichnet und herausgegeben von Aniela Jaffé* (Olten: Walter, 1971), 186. See also Shamdasani, "Liber Novus," 201–202, with reference to Jung's report to Mircea Eliade that his 1914 dream events had convinced him that the information came from the collective unconscious, and that he only had to confirm and deepen these insights—work that had occupied him for the last forty years.
31. Shamdasani, "Liber Novus," 202.
32. Ludwig Klages, *Die psychologischen Errungenschaften Nietzsches* (Leipzig: Johann Ambrosius Barth, 1926), 10.
33. Klages, 10.
34. *Mysterium Coniunctionis: Untersuchungen über die Trennung und Zusammensetzung der seelischen Gegensätze in der Alchemie*, in Jung, *Gesammelte Werke*, 14/1: 11.
35. Jung, *Gesammelte Werke*, 14/1:11.

36. Jung, 14/1:12, with reference to Lucien Lévy-Bruhl and his related concept of *représentations collectives*.
37. See Kocku von Stuckrad, *The Scientification of Religion: An Historical Study of Discursive Change, 1800–2000* (Berlin: De Gruyter, 2014), 56–75.
38. Wouter J. Hanegraaff, *Esotericism and the Academy: Rejected Knowledge in Western Culture* (Cambridge: Cambridge University Press, 2012), 294.
39. Mark S. Morrisson, *Modern Alchemy: Occultism and the Emergence of Atomic Theory* (Oxford: Oxford University Press, 2007), 5.
40. *Der philosophische Baum*, in Jung, *Gesammelte Werke* 13:§305.
41. Jung, 13:§305.
42. Jung, 13:§356–357 (emphasis original).
43. For criticism of Jung, Eliade, and others, see Lawrence M. Principe and William R. Newman, "Some Problems with the Historiography of Alchemy," in *Secrets of Nature: Astrology and Alchemy in Early Modern Europe*, ed. William R. Newman and Anthony Grafton (Cambridge, MA: MIT Press, 2001), 385–431.
44. Thomas Arzt, Maria Hippius-Gräfin Dürckheim, and Roland Dollinger, eds., *Unus Mundus: Kosmos und Sympathie. Beiträge zum Gedanken der Einheit von Mensch und Kosmos* (Frankfurt am Main: Peter Lang, 1991), 14.
45. See especially Wolfgang Pauli, *Writings on Physics and Philosophy*, ed. Charles P. Enz and Karl von Meyenn (Berlin: Springer, 1994).
46. Kalervo Vihtori Laurikainen, *The Philosophical Thought of Wolfgang Pauli* (Berlin: Springer, 1988); F. David Peat, *Synchronicity: The Bridge Between Matter and Mind* (Toronto: Bantam, 1987).
47. Wolfgang Pauli, "Die Wissenschaft und das abendländische Denken," in *Europa—Erbe und Aufgabe: Internationaler Gelehrtenkongress Mainz 1955*, ed. Martin Göhring (Wiesbaden: Franz Steiner, 1956), 71–79, p. 79.
48. Carl Gustav Jung and Wolfgang Pauli, *Naturerklärung und Psyche* (Zurich: Rascher, 1952), 115.
49. This essay is also included in Jung, *Gesammelte Werke*, vol. 8.
50. On Jung and Pauli's joint work on the concept of synchronicity, see Marialuisa Donati, "Beyond Synchronicity: The Worldview of Carl Gustav Jung and Wolfgang Pauli," *Journal of Analytical Psychology* 49 (2004): 707–728.
51. Jung, *Gesammelte Werke*, 8:§827.
52. Jung and Pauli, *Naturerklärung und Psyche*, 44–69.
53. He did so, for instance, in his treatise on tree symbolism: Jung, *Gesammelte Werke* 13:§337n16.
54. Jung, *Gesammelte Werke*, 13:§263.
55. Jung, 13:§378.
56. On the development of the text, see Shamdasani, *Jung and the Making of Modern Psychology*, 243–249.
57. *Über die Energetik der Seele*, in Jung, *Gesammelte Werke*, 8:§§1–3.
58. Jung, *Gesammelte Werke*, 8:§3 (emphasis original).
59. Jung, 8:§4.
60. Jung, 8:§7.
61. Jung, 8:§28.
62. Jung, 8:§28 (emphasis original).

63. Jung, 8:§32 (emphasis original).
64. Jung, 8:§33.
65. Nagy, *Philosophical Issues*, 255; see the detailed treatment of this topic on pp. 237–264.
66. Jung, *Gesammelte Werke*, 8:§33.
67. Jung, 8:§5n6. See also Bair, *Jung*, 744n56.

5. OCCULTISM, THE NATURAL SCIENCES, AND SPIRITUALITY

1. See Robert J. Richards, *The Romantic Conception of Life: Science and Philosophy in the Age of Goethe* (Chicago: University of Chicago Press, 2002); Peter Hanns Reill, *Vitalizing Nature in the Enlightenment* (Berkeley: University of California Press, 2005).
2. Kurt Danziger, "Mid-Nineteenth-Century British Psycho-Physiology: A Neglected Chapter in the History of Psychology," in *The Problematic Science: Psychology in Nineteenth-Century Thought*, ed. William R. Woodward and Mitchell G. Ash (New York: Praeger, 1982), 119–146, p. 120.
3. Danziger, 119.
4. As one of the best works on this topic, see Robert J. Richards, *The Tragic Sense of Life: Ernst Haeckel and the Struggle Over Evolutionary Thought* (Chicago: University of Chicago Press, 2008).
5. Ernst Haeckel, *Die Welträthsel: Gemeinverständliche Studien über Monistische Philosophie*. Volksausgabe (151.–170. Tausend) (Stuttgart: Kröner, 1903), 47 (emphasis original); first edition published in 1899.
6. Haeckel, 39–86.
7. Haeckel, 93.
8. Ernst Haeckel, *Kristallseelen: Studien über das anorganische Leben* (Leipzig: Kröner, 1917), vii (emphasis original).
9. Haeckel, viii (emphasis original).
10. Johann Wolfgang von Goethe, quoted in Haeckel, ii (emphasis original). The original quotation (not referenced by Haeckel) is taken from a letter Goethe wrote to Karl Ludwig von Knebel, dated April 8, 1812; see Johann Wolfgang von Goethe, *Goethes Briefe*, vol. 3, *1805–1821* (Hamburger Ausgabe), ed. Karl Robert Mandelkow and Bodo Morawe (Munich: C. H. Beck, 1965), 180 (without emphasis in the original).
11. Ernst Haeckel, *Kunstformen der Natur: Hundert Illustrationstafeln mit beschreibendem Text, Allgemeine Erläuterungen und Systematische Übersicht* (Leipzig: Bibliographisches Institut, 1904).
12. Arthur Titius, *Natur und Gott: Ein Versuch zur Verständigung zwischen Naturwissenschaft und Theologie*, 2nd ed. (Göttingen: Vandenhoeck und Ruprecht, 1931), 14.
13. Haeckel, *Kristallseelen*, 2.
14. Haeckel, 96 (emphasis original).
15. Rosemarie Nöthlich, Heiko Weber, Uwe Hoßfeld, Olaf Breidbach, and Erika Krauße, eds., *"Substanzmonismus" und/oder "Energetik": Der Briefwechsel von Ernst Haeckel und Wilhelm Ostwald, 1910–1918* (Berlin: Verlag für Wissenschaft und Bildung, 2006); see also the historical overview on pp. 1–40.
16. As the most recent analysis (with further literature), see Christoffer Leber, "Integration Through Science? Nationalism and Internationalism in the German Monist Movement

(1906–1918)," in *Freethinkers in Europe: National and Transnational Secularities, 1789–1920s*, ed. Carolin Kosuch (Berlin: De Gruyter, 2020), 181–202.

17. On Ostwald, see Eckard Daser, "Ostwalds energetischer Monismus" (PhD diss., University of Konstanz, 1980); Andreas Braune, *Fortschritt als Ideologie: Wilhelm Ostwald und der Monismus* (Leipzig: Leipziger Universitätsverlag, 2009); Kocku von Stuckrad, *The Scientification of Religion: An Historical Study of Discursive Change, 1800–2000* (Berlin: De Gruyter, 2014), 80–85. For the general context, see Eric Paul Jacobsen, *From Cosmology to Ecology: The Monist World-View in Germany from 1770 to 1930* (Oxford: Peter Lang, 2005).
18. Wilhelm Ostwald, *Die Forderung des Tages* (Leipzig: Akademische Verlagsgesellschaft, 1910), 22.
19. Wilhelm Ostwald, *Monistische Sonntagspredigten*, second series (Leipzig: Akademische Verlagsgesellschaft, 1912), 277.
20. Ostwald, 279.
21. Ostwald, *Forderung des Tages*, 211.
22. Wilhelm Ostwald, *Monistische Sonntagspredigten*, first series (Leipzig: Akademische Verlagsgesellschaft, 1911), 186–187 (emphasis original).
23. Wilhelm Ostwald, *Religion und Monismus* (Leipzig: Unesma, 1914), 105.
24. Wilhelm Ostwald, *Das Christentum als Vorstufe zum Monismus* (Leipzig: Unesma, 1914), 53.
25. Ostwald, *Monistische Sonntagspredigten*, first series, 88.
26. Marilyn Nagy, *Philosophical Issues in the Psychology of C. G. Jung* (Albany: State University of New York Press, 1991), 245.
27. Hans Driesch, *Ordnungslehre: Ein System des nichtmetaphysischen Teiles der Philosophie*, new, improved, and revised ed. (Jena: Eugen Diederichs, 1923), 290–299; from p. 300 on, he combines these with the basic assumptions of vitalism.
28. For the scientific-theoretical and philosophical significance of the discussion behind it, see Lorraine Daston, "The Theory of Will Versus the Science of Mind," in *The Problematic Science: Psychology in Nineteenth-Century Thought*, ed. William R. Woodward and Mitchell G. Ash (New York: Praeger, 1982), 88–115, pp. 100–103.
29. Hans Driesch, *Leib und Seele: Eine Untersuchung über das psychophysische Grundproblem*, 3rd ed., based on the second and partly revised ed. (Leipzig: Emmanuel Reinicke, 1923), 2 (emphasis removed).
30. Driesch, 107 (emphasis original).
31. Driesch, 107 (emphasis original).
32. Driesch, *Ordnungslehre*, 364–371.
33. Hans Driesch, *Lebenserinnerungen: Aufzeichnungen eines Forschers und Denkers in entscheidender Zeit* (Munich: Ernst Reinhardt, 1951), 274.
34. Von Stuckrad, *Scientification of Religion*, 64–70; on Rudolf Steiner's role in this movement, see von Stuckrad, 110–112; see also the detailed analysis of this discourse in Egil Asprem, *The Problem of Disenchantment: Scientific Naturalism and Esoteric Discourse 1900–1939* (Leiden: Brill, 2014).
35. Hans Driesch, *Parapsychologie: Die Wissenschaft von den "okkulten" Erscheinungen* (Munich: F. Bruckmann, 1932), 6.
36. See Andreas Sommer, "Crossing the Boundaries of Mind and Body: Psychical Research and the Origins of Modern Psychology," PhD diss., University College London, 2013; Sommer, "Normalizing the Supernormal: The Formation of the 'Gesellschaft für

Psychologische Forschung' ('Society for Psychological Research'), c. 1886–1890," *Journal of the History of the Behavioral Sciences* 49 (2013): 18–44.

37. Driesch, *Parapsychologie*, 123 (emphasis original).
38. Driesch, 58–59.
39. Asprem, *Problem of Disenchantment*, 317–412.
40. Richard Baerwald, "Psychologische Faktoren des modernen Zeitgeistes," *Schriften der Gesellschaft für psychologische Forschung* 15 (1905): 583–667, p. 583.
41. Baerwald, 584.
42. Baerwald, "Psychologische Faktoren," 585.
43. Richard Baerwald, *Okkultismus, Spiritismus und unterbewußte Seelenzustände* (Leipzig: B. G. Teubner, 1920), 5 (emphasis removed).
44. Baerwald, 103–125.
45. Baerwald, 125.
46. Baerwald, 11.
47. Richard Baerwald, *Okkultismus und Spiritismus und ihre weltanschaulichen Folgerungen* (Berlin: Deutsche Buch-Gemeinschaft, 1926), 7–8.
48. Baerwald, 9 and 11, respectively.
49. Traugott Konstantin Oesterreich, *Die philosophische Bedeutung der mediumistischen Phänomene*. Erweiterte Fassung des auf dem Zweiten Internationalen Kongress für Parapsychologische Forschung in Warschau gehaltenen Vortrags (Stuttgart: W. Kohlhammer, 1924), v.
50. Traugott Konstantin Oesterreich, *Der Okkultismus im modernen Weltbild*, third, expanded ed. (Dresden: Sybillen-Verlag, 1923), 14; first edition published in 1921.
51. Oesterreich, 15.
52. Oesterreich, 16–17.
53. Oesterreich, 20.
54. See Oesterreich, 21.
55. Oesterreich, 246.
56. Rudolf Tischner, *Einführung in den Okkultismus und Spiritismus*, 2nd, revised and improved ed. (Munich: J. F. Bergmann, 1923), v; first edition published in 1921.
57. Tischner, 119.
58. Tischner, 119.
59. Max Dessoir, *Vom Jenseits der Seele: Die Geheimwissenschaften in kritischer Betrachtung*, 4th and 5th ed. (Stuttgart: Ferdinand Enke, 1920), iv; first edition published in 1917. On Dessoir, see Sommer, "Crossing the Boundaries of Mind and Body," 95–98.
60. Sommer, "Normalizing the Supernormal," 19.
61. Carl Ludwig Schleich, *Dichtungen* (Berlin: Ernst Rowohlt, 1924), 46. The original German poem reads as follows:

EINEM "EXAKTEN" NATURFORSCHER

Was du nicht im Rohr erschaut,
Nahe vor die Stirn gebaut,
War nie ganz für dich vorhanden,
Und so hast du nie verstanden
Eine Welt von feineren Sinnen
Über uns, um uns und innen.

Das Organische zerpflücken
Heißt ein Kunstwerk kühn zerstücken.
Doch es gilt die Welt im kleinen
Mit dem Höchsten zu vereinen!
Auch die Zelle ist am End'
Unbegreiflich, transzendent,
Und die letzte Lebenseinheit
Schaut nur, der sie schuf, in Reinheit!
Sinne können doch nur streifen
Die Symbole, und begreifen
Jene Welt mit sieben Siegeln
Kann man nur aus Zauberspiegeln,
Die die Ehrfurcht still gestaltet,
Drin ein Lichtrad: Dichtung, waltet.
Was im Bild die Welle hebt,
Ist nicht, was im Grunde lebt:
Nur die Ahnung spinnt ein Band
Zu dem Eiland Unbekannt.

62. Carl Ludwig Schleich, *Besonnte Vergangenheit: Lebenserinnerungen, 1859–1919* (Berlin: Ernst Rowohlt, 1922), 93.
63. Schleich, 93–94.
64. Carl Ludwig Schleich, *Zwei Jahre kriegschirurgischer Erfahrungen aus einem Berliner Lazarett* (Stuttgart: Deutsche Verlags-Anstalt, 1916), 3.
65. Schleich, 21.
66. Schleich, 22.
67. Carl Ludwig Schleich, *Vom Schaltwerk der Gedanken: Neue Einsichten und Betrachtungen über die Seele* (Berlin: S. Fischer, 1917), 252.
68. Schleich, 256.
69. Carl Ludwig Schleich, *Gedankenmacht und Hysterie* (Berlin: Ernst Rowohlt, 1920), 5–6.
70. Schleich, 6.
71. Schleich, 268.
72. Carl Ludwig Schleich, *Das Ich und die Dämonien*, 10th–12th ed. (Berlin: S. Fischer, 1924), 7; first edition published in 1920.
73. Schleich, 139–140.
74. Carl Ludwig Schleich, *Von der Seele: Essays*, 19th–23rd ed. (Berlin: S. Fischer, 1922), 14–15 (emphasis original); first edition published 1910.
75. Schleich, 294.
76. Schleich, 296.
77. Carl Ludwig Schleich, *Die Wunder der Seele*, with a preface by C. G. Jung (Frankfurt am Main: S. Fischer, 1951), 5.
78. Jung in Schleich, 6–7.
79. Jung in Schleich, 11.
80. See, for instance, Hans D. Mummendey, *Die Psychologie des "Selbst": Theorien, Methoden und Ergebnisse der Selbstkonzeptforschung* (Göttingen: Hogrefe, 2006). Another example is the "psychology of the self" developed by Heinz Kohut; see Allen M. Siegel, *Heinz Kohut and the Psychology of the Self* (London: Routledge, 1996). From the point

of view of discourse history, it would be very interesting to take a closer look at the entanglement of the prefix "self-" with complementary terms both within and outside the psychological disciplines, because such terms have filled the voids left by a psychology without a soul.

81. See, for instance, the "Gesellschaft für Parapsychologie und Grenzgebiete der Psychologie," the "Freie Forschungsgemeinschaft für Psychologie und Grenzgebiete des Wissens," and others.
82. Kurt Danziger, *Naming the Mind: How Psychology Found Its Language* (London: Sage, 1997), 17.
83. Dietmar Kamper and Christoph Wulf, "Vexierbild und transitorische Metapher—Die Seele als das Andere ihrer selbst," in *Die erloschene Seele: Disziplin, Geschichte, Kunst, Mythos*, ed. Dietmar Kamper and Christoph Wulf (Berlin: Reimer, 1988), 1–14, p. 1.
84. Hans Thomas Hakl, *Eranos: An Alternative Intellectual History of the Twentieth Century*, revised and expanded ed., trans. Christopher McIntosh with the collaboration of Hereward Tilton (Montréal: McGill-Queen's University Press, 2013), 154–168; on Jung's central role in the Eranos conferences, see pp. 43–49. See also Steven M. Wasserstrom, *Religion After Religion: Gershom Scholem, Mircea Eliade and Henry Corbin at Eranos* (Princeton: Princeton University Press, 1999); Wouter J. Hanegraaff, *Esotericism and the Academy: Rejected Knowledge in Western Culture* (Cambridge: Cambridge University Press, 2012), 295–314.

6. TRANSPERSONAL PSYCHOLOGY

1. Erhardt Hanefeld, "Vorwort zur deutschen Ausgabe: Psychosynthesis und Transpersonale Psychotherapie," in *Handbuch der Psychosynthesis: Angewandte transpersonale Psychologie*, by Roberto Assagioli, ed. Erhardt Hanefeld (Freiburg: Aurum, 1978), 9–34, p. 17.
2. This passage also serves as an epigraph for Charles T. Tart, *Transpersonal Psychologies* (London: Routledge and Kegan Paul, 1975).
3. For his biography, see Paola Giovetti, *Roberto Assagioli: La vita e l'opera del fondatore della Psicosintesi* (Rome: Edizioni Mediterranee, 1995); Massimo Rosselli, "Roberto Assagioli: A Bright Star," *International Journal of Psychotherapy* 16 (2012): 7–19. On the early phase of his work, see also Alessandro Berti, *Roberto Assagioli: Profilo biografico degli anni di formazione* (Florence: Istituto di Psicosintesi, 1988).
4. Massimo Rosselli and Duccio Vanni, "Roberto Assagioli and Carl Gustav Jung," *Journal of Transpersonal Psychology* 46 (2014): 7–34, p. 13.
5. See Rosselli and Vanni, 14–15.
6. The following overview is based on Rosselli and Vanni, 8–11.
7. Rosselli and Vanni, 11.
8. Roberto Assagioli, *Psychosynthese und transpersonale Entwicklung*, trans. Hans Dellefant (Paderborn: Junfermann, 1992), 20; Italian original edition published in 1988.
9. Assagioli, 150–151. This assessment resonates with Schleich's critique of the gendered understanding of hysteria, as discussed earlier.
10. Assagioli, 153.
11. Assagioli, 159.
12. Assagioli, 166.

13. Assagioli, 175.
14. Described in detail in Roberto Assagioli, *Psychosynthesis* (London: Penguin, 1971).
15. See Rosselli and Vanni, "Roberto Assagioli," 24–25.
16. Bruno Huber and Louise Huber, *Transformationen: Astrologie als geistiger Weg* (Adliswil: Astrologisch-Psychologisches Institut API, 1996), 13.
17. Louise Huber, *Die Tierkreiszeichen: Reflexionen—Meditationen*, 3rd ed. (Adliswil: Astrologisch-Psychologisches Institut API, 1989), 401–402.
18. Abraham H. Maslow, *Motivation and Personality*, 2nd ed. (New York: Harper and Row, 1970), ix; first edition published in 1954.
19. See Maslow, x.
20. Abraham H. Maslow, *Toward a Psychology of Being*, 2nd, rev. ed. (New York: D. van Nostrand, 1968), iii; first edition published in 1962.
21. Maslow, iii.
22. Maslow, iii–iv.
23. Maslow, iv.
24. Maslow, 3.
25. Maslow, 4.
26. Maslow, 5.
27. Maslow, 11 (emphasis original).
28. Dave Vliegenthart, *The Secular Religion of Franklin Merrell-Wolff: An Intellectual History of Anti-Intellectualism in Modern America* (Leiden: Brill, 2018).
29. Roger N. Walsh and Frances Vaugah, eds., *Beyond Ego: Transpersonal Dimensions in Psychology* (Los Angeles: J. P. Tarcher, 1980).
30. See the entire volume 11 of Jung's *Gesammelte Werke* with the title *Zur Psychologie westlicher und östlicher Religion* (On the Psychology of Western and Eastern Religion). Carl Gustav Jung, *Gesammelte Werke*, 18 vols. (Zurich: Rascher and Olten: Walter, 1958–1981).
31. Jung, *Gesammelte Werke*, 11:§907.
32. Jeffrey J. Kripal, *Esalen: America and the Religion of No Religion* (Chicago: University of Chicago Press, 2007).
33. Marion S. Goldman, *The American Soul Rush: Esalen and the Rise of Spiritual Privilege* (New York: New York University Press, 2012). See also Vliegenthart, *Secular Religion of Franklin Merrell-Wolff*, 202–214.
34. Roger N. Walsh, "Die Transpersonale Bewegung: Geschichte und derzeitiger Entwicklungsstand," *Transpersonale Psychologie und Psychotherapie* 1 (1995): 6–21, p. 8.
35. Stanislav Grof, "Revision and Re-Enchantment of the Legacy of Psychology from a Half Century of Consciousness Research," *Journal of Transpersonal Psychology* 44 (2012): 137–163, p. 138.
36. Stanislav Grof, *Psychology for the Future: Lessons from Modern Consciousness Research* (Albany: State University of New York Press, 2000), 207.
37. Grof, 208–209.
38. Grof, 209–210.
39. Grof, 210–211 (emphasis original).
40. Grof, 213.
41. Grof, 293.
42. Grof, 319.
43. See also Grof, 321.

44. Ken Wilber, *The Atman Project: A Transpersonal View of Human Development* (Wheaton: Theosophical Publishing House, 1980); Ken Wilber, *Sex, Ecology, Spirituality: The Spirit of Evolution*, 2nd, rev. ed. (Boston: Shambhala, 2000); 1st published in 1995.
45. Wilber, *Sex, Ecology, Spirituality*, 210–213.
46. Ken Wilber, *The Spectrum of Consciousness*, 2nd ed. (Wheaton: Theosophical Publishing House, 1993); first edition published in 1977. See also the discussion of Wilber's theory in Stanislav Grof, *Beyond the Brain: Birth, Death and Transcendence in Psychotherapy* (Albany: State University of New York Press, 1985), 131–137.
47. Roger N. Walsh, *The Spirit of Shamanism* (Los Angeles: Jeremy P. Tarcher, 1990), 6.
48. Wilber, *Sex, Ecology, Spirituality*, 600. He adds: "Walsh is one of the leading lights of the transpersonal movement, and his balanced and sane overview, decisive in many ways, is a major contribution to the field."
49. See Walsh, *Spirit of Shamanism*, 238–239.
50. Walsh, 241.
51. Stanislav Grof and Christina Grof, eds., *Spiritual Emergency: When Personal Transformation Becomes a Crisis* (Los Angeles: Jeremy P. Tarcher, 1989).
52. Robert Ornstein, quoted in Charles T. Tart, "Introduction," in *Transpersonal Psychologies*, ed. Charles T. Tart (New York: Harper and Row, 1975), 1–7, p. 3.
53. Tart, "Introduction," 3–4 (emphasis original).
54. Tart, 7.
55. Charles T. Tart, *The End of Materialism: How Evidence of the Paranormal Is Bringing Science and Spirit Together* (Oakland: New Harbinger, 2009).
56. Tart, "Introduction," 4 (emphasis original).
57. Kripal, *Esalen*, 378.
58. Richard Tarnas, *The Passion of the Western Mind: Understanding the Ideas That Have Shaped Our Word View* (London: Pimlico/Random House, 2010), xi–xii; first edition published in 1991.
59. Tarnas, 445.
60. Tarnas, 458–459.
61. Tarnas, 476–477.
62. Tarnas, 477–478.
63. Tarnas, 479.
64. Richard Tarnas, *Cosmos and Psyche: Intimations of a New World View* (New York: Plume, 2007), xv.
65. Tarnas, 80.
66. Tarnas, 82.
67. Tarnas, 82–83.
68. Tarnas, 85.
69. Tarnas, 28.
70. Tarnas, 33.
71. Tarnas, 39.
72. Tarnas, 353–451.
73. Tarnas, 453–490.
74. Tarnas, 486.
75. Tarnas, 487.

7. THE RENAISSANCE OF *NATURPHILOSOPHIE*

1. David Kaiser, *How the Hippies Saved Physics: Science, Counterculture, and the Quantum Revival* (New York: W. W. Norton, 2011), xxiii.
2. Kaiser, xxiv.
3. Kaiser, xxv.
4. Kaiser, xxv.
5. Mary-Jane Rubenstein, *Worlds Without End: The Many Lives of the Multiverse* (New York: Columbia University Press, 2014), 146.
6. Kaiser, *How the Hippies Saved Physics*, 2.
7. F. David Peat in Thomas Arzt, Maria Hippius-Gräfin Dürckheim, and Roland Dollinger, eds., *Unus Mundus: Kosmos und Sympathie: Beiträge zum Gedanken der Einheit von Mensch und Kosmos* (Frankfurt am Main: Peter Lang, 1991), 211–212.
8. For a recent discussion that also engages with the philosophical implications, see Wayne Myrvold, Marco Genovese, and Abner Shimony, "Bell's Theorem," in *The Stanford Encyclopedia of Philosophy* (Spring 2019 edition), ed. Edward N. Zalta, https://plato.stanford.edu/archives/spr2019/entries/bell-theorem/.
9. Steven Weinberg, *Dreams of a Final Theory* (New York: Pantheon, 1992), 81.
10. See Kaiser, *How the Hippies Saved Physics*, 25–41.
11. Nick Herbert, *Quantum Reality: Beyond the New Physics* (Garden City, NY: Anchor Press/Doubleday, 1987), 249.
12. Herbert, 250.
13. See David Lindley, *Uncertainty: Einstein, Heisenberg, Bohr, and the Struggle for the Soul of Science* (New York: Anchor, 2007).
14. Kaiser, *How the Hippies Saved Physics*, 155.
15. Fritjof Capra, *The Tao of Physics: An Exploration of the Parallels Between Modern Physics and Eastern Mysticism* (Boulder, CO: Shambhala, 1975), 26–27.
16. Capra, 28.
17. Capra, 29–30. This is followed by a quotation from William James.
18. Capra, 140.
19. Capra, 142.
20. F. David Peat, *Infinite Potential: The Life and Times of David Bohm* (Reading: Helix Books / Addison-Wesley, 1997), 195.
21. Peat, 199.
22. See David Bohm, *Wholeness and the Implicate Order* (London: Routledge and Kegan Paul, 1981), 19–26; 196–213; first edition published in 1980.
23. Karen Barad, *Meeting the Universe Halfway: Quantum Physics and the Entanglement of Matter and Meaning* (Durham, NC: Duke University Press, 2006).
24. Michael B. Mensky, *Consciousness and Quantum Mechanics: Life In Parallel Worlds: Miracles of Consciousness from Quantum Reality* (Singapore: World Scientific, 2010), 215–240.
25. Lothar Schäfer and Diogo Valadas Ponte, "Carl Gustav Jung, Quantum Physics and the Spiritual Mind: A Mystical Vision of the Twenty-First Century," *Behavioral Sciences* 3 (2013): 601–618.
26. Juan Miguel Marin, "'Mysticism' in Quantum Mechanics: The Forgotten Controversy," *European Journal of Physics* 30 (2009): 807–822.

27. Rubenstein, *Worlds Without End*, 17.
28. See Arne Naess, "The Shallow and the Deep, Long-Range Ecology Movement: A Summary," *Inquiry* 16 (1973): 95–100; for a more detailed account, see Arne Naess, *Ecology, Community and Lifestyle: Outline of an Ecosophy* (Cambridge: Cambridge University Press, 1989).
29. Roger S. Gottlieb, "The Transcendence of Justice and the Justice of Transcendence: Mysticism, Deep Ecology, and Political Life," *Journal of the American Academy of Religion* 67 (1999): 149–166, p. 155.
30. Paul W. Taylor, "Die Ethik der Achtung für die Natur (1981)," in *Ökophilosophie*, ed. Dieter Birnbacher (Stuttgart: Philipp Reclam jun., 1997), 77–116, p. 97. See also Christoph Schorsch, *Die Große Vernetzung: Wege zu einer ökologischen Philosophie* (Freiburg: Bauer, 1987). For biological and ecological interpretations, see also chapter 10 of this book. While an "ecocentric" position overlaps with a "'biocentric" one to some extent, "ecocentric" approaches focus more on the intersection of all ecosystems on the planet, while "biocentric" approaches tend to highlight the 'living' (from Greek *bio*) aspects of the natural world.
31. In Bron Taylor's historical reconstruction, the celebration of the first Earth Day also coincided with the renewal of and upswing in environmental movements in North America, as well as what can be called "nature religion" or "nature-as-sacred religion." See Bron Taylor, *Dark Green Religion: Nature Spirituality and the Planetary Future* (Berkeley: University of California Press, 2010), 5.
32. "Vorbemerkung," in Dieter Birnbacher, ed., *Ökophilosophie* (Stuttgart: Philipp Reclam jun., 1997), 9.
33. One of the most influential publications to be mentioned is John Seed, Joanna Macy, Pat Fleming, and Arne Naess, eds., *Thinking Like a Mountain: Towards a Council of All Beings* (Philadelphia: New Society, 1988). See also Shirley Nicholson and Brenda Rosen, eds., *Gaia's Hidden Life: The Unseen Intelligence of Nature* (Wheaton, IL: Theosophical Publishing House, 1992), who link this discourse to discourses on Gaia. Two German volumes published with Diederichs make a similar point: Franz-Theo Gottwald and Andrea Klepsch, eds., *Tiefenökologie: Wie wir in Zukunft leben wollen* (Munich: Diederichs, 1995); Hans-Peter Dürr and Walther Ch. Zimmerli, eds., *Geist und Natur: Über den Widerspruch zwischen naturwissenschaftlicher Erkenntnis und philosophischer Welterfahrung* (Bern: Scherz, 1989).
34. Franz-Theo Gottwald and Christian Rätsch, eds., *Schamanische Wissenschaft: Ökologie, Naturwissenschaft und Kunst* (Munich: Diederichs, 1998), 7. See also the analyses in another Diederichs publication, which even has the bridging term *consciousness* in the title: Gerardo Reichel-Dolmatoff, ed., *Das Schamanische Universum: Schamanismus, Bewußtsein und Ökologie in Südamerika* (Munich: Diederichs, 1996).
35. Jonathan Horwitz, "The Absence of 'Performance' in the Shamanic Rite," in *Shamanism in Performing Arts*, ed. Tae-Gon Kim and Mihály Hoppál (Budapest: Akadémiai Kiadó, 1995), 231–242, p. 234.
36. Franz-Theo Gottwald, "Hören, Wissen, Handeln—Schamanische und tiefenökologische Anregungen für eine konviviale Wissenschaft," in *Schamanische Wissenschaft: Ökologie, Naturwissenschaft und Kunst*, ed. Franz-Theo Gottwald and Christian Rätsch (Munich: Diederichs, 1998), 11–23, p. 23.
37. Quoted from the course brochure of the Scandinavian Center for Shamanic Studies, Summer 1998.

38. Joan Halifax, *The Fruitful Darkness: Reconnecting with the Body of the Earth* (San Francisco: HarperCollins, 1994), xxx.
39. See the respective websites with further information at https://ojaifoundation.org/ and www.upaya.org/.
40. Stanislav Grof, "Ervin Laszlo's Akashic Field and the Dilemmas of Modern Consciousness Research," *World Futures* 62 (2006): 86–102, p. 87.
41. Grof, 87. On this topic see, Anna Pokazanyeva, "Mind Within Matter: Science, the Occult, and the (Meta)physics of Ether and Akasha," *Zygon* 51 (2016): 318–346. Pokazanyeva interprets the equation ether—Akasha—mind as a panpsychism leading to monistic quantum mysticism.
42. Grof, "Ervin Laszlo's Akashic Field," 99–100.
43. Ervin Laszlo, *The Systems View of the World: The Natural Philosophy of the New Developments in the Sciences* (Oxford: Basil Blackwell, 1972), 19–75. It is noteworthy that the German translation of this book (1998) was published in the Diederichs New Science series; with publications such as this, Eugen Diederichs press carries on a tradition of mysticism and *Naturphilosophie* that goes back to the beginning of the twentieth century.
44. Laszlo, *Systems View of the World*, 85.
45. Laszlo, 85 and 86, respectively.
46. For his concept of consciousness, see Laszlo, 86–100. Laszlo had already formulated a theory of mind, which referred to Gestalt psychology (among other traditions); see Ervin Laszlo, *System, Structure, and Experience: Toward a Scientific Theory of Mind* (New York: Gordon and Breach Science, 1969).
47. Laszlo, *Systems View of the World*, 119.
48. Laszlo, 119.
49. Laszlo, 120 (both quotations).
50. Ervin Laszlo, preface to *Gaia Project—A New Paradigm in Education—Planetary Consciousness and Self Awareness Development Program and Psychosomatic Health Promotion in Accordance with WHO guidelines*, by Federico Nitamo Montecucco and Silvia Ghiroldi. Approved and funded by the Italian Ministry of Labour and Social Policies, in collaboration with the Club UNESCO Lucca (2015); www.progettogaia.eu/documenti/docenti/gaia_project_presentation_2019_english.pdf.

8. THE SOUL AS THE LODESTAR OF NEW SPIRITUAL PRACTICES

1. Bron Taylor, *Dark Green Religion: Nature Spirituality and the Planetary Future* (Berkeley: University of California Press, 2010); Roderick Nash, *The Rights of Nature: A History of Environmental Ethics* (Madison: University of Wisconsin Press, 1989), 87–120.
2. Hans G. Kippenberg, *Discovering Religious History in the Modern Age*, trans. Barbara Harshav (Princeton: Princeton University Press, 2002), 51–64. See also Hans G. Kippenberg and Brigitte Luchesi, eds., *Magie: Die sozialwissenschaftliche Kontroverse über das Verstehen fremden Denkens* (Frankfurt am Main: Suhrkamp, 1987), 14–17.
3. Jason Ā. Josephson-Storm, *The Myth of Disenchantment: Magic, Modernity, and the Birth of the Human Sciences* (Chicago: University of Chicago Press, 2017), 98–101.

4. For an excellent critical review, combined with the comparison of an Indian example of exactly the kind of animism that European fantasies dubbed "primitive," see David L. Haberman, *Loving Stones: Making the Impossible Possible in the Worship of Mount Govardhan* (London: Oxford University Press, 2020).
5. Gerhard Schlatter, "Animism," in *The Brill Dictionary of Religion*, ed. Kocku von Stuckrad, 4 vols. (Leiden: Brill), 1:77–78. The original German version from 1999 also mentioned "esoteric literature" as a "trivial connection" of the use of animism.
6. Nurit Bird-David, "'Animism' Revisited: Personhood, Environment, and Relational Epistemology," *Current Anthropology* 40 (1999): 67–79.
7. Anne-Christine Hornborg, "Objects as Subjects: Agency and Performativity in Rituals," in *The Relational Dynamics of Enchantment and Sacralization*, ed. Peik Ingman, Måns Broo, Tuija Hovi, and Terhi Utriainen (Sheffield: Equinox, 2016), 27–43, p. 27. See the entire first part of that volume, pp. 27–105.
8. Graham Harvey, *Animism: Respecting the Living World* (Kent Town: Wakefield, 2005), xi.
9. Taylor defines the term as follows: "Today it commonly refers to perceptions that natural entities, forces, and nonhuman life-forms have one or more of the following: a soul or vital lifeforce or spirit, personhood (an affective life and personal intentions), and consciousness, often but not always including special spiritual intelligence or powers. Animistic perceptions are often accompanied by ethical mores specifying the sorts of relationships that human beings should have, or avoid having, with nature's diverse forces and beings." Taylor, *Dark Green Religion*, 15. See also his differentiation between spiritual animism and naturalistic animism on pp. 15–16.
10. Nevill Drury, *The Elements of Shamanism* (Longmead, UK: Element, 1989), 5.
11. Jonathan Horwitz, "Animism—Everyday Magic," *Sacred Hoop* 9 (1995): 6–10, p. 7.
12. Quoted in Shirley Nicholson, ed., *Shamanism*, 5th ed. (Wheaton, IL: Theosophical Publishing House, 1996), 5.
13. Jonathan Horwitz, "Apprentice to the Spirits: The Shaman's Spiritual Path," in *Was ist ein Schamane? Schamanen, Heiler, Medizinleute im Spiegel westlichen Denkens / What Is a Shaman? Shamans, Healers, and Medicine Men from a Western Point of View*, ed. Amelie Schenk and Christian Rätsch (Berlin: Verlag für Wissenschaft und Bildung, 1999), 215–221, p. 217.
14. Jonathan Horwitz, "The Absence of 'Performance' in the Shamanic Rite," in *Shamanism in Performing Arts*, ed. Tae-Gon Kim and Mihály Hoppál (Budapest: Akadémiai Kiadó, 1995), 231–242, p. 234.
15. For a detailed analysis of the following, see Kocku von Stuckrad, *Schamanismus und Esoterik: Kultur- und wissenschaftsgeschichtliche Betrachtungen* (Leuven: Peeters, 2003); Stuckrad, *The Scientification of Religion: An Historical Study of Discursive Change, 1800–2000* (Berlin: De Gruyter, 2014), 159–177.
16. Roger N. Walsh, *The Spirit of Shamanism* (Los Angeles: Jeremy P. Tarcher, 1990), 11.
17. Paul Uccusic, *Der Schamane in uns: Schamanismus als neue Selbsterfahrung, Hilfe und Heilung* (Munich: Goldmann, 1993), 147.
18. Uccusic, 149.
19. Sandra Ingerman, *Soul Retrieval: Mending the Fragmented Self*, new ed. (San Francisco: HarperCollins, 1998), 22; first edition published in 1991.
20. Ingerman, 22.
21. Ingerman, 23.

22. Gloria Flaherty, *Shamanism and the Eighteenth Century* (Princeton, NJ: Princeton University Press, 1992), 183. See also the discussion in von Stuckrad, *Schamanismus und Esoterik*, 66–75.
23. See particularly Ronald Hutton, *The Triumph of the Moon: A History of Modern Pagan Witchcraft* (Oxford: Oxford University Press, 1999); Ronald Hutton, *Shamans: Siberian Spirituality and the Western Imagination* (London: Hambledon and London, 2001).
24. Israel Regardie, *The Tree of Life: An Illustrated Study of Magic*, edited and annotated by Chic Cicero and Sandra Tabatha Cicero (St. Paul: Llewellyn, 2002), 25; first edition published in 1932.
25. Aleister Crowley, *Magick in Theory and Practice* (New York: Castle, 1929), ix–x (emphasis original). See also Bernd-Christian Otto, *Magie: Rezeptions- und diskursgeschichtliche Analysen von der Antike bis zur Neuzeit* (Berlin: De Gruyter, 2011), 602 (who accidentally attributes this quote to Crowley himself).
26. Crowley, *Magick in Theory and Practice*, xii (emphasis original).
27. Otto, *Magie*, 601–611.
28. Josephson-Storm, *The Myth of Disenchantment*, 152; on Frazer see pp. 125–152, on Crowley pp. 153–176.
29. Josephson-Storm, 175.
30. Graham Harvey, *Contemporary Paganism: Listening People, Speaking Earth* (New York: New York University Press, 1997), 88 (the quotation from Dion Fortune is on the same page).
31. David Ray Griffin, *Parapsychology, Philosophy, and Spirituality: A Postmodern Exploration* (Albany: State University of New York Press, 1997), 273 (all four quotations).
32. See Brigitte Röder, Juliane Hummel, and Brigitta Kunz, *Göttinnendämmerung: Das Matriarchat aus archäologischer Sicht* (Munich: Droemer Knaur, 1996); Anna Fedele and Kim E. Knibbe, eds., *Gender and Power in Contemporary Spirituality: Ethnographic Approaches* (New York: Routledge, 2013).
33. Hutton, *Triumph of the Moon*, 373.
34. Prudence Jones and Caitlín Matthews, eds., *Voices from the Circle: The Heritage of Western Paganism* (Hammersmith, UK: Aquarian, 1990), 40.

9. THE SOUL AS A CENTRAL MOTIF IN LITERATURE AND FILM

1. Philip J. Deloria, *Playing Indian* (New Haven, CT: Yale University Press, 1998).
2. Joseph L. Esposito, *Schelling's Idealism and Philosophy of Nature* (Lewisburg, PA: Bucknell University Press; London: Associated University Presses, 1977), 189.
3. Evan Berry, *Devoted to Nature: The Religious Roots of American Environmentalism* (Oakland: University of California Press, 2015), 5.
4. For detailed overviews (with differences in focus and argumentation), see Roderick Nash, *Wilderness and the American Mind*, 3rd ed. (New Haven, CT: Yale University Press, 1982); Max Oelschlaeger, *The Idea of Wilderness: From Prehistory to the Age of Ecology* (New Haven, CT: Yale University Press, 1991); Catherine L. Albanese, *Nature Religion in America: From the Algonkian Indians to the New Age*, 2nd ed. (Chicago: University of Chicago Press, 1991); Lawrence Buell, *The Environmental Imagination: Thoreau, Nature Writing, and the Formation of American Culture* (Cambridge, MA: The

Belknap Press of Harvard University Press, 1995); Daniel J. Philippon, *Conserving Words: How American Nature Writers Shaped the Environmental Movement* (Athens: University of Georgia Press, 2004). I will discuss more recent literature that also engages with these "classic" works in the course of my argumentation.

5. Ralph Waldo Emerson, *The Collected Works of Ralph Waldo Emerson*, ed. Alfred R. Ferguson, vol. 1, *Nature, Addresses, and Lectures* (Cambridge, MA: Belknap Press of Harvard University Press, 1971), 3.
6. Bron Taylor, *Dark Green Religion: Nature Spirituality and the Planetary Future* (Berkeley: University of California Press, 2010), 49.
7. Emerson, *Collected Works*, 1:8.
8. Emerson, 1:21; see also pp. 31–33.
9. Dieter Schulz, *Amerikanischer Transzendentalismus: Ralph Waldo Emerson, Henry David Thoreau, Margaret Fuller* (Darmstadt: Wissenschaftliche Buchgesellschaft, 1997), 121.
10. Buell, *Environmental Imagination*, 115.
11. Henry David Thoreau, *The Writings of Henry D. Thoreau: Walden*, ed. B. Torrey and F. H. Allen (Boston: Houghton Mifflin, 1971), 42.
12. Thoreau, 313.
13. Thoreau, 86, 272, and 194, respectively.
14. Thoreau, 282; on the eye and the iris, see pp. 186 and 176.
15. Thoreau, 311.
16. Thoreau, 193.
17. Buell, *Environmental Imagination*, 208.
18. Thoreau, *Walden*, 505.
19. Taylor, *Dark Green Religion*, 57. And he adds: "One thing is clear: many who have been engaged in the production and spread of dark green religion have taken inspiration from Thoreau and consider him an ecospiritual elder. Certainly, deep ecologists and radical environmentalists have enthusiastically embraced him." See also Taylor's overview of Thoreau's themes and their scholarly interpretations on pp. 50–58, 227–247.
20. Buell, *Environmental Imagination*, 192.
21. John Muir, *The Wilderness World of John Muir*, ed. Edwin Way Teale (Boston: Houghton Mifflin, 1954), 312.
22. John Muir, *Works: The Sierra Edition*, 10 vols., ed. William Frederick Badé (Boston: Houghton Mifflin, 1915–1924), 1:343 (from *A Thousand-Mile Walk to the Gulf*).
23. Bron Taylor, "Resacralizing Earth: Pagan Environmentalism and the Restoration of Turtle Island," in *American Sacred Space*, ed. David Chidester and E. T. Linenthal (Bloomington: Indiana University Press, 1995), 97–151, p. 101.
24. Muir, *Works*, 1:416.
25. Susan L. Flader, *Thinking Like a Mountain: Aldo Leopold and the Evolution of an Ecological Attitude Toward Deer, Wolves, and Forests* (Columbia: University of Missouri Press, 1974); Buell, *Environmental Imagination*, 171–174. See also Leopold's biography in Curt Meine, *Aldo Leopold: His Life and Work* (Madison: University of Wisconsin Press, 1988).
26. Joan Halifax, *The Fruitful Darkness: Reconnecting with the Body of the Earth* (San Francisco: HarperCollins, 1994), 92.
27. Bron Taylor, "Earth and Nature-Based Spirituality: From Deep Ecology to Radical Environmentalism," *Religion* 31 (2001): 175–193, p. 183.

28. Taylor, "Resacralizing Earth," 110–115; see also the detailed analysis in Jason M. Wirth, *Mountains, Rivers, and the Great Earth: Reading Gary Snyder and Dōgen in an Age of Ecological Crisis* (Albany: State University of New York Press, 2017).
29. Gary Snyder, *The Old Ways* (San Francisco: City Lights, 1977), 13–14.
30. Quoted in Taylor, "Resacralizing Earth," 113.
31. For her biography, see Donna Krolik Hollenberg, *A Poet's Revolution: The Life of Denise Levertov* (Berkeley: University of California Press, 2013).
32. Hollenberg, 67.
33. Hollenberg, 384; see also Edward Zlotkowski, "Levertov and Rilke: A Sense of Aesthetic Ethics," *Twentieth Century Literature* 38 (1992): 324–342.
34. Hollenberg, *A Poet's Revolution*, 4.
35. Denise Levertov, *A Tree Telling of Orpheus* (Los Angeles: Black Sparrow, 1968). The poem has been repeatedly published online. In the following, I quote the poem from https://allpoetry.com/A-Tree-Telling-Of-Orpheus.
36. See John Gatta, *Making Nature Sacred: Literature, Religion, and Environment in America from the Puritans to the Present* (Oxford: Oxford University Press, 2004), 239.
37. Denise Levertov, *Evening Train* (New York: New Directions, 1992), 14.
38. Gatta, *Making Nature Sacred*, 242.
39. Gatta, 241; see also Hollenberg, *A Poet's Revolution*, 403.
40. David Abram, *Becoming Animal: An Earthly Cosmology* (New York: Pantheon, 2010), 10.
41. Abram, 58.
42. On the larger theme of the internalization of external space, see also Ewa Lajer-Burcharth and Beate Söntgen, eds., *Interiors and Interiority* (Berlin: De Gruyter, 2016).
43. See the overview in Burkhard Gladigow, "'Tiefe der Seele' und 'inner space': Zur Geschichte eines Topos von Heraklit bis zur Science Fiction," in *Die Erfindung des inneren Menschen: Studien zur religiösen Anthropologie*, ed. Jan Assmann (Gütersloh: Gütersloher Verlagshaus Mohn, 1993), 114–132. See also Karl S. Guthke, *Der Mythos der Neuzeit: Das Thema der Mehrheit der Welten in der Literatur- und Geistesgeschichte von der kopernikanischen Wende bis zur Science Fiction* (Bern: Francke, 1983).
44. Karl Philipp Moritz, *Anton Reiser: A Psychological Novel*, trans. John Raymond Russell (Columbia: Camden House, 1996), 169.
45. "Es winkt zu Fühlung fast aus allen Dingen," in Rainer Maria Rilke, *Die Gedichte*, 11th ed. (Frankfurt am Main: Insel, 1999), 879 (my trans., emphasis original). The original reads: "Durch alle Wesen reicht der *eine* Raum: / Weltinnenraum. Die Vögel fliegen still / durch uns hindurch. O, der ich wachsen will, / ich seh hinaus, und *in* mir wächst der Baum."
46. Hans Joachim Alpers, Joachim Fuchs, et al., *Lexikon der Science Fiction Literatur*, new and enlarged ed. (Munich: Wilhelm Heyne, 1988), 142; see the entire chapter "Landscapes of the Psyche: Inner-Space Literature," pp. 142–152. See also Gary Westfahl, ed., *Science Fiction Quotations: From the Inner Mind to the Outer Limits* (New Haven, CT: Yale University Press, 2005), 291–296 (on "Psychic Powers" and "Psychology").
47. Alpers, Fuchs, et al., *Lexikon der Science Fiction Literatur*, 148.
48. See Joseph V. Francavilla, "Promethean Bound: Heroes and Gods in Roger Zelazny's Science Fiction," in *The Transcendent Adventure: Studies of Religion in Science Fiction/Fantasy*, ed. Robert Reilly (Westport, CT: Greenwood, 1985), 207–222.
49. Samuel R. Delany, *The Einstein Intersection* (Middletown, CT: Wesleyan University Press, 1967), 56.

50. Ursula K. Le Guin, *The Language of the Night: Essays on Fantasy and Science Fiction*, ed. Susan Wood (New York: G. P. Putnam's Sons, 1979), 81.
51. Le Guin, 77.
52. Le Guin, 77.
53. Le Guin, 77.
54. Le Guin, 78.
55. Le Guin, 78.
56. Le Guin, 80.
57. Ian Watson, "The Forest as Metaphor for Mind: 'The Word for World Is Forest' and 'Vaster Than Empires and More Slow,'" in *Ursula K. Le Guin (Modern Critical Views)*, ed. Harold Bloom (New York: Chelsea House, 1986), 47–55, p. 49.
58. Watson, "The Forest as Metaphor of Mind," 51.
59. For a comparison of those two works, see David L. Barnhill, "Spirituality and Resistance: Ursula Le Guin's *The Word for World Is Forest* and the Film *Avatar*," *Journal for the Study of Religion, Nature and Culture* 4 (2010): 478–498. For the link between ecology and spirituality in *Avatar* generally, see Bron Taylor, ed., *Avatar and Nature Spirituality* (Waterloo: Wilfrid Laurier University Press, 2013).
60. On the following, see also Scott Sehon, "The Soul in Harry Potter," in *The Ultimate Harry Potter and Philosophy: Hogwarts for Muggles*, ed. William Irwin and Gregory Bassham (Hoboken, NJ: Wiley, 2010), 7–21.
61. J. K. Rowling, *Harry Potter and the Deathly Hallows* (New York: Scholastic, 2007), 104.
62. J. K. Rowling, *Harry Potter and the Goblet of Fire* (New York: Scholastic, 2000), 653.
63. J. K. Rowling, *Harry Potter and the Prisoner of Azkaban* (New York: Scholastic, 1999), 247.
64. J. K. Rowling, *Harry Potter and the Half-Blood Prince* (New York: Scholastic, 2005), 498.
65. Rowling, 498.
66. Rowling, 509.
67. Rowling, 502.
68. Rowling, *Harry Potter and the Goblet of Fire*, 643.
69. Franz X. Eder, "Historische Diskurse und ihre Analyse—eine Einleitung," in *Historische Diskursanalysen: Genealogie, Theorien, Anwendungen*, ed. Franz X. Eder (Wiesbaden: VS Verlag für Sozialwissenschaft, 2006), 9–23, p. 13.

10. ECOLOGICAL MOVEMENTS AND THE SACRALIZATION OF THE EARTH

1. On the history of this event, see Fred Turner, *From Counterculture to Cyberculture: Stewart Brand, the Whole Earth Network and the Rise of Digital Utopianism* (Chicago: University of Chicago Press, 2006); Andrew G. Kirk, *Counterculture Green: The Whole Earth Catalog and American Environmentalism* (Lawrence: University Press of Kansas, 2007); Neil M. Maher, *Apollo in the Age of Aquarius* (Cambridge, MA: Harvard University Press, 2017).
2. Christopher Potter, *The Earth Gazers: On Seeing Ourselves* (New York: Pegasus, 2018), 7.
3. Potter, 7.
4. www.youtube.com/watch?v=JZXErLns1mM.

5. https://svs.gsfc.nasa.gov/.
6. For the analytical concepts, see Arianna Borelli and Alexandra Grieser, "Recent Research on the Aesthetics of Knowledge in Science and in Religion," *Approaching Religion* 7 (2017): 4–21; Alexandra Grieser and Jay Johnston, eds., *Aesthetics of Religion: A Connective Concept* (Berlin: De Gruyter, 2017). Another telling example is the aesthetic modification of data received from the NASA Hubble Space Telescope; these aestheticizations follow Romantic color theories of beauty and the sublime. See Alexandra Grieser, "Imaginationen des Nichtwissens: Zur Hubble Space Imagery und den Figurationen des schönen Universums zwischen Wissenschaft, Kunst und Religion," in *Religion—Imagination—Ästhetik: Vorstellungs- und Sinneswelten in Religion und Kultur*, ed. Annette Wilke and Lucia Traut (Göttingen: Vandenhoeck und Ruprecht, 2015), 451–485.
7. Lisa H. Sideris, *Consecrated Science: Wonder, Knowledge, and the Natural World* (Oakland: University of California Press, 2017).
8. See Daniel J. Philippon, *Conserving Words: How American Nature Writers Shaped the Environmental Movement* (Athens: University of Georgia Press, 2004).
9. Evan Berry, *Devoted to Nature: The Religious Roots of American Environmentalism* (Oakland: University of California Press, 2015), 8.
10. Linda Lear, *Rachel Carson: Witness for Nature* (New York: Henry Holt, 1997), 4–5.
11. See also Lisa H. Sideris and Kathleen Dean Moore, eds., *Rachel Carson: Legacy and Challenge* (Albany: State University of New York Press, 2008).
12. Rachel Carson, *Chincoteague: A National Wildlife Refuge*, Conservation in Action 1 (Washington, DC: US Government Printing Office, 1947); quoted in William Souder, *On a Farther Shore: The Life and Legacy of Rachel Carson* (New York: Crown, 2012), 115.
13. See Souder, *On a Farther Shore*, 212.
14. Rachel Carson, *The Edge of the Sea* (Boston: Houghton Mifflin, 1955), vii–viii.
15. Carson, 5.
16. Carson, 7.
17. Carson, 250.
18. Carson, 250.
19. Linda Lear in Rachel Carson, *The Sense of Wonder*, introduction by Linda Lear (New York: HarperCollins, 1998), 10; first edition published in 1965.
20. The website www.barrylopez.com gives a good insight into his thinking and work.
21. Barry Lopez, *Arctic Dreams: Imagination and Desire in a Northern Landscape* (Toronto: Bantam, 1989), 273–274.
22. Lopez, 257.
23. Lopez, 257.
24. Lopez, xx. Note that the concept of breath and breathing is a direct link to discourses on the soul.
25. John Gatta, *Making Nature Sacred: Literature, Religion, and Environment in America from the Puritans to the Present* (Oxford: Oxford University Press, 2004), 182; see the entire section on Lopez on pp. 181–187.
26. Lopez, *Arctic Dreams*, 414.
27. Lopez, 36 and 37, respectively.
28. Barry Lopez, *Horizon* (New York: Alfred A. Knopf, 2019), 263.
29. Hermann Hesse, *News from the Universe*, trans. Robert Bly (San Francisco: Sierra Club Books, 1980), 86.

30. On Lopez's involvement with environmental milieus, see also Bron Taylor, *Dark Green Religion: Nature Spirituality and the Planetary Future* (Berkeley: University of California Press, 2010), 93.
31. Lopez, *Arctic Dreams*, 250 (emphasis original).
32. In the light of his discussions with artists in the Galápagos, Lopez notes that these have helped him to understand the "essence of a place," which transgresses the image itself: "The image did not have to have meaning. This was only the *presence* of the place, in the middle of a March afternoon on the equator." Lopez, *Horizon*, 241 (emphasis original). See also p. 169 on the Indigenous way of observing the landscape, and pp. 144–145 on an Indigenous (in this case Navajo) understanding of "beauty" as the integration of color, line, proportionality, sound, smell, and texture: "I was aware of its effect on me, and of how my vulnerability to it enhanced a feeling of health in me, of being in harmony with the world that existed outside my own thoughts and beyond my understanding" (p. 145).
33. Lopez, *Horizon*, 28. See also his implicit comment on the "Anthropocene," when he writes about ancient Indigenous petroglyphs and pictographs as having "both a sense of wonder about the nature of the world and, more subtly, an understanding that human beings do not control their own fate, that in some fundamental way humans are powerless to do so" (p. 369).
34. See Sideris, *Consecrated Science*, 2–9.
35. Martin Eger, "The New Epic of Science and the Problem of Communication," in *Science, Understanding, and Justice: The Philosophical Essays of Martin Eger*, ed. Abner Shimony (Chicago: Open Court, 2006), 281–296, p. 287.
36. Sideris, *Consecrated Science*, 5.
37. Sideris, 6.
38. Cathy McGowan Russell, "The Epic of Evolution," http://epicofevolution.com/about/about-the-epic. We find almost exactly the same sentences elsewhere, for instance, in Loyal Rue, "Epic of Evolution," in *Encyclopedia of Religion and Nature*, ed. Bron R. Taylor (London: Continuum, 2005), 612–615, p. 612.
39. Rue, "Epic of Evolution," 612.
40. Loyal D. Rue, *Everybody's Story: Wising Up to the Epic of Evolution* (Albany: State University of New York Press, 2000), 130–131.
41. Brian Thomas Swimme and Mary Evelyn Tucker, *Journey of the Universe* (New Haven, CT: Yale University Press, 2011). See Sideris, *Consecrating Science*, 118; on Swimme and Tucker see pp. 123 and 165.
42. Taylor, *Dark Green Religion*, 10.
43. Taylor, 105 (Taylor quotes from the Internet here).
44. UNESCO (United Nations Educational, Scientific and Cultural Organization), *Man Belongs to the Earth: International Cooperation in Environmental Research* (Paris: UNESCO, 1988), https://unesdoc.unesco.org/ark:/48223/pf0000080638, 8.
45. UNESCO, 8.
46. UNESCO, 10. See also Taylor, *Dark Green Religion*, 175.
47. UNESCO, *Man Belongs to the Earth*, 48.
48. UNESCO, 62.
49. United Nations, *Report of the World Commission on Environment and Development: Our Common Future*, transmitted to the General Assembly as an Annex to document

A/42/427—Development and International Co-Operation: Environment, 1987, www.un-documents.net/our-common-future.pdf; no pagination, but the quote is from p. 33 of the PDF.

50. United Nations, p. 52 of PDF.
51. Taylor, *Dark Green Religion*, 174.
52. United Nations, *Our Common Future*, p. 93 of PDF.
53. Taylor, *Dark Green Religion*, 176.
54. See Taylor's definitions in *Dark Green Religion*, 14–16.
55. https://en.wikipedia.org/wiki/Gaia_hypothesis.
56. See the useful overview in Alexander Friedrich, Petra Löffler, Niklas Schrape, and Florian Sprenger, *Ökologien der Erde: Zur Wissensgeschichte und Aktualität der Gaia-Hypothese* (Lüneburg: meson press, 2018).
57. Quoted in Taylor, *Dark Green Religion*, 94. See also Julia Butterfly Hill's website at www.juliabutterflyhill.com for further publications and information.
58. John Seed, Joanna Macy, Pat Fleming, and Arne Naess, eds., *Thinking Like a Mountain: Towards a Council of All Beings* (Philadelphia: New Society, 1988), 91–92.
59. Taylor, *Dark Green Religion*, 96.
60. Taylor, 96.
61. For this and other reviews and information, see the author's website at www.richardpowers.net/the-overstory.
62. Richard Powers, *The Overstory: A Novel* (New York: W. W. Norton, 2018), 4 (emphasis original).
63. Powers, 17 and 54, respectively.
64. Powers, 56.
65. Powers, 97.
66. Powers, 110–111.
67. Everett Hamner, "Here's to Unsuicide: An Interview with Richard Powers," *Los Angeles Review of Books*, April 7, 2018, https://lareviewofbooks.org/article/heres-to-unsuicide-an-interview-with-richard-powers/#!
68. Powers, *The Overstory*, 115.
69. Powers, 118.
70. Powers, 124.
71. Powers, 190 and 211, respectively.
72. All the following titles feed into this discursive arrangement, each one in its own way: Colin Tudge, *The Secret Life of Trees: How They Live and Why They Matter* (London: Allen Lane, 2005); Nalini Nadkarni, *Between Earth and Sky: Our Intimate Connections to Trees* (Berkeley: University of California Press, 2008); Matthew Hall, *Plants as Persons: A Philosophical Botany* (Albany: State University of New York Press, 2011); Robin Wall Kimmerer, *Braiding Sweetgrass: Indigenous Wisdom, Scientific Knowledge and the Teachings of Plants* (Minneapolis: Milkweed, 2013); David George Haskell, *The Forest Unseen: A Year's Watch in Nature* (New York: Penguin, 2013); David George Haskell, *The Songs of Trees: Stories from Nature's Great Connectors* (New York: Penguin, 2018); Stefano Mancuso, *The Revolutionary Genius of Plants* (New York: Atria, 2018); Max Porter, *Lanny: A Novel* (Minneapolis: Graywolf, 2019).
73. More information about his work can be found on his homepage at www.peter-wohlleben.de.

74. Martin Ebel, "Mein Held, der Wald," *Süddeutsche Zeitung* online, October 23, 2018, www.sueddeutsche.de/kultur/amerikanische-literatur-mein-held-der-wald-1.4182004.
75. Peter Wohlleben, *Das geheime Leben der Bäume: Was sie fühlen, wie sie kommunizieren—die Entdeckung einer verborgenen Welt* (Munich: Ludwig, 2015), 218.
76. Peter Wohlleben, *Das Seelenleben der Tiere: Liebe, Trauer, Mitgefühl—erstaunliche Einblicke in eine verborgene Welt* (Munich: Ludwig, 2016), 9.
77. Wohlleben, 228.
78. Wohlleben, 224.
79. Jane Goodall, "Primate Spirituality," in *Encyclopedia of Religion and Nature*, 2 vols., ed. Bron Taylor (London: Continuum International, 2005), 1303–1306, p. 1303. The most relevant book documenting her spiritual convictions is Jane Goodall, *Reason for Hope: A Spiritual Journey* (New York: Time Warner, 1999). On her strong contribution to environmental spiritualities, see Taylor, *Dark Green Religion*, 24–31.
80. For a recent analysis that makes a very similar point, see Christopher M. Driscoll and Monica R. Miller, *Method as Identity: Manufacturing Discourse in the Academic Study of Religion* (Lanham, MD: Lexington, 2018).
81. Elizabeth Kolbert, *The Sixth Extinction: An Unnatural History* (London: Bloomsbury, 2014).
82. See, for instance, Rodolfo Dirzo, Hillary S. Young, Mauro Galetti, Gerardo Ceballos, Nick J. B. Isaac, and Ben Collen, "Defaunation in the Anthropocene," *Science* 345, no. 6195 (2014): 401–406.
83. Arianne Françoise Conty, "The Politics of Nature: New Materialist Responses to the Anthropocene." *Theory, Culture and Society* 35 (2018): 73–96, p. 73. On the use of the term *indiscretion* in this quotation, and on the broader context of the argument, see Jay Johnston, "'Beyond' Language?: Ecology, Ontology, and Aesthetics," in *Religion and Discourse Research: Disciplinary Use and Interdisciplinary Dialogues*, ed. Jay Johnston and Kocku von Stuckrad (Berlin: De Gruyter, 2021), 231–242, p. 234. For a religious studies and theology point of view, see also Catherine Keller and Mary-Jane Rubenstein, eds., *Entangled Worlds: Religion, Science, and New Materialisms* (New York: Fordham University Press, 2018).
84. Manuel de Landa, *A Thousand Years of Nonlinear History* (Cambridge, MA: MIT Press/Zone, 1997); Rosi Braidotti, *The Posthuman* (Cambridge, MA: Polity, 2013); Rosi Braidotti, *Posthuman Knowledge* (Cambridge, MA: Polity, 2019).
85. Jonathan K. Crane, "Beastly Morality: A Twisting Tale," in *Beastly Morality: Animals as Ethical Agents*, ed. Jonathan K. Crane (New York: Columbia University Press, 2016), 3–27, p. 20.
86. Peter Singer, *Animal Liberation: A New Ethics for Our Treatment of Animals* (New York: New York Review/Random House, 1975).
87. See, for instance, Paola Cavalieri, *The Animal Question: Why Nonhuman Animals Deserve Human Rights* (Oxford: Oxford University Press, 2004); Matthew Calarco, *Zoographies: The Question of the Animal from Heidegger to Derrida* (New York: Columbia University Press, 2008); Carl Safina, *Beyond Words: What Animals Think and Feel*, 2nd ed. (New York: Macmillan/Henry Holt, 2015).
88. Paola Cavalieri, *The Death of the Animal: A Dialogue* (New York: Columbia University Press, 2012).
89. Crane, "Beastly Morality," 10.

90. Jane Bennett, *Vibrant Matter: A Political Ecology of Things* (Durham, NC: Duke University Press, 2010), 32.
91. Ian Hodder, *Entangled: An Archaeology of the Relationships Between Humans and Things* (Hoboken, NJ: Wiley-Blackwell, 2012), 215.
92. See Peik Ingman, Måns Broo, Tuija Hovi, and Terhi Utriainen, eds., *The Relational Dynamics of Enchantment and Sacralization* (Sheffield: Equinox, 2016).
93. Bruno Latour and Steve Woolgar, *Laboratory Life: The Construction of Scientific Facts* (Princeton, NJ: Princeton University Press, 1986); first edition published in 1979.
94. Bruno Latour, *We Have Never Been Modern* (Cambridge, MA: Harvard University Press, 1993); Bruno Latour, *On the Modern Cult of the Factish Gods*, trans. Heather MacLean and Catherine Porter (Durham, NC: Duke University Press, 2010); Bruno Latour, "Fetish-Factish," *Material Religion* 7 (2011): 42–49.
95. Bruno Latour, *Facing Gaia: Eight Lectures on the New Climatic Regime*, trans. Catherine Porter (Cambridge: Polity, 2017), 58 (emphasis original). Note also his equation of "soul" and "consciousness."
96. Latour, 86 (emphasis original). See also the discussion in Alexander Friedrich, Petra Löffler, Niklas Schrape, and Florian Sprenger, *Ökologien der Erde: Zur Wissensgeschichte und Aktualität der Gaia-Hypothese* (Lüneburg: meson press, 2018), 63–92; and Petra Löffler's comment on "Latour's strategically quite arbitrary adaptation, if not expropriation, of Lovelock and Margulis's concept of Gaia as a self-regulating system" (p. 118).
97. Latour, *Facing Gaia*, 70.
98. Donna J. Haraway, *Staying with the Trouble: Making Kin in the Chthulucene* (Durham, NC: Duke University Press, 2016), loc. 512–513 (Kindle edition).
99. Donna J. Haraway, *When Species Meet* (Minneapolis: University of Minnesota Press, 2008), 19.
100. Haraway, *Staying with the Trouble*, loc. 1157–1159; see also loc. 315–318.
101. Haraway, loc. 1159.
102. Marc Bekoff and Jessica Pierce, *The Animals' Agenda: Freedom, Compassion, and Coexistence in the Human Age* (Boston: Beacon, 2017), 7.
103. Lopez, *Horizon*, 297.
104. Latour, *Facing Gaia*, 150.
105. Diana Coole and Samantha Frost, eds., *New Materialisms: Ontology, Agency, and Politics* (Durham, NC: Duke University Press, 2010), 6.
106. Diana Coole in Coole and Frost, *New Materialisms*, 92.
107. Wendy Wheeler, "A Feeling for Life: Biosemiotics, Autopoiesis and the Orders of Discourse," *Anglia* 133 (2015): 53–68.
108. Serenella Iovino and Serpil Oppermann, "Introduction: Stories Come to Matter," in *Material Ecocriticism*, ed. Serenella Iovino and Serpil Oppermann (Bloomington: Indiana University Press, 2014), 1–17, pp. 1–2.
109. See also Kate Rigby, *Reclaiming Romanticism: Towards an Ecopoetics of Decolonization* (London: Bloomsbury Academic, 2020).
110. Ursula K. Le Guin, *Late in the Day: Poems, 2010–2014* (Oakland: PM, 2016), viii.
111. Le Guin, viii.
112. Le Guin, ix.
113. Le Guin, 10. The poem is also available online at www.ursulakleguin.com/late-day-index; see also the links to podcasts and further material provided there.

114. There are other examples of poems in *Late in the Day* that express similar sentiments, including the Anthropocene. In "Geology of the Northwest Coast," for instance, Le Guin describes how the sea returns and takes back the land, with collapsing headlands and falling cliffs, preparing the way for a "beautiful, remorseless morning" (Le Guin, 21).
115. Le Guin, ix.

BIBLIOGRAPHY

Abram, David. *Becoming Animal: An Earthly Cosmology*. New York: Pantheon, 20[illegible]

Akademie der Künste, Berlin. *Waldungen: Die Deutschen und ihr Wald*. Ausstellung d[illegible]d-emie der Künste vom 20. September bis 15. November 1987. Berlin: Nicolaische Verla[illegible]chhandlung, 1987.

Albanese, Catherine L. *Nature Religion in America: From the Algonkian Indians to the New Age*. 2nd ed. Chicago: University of Chicago Press, 1991.

Alpers, Hans Joachim, Joachim Fuchs, et al. *Lexikon der Science Fiction Literatur*. New and enlarged ed. Munich: Wilhelm Heyne, 1988.

Anders, Günther. *Die Antiquiertheit des Menschen: Über die Seele im Zeitalter der zweiten industriellen Revolution*. 5th enlarged ed. Munich: C. H. Beck, 1980. First edition published in 1956.

Anderson, Benedict. *Imagined Communities: Reflections on the Origin and Spread of Nationalism*. Rev. ed. London: Verso, 2006. First edition published in 1983.

Arzt, Thomas, ed. *Das Rote Buch: C. G. Jungs Reise zum "anderen Pol der Welt."* Würzburg: Königshausen und Neumann, 2015.

Arzt, Thomas, Maria Hippius-Gräfin Dürckheim, and Roland Dollinger, eds. *Unus Mundus: Kosmos und Sympathie: Beiträge zum Gedanken der Einheit von Mensch und Kosmos*. Frankfurt am Main: Peter Lang, 1991.

Aschheim, Steven E. *Brothers and Strangers: The East European Jew in German and German Jewish Consciousness, 1800–1932*. Madison: University of Wisconsin Press, 1982.

Asprem, Egil. *The Problem of Disenchantment: Scientific Naturalism and Esoteric Discourse, 1900–1939*. Leiden: Brill, 2014.

Assagioli, Roberto. *Psychosynthese und transpersonale Entwicklung*. Translated from the Italian by Hans Dellefant. Paderborn: Junfermann, 1992. Italian original edition published in 1988.

——. *Psychosynthesis*. London: Penguin, 1971.

Assmann, Jan, ed. *Die Erfindung des inneren Menschen: Studien zur religiösen Anthropologie*. Gütersloh: Gütersloher Verlagshaus Mohn, 1993.

Baerwald, Richard. *Okkultismus, Spiritismus und unterbewußte Seelenzustände*. Leipzig: B. G. Teubner, 1920.

——. *Okkultismus und Spiritismus und ihre weltanschaulichen Folgerungen*. Berlin: Deutsche Buch-Gemeinschaft, 1926.

——. "Psychologische Faktoren des modernen Zeitgeistes." *Schriften der Gesellschaft für psychologische Forschung* 15 (1905): 583–667.

Bair, Deirdre. *Jung: A Biography*. London: Little, Brown, 2004.

Baker, Mark. *The Soul Hypothesis: Investigations Into the Existence of the Soul*. London: Continuum, 2011.

Balmer, Heinrich, ed. *Die Psychologie des 20. Jahrhunderts*. Vol. 1, *Die europäische Tradition: Tendenzen, Schulen, Entwicklungslinien*. Zurich: Kindler, 1976.

Barad, Karen. *Meeting the Universe Halfway: Quantum Physics and the Entanglement of Matter and Meaning*. Durham, NC: Duke University Press, 2006.

Barnhill, David L. "Spirituality and Resistance: Ursula Le Guin's *The Word for World Is Forest* and th[illegible] Film *Avatar*." *Journal for the Study of Religion, Nature and Culture* 4 (2010): 478–[illegible].

Baudu[illegible]ssel M. *Surrealism and the Occult: Occultism and Western Esotericism in the Work a[illegible]ement of André Breton*. Amsterdam: Amsterdam University Press, 2015.

Bau[illegible]ssel M., and Henrik Johnsson, eds. *The Occult in Modernist Art, Literature, and* [illegible] Cham: Palgrave Macmillan / Springer, 2017.

B[illegible]Max L. "Das moderne Phänomen des Dionysischen und seine 'Entdeckung' durch [illegible]ietzsche." *Nietzsche-Studien* 6 (1977): 123–153.

[illegible]umgarten, Albert I., Jan Assmann, and Guy G. Stroumsa, eds. *Self, Soul and Body in Religious Experience*. Leiden: Brill, 1998.

Beck, Joseph. *Grundriß der Empirischen Psychologie und Logik*. 2nd ed. Stuttgart: Verlag der J. B. Metzler'schen Buchhandlung, 1846.

Beetz, K. O. *Einführung in die moderne Psychologie*. Pt. 1, *Allgemeine Grundlegung*. Osterwieck/Harz: A. W. Zickfeldt, 1900.

Bekoff, Marc, and Jessica Pierce. *The Animals' Agenda: Freedom, Compassion, and Coexistence in the Human Age*. Boston: Beacon, 2017.

Bender, Courtney. *The New Metaphysicals: Spirituality and the American Religious Imagination*. Chicago: University of Chicago Press, 2010.

Beneke, Eduard. *Lehrbuch der pragmatischen Psychologie oder der Seelenlehre in der Anwendung auf das Leben*. Berlin: E. S. Mittler, 1853.

——. *Lehrbuch der Psychologie als Naturwissenschaft*. 4th ed. Berlin: E. S. Mittler, 1877. First edition published in 1833.

Bennett, Jane. *Vibrant Matter: A Political Ecology of Things*. Durham, NC: Duke University Press, 2010.

Bernitz, Anna Maria. "Hilma af Klint and the New Art of Seeing." In *A Cultural History of the Avant-Garde in the Nordic Countries, 1900–1925*, edited by Hubert van den Berg and Marianne Ølholm, 587–597. Amsterdam: Brill / Rodopi, 2012.

Bernoulli, Christoph, and Hans Kern, eds. *Romantische Naturphilosophie*. Jena: Eugen Diederichs, 1926.

Berry, Evan. *Devoted to Nature: The Religious Roots of American Environmentalism*. Oakland: University of California Press, 2015.

Berti, Alessandro. *Roberto Assagioli: Profilo biografico degli anni di formazione*. Florence: Istituto di Psicosintesi, 1988.

Beßlich, Barbara. *Wege in den "Kulturkrieg": Zivilisationskritik in Deutschland, 1890–1914*. Darmstadt: Wissenschaftliche Buchgesellschaft, 2000.

Betz, Joseph. *Grundriß der Empirischen Psychologie und Logik*. 6th improved ed. Stuttgart: Verlag der J. B. Metzler'schen Buchhandlung, 1860.

Bhabha, Homi K., ed. *Nation and Narration*. London: Routledge, 1990.

Biale, David. *Gershom Scholem: Kabbalah and Counter-History*. Cambridge, MA: Harvard University Press, 1979.

Bird-David, Nurit. "'Animism' Revisited: Personhood, Environment, and Relational Epistemology." *Current Anthropology* 40 (1999): 67–79.

Birnbacher, Dieter, ed. *Ökophilosophie*. Stuttgart: Philipp Reclam jun., 1997.

Blok, Gemma, Vincent Kuitenbrouwer, and Claire Weeda, eds. *Imagining Communities: Historical Reflections on the Process of Community Formation*. Amsterdam: Amsterdam University Press, 2018.

Bohm, David. *Wholeness and the Implicate Order*. Reprinted and first published in paperback with corrections. London: Routledge and Kegan Paul, 1981. First edition published in 1980.

Böhme, Hartmut. *Fetischismus und Kultur: Eine andere Theorie der Moderne*. Reinbek: Rowohlt, 2006.

Borchmeyer, Dieter. *Was ist deutsch? Variationen eines Themas von Schiller über Wagner zu Thomas Mann*. Eichstätt: Katholische Universität Eichstätt-Ingolstadt, 2010.

Borelli, Arianna, and Alexandra Grieser. "Recent Research on the Aesthetics of Knowledge in Science and in Religion." *Approaching Religion* 7 (2017): 4–21.

Bosch, Aida. *Konsum und Exklusion: Eine Kultursoziologie der Dinge*. Bielefeld: transcript, 2010.

Boyarin, Jonathan, and Daniel Boyarin, eds. *Jews and Other Differences: The New Jewish Cultural Studies*. Minneapolis: University of Minnesota Press, 1997.

Braidotti, Rosi. *The Posthuman*. Cambridge: Polity, 2013.

——. *Posthuman Knowledge*. Cambridge: Polity, 2019.

Braune, Andreas. *Fortschritt als Ideologie: Wilhelm Ostwald und der Monismus*. Leipzig: Leipziger Universitätsverlag, 2009.

Bremmer, Jan N. *The Early Greek Concept of the Soul*. Princeton: Princeton University Press, 1983.

——. *The Rise and Fall of the Afterlife: The 1995 Read-Tuckwell Lectures at the University of Bristol*. London: Routledge, 2002.

Brenner, Michael. "Gnosis and History: Polemics of German-Jewish Identity from Graetz to Scholem." *New German Critique* 77 (1999): 45–60.

Breuninger, Renate. *Wirklichkeit in der Dichtung Rilkes*. Frankfurt am Main: Peter Lang, 1991.

Breysig, Kurt. *Die Geschichte der Seele im Werdegang der Menschheit*. Breslau: M. und H. Marcus, 1931.

Bruder, Klaus-Jürgen. "Zwischen Kant und Freud: Die Institutionalisierung der Psychologie als selbständige Wissenschaft." In *Die Seele: Ihre Geschichte im Abendland*, edited by Gerd Jüttemann, Michael Sonntag, and Christoph Wulf, 319–339. Weinheim: Psychologie Verlags Union, 1991.

Brunotte, Ulrike. *Dämonen des Wissens: Gender, Performativität und materielle Kultur im Werk von Jane Ellen Harrison*. Würzburg: Ergon, 2013.

Buber, Martin. *Drei Reden über das Judentum*. Frankfurt am Main: Literarische Anstalt Rütten und Loening, 1919.

——. *Ekstatische Konfessionen: Gesammelt von Martin Buber*. Berlin: Schocken, 1923. First edition published in Jena by Diederichs in 1909.

Buell, Lawrence. *The Environmental Imagination: Thoreau, Nature Writing, and the Formation of American Culture*. Cambridge: Belknap Press of Harvard University Press, 1995.

Calarco, Matthew. *Zoographies: The Question of the Animal from Heidegger to Derrida*. New York: Columbia University Press, 2008.

Canetti, Elias. *Masse und Macht*. Frankfurt am Main: Fischer, 1998. First edition published in 1960.

Capra, Fritjof. *The Tao of Physics: An Exploration of the Parallels Between Modern Physics and Eastern Mysticism*. Boulder: Shambhala, 1975.

Carson, Rachel. *Chincoteague: A National Wildlife Refuge*. Conservation in Action 1. Washington, DC: US Government Printing Office, 1947.

——. *The Edge of the Sea*. Boston: Houghton Mifflin, 1955.

——. *The Sense of Wonder*. Introduction by Linda Lear. New York: HarperCollins, 1998. First edition published in 1965.

——. *Silent Spring*. New York: Houghton Mifflin, 1962.

Cavalieri, Paola. *The Animal Question: Why Nonhuman Animals Deserve Human Rights*. Oxford: Oxford University Press, 2004.

——. *The Death of the Animal: A Dialogue*. New York: Columbia University Press, 2012.

Clair, Jean, Cathrin Pichler, and Wolfgang Pircher, eds. *Wunderblock: Eine Geschichte der modernen Seele*. Katalog zur Ausstellung der Wiener Festwochen in Zusammenarbeit mit dem Historischen Museum der Stadt Wien, 27. April bis 6. August 1989. Edited by the Wiener Festwochen. Vienna: Löcker, 1989.

Cobb, John B., and David Ray Griffin, eds. *Mind in Nature: Essays on the Interface of Science and Philosophy*. Washington: University Press of America, 1977.

Colman, Andrew M. *A Dictionary of Psychology*. Oxford: Oxford University Press, 2015. www.oxfordreference.com/view/10.1093/acref/9780199657681.001.0001/acref-9780199657681.

Conty, Arianne Françoise. "The Politics of Nature: New Materialist Responses to the Anthropocene." *Theory, Culture and Society* 35 (2018): 73–96.

Coole, Diana, and Samantha Frost, eds. *New Materialisms: Ontology, Agency, and Politics*. Durham, NC: Duke University Press, 2010.

Corcilius, Klaus, and Dominik Perler, eds. *Partitioning the Soul: Debates from Plato to Leibniz*. Berlin: De Gruyter, 2014.

Crane, Jonathan K. "Beastly Morality: A Twisting Tale." In *Beastly Morality: Animals as Ethical Agents*, edited by Jonathan K. Crane, 3–27. New York: Columbia University Press, 2016.

Crisp, Thomas M., Steven Porter, and Gregg A. Ten Elshof, eds. *Neuroscience and the Soul: The Human Person in Philosophy, Science, and Theology*. Grand Rapids, MI: Eerdmans, 2016.

Crowley, Aleister. *Magick in Theory and Practice*. New York: Castle, 1929.

Danziger, Kurt. *Constructing the Subject: Historical Origins of Psychological Research*. Cambridge: Cambridge University Press, 1990.

——. "Mid-Nineteenth-Century British Psycho-Physiology: A Neglected Chapter in the History of Psychology." In *The Problematic Science: Psychology in Nineteenth-Century Thought*, edited by William R. Woodward and Mitchell G. Ash, 119–146. New York: Praeger, 1982.

——. *Naming the Mind: How Psychology Found Its Language*. London: Sage, 1997.

Daser, Eckard. "Ostwalds energetischer Monismus." PhD diss., University of Konstanz, 1980.

Daston, Lorraine. "The Theory of Will Versus the Science of Mind." In *The Problematic Science: Psychology in Nineteenth-Century Thought*, edited by William R. Woodward and Mitchell G. Ash, 88–115. New York: Praeger, 1982.

Daston, Lorraine, and Peter Galison. *Objectivity*. New York: Zone, 2007.

Davidowicz, Klaus Samuel. *Gershom Scholem und Martin Buber: Die Geschichte eines Mißverständnisses*. Neukirchen-Vluyn: Neukirchener Verlag, 1995.

de Landa, Manuel. *A Thousand Years of Nonlinear History*. Cambridge, MA: MIT Press/Zone Books, 1997.

Delany, Samuel R. *The Einstein Intersection*. Middletown, CT: Wesleyan University Press, 1967.

Deloria, Philip J. *Playing Indian*. New Haven, CT: Yale University Press, 1998.

Descartes, René. *Discours de la méthode: Texte et commentaire*, edited by Etienne Gilson. 5th ed. 1627; Paris: Vrin, 1976.

Descola, Philippe. *Jenseits von Natur und Kultur*. Frankfurt am Main: Suhrkamp, 2011.

——. *Die Ökologie der Anderen*. Berlin: Matthes und Seitz, 2014.

Dessoir, Max. *Vom Jenseits der Seele: Die Geheimwissenschaften in kritischer Betrachtung*. 4th and 5th eds. Stuttgart: Ferdinand Enke, 1920. First edition published in 1917.

Dilthey, Wilhelm. "Ideen über eine beschreibende und zergliedernde Psychologie." In *Gesammelte Schriften*, vol. 5, 139–240. Stuttgart: Teubner; Göttingen: Vandenhoeck und Ruprecht, 1894.

Dirzo, Rodolfo, Hillary S. Young, Mauro Galetti, Gerardo Ceballos, Nick J. B. Isaac, and Ben Collen. "Defaunation in the Anthropocene." *Science* 345, no. 6195 (2014): 401–406.

Dodds, E. R. *The Greeks and the Irrational*. Berkeley: University of California Press, 1963.

Donati, Marialuisa. "Beyond Synchronicity: The Worldview of Carl Gustav Jung and Wolfgang Pauli." *Journal of Analytical Psychology* 49 (2004): 707–728.

Dörrenbächer, Judith, and Kerstin Plüm, eds. *Beseelte Dinge: Design aus Perspektive des Animismus*. Bielefeld: transcript, 2016.

Dreßen, Wolfgang. "Mobilisierung der Seele. Jugend in Deutschland: 1880–1930." In *Die Seele: Ihre Geschichte im Abendland*, edited by Gerd Jüttemann, Michael Sonntag, and Christoph Wulf, 424–447. Weinheim: Psychologie Verlags Union, 1991.

Driesch, Hans. *The Crisis in Psychology*. Princeton: Princeton University Press, 1925.

——. *Lebenserinnerungen: Aufzeichnungen eines Forschers und Denkers in entscheidender Zeit*. Munich: Ernst Reinhardt, 1951.

——. *Leib und Seele: Eine Untersuchung über das psychophysische Grundproblem*. 3rd ed., based on the second and partly revised ed. Leipzig: Emmanuel Reinicke, 1923.

——. *Ordnungslehre: Ein System des nichtmetaphysischen Teiles der Philosophie*. New, improved and revised ed. Jena: Eugen Diederichs, 1923.

——. *Parapsychologie: Die Wissenschaft von den "okkulten" Erscheinungen*. Munich: F. Bruckmann, 1932.

——. *Der Vitalismus als Geschichte und als Lehre*. Leipzig: Barth, 1905.

Driscoll, Christopher M., and Monica R. Miller. *Method as Identity: Manufacturing Discourse in the Academic Study of Religion*. Lanham, MD: Lexington, 2018.

Drury, Nevill. *The Elements of Shamanism*. Longmead, UK: Element, 1989.

Du Bois, W. E. B. *The Souls of Black Folk*. Edited with an Introduction and Notes by Brent Hayes Edwards. Oxford: Oxford University Press, 2007. First edition published in 1903.

du Prel, Carl. "Der Dämon des Sokrates." *Sphinx* 4 (1887): 217–227, 329–335, 391–400.

——. "Moderner Tempelschlaf." *Sphinx* 9 (1890): 1–6, 105–111.

——. *Die Mystik der alten Griechen*. Leipzig: Günther, 1888.

——. *The Philosophy of Mysticism*. Trans. C. C. Massey. 2 vols. London: George Redway, 1898. German original *Die Philosophie der Mystik*. Leipzig: Günther, 1885.

Dürr, Hans-Peter, and Walther Ch. Zimmerli, eds. *Geist und Natur: Über den Widerspruch zwischen naturwissenschaftlicher Erkenntnis und philosophischer Welterfahrung*. Bern: Scherz, 1989.

Ebel, Martin. "Mein Held, der Wald." *Süddeutsche Zeitung* online, October 23, 2018. www.sueddeutsche.de/kultur/amerikanische-literatur-mein-held-der-wald-1.4182004.

Eckel, Winfried. *Wendung: Zum Prozeß der poetischen Reflexion im Werk Rilkes.* Würzburg: Königshausen und Neumann, 1994.

Eder, Franz X. "Historische Diskurse und ihre Analyse—eine Einleitung." In *Historische Diskursanalysen: Genealogie, Theorien, Anwendungen*, edited by Franz X. Eder, 9–23. Wiesbaden: VS Verlag für Sozialwissenschaft, 2006.

Eger, Martin. "The New Epic of Science and the Problem of Communication." In *Science, Understanding, and Justice: The Philosophical Essays of Martin Eger*, edited by Abner Shimony, 281–296. Chicago: Open Court, 2006.

Ellenberger, Henri F. *The Discovery of the Unconscious: The History and Evolution of Dynamic Psychiatry.* London: Allen Lane / Penguin, 1970.

Emerson, Ralph Waldo. *The Collected Works of Ralph Waldo Emerson*, edited by Alfred R. Ferguson. Vol. 1, *Nature, Addresses, and Lectures.* Cambridge: Belknap Press of Harvard University Press, 1971.

Engelhard, Dietrich von. "Schuberts Stellung in der romantischen Naturforschung." In *Gotthilf Heinrich Schubert: Gedenkschrift zum 200. Geburtstag des romantischen Naturforschers*, edited by Universitätsbund Erlangen-Nürnberg e.V., 11–36. Nuremberg, 1980.

Erdbeer, Robert Matthias. *Die Signatur des Kosmos: Epistemische Poetik und die Genealogie der Esoterischen Moderne.* Berlin: De Gruyter, 2010.

Esposito, Joseph L. *Schelling's Idealism and Philosophy of Nature.* Lewisburg: Bucknell University Press; London: Associated University Presses, 1977.

Faivre, Antoine. "Occultism." In *The Encyclopedia of Religion*, edited Mircea Eliade (editor in chief), vol. 11, 36–40. New York: Macmillan, 1987.

Fedele, Anna, and Kim E. Knibbe, eds. *Gender and Power in Contemporary Spirituality: Ethnographic Approaches.* New York: Routledge, 2013.

Figl, Johann, and Hans-Dieter Klein, eds. *Der Begriff der Seele in der Religionswissenschaft.* Würzburg: Königshausen und Neumann, 2002.

Finger, Otto. *Von der Materialität der Seele: Beitrag zur Geschichte des Materialismus und Atheismus im Deutschland der zweiten Hälfte des 18. Jahrhunderts.* Berlin: Akademie-Verlag, 1961.

Flader, Susan L. *Thinking Like a Mountain: Aldo Leopold and the Evolution of an Ecological Attitude Toward Deer, Wolves, and Forests.* Columbia: University of Missouri Press, 1974.

Flaherty, Gloria. *Shamanism and the Eighteenth Century.* Princeton: Princeton University Press, 1992.

Francavilla, Joseph V. "Promethean Bound: Heroes and Gods in Roger Zelazny's Science Fiction." In *The Transcendent Adventure: Studies of Religion in Science Fiction/Fantasy*, edited by Robert Reilly, 207–222. Westport, CT: Greenwood, 1985.

Friedrich, Alexander, Petra Löffler, Niklas Schrape, and Florian Sprenger. *Ökologien der Erde: Zur Wissensgeschichte und Aktualität der Gaia-Hypothese.* Lüneburg: meson press, 2018.

Friedrich, Janette, ed. *Karl Bühlers* Krise der Psychologie: *Positionen, Bezüge und Kontroversen im Wien der 1920er/30er Jahre.* Cham: Springer, 2018.

Fuller, Michael, ed. *The Concept of the Soul: Scientific and Religious Perspectives.* Science and Religion Forum. Newcastle Upon Tyne: Cambridge Scholars, 2014.

Gale, Richard M. *The Philosophy of William James: An Introduction.* New York: Cambridge University Press, 2005.

Gamper, Michael. "Charisma, Hypnose, Nachahmung. Massenpsychologie und Medientheorie." In *Trancemedien und Neue Medien um 1900: Ein anderer Blick auf die Moderne*, edited by Marcus Hahn and Erhard Schüttpelz, 351–373. Bielefeld: transcript, 2009.

Gatta, John. *Making Nature Sacred: Literature, Religion, and Environment in America from the Puritans to the Present.* Oxford: Oxford University Press, 2004.

Gerson, Lloyd. "Plotinus." In *The Stanford Encyclopedia of Philosophy* (Fall 2018 edition), edited by Edward N. Zalta, https://plato.stanford.edu/archives/fall2018/entries/plotinus/.

Giovetti, Paola. *Roberto Assagioli: La vita e l'opera del fondatore della Psicosintesi.* Rome: Edizioni Mediterranee, 1995.

Gladigow, Burkhard. "'Tiefe der Seele' und 'inner space': Zur Geschichte eines Topos von Heraklit bis zur Science Fiction." In *Die Erfindung des inneren Menschen: Studien zur religiösen Anthropologie*, edited by Jan Assmann, 114–132. Gütersloh: Gütersloher Verlagshaus Mohn, 1993.

Goethe, Johann Wolfgang von. *Goethes Briefe.* Vol. 3, *1805–1821.* Hamburger Ausgabe. Edited by Karl Robert Mandelkow and Bodo Morawe. Munich: C. H. Beck, 1965.

——. *Wilhelm Meisters Wanderjahre.* Frankfurt am Main: Insel, 1982. First edition published in 1821.

Goetz, Stewart, and Charles Taliaferro. *A Brief History of the Soul.* Hoboken, NJ: Wiley-Blackwell, 2011.

Goldman, Marion S. *The American Soul Rush: Esalen and the Rise of Spiritual Privilege.* New York: New York University Press, 2012.

Goldstein, Amanda Jo. *Sweet Science: Romantic Materialism and the New Logics of Life.* Chicago: University of Chicago Press, 2017.

Golomb, Jacob. *Nietzsche and Zion.* Ithaca: Cornell University Press, 2004.

Goodall, Jane. "Primate Spirituality." In *Encyclopedia of Religion and Nature*, 2 vols., edited by Bron Taylor, 1303–1306. London: Continuum International, 2005.

——. *Reason for Hope: A Spiritual Journey.* New York: Time Warner, 1999.

Gottlieb, Roger S. "The Transcendence of Justice and the Justice of Transcendence: Mysticism, Deep Ecology, and Political Life." *Journal of the American Academy of Religion* 67 (1999): 149–166.

Gottwald, Franz-Theo. "Hören, Wissen, Handeln—Schamanische und tiefenökologische Anregungen für eine konviviale Wissenschaft." In *Schamanische Wissenschaft: Ökologie, Naturwissenschaft und Kunst*, edited by Franz-Theo Gottwald and Christian Rätsch, 11–23. Munich: Diederichs, 1998.

Gottwald, Franz-Theo, and Andrea Klepsch, eds. *Tiefenökologie: Wie wir in Zukunft leben wollen.* Munich: Diederichs, 1995.

Gottwald, Franz-Theo, and Christian Rätsch, eds. *Schamanische Wissenschaft: Ökologie, Naturwissenschaft und Kunst.* Munich: Diederichs, 1998.

Gräber-Magocsi, Sonja. "Die Vermessung 'Neu-Seellands': Schreibweisen der Psychologien in der deutschsprachigen Literatur der Jahrhundertwende." PhD diss., Harvard University, 2012.

Greene, Liz. *The Astrological World of Jung's 'Liber Novus': Daimons, Gods, and the Planetary Journey.* London: Routledge, 2018.

——. *Jung's Studies in Astrology: Prophecy, Magic and the Qualities of Time.* London: Routledge, 2018.

Greisiger, Lutz, Sebastian Schüler, and Alexander van der Haven, eds. *Religion und Wahnsinn um 1900: Zwischen Pathologisierung und Selbstermächtigung / Religion and Madness Around 1900: Between Pathology and Self-Empowerment.* Würzburg: Ergon, 2017.

Grieser, Alexandra. "Imaginationen des Nichtwissens: Zur Hubble Space Imagery und den Figurationen des schönen Universums zwischen Wissenschaft, Kunst und Religion." In *Religion—Imagination—Ästhetik: Vorstellungs- und Sinneswelten in Religion und Kultur,* edited by Annette Wilke and Lucia Traut, 451–485. Göttingen: Vandenhoeck und Ruprecht, 2015.

Grieser, Alexandra, and Jay Johnston, eds. *Aesthetics of Religion: A Connective Concept*. Berlin: De Gruyter, 2017.

Griffin, David Ray. *Parapsychology, Philosophy, and Spirituality: A Postmodern Exploration*. Albany: State University of New York Press, 1997.

——. *Reenchantment Without Supernaturalism: A Process Philosophy of Religion*. Ithaca: Cornell University Press, 2018.

——. *Unsnarling the World-Knot: Consciousness, Freedom, and the Mind-Body Problem*. Berkeley: University of California Press, 1998.

Gripentrog, Stephanie. *Anormalität und Religion: Zur Entstehung der Psychologie im Kontext der europäischen Religionsgeschichte des 19. und frühen 20. Jahrhunderts*. Würzburg: Ergon-Verlag, 2016.

Grof, Stanislav. *Beyond the Brain: Birth, Death and Transcendence in Psychotherapy*. Albany: State University of New York Press, 1985.

——. "Ervin Laszlo's Akashic Field and the Dilemmas of Modern Consciousness Research." *World Futures* 62 (2006): 86–102.

——. *Psychology for the Future: Lessons from Modern Consciousness Research*. Albany: State University of New York Press, 2000.

——. "Revision and Re-Enchantment of the Legacy of Psychology from a Half Century of Consciousness Research." *Journal of Transpersonal Psychology* 44 (2012): 137–163.

Grof, Stanislav, and Christina Grof, eds. *Spiritual Emergency: When Personal Transformation Becomes a Crisis*. Los Angeles: Jeremy P. Tarcher, 1989.

Großheim, Michael. *Ludwig Klages und die Phänomenologie*. Berlin: Akademie-Verlag, 1994.

Guenther, Konrad. *Deutsches Naturerleben*. Stuttgart: J. F. Steinkopf, 1935.

Guldin, Rainer. *Politische Landschaften: Zum Verhältnis von Raum und nationaler Identität*. Bielefeld: transcript, 2014.

Guthke, Karl S. *Der Mythos der Neuzeit: Das Thema der Mehrheit der Welten in der Literatur- und Geistesgeschichte von der kopernikanischen Wende bis zur Science Fiction*. Bern: Francke, 1983.

Haberman, David L. *Loving Stones: Making the Impossible Possible in the Worship of Mount Govardhan*. London: Oxford University Press, 2020.

Habermas, Jürgen. *Der philosophische Diskurs der Moderne: Zwölf Vorlesungen*. 6th ed. Frankfurt am Main: Suhrkamp, 1998. First edition published in 1988.

Haeckel, Ernst. *Generelle Morphologie der Organismen: Allgemeine Grundzüge der organischen Formen-Wissenschaft, mechanisch begründet durch die von Charles Darwin reformirte Descendenz-Theorie*. Vol. 2, *Allgemeine Entwicklungsgeschichte der Organismen: Kritische Grundzüge der mechanistischen Wissenschaft von den entstehenden Formen der Organismen, begründet durch die Descendenz-Theorie*. Berlin: Reimer, 1866.

——. *Kristallseelen: Studien über das anorganische Leben*. Leipzig: Kröner, 1917.

——. *Kunstformen der Natur: Hundert Illustrationstafeln mit beschreibendem Text, Allgemeine Erläuterungen und Systematische Übersicht*. Leipzig: Bibliographisches Institut, 1904.

——. *Die Welträthsel: Gemeinverständliche Studien über Monistische Philosophie*. Volksausgabe (151.–170. Tausend). Stuttgart: Kröner, 1903. First edition published in 1899.

Hagelstange, Rudolf, Carl Georg Heise, and Paul Appel, eds. *Renée Sintenis*. With contributions from Rudolf Hagelstange, Carl Georg Heise, and Paul Appel. Berlin: Aufbau-Verlag, 1947.

Hahn, Marcus, and Erhard Schüttpelz, eds. *Trancemedien und Neue Medien um 1900: Ein anderer Blick auf die Moderne*. Bielefeld: transcript, 2009.

Hakl, Hans Thomas. *Eranos: An Alternative Intellectual History of the Twentieth Century*. Revised and expanded ed. Translated by Christopher McIntosh with the collaboration of Hereward Tilton. Montréal: McGill-Queen's University Press, 2013.

Hales, Barbara. "Mediating Worlds: The Occult as Projection of the New Woman in Weimar Culture." *German Quarterly* 83, no. 3 (2010): 317–332.

Halifax, Joan. *The Fruitful Darkness: Reconnecting with the Body of the Earth*. San Francisco: HarperCollins, 1994.

Hall, Matthew. *Plants as Persons: A Philosophical Botany*. Albany: State University of New York Press, 2011.

Hamner, Everett. "Here's to Unsuicide: An Interview with Richard Powers." *Los Angeles Review of Books*, April 7, 2018. https://lareviewofbooks.org/article/heres-to-unsuicide-an-interview-with-richard-powers/#!

Hanefeld, Erhardt. "Vorwort zur deutschen Ausgabe: Psychosynthesis und Transpersonale Psychotherapie." In *Handbuch der Psychosynthesis: Angewandte transpersonale Psychologie*, by Roberto Assagioli, edited by Erhardt Hanefeld, 9–34. Freiburg: Aurum, 1978.

Hanegraaff, Wouter J. *Esotericism and the Academy: Rejected Knowledge in Western Culture*. Cambridge: Cambridge University Press, 2012.

——. "The Great War of the Soul: Divine and Human Madness in Carl Gustav Jung's Liber Novus." In *Religion und Wahnsinn um 1900: Zwischen Pathologisierung und Selbstermächtigung / Religion and Madness Around 1900: Between Pathology and Self-Empowerment*, edited by Lutz Greisiger, Sebastian Schüler, and Alexander van der Haven, 101–135. Würzburg: Ergon, 2017.

Haraway, Donna J. *Staying with the Trouble: Making Kin in the Chthulucene*. Durham, NC: Duke University Press, 2016. Kindle.

——. *When Species Meet*. Minneapolis: University of Minnesota Press, 2008.

Harrison, Jane Ellen. Review of Erwin Rohde, *Seelencult und Unsterblichkeitsglaube der Griechen*, 2 vols. *Classical Review* 4 (1890): 376–377 (vol. 1); 8 (1894): 165–166 (vol. 2).

——. *Themis: A Study of the Social Origins of Greek Religion. With an Excursus on the Ritual Forms Preserved in Greek Tragedy by Gilbert Murray and a Chapter on the Origin of the Olympic Games by F. M. Cornford*. 2nd ed. Cambridge: Cambridge University Press, 1927. First edition published in 1912.

Harvey, Graham. *Animism: Respecting the Living World*. Kent Town: Wakefield, 2005.

——. *Contemporary Paganism: Listening People, Speaking Earth*. New York: New York University Press, 1997.

Haskell, David George. *The Forest Unseen: A Year's Watch in Nature*. New York: Penguin, 2013.

——. *The Songs of Trees: Stories from Nature's Great Connectors*. New York: Penguin, 2018.

Heibach, Christiane, and Carsten Rohde, eds. *Ästhetik der Materialität*. Munich: Fink, 2014.

Herbart, Johann Friedrich. *Lehrbuch zur Psychologie*. 2nd, improved ed. Königsberg: August Wilhelm Unzer, 1834.

Herbert, Nick. *Quantum Reality: Beyond the New Physics*. Garden City, NY: Anchor Press/Doubleday, 1987.

Herder, Johann Gottfried. *Sämmtliche Werke: Zur schönen Literatur und Kunst*. Vol. 3/1, *Gedichte*. Stuttgart: J. G. Cotta, 1827.

Hess, Jonathan. "Sugar Island Jews? Jewish Colonialism and the Rhetoric of 'Civic Improvement' in Eighteenth-Century Germany." *Eighteenth-Century Studies* 32 (1998): 92–100.

Hesse, Hermann. *Die Gedichte*. Edited by Volker Michels. 5th ed. Frankfurt am Main: Suhrkamp, 1998.

——. *News from the Universe*. Translated by Robert Bly. San Francisco: Sierra Club Books, 1980.

Hickman, Louise. "The Nature of the Self and the Contemplation of Nature: Ecotheology and the History of the Soul." In *The Concept of the Soul: Scientific and Religious Perspectives* (Science and Religion Forum), edited by Michael Fuller, 5–28. Newcastle Upon Tyne, UK: Cambridge Scholars, 2014.

Hodder, Ian. *Entangled: An Archaeology of the Relationships Between Humans and Things*. Hoboken, NJ: Wiley-Blackwell, 2012.

Hoheisel, Karl. "Okkultismus I." In *Religion in Geschichte und Gegenwart*, 4th, thoroughly rev. ed., edited by Hans Dieter Betz et al., 498–499. Tübingen: Mohr Siebeck, 2003.

Hollenberg, Donna Krolik. *A Poet's Revolution: The Life of Denise Levertov*. Berkeley: University of California Press, 2013.

Holz, Klaus. "Der Jude: Dritter der Nationen." In *Die Figur des Dritten: Ein kulturwissenschaftliches Paradigma*, edited by Eva Eßlinger et al., 292–303. Frankfurt am Main: Suhrkamp, 2010.

Hornborg, Anne-Christine. "Objects as Subjects: Agency and Performativity in Rituals." In *The Relational Dynamics of Enchantment and Sacralization*, edited by Peik Ingman, Måns Broo, Tuija Hovi, and Terhi Utriainen, 27–43. Sheffield: Equinox, 2016.

Horwitz, Jonathan. "The Absence of 'Performance' in the Shamanic Rite." In *Shamanism in Performing Arts*, edited by Tae-Gon Kim and Mihály Hoppál, 231–242. Budapest: Akadémiai Kiadó, 1995.

——. "Animism—Everyday Magic." *Sacred Hoop* 9 (1995): 6–10.

——. "Apprentice to the Spirits: The Shaman's Spiritual Path." In *Was ist ein Schamane? Schamanen, Heiler, Medizinleute im Spiegel westlichen Denkens / What Is a Shaman? Shamans, Healers, and Medicine Men from a Western Point of View*, edited by Amelie Schenk and Christian Rätsch, 215–221. Berlin: Verlag für Wissenschaft und Bildung, 1999.

Huber, Bruno, and Louise Huber. *Transformationen: Astrologie als geistiger Weg*. Adliswil: Astrologisch-Psychologisches Institut API, 1996.

Huber, Louise. *Die Tierkreiszeichen: Reflexionen—Meditationen*. 3rd ed. Adliswil: Astrologisch-Psychologisches Institut API, 1989.

Hübinger, Gangolf, ed. *Versammlungsort moderner Geister: Der Eugen Diederichs Verlag—Aufbruch ins Jahrhundert der Extreme*. Munich: Eugen Diederichs, 1996.

Hunter, Peter. "Catholicism, Materialism and the Soul." In *The Concept of the Soul: Scientific and Religious Perspectives* (Science and Religion Forum), edited by Michael Fuller, 29–37. Newcastle Upon Tyne, UK: Cambridge Scholars, 2014.

Hutten, Kurt. *Christus oder Deutschglaube? Ein Kampf um die deutsche Seele*. Stuttgart: J. F. Steinkopf, 1935.

Hutton, Ronald. *Shamans: Siberian Spirituality and the Western Imagination*. London: Hambledon and London, 2001.

——. *The Triumph of the Moon: A History of Modern Pagan Witchcraft*. Oxford: Oxford University Press, 1999.

Ingerman, Sandra. *Soul Retrieval: Mending the Fragmented Self*. New ed. San Francisco: HarperCollins, 1998. First edition published in 1991.

Ingman, Peik, Måns Broo, Tuija Hovi, and Terhi Utriainen, eds. *The Relational Dynamics of Enchantment and Sacralization*. Sheffield: Equinox, 2016.

Iovino, Serenella, and Serpil Oppermann. "Introduction: Stories Come to Matter." In *Material Ecocriticism*, edited by Serenella Iovino and Serpil Oppermann, 1–17. Bloomington: Indiana University Press, 2014.

Jacobsen, Eric Paul. *From Cosmology to Ecology: The Monist World-View in Germany from 1770 to 1930*. Oxford: Peter Lang, 2005.

Jaffé, Aniela. *Erinnerungen, Träume, Gedanken von C. G. Jung: Aufgezeichnet und herausgegeben von Aniela Jaffé*. Olten: Walter, 1971.

James, William. "The Hidden Self." *Scribner's Magazine* 7 (1890): 361–373.

——. *The Principles of Psychology*, 2 vols. New York: Dover, 1950. First edition published in 1890.

——. *Psychology: Briefer Course*. New York: Henry Holt, 1910. First edition published in 1892.

——. *The Varieties of Religious Experience*. New York: New American Library, 1958. First edition published in 1902.

Jerusalem, Wilhelm. *Lehrbuch der Psychologie*. Third, completely revised edition. Vienna: Wilhelm Braumüller, 1902.

Jodl, Friedrich. *Lehrbuch der Psychologie*. 3rd ed. Stuttgart: J. G. Cotta'sche Buchhandlung Nachfolger, 1908. First edition published in 1896.

Joël, Karl. *Seele und Welt: Versuch einer organischen Auffassung*. Jena: Eugen Diederichs, 1912.

——. *Der Ursprung der Naturphilosophie aus dem Geiste der Mystik*. Jena: Eugen Diederichs, 1906.

Johnston, Jay. "'Beyond' Language? Ecology, Ontology, and Aesthetics." In *Religion and Discourse Research: Disciplinary Use and Interdisciplinary Dialogues*, edited by Jay Johnston and Kocku von Stuckrad, 231–242. Berlin: De Gruyter, 2021.

Jones, Prudence, and Caitlín Matthews, eds. *Voices from the Circle: The Heritage of Western Paganism*. Hammersmith, London: Aquarian Press, 1990.

Josephson-Storm, Jason Ā. "Max Weber in the Realm of Enchantment." Blog post for *Forbidden Histories*, April 4, 2018. www.forbiddenhistories.com/weber-josephson-storm/.

——. *The Myth of Disenchantment: Magic, Modernity, and the Birth of the Human Sciences*. Chicago: University of Chicago Press, 2017.

Jung, Carl Gustav. *Gesammelte Werke*. 18 vols. Zurich: Rascher: Walter, 1958–1981.

——. *Psychologie und Religion*. 3rd, significantly expanded ed. In *Gesammelte Werke*, vol. 11 (1963). Olten: Walter, 1971.

——. *The Red Book. Liber Novus*. Edited by Sonu Shamdasani. Translated by Mark Kyburz, John Peck, and Sonu Shamdasani. New York: W. W. Norton, 2009.

Jung, Carl Gustav, and Wolfgang Pauli. *Naturerklärung und Psyche*. Zurich: Rascher, 1952.

Jüttemann, Gerd, ed. *Die Geschichtlichkeit des Seelischen: Der historische Zugang zum Gegenstand der Psychologie*. Weinheim: Psychologie Verlags Union / Beltz, 1986.

Jüttemann, Gerd, Michael Sonntag, and Christoph Wulf, eds. *Die Seele: Ihre Geschichte im Abendland*. Weinheim: Psychologie Verlags Union, 1991.

Kaden, Tom, Stephen Jones, Rebecca Catto, and Fern Elsdon-Baker. "Knowledge as Explanandum: Disentangling Lay and Professional Perspectives on Science and Religion." *Studies in Religion/Sciences Religieuses* (2017). doi: 000842981774144. 10.1177/0008429817741448.

Kaiser, David. *How the Hippies Saved Physics: Science, Counterculture, and the Quantum Revival*. New York: W. W. Norton, 2011.

Kalmar, Ivan Davidson, and Derek J. Penslar, eds. *Orientalism and the Jews*. Waltham: Brandeis University Press, 2005.

Kamper, Dietmar, and Christoph Wulf, eds. *Die erloschene Seele: Disziplin, Geschichte, Kunst, Mythos*. Berlin: Reimer, 1988.

——. "Vexierbild und transitorische Metapher—Die Seele als das Andere ihrer selbst." In *Die erloschene Seele: Disziplin, Geschichte, Kunst, Mythos*, edited by Dietmar Kamper and Christoph Wulf, 1–14. Berlin: Reimer, 1988.

Kantor, J. R. *The Scientific Evolution of Psychology*. Vol. 1. Chicago: Principia, 1963.

Kästner, Erhart. *Der Aufstand der Dinge. Byzantinische Aufzeichnungen*. Frankfurt am Main: Insel, 1973.

Keller, Catherine. *On the Mystery: Discerning Divinity in Process*. Minneapolis: Fortress, 2008.

Keller, Catherine, and Mary-Jane Rubenstein, eds. *Entangled Worlds: Religion, Science, and New Materialisms*. New York: Fordham University Press, 2018.

Kerr, Howard, and Charles L. Crow, eds. *The Occult in America: New Historical Perspectives*. Urbana: University of Illinois Press, 1983.

Kettelhake, Silke. *Renée Sintenis: Berlin, Boheme und Ringelnatz*. Berlin: Osburg, 2010.

Kiesewetter, Karl. *Die Geheimwissenschaften*. 2nd ed. Leipzig: Wilhelm Friedrich, 1894.

——. *Geschichte des neueren Occultismus: Geheimwissenschaftliche Systeme von Agrippa von Nettesheim bis zu Karl du Prel*. 2nd, updated, and expanded ed. Edited by Robert Blum. Leipzig: Max Altmann, 1909.

——. *Der Occultismus des Altertums*. Leipzig: Wilhelm Friedrich, 1896.

Kimmerer, Robin Wall. *Braiding Sweetgrass: Indigenous Wisdom, Scientific Knowledge and the Teachings of Plants*. Minneapolis: Milkweed, 2013.

Kippenberg, Hans G. *Discovering Religious History in the Modern Age*. Translated by Barbara Harshav. Princeton: Princeton University Press, 2002.

Kippenberg, Hans G., Yme B. Kuiper, and Andy F. Sanders, eds. *Concepts of Person in Religion and Thought*. Berlin: Mouton de Gruyter, 1990.

Kippenberg, Hans G., and Brigitte Luchesi, eds. *Magie: Die sozialwissenschaftliche Kontroverse über das Verstehen fremden Denkens*. Frankfurt am Main: Suhrkamp, 1987.

Kippenberg, Katharina. *Rainer Maria Rilke: Ein Beitrag*. Leipzig: Insel Verlag, 1935.

Kirk, Andrew G. *Counterculture Green: The Whole Earth Catalog and American Environmentalism*. Lawrence: University Press of Kansas, 2007.

Klages, Ludwig. *The Biocentric Worldview: Selected Essays and Poems of Ludwig Klages*. Translated by Joseph Pryce. London: Arktos, 2013.

——. *Cosmogonic Reflections: Selected Aphorisms from Ludwig Klages*. Translated by Joseph Pryce. London: Arktos, 2015.

——. *Der Mensch und das Leben*. Edition of "Mensch und Erde" (1913) and "Bewußtsein und Leben" (1915). Jena: Eugen Diederichs, 1937.

——. *Die psychologischen Errungenschaften Nietzsches*. Leipzig: Johann Ambrosius Barth, 1926.

——. *Vom kosmogonischen Eros*. 6th, corrected ed. Bonn: H. Bouvier, 1963. First edition published in 1921.

Klemm, Otto. *Geschichte der Psychologie*. Leipzig: B. G. Teubner, 1911.

Klingsöhr-Leroy, Cathrin, and Andrea Firmenich, eds. *Franz Marc und Joseph Beuys: Im Einklang mit der Natur*. Munich: Schirmer/Mosel, Franz Marc Museum, 2011.

Knapp, Krister Dylan. *William James: Psychical Research and the Challenge of Modernity*. Chapel Hill: University of North Carolina Press, 2017.

Kolbert, Elizabeth. *The Sixth Extinction: An Unnatural History*. London: Bloomsbury, 2014.

Kripal, Jeffrey J. *Esalen: America and the Religion of No Religion*. Chicago: University of Chicago Press, 2007.

Küchler, Walther. *Ernest Renan: Der Dichter und der Künstler*. Gotha: Friedrich Andreas Perthes, 1921.

Külpe, Oswald. *Grundriss der Psychologie: Auf experimenteller Grundlage dargestellt*. Leipzig: Wilhelm Engelmann, 1893.

Kunz, Hans. *Martin Heidegger und Ludwig Klages: Daseinsanalytik und Metaphysik*. Munich: Kindler, 1976.

Lajer-Burcharth, Ewa, and Beate Söntgen, eds. *Interiors and Interiority*. Berlin: De Gruyter, 2016.

LaMothe, Kimerer Lewis. *Nietzsche's Dancers: Isadora Duncan, Martha Graham, and the Revaluation of Christian Values*. New York: Palgrave-Macmillan, 2006.

Laszlo, Ervin. "Preface." In *Gaia Project—A New Paradigm in Education—Planetary Consciousness and Self Awareness Development Program and Psychosomatic Health Promotion in Accordance with WHO guidelines*, by Federico Nitamo Montecucco and Silvia Ghiroldi. Approved and funded by the Italian Ministry of Labour and Social Policies, in collaboration with the Club UNESCO Lucca (2015); www.progettogaia.eu/documenti/docenti/gaia_project_presentation_2019_english.pdf.

——. *System, Structure, and Experience: Toward a Scientific Theory of Mind*. New York: Gordon and Breach Science, 1969.

——. *The Systems View of the World: The Natural Philosophy of the New Developments in the Sciences*. Oxford: Basil Blackwell, 1972.

Latour, Bruno. *Facing Gaia: Eight Lectures on the New Climatic Regime*. Translated by Catherine Porter. Cambridge: Polity, 2017.

——. "Fetish-Factish." *Material Religion* 7 (2011): 42–49.

——. *On the Modern Cult of the Factish Gods*. Translated by Heather MacLean and Catherine Porter. Durham, NC: Duke University Press, 2010.

——. "The Recall of Modernity: Anthropological Approaches." *Cultural Studies Review* 13 (2011): 11–30.

——. *We Have Never Been Modern*. Cambridge, MA: Harvard University Press, 1993.

Latour, Bruno, and Steve Woolgar. *Laboratory Life: The Construction of Scientific Facts*. Princeton: Princeton University Press, 1986. First edition published in 1979.

Laurikainen, Kalervo Vihtori. *The Philosophical Thought of Wolfgang Pauli*. Berlin: Springer, 1988.

Lauster, Jörg, Peter Schüz, Roderich Bart, and Christian Danz, eds. *Rudolf Otto: Theologie—Religionsphilosophie—Religionsgeschichte*. Berlin: De Gruyter, 2014.

Lear, Linda. *Rachel Carson: Witness for Nature*. New York: Henry Holt, 1997.

Leber, Christoffer. "Integration Through Science? Nationalism and Internationalism in the German Monist Movement (1906–1918)." In *Freethinkers in Europe: National and Transnational Secularities, 1789–1920s*, edited by Carolin Kosuch, 181–202. Berlin: De Gruyter, 2020.

Lebovic, Nitzan. *The Philosophy of Life and Death: Ludwig Klages and the Rise of a Nazi Biopolitics*. New York: Palgrave Macmillan, 2013.

Lecznar, Adam. *Dionysus After Nietzsche:* The Birth of Tragedy *in Twentieth-Century Literature and Thought*. Cambridge: Cambridge University Press, 2020.

Leeder, Karen J., and Robert Vilain, eds. *The Cambridge Companion to Rilke*. Cambridge: Cambridge University Press, 2010.

Leeuw, Gerardus van der. *Mystiek*. Baarn: Hollandia-Drukkerij, 1924.

——. *Sacred and Profane Beauty: The Holy in Art*. Translated by David E. Green, with a preface by Mircea Eliade and a new introduction and bibliography by Diane Apostolos-Capadona. New York: Oxford University Press, 2006. First English translation published in 1963; Dutch original published in 1932.

——. *Sakramentales Denken: Erscheinungsformen und Wesen der außerchristlichen und christlichen Sakramente*. Kassel: Johannes Stauda-Verlag, 1959.

Le Guin, Ursula K. *The Language of the Night: Essays on Fantasy and Science Fiction*. Edited and with introductions by Susan Wood. New York: G. P. Putnam's Sons, 1979.

——. *Late in the Day: Poems, 2010–2014*. Oakland: PM Press, 2016.

Leslie, Ian R. "Betrachtungen über Religion und Kunst in den Schriften von R. M. Rilke und D. H. Lawrence." PhD diss., Freie Universität Berlin, 1990.

LeVasseur, Todd, and Anna Peterson, eds. *Religion and Ecological Crisis: The "Lynn White Thesis" at Fifty*. New York: Routledge, 2017.

Levertov, Denise. *Evening Train*. New York: New Directions, 1992.

——. *A Tree Telling of Orpheus*. Los Angeles: Black Sparrow, 1968.

Lewis, David Levering. *W. E. B. Du Bois: Biography of a Race, 1868–1919*. New York: Henry Holt, 1993.

Lichtblau, Klaus. *Kulturkrise und Soziologie um die Jahrhundertwende: Zur Genealogie der Kultursoziologie in Deutschland*. Frankfurt am Main: Suhrkamp, 1996.

Lindley, David. *Uncertainty: Einstein, Heisenberg, Bohr, and the Struggle for the Soul of Science*. New York: Anchor, 2007.

Linse, Ulrich. *Geisterseher und Wunderwirker: Heilssuche im Industriezeitalter*. Frankfurt am Main: Fischer, 1996.

Lopez, Barry. *Arctic Dreams: Imagination and Desire in a Northern Landscape*. Toronto: Bantam, 1989.

——. *Horizon*. New York: Alfred A. Knopf, 2019.

Lorenz, Hendrik. "Ancient Theories of Soul." In *The Stanford Encyclopedia of Philosophy* (Summer 2009 edition), edited by Edward N. Zalta, https://plato.stanford.edu/archives/sum2009/entries/ancient-soul/.

Magnússon, Gísli. *Dichtung als Erfahrungsmetaphysik—Esoterische und okkultistische Modernität bei R. M. Rilke*. Würzburg: Königshausen und Neumann, 2009.

Maher, Neil M. *Apollo in the Age of Aquarius*. Cambridge, MA: Harvard University Press, 2017.

Mancuso, Stefano. *The Revolutionary Genius of Plants*. New York: Atria, 2018.

Marin, Juan Miguel. " 'Mysticism' in Quantum Mechanics: The Forgotten Controversy." *European Journal of Physics* 30 (2009): 807–822.

Marquard, Odo. *Transzendentaler Idealismus—Romantische Naturphilosophie—Psychoanalyse*. Cologne: Verlag für Philosophie Jürgen Dinter, 1987.

Maslow, Abraham H. *Motivation and Personality*. 2nd ed. New York: Harper and Row, 1970. First edition published in 1954.

——. *Toward a Psychology of Being*. 2nd, rev. ed. New York: D. van Nostrand, 1968. First edition published in 1962.

McDonnell, Lytton Naegele. "Ecstatic Anthems." PhD diss., Rutgers University, 2018. doi:10.7282/T3GFoXQH.

McGowan Russell, Cathy. "The Epic of Evolution." http://epicofevolution.com/about/about-the-epic.

Meine, Curt. *Aldo Leopold: His Life and Work*. Madison: University of Wisconsin Press, 1988.

Mendes-Flohr, Paul R. "Fin de Siècle Orientalism, the *Ostjuden*, and the Aesthetics of Jewish Self-Affirmation." In *Divided Passions: Jewish Intellectuals and the Experience of Modernity*, edited by Paul R. Mendes-Flohr, 77–132. Detroit: Wayne State University Press, 1991.

——. *From Mysticism to Dialogue: Martin Buber's Transformation of German Social Thought*. Detroit: Wayne State University Press, 1989.

Mensky, Michael B. *Consciousness and Quantum Mechanics: Life In Parallel Worlds. Miracles of Consciousness from Quantum Reality*. Singapore: World Scientific, 2010.

Metzger, Birgit. *"Erst stirbt der Wald, dann du!" Das Waldsterben als westdeutsches Politikum (1978–1986)*. Frankfurt am Main: Campus, 2015.

Mickey, Sam, Sean M. Kelly, and Adam Robbert, eds. *The Variety of Integral Ecologies: Nature, Culture, and Knowledge in the Planetary Era*. Albany: State University of New York Press, 2017.

Millepierres, François. *La vie d'Ernest Renan, sage d'Occident*. Paris: Librairie Marcel Rivière et Cie, 1961.

Moffitt, John F. "'Fighting Forms: The Fate of the Animals': The Occultist Origins of Franz Marc's 'Farbentheorie.'" *Artibus et Historiae* 6, no. 12 (1985): 107–126.

Moritz, Karl Philipp. *Anton Reiser: A Psychological Novel*. Translated by John Raymond Russell. Columbia: Camden House, 1996.

Morrisson, Mark S. *Modern Alchemy: Occultism and the Emergence of Atomic Theory*. Oxford: Oxford University Press, 2007.

Muir, John. *The Wilderness World of John Muir*. Edited by Edwin Way Teale. Boston: Houghton Mifflin, 1954.

——. *Works: The Sierra Edition*. 10 vols., edited by William Frederick Badé. Boston: Houghton Mifflin, 1915–1924.

Mukhopadhyay, Ranjan. "Quantum Mechanics, Objective Reality, and the Problem of Consciousness." *Journal of Consciousness Studies* 21 (2014): 57–80.

Müller, Günther. *Geschichte der deutschen Seele: Vom Faustbuch zu Goethes Faust*. Freiburg: Herder, 1939.

Müller, Lothar G. "Mikroskopie der Seele—Zur Entstehung der Psychologie aus dem Geist der Beobachtungskunst im 18. Jahrhundert." In *Die Geschichtlichkeit des Seelischen: Der historische Zugang zum Gegenstand der Psychologie*, edited by Gerd Jüttemann, 185–208. Weinheim: Psychologie Verlags Union / Beltz, 1986.

Müller-Westermann, Iris, and Jo Widoff, eds. *Hilma af Klint: A Pioneer of Abstraction*. Ostfildern: Hatje Cantz, 2013.

Mummendey, Hans D. *Die Psychologie des "Selbst": Theorien, Methoden und Ergebnisse der Selbstkonzeptforschung*. Göttingen: Hogrefe, 2006.

Murphy, Nancey. "What Happened to the Soul? Theological Perspectives on Neuroscience and the Self." *Annals of the New York Academy of Sciences* 1001, no. 1 (2003): 51–64.

Myrvold, Wayne, Marco Genovese, and Abner Shimony. "Bell's Theorem." In *The Stanford Encyclopedia of Philosophy* (Spring 2019 edition), edited by Edward N. Zalta. https://plato.stanford.edu/archives/spr2019/entries/bell-theorem/.

Nadkarni, Nalini. *Between Earth and Sky: Our Intimate Connections to Trees*. Berkeley: University of California Press, 2008.

Naess, Arne. *Ecology, Community and Lifestyle: Outline of an Ecosophy*. Cambridge: Cambridge University Press, 1989.

——. "The Shallow and the Deep, Long-Range Ecology Movement: A Summary." *Inquiry* 16 (1973): 95–100.

Nagy, Marilyn. *Philosophical Issues in the Psychology of C. G. Jung*. Albany: State University of New York Press, 1991.

Nannini, Sandro. *Seele, Geist und Körper: Historische Wurzeln und philosophische Grundlagen der Kognitionswissenschaften*. Frankfurt am Main: Peter Lang, 2006.

Nash, Roderick. *The Rights of Nature: A History of Environmental Ethics*. Madison: University of Wisconsin Press, 1989.

——. *Wilderness and the American Mind*. 3rd ed. New Haven, CT: Yale University Press, 1982.

Nicholson, Shirley, ed. *Shamanism*. 5th ed. Wheaton, IL: Theosophical Publishing House, 1996.

Nicholson, Shirley, and Brenda Rosen, eds. *Gaia's Hidden Life: The Unseen Intelligence of Nature*. Wheaton, IL: Theosophical Publishing House, 1992.

Niebylski, Dianna C. *The Poem on the Edge of the Word: The Limits of Language and the Uses of Silence in the Poetry of Mallarmé, Rilke, and Vallejo*. New York: P. Lang, 1993.

Nietzsche, Friedrich. *Friedrich Nietzsches Briefwechsel mit Erwin Rohde*. Edited by Elisabeth Förster-Nietzsche and Fritz Schöll. Leipzig: Insel, 1923.

——. *Sämtliche Werke*. 15 vols. Edited by Giorgio Colli and Mazzino Montinari. Munich: dtv, 1999. New edition on the basis of the second edition from 1988.

Noakes, Richard. *Physics and Psychics: The Occult and the Sciences in Modern Britain*. Cambridge: Cambridge University Press, 2019.

Nöthlich, Rosemarie, Heiko Weber, Uwe Hoßfeld, Olaf Breidbach, and Erika Krauße, eds. *"Substanzmonismus" und/oder "Energetik": Der Briefwechsel von Ernst Haeckel und Wilhelm Ostwald (1910–1918)*. Berlin: Verlag für Wissenschaft und Bildung, 2006.

Novalis (Friedrich von Hardenberg). *Novalis: Werke, Tagebücher und Briefe Friedrich von Hardenbergs*. Edited by Hans-Joachim Mähl and Richard Samuel. 3 vols. Darmstadt: Wissenschaftliche Buchgesellschaft.

Oelschlaeger, Max. *The Idea of Wilderness: From Prehistory to the Age of Ecology*. New Haven, CT: Yale University Press, 1991.

Oesterreich, Traugott Konstantin. *Der Okkultismus im modernen Weltbild*. 3rd, expanded ed. Dresden: Sybillen-Verlag, 1923. First edition published in 1921.

——. *Die philosophische Bedeutung der mediumistischen Phänomene*. Erweiterte Fassung des auf dem Zweiten Internationalen Kongress für Parapsychologische Forschung in Warschau gehaltenen Vortrags. Stuttgart: W. Kohlhammer, 1924.

Oken, Lorenz. *Lehrbuch der Naturphilosophie*. 3rd, rev. ed. Zurich: Friedrich Schultheß, 1843. Reprinted in Hildesheim by Georg Olm in 1991. First edition published in 1809.

Ostwald, Wilhelm. *Das Christentum als Vorstufe zum Monismus*. Leipzig: Unesma, 1914.

——. *Die Forderung des Tages*. Leipzig: Akademische Verlagsgesellschaft, 1910.

——. *Monistische Sonntagspredigten*. First series. Leipzig: Akademische Verlagsgesellschaft, 1911.

——. *Monistische Sonntagspredigten*. Second series. Leipzig: Akademische Verlagsgesellschaft, 1912.

——. *Religion und Monismus*. Leipzig: Unesma, 1914.

Otto, Bernd-Christian. *Magie: Rezeptions- und diskursgeschichtliche Analysen von der Antike bis zur Neuzeit*. Berlin: De Gruyter, 2011.

Otto, Rudolf. *Das Heilige: Über das Irrationale in der Idee des Göttlichen und sein Verhältnis zum Rationalen*. Munich: C. H. Beck, 2004. English translation: *The Idea of the Holy*. Translated by J. W. Harvey. New York: Oxford University Press, 1923. First edition published in 1917.

Owen, Alex. *The Place of Enchantment: British Occultism and the Culture of the Modern*. Chicago: University of Chicago Press, 2004.

Paglia, Camille. *Sexual Personae: Art and Decadence from Nefertiti to Emily Dickinson*. New Haven, CT: Yale University Press, 1990.

Papapetros, Spyros. "Movements of the Soul: Traversing Animism, Fetishism, and the Uncanny." *Discourse* 34, nos. 2–3 (2012): 185–208.

Pauli, Wolfgang. "Die Wissenschaft und das abendländische Denken." In *Europa—Erbe und Aufgabe: Internationaler Gelehrtenkongress Mainz 1955*, edited by Martin Göhring, 71–79. Wiesbaden: Franz Steiner, 1956.

——. *Writings on Physics and Philosophy*. Edited by Charles P. Enz and Karl von Meyenn. Berlin: Springer, 1994.

Peat, F. David. *Infinite Potential: The Life and Times of David Bohm*. Reading: Helix / Addison-Wesley, 1997.

——. *Synchronicity: The Bridge Between Matter and Mind*. Toronto: Bantam, 1987.

Peleg, Yaron. *Orientalism and the Hebrew Imagination*. Ithaca: Cornell University Press, 2005.

Philippon, Daniel J. *Conserving Words: How American Nature Writers Shaped the Environmental Movement*. Athens: University of Georgia Press, 2004.

Piper, Ernst. *Alfred Rosenberg: Hitlers Chefideologe*. Munich: Karl Blessing, 2005.

Pircher, Wolfgang. "Beseelte Maschinen. Über ein mögliches Wechselspiel von Technik und Seele." In *Die Seele: Ihre Geschichte im Abendland*, edited by Gerd Jüttemann, Michael Sonntag, and Christoph Wulf, 477–492. Weinheim: Psychologie Verlags Union, 1991.

Platzhoff, Eduard. *Ernest Renan: Ein Lebensbild*. Dresden: Carl Reißner, 1900.

Pokazanyeva, Anna. "Mind Within Matter: Science, the Occult, and the (Meta)physics of Ether and Akasha." *Zygon* 51 (2016): 318–346.

Pomerleau, Wayne P. "William James (1842–1910)." *Internet Encyclopedia of Philosophy*, www.iep.utm.edu/james-o/.

Porter, Max. *Lanny: A Novel*. Minneapolis: Graywolf, 2019.

Potter, Christopher. *The Earth Gazers: On Seeing Ourselves*. New York: Pegasus, 2018.

Powers, Richard. *The Overstory: A Novel*. New York: W. W. Norton, 2018.

Principe, Lawrence M., and William R. Newman. "Some Problems with the Historiography of Alchemy." In *Secrets of Nature: Astrology and Alchemy in Early Modern Europe*, edited by William R. Newman and Anthony Grafton, 385–431. Cambridge, MA: MIT Press, 2001.

Rauch, Frederick A. *Psychology or A View of the Human Soul, Including Anthropology*. A Facsimile Reproduction with an introduction by Eric T. Carlson, M. D. Delmar. 1841; New York: Scholars' Facsimiles and Reprints, 1975.

Regardie, Israel. *The Tree of Life: An Illustrated Study of Magic*. Edited and annotated by Chic Cicero and Sandra Tabatha Cicero. St. Paul: Llewellyn, 2002. First edition published in 1932.

Reichel-Dolmatoff, Gerardo, ed. *Das Schamanische Universum: Schamanismus, Bewußtsein und Ökologie in Südamerika*. Munich: Diederichs, 1996.

Reill, Peter Hanns. *Vitalizing Nature in the Enlightenment*. Berkeley: University of California Press, 2005.

Renan, Ernest. *Qu'est-ce qu'une Nation? et autres écrits politiques*. Edited by Raoul Girardet. Paris: Imprimerie nationale Éditions, 1996.

——. "Was ist eine Nation? Vortrag in der Sorbonne am 11. März 1882." Translated from the French by Henning Ritter. In *Grenzfälle—Über neuen und alten Nationalismus*, edited by Michael Jeismann and Henning Ritter, 290–311. Leipzig: Reclam, 1993.

Richards, Graham. *Psychology, Religion, and the Nature of the Soul: A Historical Entanglement*. New York: Springer Science + Business Media, 2011.

Richards, Robert J. *The Romantic Conception of Life: Science and Philosophy in the Age of Goethe*. Chicago: University of Chicago Press, 2002.

——. *The Tragic Sense of Life: Ernst Haeckel and the Struggle Over Evolutionary Thought*. Chicago: University of Chicago Press, 2008.

Richardson, Robert D. *William James: In the Maelstrom of American Modernism*. Boston: Houghton Mifflin, 2006.

Rigby, Kate. *Reclaiming Romanticism: Towards an Ecopoetics of Decolonization*. London: Bloomsbury Academic, 2020.

Rilke, Rainer Maria. *Briefe aus Muzot 1921 bis 1926*. Vol. 6 of *Briefe*. Edited by Ruth Sieber-Rilke and Carl Sieber. Leipzig: Insel, 1935.

——. *Die Gedichte*. 11th ed. Frankfurt am Main: Insel, 1999.

——. *In Praise of Mortality: Selections from Rainer Maria Rilke's* Duino Elegies *and* Sonnets to Orpheus. Translated and edited by Anita Barrows and Joanna Macy. Brattleboro: Echo Point, 2005.

——. *Selected Poems of Rainer Maria Rilke*. Translated from the German and commentary by Robert Bly. New York: Harper and Row, 1981.

——. *The Selected Poetry of Rainer Maria Rilke*. Edited and translated by Stephen Mitchell. New York: Vintage International, 1989.

——. *Sonnets to Orpheus and Duino Elegies*. Translated by Jessie Lemont. Newburyport: Dover, 2020.

Robinson, Annabel. *The Life and Work of Jane Ellen Harrison*. Oxford: Oxford University Press, 2002.

Röder, Brigitte, Juliane Hummel, and Brigitta Kunz. *Göttinnendämmerung: Das Matriarchat aus archäologischer Sicht*. Munich: Droemer Knaur, 1996.

Roemer, Nils. "Reading Nietzsche—Thinking About God: Martin Buber, Gershom Scholem, and Franz Rosenzweig." *American Catholic Philosophical Quarterly* 84 (2010): 427–441.

Rohde, Erwin. *Psyche: Seelencult und Unsterblichkeitsglaube der Griechen*. 2 vols. 5th/6th ed. Tübingen: Mohr-Siebeck, 1910. First edition published in 1894.

Rosenberg, Alfred. *Der Mythus des 20. Jahrhunderts: Eine Wertung der seelisch-geistigen Gestaltenkämpfe unserer Zeit*. 13th–16th ed. Munich: Hoheneichen-Verlag, 1933. First edition published in 1930.

Rosselli, Massimo. "Roberto Assagioli: A Bright Star." *International Journal of Psychotherapy* 16 (2012): 7–19.

Rosselli, Massimo, and Duccio Vanni. "Roberto Assagioli and Carl Gustav Jung." *Journal of Transpersonal Psychology* 46 (2014): 7–34.

Rothe, Friedrich. "Deutscher Wald um 1900." In *Waldungen: Die Deutschen und ihr Wald*, edited by Akademie der Künste, Berlin, 69–73. Berlin: Nicolaische Verlagsbuchhandlung, 1987.

Rowling, J. K. *Harry Potter and the Deathly Hallows*. New York: Scholastic, 2007.

——. *Harry Potter and the Goblet of Fire*. New York: Scholastic, 2000.

——. *Harry Potter and the Half-Blood Prince*. New York: Scholastic, 2005.

——. *Harry Potter and the Prisoner of Azkaban*. New York: Scholastic, 1999.

Rubenstein, Mary-Jane. *Pantheologies: Gods, Worlds, Monsters*. New York: Columbia University Press, 2018.

——. *Worlds Without End: The Many Lives of the Multiverse*. New York: Columbia University Press, 2014.

Rue, Loyal. "Epic of Evolution." In *Encyclopedia of Religion and Nature*, edited by Bron R. Taylor, 612–615. London: Continuum, 2005.

——. *Everybody's Story: Wising Up to the Epic of Evolution*. Albany: State University of New York Press, 2000.

Safina, Carl. *Beyond Words: What Animals Think and Feel*. 2nd ed. New York: Macmillan/Henry Holt, 2015.

Safranski, Rüdiger. *Nietzsche: Biographie seines Denkens*. Munich: Hanser, 2000.

Schäfer, Lothar, and Diogo Valadas Ponte. "Carl Gustav Jung, Quantum Physics and the Spiritual Mind: A Mystical Vision of the Twenty-First Century." *Behavioral Sciences* 3 (2013): 601–618.

Schama, Simon. *Landscape and Memory*. New York: A. A. Knopf, 1995.

Schlatter, Gerhard. "Animism." In *The Brill Dictionary of Religion*, edited by Kocku von Stuckrad, 4 vols., 1:77–78. Leiden: Brill, 2007.

Schleich, Carl Ludwig. *Besonnte Vergangenheit: Lebenserinnerungen, 1859–1919*. Berlin: Ernst Rowohlt, 1922.

——. *Dichtungen*. Berlin: Ernst Rowohlt, 1924.

——. *Gedankenmacht und Hysterie*. Berlin: Ernst Rowohlt, 1920.

——. *Das Ich und die Dämonien*. 10th–12th ed. Berlin: S. Fischer, 1924. First edition published in 1920.

——. *Vom Schaltwerk der Gedanken: Neue Einsichten und Betrachtungen über die Seele*. Berlin: S. Fischer, 1917.

——. *Von der Seele: Essays*. 19th–23rd ed. Berlin: S. Fischer, 1922. First edition published in 1910.

——. *Die Wunder der Seele*. With a preface by C. G. Jung. Frankfurt am Main: S. Fischer, 1951.

——. *Zwei Jahre kriegschirurgischer Erfahrungen aus einem Berliner Lazarett*. Stuttgart: Deutsche Verlags-Anstalt, 1916.

Schlieter, Jens. *What Is It Like to Be Dead? Near-Death Experiences, Christianity, and the Occult*. New York: Oxford University Press, 2018.

Schmidt-Biggemann, Wilhelm. *Philosophia perennis: Historische Umrisse abendländischer Spiritualität in Antike, Mittelalter und Früher Neuzeit*. Frankfurt am Main: Suhrkamp, 1998.

Scholem, Gershom. *Tagebücher, nebst Aufsätzen und Entwürfen bis 1923*. Vol. 1. Edited by Karlfried Gründer and Friedrich Niewöhner, in collaboration with Herbert Kopp-Oberstebrink. Frankfurt am Main: Jüdischer Verlag, 1995.

——. *Tagebücher, nebst Aufsätzen und Entwürfen bis 1923*. 2nd half binding 1917–1923. Edited by Karlfried Gründer, Herbert Kopp-Oberstebrink, and Friedrich Niewöhner, in collaboration with Karl E. Grözinger. Frankfurt am Main: Jüdischer Verlag, 2000.

Schorsch, Christof. *Die Große Vernetzung: Wege zu einer ökologischen Philosophie*. Freiburg: Bauer, 1987.

Schubert, Gotthilf Heinrich von. *Die Geschichte der Seele*. 4th ed. Stuttgart: J. G. Cotta, 1850. First edition published in 1830.

——. *Die Symbolik des Traumes*. 2nd ed. Bamberg: Carl Friedrich Kunz, 1821. First edition published in 1814.

Schulz, Dieter. *Amerikanischer Transzendentalismus: Ralph Waldo Emerson, Henry David Thoreau, Margaret Fuller*. Darmstadt: Wissenschaftliche Buchgesellschaft, 1997.

Seed, John, Joanna Macy, Pat Fleming, and Arne Naess, eds. *Thinking Like a Mountain: Towards a Council of All Beings*. Philadelphia: New Society, 1988.

Sehon, Scott. "The Soul in Harry Potter." In *The Ultimate Harry Potter and Philosophy: Hogwarts for Muggles*, edited by William Irwin and Gregory Bassham, 7–21. Hoboken, NJ: Wiley, 2010.

Shamdasani, Sonu. *C. G. Jung: A Biography in Books*. New York: W. W. Norton, 2012.

——. *Cult Fictions: C. G. Jung and the Founding of Analytical Psychology*. London: Routledge, 1998.

——. *Jung and the Making of Modern Psychology: The Dream of a Science*. Cambridge: Cambridge University Press, 2003.

——. *Jung Stripped Bare by His Biographers, Even*. London: Karnac, 2005.

——. "Liber Novus: The 'Red Book' of C. G. Jung." In *The Red Book: Liber Novus*, edited by Sonu Shamdasani, 193–221. New York: W. W. Norton, 2009.

Shapin, Steven. *A Social History of Truth: Civility and Science in Seventeenth-Century England.* Chicago: University of Chicago Press, 1994.

Sideris, Lisa H. "Biosphere, Noosphere, and the Anthropocene: Earth's Perilous Prospects in a Cosmic Context." *Journal for the Study of Religion, Nature and Culture* 11 (2018): 399–419.

——. *Consecrated Science: Wonder, Knowledge, and the Natural World.* Oakland: University of California Press, 2017.

——. "Evolving Environmentalism: The Role of Ecotheology in Creation/Evolution Controversies." *Worldviews: Global Religions, Culture, and Ecology* 11 (2007): 58–82.

——. "Fact and Fiction, Fear and Wonder: The Legacy of Rachel Carson." *Soundings: An Interdisciplinary Journal* 91 (2008): 335–369.

——. "Science as Sacred Myth? Ecospirituality in the Anthropocene Age." *Journal for the Study of Religion, Nature and Culture* 9 (2015): 136–153.

Sideris, Lisa H., and Kathleen Dean Moore, eds. *Rachel Carson: Legacy and Challenge.* Albany: State University of New York Press, 2008.

Siegel, Allen M. *Heinz Kohut and the Psychology of the Self.* London: Routledge, 1996.

Singer, Peter. *Animal Liberation: A New Ethics for our Treatment of Animals.* New York: New York Review/Random House, 1975.

Sloterdijk, Peter, and Thomas H. Macho, eds. *Weltrevolution der Seele: Ein Lese- und Arbeitsbuch der Gnosis von der Spätantike bis zur Gegenwart.* 2 vols. Munich: Artemis und Winkler, 1991.

Smith, Roger. *The Fontana History of the Human Sciences.* London: Fontana, 1997.

Snyder, Gary. *The Old Ways.* San Francisco: City Lights, 1977.

Sommer, Andreas. "Crossing the Boundaries of Mind and Body: Psychical Research and the Origins of Modern Psychology." PhD diss., Science and Technology Studies, University College London, 2013.

——. "Normalizing the Supernormal: The Formation of the 'Gesellschaft für Psychologische Forschung' ('Society for Psychological Research'), c. 1886–1890." *Journal of the History of the Behavioral Sciences* 49 (2013): 18–44.

Sonntag, Michael. "Die Seele und das Wissen vom Lebenden: Zur Entstehung der Biologie im 19. Jahrhundert." In *Die Seele: Ihre Geschichte im Abendland,* edited by Gerd Jüttemann, Michael Sonntag, and Christoph Wulf, 293–318. Weinheim: Psychologie Verlags Union, 1991.

——. "'Zeitlose Dokumente der Seele'—Von der Abschaffung der Geschichte in der Geschichtsschreibung der Psychologie." In *Die Geschichtlichkeit des Seelischen: Der historische Zugang zum Gegenstand der Psychologie,* edited by Gerd Jüttemann, 116–142. Weinheim: Psychologie Verlags Union / Beltz, 1986.

Sorabji, Richard. "Soul and Self in Ancient Philosophy." In *From Soul to Self,* edited by James C. Crabbe, 8–32. London: Routledge, 1999.

Souder, William. *On a Farther Shore: The Life and Legacy of Rachel Carson.* New York: Crown, 2012.

Staudenmaier, Ludwig. *Die Magie als experimentelle Naturwissenschaft.* Leipzig: Akademische Verlagsgesellschaft, 1912.

Stojilkov, Andrea. "Life(and)death in Harry Potter: The Immortality of Love and Soul." *Mosaic: A Journal for the Interdisciplinary Study of Literature* 48, no. 2 (2015): 133–148.

Strauss, Walter A. *Descent and Return: The Orphic Theme in Modern Literature.* Cambridge, MA: Harvard University Press, 1971.

Stuckrad, Kocku von. "Historical Discourse Analysis: The Entanglement of Past and Present." In *Religion and Discourse Research: Disciplinary Use and Interdisciplinary Dialogues*, edited by Jay Johnston and Kocku von Stuckrad, 77–87. Berlin: De Gruyter, 2021.

——. *Locations of Knowledge in Medieval and Early Modern Europe: Esoteric Discourse and Western Identities*. Leiden: Brill, 2010.

——. *Schamanismus und Esoterik: Kultur- und wissenschaftsgeschichtliche Betrachtungen*. Leuven: Peeters, 2003.

——. *The Scientification of Religion: An Historical Study of Discursive Change, 1800–2000*. Berlin: De Gruyter, 2014.

——. "Utopian Landscapes and Ecstatic Journeys: Friedrich Nietzsche, Hermann Hesse, and Mircea Eliade on the Terror of Modernity." *Numen: International Review for the History of Religions* 57 (2010): 78–102.

Swimme, Brian Thomas, and Mary Evelyn Tucker. *Journey of the Universe*. New Haven, CT: Yale University Press, 2011.

Swinburne, Richard. *The Evolution of the Soul*. Rev. ed. Gifford Lectures, 1983–1984. Oxford: Clarendon, 1997.

Tarnas, Richard. *Cosmos and Psyche: Intimations of a New World View*. New York: Plume, 2007.

——. *The Passion of the Western Mind: Understanding the Ideas That Have Shaped Our Word View*. London: Pimlico/Random House, 2010. First edition published in 1991.

Tart, Charles T. *The End of Materialism: How Evidence of the Paranormal Is Bringing Science and Spirit Together*. Oakland: New Harbinger, 2009.

——. "Introduction." In *Transpersonal Psychologies*, edited by Charles T. Tart, 1–7. New York: Harper and Row, 1975.

——, ed. *Transpersonal Psychologies*. New York: Harper and Row, 1975.

Taylor, Bron, ed. *Avatar and Nature Spirituality*. Waterloo: Wilfrid Laurier University Press, 2013.

——. *Dark Green Religion: Nature Spirituality and the Planetary Future*. Berkeley: University of California Press, 2010.

——. "Earth and Nature-Based Spirituality: From Deep Ecology to Radical Environmentalism." *Religion* 31 (2001): 175–193.

——. "Resacralizing Earth: Pagan Environmentalism and the Restoration of Turtle Island." In *American Sacred Space*, edited by David Chidester and E. T. Linenthal, 97–151. Bloomington: Indiana University Press, 1995.

Taylor, Eugene. "Jung and William James." *Spring: A Journal for Archetypal Psychology and Jungian Thought* 20 (1980): 157–169.

Taylor, Paul W. "Die Ethik der Achtung für die Natur (1981)." In *Ökophilosophie*, edited by Dieter Birnbacher, 77–116. Stuttgart: Philipp Reclam jun., 1997.

Thoreau, Henry David. *The Writings of Henry D. Thoreau: Walden*. Edited by B. Torrey and F. H. Allen. Boston: Houghton Mifflin, 1971.

Tischner, Rudolf. *Einführung in den Okkultismus und Spiritismus*. 2nd, rev. and improved ed. Munich: J. F. Bergmann, 1923. First edition published in 1921.

Titius, Arthur. *Natur und Gott: Ein Versuch zur Verständigung zwischen Naturwissenschaft und Theologie*. 2nd ed. Göttingen: Vandenhoeck und Ruprecht, 1931.

Treitel, Corinna. *A Science for the Soul: Occultism and the Genesis of the German Modern*. Baltimore: Johns Hopkins University Press, 2004.

Tudge, Colin. *The Secret Life of Trees: How They Live and Why They Matter*. London: Allen Lane, 2005.

Turner, Fred. *From Counterculture to Cyberculture: Stewart Brand, the Whole Earth Network and the Rise of Digital Utopianism*. Chicago: University of Chicago Press, 2006.

Uccusic, Paul. *Der Schamane in uns: Schamanismus als neue Selbsterfahrung, Hilfe und Heilung.* Munich: Goldmann, 1993.

UNESCO (United Nations Educational, Scientific and Cultural Organization). *Man Belongs to the Earth: International Cooperation in Environmental Research.* Paris: UNESCO, 1988. https://unesdoc.unesco.org/ark:/48223/pf0000080638.

United Nations. *Report of the World Commission on Environment and Development: Our Common Future.* Transmitted to the General Assembly as an Annex to document A/42/427—Development and International Co-operation: Environment, 1987. http://www.un-documents.net/our-common-future.pdf.

Vitebsky, Piers. *The Shaman.* Boston: Little, Brown, 1995.

Vliegenthart, Dave. *The Secular Religion of Franklin Merrell-Wolff: An Intellectual History of Anti-Intellectualism in Modern America.* Leiden: Brill, 2018.

Walsh, Roger N. *The Spirit of Shamanism.* Los Angeles: Jeremy P. Tarcher, 1990.

——. "Die Transpersonale Bewegung: Geschichte und derzeitiger Entwicklungsstand." *Transpersonale Psychologie und Psychotherapie* 1 (1995): 6–21.

Walsh, Roger N., and Frances Vaugah, eds. *Beyond Ego: Transpersonal Dimensions in Psychology.* Los Angeles: J. P. Tarcher, 1980.

Wasserstrom, Steven M. *Religion After Religion: Gershom Scholem, Mircea Eliade and Henry Corbin at Eranos.* Princeton: Princeton University Press, 1999.

Watson, Ian. "The Forest as Metaphor for Mind: 'The Word for World Is Forest' and 'Vaster Than Empires and More Slow.'" In *Ursula K. Le Guin (Modern Critical Views)*, edited by Harold Bloom, 47–55. New York: Chelsea House, 1986.

Weinberg, Steven. *Dreams of a Final Theory.* New York: Pantheon, 1992.

Westfahl, Gary, ed. *Science Fiction Quotations: From the Inner Mind to the Outer Limits.* New Haven: Yale University Press, 2005.

Weyergraf, Bernd. "Deutsche Wälder." In *Waldungen: Die Deutschen und ihr Wald*, edited by Akademie der Künste, Berlin, 6–12. Berlin: Nicolaische Verlagsbuchhandlung, 1987.

Wheeler, Wendy. "A Feeling for Life: Biosemiotics, Autopoiesis and the Orders of Discourse." *Anglia* 133 (2015): 53–68.

White, Carol Wayne. *Black Lives and Sacred Humanity: Toward an African American Religious Naturalism.* New York: Fordham University Press, 2016.

White, Lynn, Jr. "The Historical Roots of Our Ecologic Crisis." *Science* 155, no. 3767 (1967): 1203–1207.

Wilber, Ken. *The Atman Project: A Transpersonal View of Human Development.* Wheaton, IL: Theosophical Publishing House, 1980.

——. *Sex, Ecology, Spirituality: The Spirit of Evolution.* 2nd, rev. ed. Boston: Shambhala, 2000. First edition published in 1995.

——. *The Spectrum of Consciousness.* 2nd ed. Wheaton, IL: Theosophical Publishing House, 1993. First edition published in 1977.

Williams, John A. "'The Chords of the German Soul Are Tuned to Nature': The Movement to Preserve the Natural *Heimat* from the Kaiserreich to the Third Reich." *Central European History* 29 (1996): 339–384.

——. "Giving Nature a Higher Purpose: Back-to-Nature Movements in Weimar Germany, 1918–1933." PhD diss., University of Michigan, 1996. https://deepblue.lib.umich.edu/handle/2027.42/129825.

Wirth, Jason M. *Mountains, Rivers, and the Great Earth: Reading Gary Snyder and Dōgen in an Age of Ecological Crisis.* Albany: State University of New York Press, 2017.

Wittgenstein, Ludwig. *Philosophische Untersuchungen.* Frankfurt am Main: Suhrkamp, 1958.

Wohlleben, Peter. *Das geheime Leben der Bäume: Was sie fühlen, wie sie kommunizieren—die Entdeckung einer verborgenen Welt.* Munich: Ludwig, 2015.

——. *Das Seelenleben der Tiere: Liebe, Trauer, Mitgefühl—erstaunliche Einblicke in eine verborgene Welt.* Munich: Ludwig, 2016.

Woodward, William R., and Mitchell G. Ash, eds. *The Problematic Science: Psychology in Nineteenth-Century Thought.* New York: Praeger, 1982.

Wundt, Wilhelm. *Der Spiritismus: Eine sogenannte wissenschaftliche Frage: Offener Brief an Herrn Prof. Dr. Hermann Ulrici in Halle.* Leipzig: Engelmann, 1879.

——. *Völkerpsychologie: Eine Untersuchung der Entwicklungsgesetze von Sprache, Mythus und Sitte.* 10 vols. Leipzig: Engelmann (subsequently Kröner), 1900–1920.

——. *Vorlesungen über die Menschen- und Thierseele.* 3rd ed. Hamburg: Voss, 1897.

Zander, Helmut. *Geschichte der Seelenwanderung in Europa: Alternative religiöse Traditionen von der Antike bis heute.* Darmstadt: Primus, 1999.

Zintzen, Clemens. "Bemerkungen zur neuplatonischen Seelenlehre." In *Die Seele: Ihre Geschichte im Abendland*, edited by Gerd Jüttemann, Michael Sonntag, and Christoph Wulf, 43–58. Weinheim: Psychologie Verlags Union, 1991.

Zlotkowski, Edward. "Levertov and Rilke: A Sense of Aesthetic Ethics." *Twentieth Century Literature* 38 (1992): 324–342.

Zweig, Arnold. *Das ostjüdische Antlitz: Zu fünfzig Steinzeichnungen von Hermann Struck.* Berlin: Welt-Verlag, 1920.

INDEX